SERMON ON THE MOUNT

OTHER BOOKS IN THIS SERIES:

NAC STUDIES IN BIBLE & THEOLOGY

SERMON ON THE MOUNT

RESTORING CHRIST'S MESSAGE TO THE MODERN CHURCH

CHARLES QUARLES

SERIES EDITOR: E. RAY CLENDENEN

ACADEMIC

NASHVILLE, TENNESSEE

Sermon on the Mount: Restoring Christ's Message to the Modern Church

Copyright © 2011 by Charles Quarles

All rights reserved.

ISBN: 978-0-8054-4715-6

Published by B&H Publishing Group
Brentwood, Tennessee

Dewey Decimal Classification: 226.9
Subject Heading: SERMON ON THE MOUNT \ BEATITUDES \
JESUS CHRIST—TEACHINGS

Printed in the United States of America

AZ

I dedicate this book to the honor of my parents,

Dr. Chester L. and Dorothy Denham Quarles

They have sought to model the character described in the Sermon on the Mount, and their own lives are among the most helpful commentaries I have studied on these texts. My four siblings and I will be eternally grateful for their example and the Christian instruction we received in our home.

CONTENTS

LIST OF ABBREVIATIONS

AB	Anchor Bible
ABD	*Anchor Bible Dictionary*
BAR	*Biblical Archaeology Review*
BDAG	W. Bauer, F. W. Danker, W. F. Arndt, and F. W. Gingrich, *Greek-English Lexicon of the New Testament and Other Early Christian Literature.* 3rd ed. University of Chicago Press, 2000.
BDF	F. Blass, A. Debrunner, and R. W. Funk, *A Greek Grammar of the New Testament and Other Early Christian Literature.* University of Chicago, 1961.
BECNT	Baker Exegetical Commentary on the New Testament
Bib	*Biblica*
BSac	*Bibliotheca Sacra*
BZ	*Biblische Zeitschrift*
CBC	Cornerstone Biblical Commentary
CBQ	*Catholic Biblical Quarterly*
CTR	*Criswell Theological Review*
DJG	*Dictionary of Jesus and the Gospels,* ed. J. B. Green, S. McKnight, and I. H. Marshall. Downers Grove: InterVarsity, 1992.
EvQ	*Evangelical Quarterly*
ExpTim	*Expository Times*
HALOT	Koehler, L., W. Baumgartner, and J. J. Stamm. *The Hebrew and Aramaic Lexicon of the Old Testament.* Translated and edited under the supervision of M. E. J. Richardson. 4 vols. Leiden. 1994–99.
HB	Hebrew Bible
HTR	*Harvard Theological Review*
ICC	International Critical Commentary
Int	*Interpretation*
JBL	*Journal of Biblical Literature*

JETS	*Journal of the Evangelical Theological Society*
JJS	*Journal of Jewish Studies*
JRitSt	*Journal of Ritual Studies*
JSNT	*Journal for the Study of the New Testament*
JSNTSup	Journal for the Study of the New Testament: Supplement Series
LXX	Septuagint
MT	Masoretic Text
NAC	New American Commentary
NA27	*Novum Testamentum Graece*, 27th ed., ed. B. Nestle and K. Aland.
NICNT	New International Commentary on the New Testament
NICOT	New International Commentary on the Old Testament
NIGTC	New International Greek Testament Commentary
NIVAC	NIV Application Commentary
NovT	*Novum Testamentum*
NTS	*New Testament Studies*
OTP	*The Old Testament Psuedepigripha*, ed. J. H. Charlesworth.
PNTC	Pillar New Testament Commentary
REJ	*Revue des études juives*
RevExp	*Review and Expositor*
RevQ	*Revue de Qumran*
RivB	*Rivista biblica italiana*
RJ	*Reformed Journal*
RQ	*Restoration Quarterly*
SBJT	*The Southern Baptist Journal of Theology*
SBLSPS	Society of Biblical Literature Seminar Papers
SNTSMS	Society for New Testament Studies Monograph Series
ST	*Studia theologica*
SwJT	*Southwestern Journal of Theology*

TDNT	*Theological Dictionary of the New Testament,* ed. G. Kittel and G. Friedrich, trans. G. W. Bromiley. 10 vols. Eerdmans, 1964–74.
ThZ	*Theologische Zeitschrift*
TJ	*Trinity Journal*
TNTC	Tyndale New Testament Commentaries
TS	*Theological Studies*
TWOT	*Theological Wordbook of the Old Testament*
TynBul	*Tyndale Bulletin*
UBS[4]	*The Greek New Testament,* 4th revised edition. Edited by Barbara Aland, Kurt Aland, Bruce M. Metzger. Stuttgart: United Bible Societies, 1977.
WBC	Word Biblical Commentary
ZKT	*Zeitschrift für die Katholische theologie*
ZNW	Zeitschrift für die neutestamentliche Wissenschaft und die Kunde der älteren Kirche

SERIES PREFACE

We live in an exciting era of evangelical scholarship. Many fine educational institutions committed to the inerrancy of Scripture are training men and women to serve Christ in the church and to advance the gospel in the world. Many church leaders and professors are skillfully and fearlessly applying God's Word to critical issues, asking new questions, and developing new tools to answer those questions from Scripture. They are producing valuable new resources to thoroughly equip current and future generations of Christ's servants.

The Bible is an amazing source of truth and an amazing tool when wielded by God's Spirit for God's glory and our good. It is a bottomless well of living water, a treasure-house of endless proportions. Like an ancient tell, exciting discoveries can be made on the surface, but even more exciting are those to be found by digging. The books in this series, NAC Studies in Bible and Theology, often take a biblical difficulty as their point of entry, remembering B. F. Westcott's point that "unless all past experience is worthless, the difficulties of the Bible are the most fruitful guides to its divine depths."

This new series is to be a medium through which the work of evangelical scholars can effectively reach the church. It will include detailed exegetical-theological studies of key pericopes such as the Sermon on the Mount and also fresh examinations of topics in biblical theology and systematic theology. It is intended to supplement the New American Commentary, whose exegetical and theological discussions so many have found helpful. These resources are aimed primarily at church leaders and those who are preparing for such leadership. We trust that individual Christians will find them to be an encouragement to greater progress and joy in the faith. More important, our prayer is that they will help the church proclaim Christ more accurately and effectively and that they will bring praise and glory to our great God.

It is a tremendous privilege to be partners in God's grace with the fine scholars writing for this new series as well as with those who will be helped by it. When Christ returns, may He find us "standing firm in one spirit, with one mind, working side by side for the faith that comes from the gospel" (Phil 1:27).

E. Ray Clendenen
B&H Publishing Group

PREFACE

To write a commentary on the Sermon on the Mount is a somewhat intimidating task. As will be discussed later, Christian writings from the close of the NT up until the fourth century quote texts from the Sermon on the Mount more frequently and extensively than any other section of the New Testament. Since that time more works on the Sermon on the Mount have been written than can possibly be compiled into a bibliography. One may legitimately wonder what could possibly be added to this legacy.

Nevertheless, after years of preaching and teaching through the Sermon on the Mount in churches, colleges, and seminaries, I concluded that a need for yet another work on the Sermon existed. Although the literature on Matthew 5–7 is vast, a gap in the current treatments still existed. Many of the commentaries are highly technical and seem to be written for fellow scholars rather than for the pastors and teachers who face the challenge of teaching Jesus' message to the modern church. Volumes written for pastors and teachers (because of the limited length of the volumes) often leap from the text of the sermon directly to modern application, sidestepping very important questions of interpretation. Some treatments present the sermon as containing an impossible ethic that ensured that Jesus' teaching would be ignored as an interesting but irrelevant relic of the past. On the other hand some treatments dilute Jesus' teaching so much that little ethical challenge remains. Few texts deal with the important questions of whether believers may live by the Sermon on the Mount today and, if so, how. This commentary was written to fill that perceived gap in hopes that this crucial section of our Lord's teaching may be restored to its proper place in His church.

The focus and space limitations of the commentary do not permit a treatment of issues related to source or redaction criticism. The volume of material on the sermon is far too extensive to allow interaction with all of the secondary literature in a commentary of this size. I chose, except in rare instances, to appeal to secondary literature on the Sermon in the English language only. This seemed appropriate for the primary audience of the book.

A number of people have contributed to this volume in significant ways. I thank Ray Clendenen of B&H Academic for recognizing the need for this project and encouraging my work over the last few years. I especially appreciate his patience when health issues delayed my completion of the commentary. I am grateful to Dr. Joe Aguillard, president of Louisiana College, for supporting the project by excusing me from administrative tasks so I could devote more time to research and writing. I thank the family of William Peterson Carter Sr. for establishing the research professorship which I now hold. This research professorship permitted me to receive a reduction in teaching load so that I could devote my energies to this project. I am deeply grateful to Dr. Preston Pearce of Prague for carefully proofreading the entire rough draft of the manuscript. His keen observations have saved me from a number of errors. My administrative assistant, Mrs. Allison Weaver, has contributed to the project in numerous ways as well. The support of my wife, Julie, and my children, Rachael, Hannah, and Joshua, throughout this period has been encouraging.

Writing this commentary has been a life-changing experience. Due to other writing projects and some health challenges, I have worked on this commentary off and on for the past six years. During this time I have been privileged to live with the Savior on the mountain pondering His precious teaching until I heard His voice and, I believe, felt His heart.

Throughout the process of writing this commentary, I have sought to heed the admonition of J. A. Bengel: "Te totum applica ad textum; rem totam applica ad te" ("Apply yourself totally to the text; apply the text totally to yourself"). The first prescribed exercise has often been enlightening, and I have seen and understood important elements of the text in new ways. The second prescribed exercise has led me to see myself in new ways. I have been encouraged by Jesus' promises, indicted by His rebukes, stirred by His challenges, and strengthened by His presence. I have learned the importance of seeking to live in accord with God's character and not merely His commands. I have aspired for holiness as a participant in the new exodus, a recipient of new creation, and a beneficiary of the new covenant. Jesus' words have caused my stomach to grumble with new hunger for righteousness and have parched my throat with new thirst for Christlikeness.

My prayer is that this commentary will help lead each reader to a similar experience. I sincerely hope that you will hear and respond to Jesus' teaching like a true disciple rather than like the crowds who were impressed by Jesus' authority but who ignored His instructions. As you study Christ's message, I urge you to consider whether you will be recognized as a true "son of God" whose character resembles that of the heavenly Father on the great day of judgment or dismissed as a hypocrite with the fateful words, "I never knew you." Relief is still available to the beggarly in spirit who humble themselves before Christ. Ask and the gift of salvation will be given to you. Seek the kingdom and you will find it. Knock at its gates and a gracious Savior will open them for you.

I covet each reader's prayer for my own growth in godliness. For I recognize that if my life is not as apt a commentary on Jesus' sermon as this book, I have failed to hear the true voice of the Teacher on the mountain and this book is an expression of the hypocrisy that Jesus so despised. May Christ grant to us a righteousness that surpasses that of the scribes and Pharisees and mirrors that of the Father's own heart.

To the glory of God alone,
Charles L. Quarles

INTRODUCTION

The Importance of the Sermon on the Mount

N o sermon ever preached has been more significant to the Christian church than the Sermon on the Mount (hereafter, SM). This sermon is widely recognized as the heart of the teaching of Jesus of Nazareth. Luke Timothy Johnson did not exaggerate when he wrote, "In the history of Christian thought—indeed in the history of those observing Christianity—the Sermon on the Mount has been considered an epitome of the teaching of Jesus and therefore, for many, the essence of Christianity."[1]

For those who affirm the deity and authority of the Lord Jesus, no portion of Scripture could possibly be more important for defining the nature of Christian discipleship and the lofty ethic that should characterize God's people. Although more than two thousand years have passed since Jesus uttered these words, they remain as relevant today as when they were first breathed from the Savior's lips. A. M. Hunter wrote aptly:

> After nineteen hundred years the Sermon on the Mount still haunts men. They may praise it, as Mahatma Gandhi did; or like Nietzsche, they may curse it. They cannot ignore it. Its words are winged words, quick and powerful to rebuke, to challenge, to inspire. And though some turn from it in despair, it continues, like some mighty magnetic mountain, to attract to itself the greatest spirits of our race (many not Christians), so that if some world-wide vote were taken, there is little doubt that men would account it "the most searching and powerful utterance we possess on what concerns the moral life."[2]

Tragically the serious study of the sermon has been largely neglected by contemporary America. A recent Gallup poll indicated that only one-third of adult Americans are familiar enough with the sermon to identify Jesus as its source. Many Americans think that the

---

[1] L. T. Johnson, "The Sermon on the Mount," in *The Oxford Companion to Christian Thought*, ed. Adrian Hastings (Oxford: Oxford University Press, 2000), 654.

[2] A. M. Hunter, *A Pattern for Life: An Exposition of the Sermon on the Mount* (Philadelphia: Westminster, 1965), 9.

sermon was a message preached by the evangelist Billy Graham.[3] The sermon is best known in America today as the source of what is one of the most frequently quoted Bible verses, "Do not judge, so that you won't be judged" (Matt 7:1), a verse that is normally stripped from its context and used to support an exaggerated form of tolerance.

In sharp contrast to the current neglect of the SM by the contemporary church, the early church prized Matthew 5–7 as one of the most important sections of the Scriptures. Probable allusions to Jesus' teachings preserved in the SM appear in other New Testament books including Romans (and possibly Galatians and 1 and 2 Corinthians),[4] James,[5] and 1 Peter.[6] Some of these allusions may predate the composition of Matthew and suggest that the content of the SM was emphasized in apostolic teaching in the earliest history of the church. Christian writings from the close of the New Testament up to the Council of Nicea in AD 325 quote Matthew 5 more frequently and extensively than any single chapter of the Bible and quote Matthew 5–7 more frequently and extensively than any other three chapters of the entire Bible.[7]

The lofty ethic of the SM has inspired many people who do not embrace evangelical Christianity. Many Jewish, Islamic, and Hindu readers have expressed admiration for Jesus because of His consummate

[3] T. C. Reeves, "Not So Christian America," *First Things* 66 (1996): 16–21. See also G. Gallup Jr. and J. Castelli, *The People's Religion: American Faith in the 90's* (New York: MacMillan, 1989), 60.

[4] Cp. Rom 12:14 with Matt 5:44; Rom 12:17,21 with Matt 5:38–42; Gal 5:14; and Rom 13:8–10 with Matt 5:43; 1 Cor 7:10–16 with Matt 5:31–32; 2 Cor 1:17 with Matt 5:37; and Rom 2:1–2; 14:10 with Matt 7:1–5. H. D. Betz argued that Paul derived his parallel statements from sources other than the Sermon on the Mount or Sermon on the Plain (*The Sermon on the Mount Including the Sermon on the Plain (Matthew 5:3–7:27 and Luke 6:20–49)*, Hermenia [Minneapolis: Augsburg Fortress, 1995], 6, n. 12).

[5] M. H. Shepherd explored a number of potential allusions of James to Matthew and the SM in "The Epistle of James and the Gospel of Matthew," *JBL* 75 (1956): 40–51, esp. 43–44. Parallels between the SM and James are numerous. Shepherd concluded: "The parallels in James to the Beatitudes of the Gospels do not, when taken by themselves, necessarily prove that the author knew either or both of the Gospels according to Matthew and to Luke. But they do suggest that James knew a group of Beatitudes about the poor, the mourners, the merciful, and the afflicted, and possibly also macarisms upon the meek, the pure in heart, and the peacemakers. This circumstance points, at least, to familiarity with the Matthean formulation. It can be further illuminated by examination of other Matthean influences upon the writer of James" (ibid., 44).

[6] Cp. 1 Pet 1:3–4 and Matt 5:5; 1 Pet 3:14 and Matt 5:10; 1 Pet 4:13–14 and Matt 5:11–12; 1 Pet 2:12 and Matt 5:16; 1 Pet 1:17 and Matt 5:45; 1 Pet 1:16 and Matt 5:48; 1 Pet 5:7 and Matt 6:25–34.

[7] W. S. Kissinger, *The Sermon on the Mount: A History of Interpretation and Bibliography* (Metuchen, NJ: Scarecrow, 1975), 6.

teaching in this sermon. On the other hand many critics of the Christian church frequently point out the disparity between Jesus' teachings in the SM and the actual conduct of those who claim to follow him.[8] Most unbelievers understandably regard modern Christianity as hypocritical, and many point to this hypocrisy as their primary reason for rejecting the Christian faith.[9] Professing Christians whose lives fail to match the descriptions of the disciples in the SM are, as Jesus warned, deemed to be good for nothing except to be cast out and trampled (5:13). Thus rediscovering the ethical and theological truths of the SM is necessary both to the revitalization of the church and to the effectiveness of the church's mission in the world.

[8] One recent poll demonstrated that 85 percent of young American adults who reject the Christian faith view present-day Christianity as hypocritical. See D. Kinnaman and G. Lyons, *Unchristian: What a New Generation Really Thinks About Christianity . . . and Why It Matters* (Grand Rapids: Baker, 2007), 42.

[9] Evangelical scholar C. Keener recently acknowledged that when he was an atheist, his primary objection to Christianity was "that Christians did not seem to take it seriously" (*The Historical Jesus of the Gospels* [Grand Rapids: Eerdmans, 2009], 387).

Chapter 1

A BRIEF HISTORY OF INTERPRETATION

The earliest sample of interpretation of the SM outside of the NT appears in the *Didache*, a church manual probably written some time between AD 60 and 80.[1] The *Didache* opens with a discussion of the "two ways," the way of life and the way of death. These two ways are comparable to the two ways described in Matt 7:13–14. At the conclusion of the description of the two ways, the author advised, "See that no one leads you astray from this way of the teaching, for such a person teaches you without regard for God. For if you are able to bear the whole yoke of the Lord, you will be perfect. But if you are not able, then do what you can."[2]

The "way" of teaching is the way of life drawn largely from the SM. The words "you will be perfect" appear in the context of a number of clear parallels to the SM and thus appear to be an allusion to 5:48. The author of the *Didache* thus viewed the SM as a description of the true righteousness that characterizes the ideal Christian disciple. The author insisted that inability to live up to the standards of the SM fully should not dissuade the Christian disciple from aspiring to do so more and more. The disciple should do what he can to obey the sermon. He should constantly strive to be "perfect even as the Father in heaven is perfect," knowing that God will grant righteousness to those who hunger and thirst for it.

Most early Christian interpreters of the SM believed that the SM was applicable to all Christians and that every believer should seek to live by its precepts. Although these early believers recognized that fulfilling the SM is difficult, they denied that fulfilling the SM was impossible for those who had experienced and were continuing to experience God's transforming grace. An example of this approach to the SM appears in the writings of John Chrysostom, the famed preacher from Antioch of the fourth century (c. 347–407). Chrysostom offered an exegesis of the SM in homilies 15–24 in his collection of 90 sermons on Matthew's Gospel. Since the first nine books of Origen's 25-book commentary on Matthew are lost except for a couple

---

[1] *Didache*, in *The Apostolic Fathers*, ed. M. W. Holmes (Grand Rapids: Baker, 1989), 146–47.
[2] Ibid., 152.

of fragments, Chrysostom's sermons on Matthew constitute the oldest complete exposition of the Gospel now in existence.[3]

Chrysostom urged his audience to seek to live by the SM more and more each day. He pointed out that some believers, from the apostolic age to his own time, had actually been characterized by the exemplary righteousness that the SM described.[4] He counseled believers to begin with the easier precepts of the SM and to seek to advance to the more difficult precepts until they had progressed to true holiness. In this fashion believers "may arrive at the very summit of all good things; unto which may we all attain, by the grace and love towards man of our Lord Jesus Christ, to whom be glory and dominion for ever and ever."[5] Chrysostom believed that divine grace would empower those who sought such righteousness to attain it. On several occasions Chrysostom clearly denied that the SM expressed an impossible ethic that believers could never attain. He urged, "Let us not consider that these commandments are impossible!"[6] Not only was it possible to live up to the standards of the SM; doing so was natural for the believer "for none of the things he has commanded are burdensome or odious."[7]

Chrysostom saw no tension between the SM and the Pauline Epistles. The refrain "so also Paul" (*kai ho Paulos*) is a hallmark of Chrysostom's treatment of Matthew 5–7 that appears 50 times in the course of his exposition of the SM.[8] This feature of Chrysostom's work demonstrates that, unlike some later commentators, he did not view the SM as belonging to the old covenant era and rendered obsolete by the gospel of grace. Chrysostom argued that Jesus' teaching applied to his own contemporaries and not just to Jesus' original audience: "For these things have been said to them, but they were written also for all those who come after."[9]

Although several important commentaries on the Gospel of Matthew were produced in the second and third centuries, Augustine

---

[3] Kissinger, *The Sermon on the Mount*, 9–10.
[4] Chrysostom, *Hom. Matt.* 21.5.
[5] Ibid., 6.24.
[6] Ibid., 18.236; 21.237.
[7] Ibid., 22.280.
[8] M. Mitchell, "John Chrysostom," in *The Sermon on the Mount Through the Centuries: From the Early Church to John Paul II*, ed. J. P. Greenman, T. Larsen, and S. R. Spencer (Grand Rapids: Brazos, 2007), 19–42, esp. 20–21.
[9] Chrysostom, *Hom. Matt.* 15.185.

(354–430) wrote the first commentary on the SM alone that has been preserved to the present day. This commentary was his first extensive exegetical work on the NT.[10] Augustine made two particularly significant contributions. First, his commentary marked the beginning of an era in which the SM became the focus of special investigation by itself, apart from the Gospel of Matthew as a whole.[11] Second, Augustine appears to have been the first to refer to this sermon as the "Sermon on the Mount" (*De Sermone Domini in Monte*).[12] This title for the sermon hints that Augustine saw the setting of the SM as significant. According to Augustine Jesus climbed a mountain to deliver the SM because Jesus wanted to teach His disciples about higher things.[13] Augustine viewed the SM as "the perfect measure of the Christian life" and "filled with all the precepts by which the Christian life is formed."[14]

Augustine emphasized that the Holy Spirit granted believers seven gifts mentioned in Isaiah 11, and these correspond to the seven virtues enumerated in the Beatitudes.[15] Augustine also recognized that the command to exhibit the character of the heavenly Father (Matt 5:48) assumed the doctrine of regeneration. The audience addressed by the SM had entered into a new relationship with God and had inherited His holy character through the new birth described in John 1:12.[16] Augustine recognized that believers would not perfectly fulfill the demands of the SM in this life. Hence the need arose for the petition, "Forgive our debts."[17] This interpretation of the SM prevailed in the early church until the time of Thomas Aquinas (1224–1274).

During the Middle Ages, Aquinas introduced the notion that not all of the SM was applicable to every believer. Aquinas distinguished between "precepts" and "evangelical counsels," a distinction first made by Ambrose. Precepts were commands that all followers of Christ were obligated to keep. "Counsels" were guides to Christlike perfection that were not obligatory but might be voluntarily adopted

---

[10] Augustine had previously written a treatise on Genesis and some notes on the Psalms. See R. L. Wilken, "Augustine," in *Sermon on the Mount Through the Centuries*, 43–57, esp. 45.

[11] Betz, *The Sermon on the Mount*, 11–12.

[12] Kissinger, *The Sermon on the Mount*, 13.

[13] Wilken, "Augustine," 43.

[14] Augustine, *Serm. Dom.* 1.1.1.

[15] Ibid., 1.4.11–12.

[16] Ibid., 1.23.78.

[17] See the use of this petition in Augustine's response to Pelagius in Augustine, *Spir. et litt.* 65.

by those who wished to attain true holiness.[18] Counsels were intended only for the spiritually elite and could be fulfilled only through withdrawal from society to monastic life. Aquinas's teaching resulted in a "double-standard view" that became basic in Roman Catholic moral theology.[19]

The Protestant Reformers rejected the Thomist interpretation of the SM. Martin Luther argued that the SM addresses those who are already Christians and that divine grace produces the life described in the sermon. He insisted that the SM said nothing "about how we become Christians, but only about the works and fruit that no one can do unless he is already a Christian and in a state of grace."[20] The righteous life described in the SM is a product of the Spirit's transforming work rather than mere human effort and is the result of salvation rather than a requirement for it.[21]

Luther argued that those who denied the possibility of ordinary Christians fulfilling the SM had failed to distinguish properly between the two kingdoms in which the Christian lives, the spiritual kingdom and the earthly kingdom, and the two persons who reside in the Christian, the spiritual person and the secular person. Susan Schreiner summarized Luther's view as follows:

> The believer will oppose every evil within the limits of his office and may go to court to remedy some violence or injustice. The Christian may go to war, be a governor or a lawyer, or work in any other occupation. Christians may maintain their households, swear oaths, and engage in secular affairs. Nonetheless, they never do these things "as Christians." The Christian is acting in these positions as a secular person. The two persons in each Christian must move in their own proper sphere.[22]

This view of the two spheres in which the Christian lives and operates was Luther's attempt to correct the idea that one fulfilled the SM by renouncing society and withdrawing from the world, an idea prominent in both Catholic monasticism and among some Anabaptists.

---

[18] On the distinction between commands and counsels, see especially Thomas Aquinas, *Summa Theologica*, Part 2.1, question 108, article 4.

[19] See the discussion in Kissinger, *The Sermon on the Mount*, 17–18.

[20] M. Luther, "Sermon on the Mount," in *Luther's Works*, vol. 21, ed. J. Pelikan (St. Louis: Concordia, 1956), 291.

[21] See W. S. Kissinger, *The Sermon on the Mount: A History of Interpretation and Bibliography* (Metuchen, NJ: Scarecrow, 1975), 20–23.

[22] S. Schreiner, "Martin Luther," in *The Sermon on the Mount Through the Centuries*, 109–27, esp. 116.

For John Calvin the SM was a compendium of Jesus' teaching that contains "the doctrine of Christ, which related to a devout and holy life."[23] Calvin taught that the purpose of the SM is to rescue the law of God from the erroneous teaching of the Pharisees who saw the law as related only to external acts and not internal attitudes.[24] The SM was intended to demonstrate the law's true purpose that had been obscured in the teaching of the Jews.[25] Against objections that the precepts were too difficult for believers to fulfill, Calvin replied, "To our weakness, indeed, everything, even to the minutest tittle of the Law, is arduous and difficult. In the Lord we have strength. . . . That Christians are under the law of grace means not that they are to wander unrestrained without law but that they are engrafted into Christ, by whose grace they have the Law written in their hearts."[26] Thus for Calvin the SM was the ethic of the New Covenant that would be fulfilled through the transforming work of the Holy Spirit. The Reformer recognized that keeping the SM was possible only through dependence on God. In the context of discussing the demands of the SM, Calvin reaffirmed the teaching of Augustine: "Let him give what he commands and command what he will."[27]

Calvin's exposition of the SM was marked by a tendency to moderate or soften its commands.[28] He reacted against the radical interpretations of the SM by the Anabaptists since these interpretations either made keeping the commands practically impossible or required one to withdraw from the world in order to fulfill the sermon's imperatives. Calvin's exegesis interpreted the commands of the SM as entirely reasonable.[29] Unfortunately sometimes Calvin moderated or softened the application of Jesus' commands too quickly without properly wrestling with important exegetical questions.[30]

[23] See the comments on Matt 5:1.

[24] J. Calvin, *Institutes of the Christian Religion*, ed. H. Beveridge (London: J. Clark, 1962), 2.8.7.

[25] J. Calvin, *A Harmony of the Gospels: Matthew, Mark, Luke*, trans. A. W. Morrison, ed. D. W. Torrance and T. F. Torrance (Grand Rapids: Eerdmans, 1972), 1:183.

[26] Calvin, *Institutes of the Christian Religion*, 2.8.57.

[27] Augustine, *Confessions*, 10.29,31,37.

[28] Z. N. Holler, "Calvin's Exegesis of the Sermon on the Mount," in *Calvin Studies III: Presented at a Colloquium on Calvin Studies at Davidson College and Davidson College Presbyterian Church*, ed. John H. Leith (Richmond, VA: Union Theological Seminary, 1986), 5–20, esp. 6.

[29] See his treatment of the disciple's response to a slap (Matt 5:39) or to litigation (5:40).

[30] S. Spencer was correct in his observations regarding Calvin's treatment of the SM: "Indeed he understands Scripture in part by means of his agenda of avoiding prevalent errors in his contemporary context. He 'calculates' the faithful path by marking the boundaries with

The Anabaptists stressed that the SM should be obeyed by all Christians in the most radical way.[31] Consequently they prohibited the use of oaths even in a court of law, personal acts of violence including self-defense or military force, legal judgments, and sometimes even the possession of personal property. Living by these standards of conduct was so difficult in an unregenerate society that some Anabaptists largely retreated from the world. Luther argued that these "enthusiasts" failed to see that believers live in two kingdoms, both secular and spiritual realms. A believer's office as a citizen may require him to take up the sword or to swear an oath. Nevertheless he is innocent if he "keeps a Christian heart."[32] Calvin objected that the extreme interpretation of the Anabaptists resulted from the failure to interpret Scripture in light of Scripture or from ignoring the context.[33]

Some dispensationalists have championed a view of the SM that is the opposite of the Anabaptist view.[34] They have argued that the SM is not applicable to believers today. They insist either that the SM belongs to the era of law rather than grace or expresses the standards of Christ's millennial reign. Lewis Sperry Chafer argued that difficulties in interpreting and applying the SM to contemporary believers resulted from a failure to discern the intended audience of the discourse. He stated, "As a rule of life, it is addressed to the Jew before the cross and to the Jew in the coming kingdom, and is therefore not now in effect."[35] After a summary of the lofty principles of the SM, Chafer wrote, "A moment's reflection will convince the mind that

---

misinterpretations and abuse. His contemporary opponents help to shape his hermeneutical lenses and establish the range of interpretation. Readings associated with them seem prejudged as discarded. He does not interpret Scripture solely in terms of itself" ("John Calvin," in *The Sermon on the Mount Through the Centuries*, 129–52, esp. 152).

[31] See Kissinger, *The Sermon on the Mount*, 29–34.

[32] Luther, "The Sermon on the Mount," 105–13.

[33] See, e.g., Calvin, *Institutes of the Christian Religion*, 2.8.26.

[34] Classical dispensationalism was popularized by the Scofield Reference Bible (1917) that said, "The Sermon on the Mount in its primary application gives neither the privilege nor the duty of the Church." Scofield later acknowledged that "there is a beautiful moral application to the Christian." However, he seems to have limited this application primarily to the Beatitudes. See for example Scofield's explanation of the condition for divine forgiveness in Matt 6:12 in which he treats the petition as belonging to the dispensation of law rather than grace. Many contemporary dispensationalists have abandoned the classical dispensationalist view of the SM and adopted the view known as "inaugurated eschatology." See C. L. Blomberg, *Matthew* (Nashville: Broadman, 1992), 94; C. Blaising, "Development of Dispensationalism by Contemporary Dispensationalists," *BSac* 145 (1988): 254–80; and R. L. Saucy, "The Presence of the Kingdom and the Life of the Church," *BSac* 145 (1988): 30–46.

[35] L. S. Chafer, *Systematic Theology* (Dallas: Dallas Theological Seminary, 1948), 5:97.

such a standard as this belongs to another social order than the present one. It is designed for a day when the King reigns upon His earthly throne and when Satan is in his abyss."[36] For Chafer, whereas the law of Moses governed the behavior of Jews before the dispensation of grace, the teachings of the kingdom, particularly the SM, will govern the behavior of God's people in the eschatological kingdom. Their application requires "the binding of Satan, a purified earth, the restoration of Israel, and the personal reign of the King."[37]

Charles Ryrie holds a more balanced dispensational position. He wrote:

> The dispensationalist does recognize the relevance and application of the teachings of the Sermon to believers today regardless of how much non-dispensationalists want to make him say otherwise. The dispensationalist, however, views the primary fulfillment of the Sermon and the full following of its laws as applicable to the Messianic kingdom.[38]

Ryrie was incorrect in his denial that some earlier dispensationalists rejected application of the SM to contemporary believers. However, Ryrie led dispensationalists to return to an interpretation of the significance of the SM that was more consistent with early Christianity.

Perhaps the prevailing interpretive approach to the SM among modern evangelical scholars is the "inaugurated eschatology" approach. This approach insists that the kingdom of God was inaugurated on earth through the ministry of Jesus. However, His kingdom will not be consummated until His return. The SM expresses a kingdom ethic. Since Jesus' kingdom has already been inaugurated, the ethic of the SM is the goal and ideal of Christian disciples here and now. However, disciples will not be fully characterized by the righteousness that the sermon describes until the kingdom is consummated at the time of the Second Coming. Thus the tension between the "already" and

---

[36] Ibid., 5:107.

[37] Ibid., 5:207.

[38] C. Ryrie, *Dispensationalism Today* (Chicago: Moody, 1965), 107–8. Others who hold this view include J. D. Pentecost, *The Sermon on the Mount: Contemporary Insights for a Christian Lifestyle* (Portland, OR: Multnomah, 1980), 17; and L. A. Barbieri Jr., "Matthew," in *The Bible Knowledge Commentary, New Testament*, ed. J. F. Walvoord and R. B. Zuck (Wheaton, IL: Victor, 1983; reprint, Colorado Springs: Cook, 1996). Barbieri writes, "The sermon did not give a 'Constitution' for the kingdom nor did it present the way of salvation. The sermon showed how a person who is in right relationship with God should conduct his life" (ibid., 28).

the "not yet" that is crucial for understanding Paul's eschatology is equally important for understanding the teaching of Jesus.[39]

This view of the SM appeared as early as the fourth century. Chrysostom wrote, "Even before heaven [Christ] commands us to make earth heaven, and while living on earth to conduct ourselves as citizens there."[40] This approach takes seriously the unwavering conviction of the church during the first millennium of its history that the SM is applicable to all believers. However, it also recognizes that the promise that "those who hunger and thirst for righteousness will be filled" is being progressively fulfilled here and now but will only be finally and completely fulfilled in the final redemption when believers are resurrected and glorified.

[39] Blomberg, *Matthew,* 95.
[40] Chrysostom, *Hom. Matt.* 19.251.

Chapter 2

THE RELATIONSHIP TO THE SERMON ON THE PLAIN

The SM (Matthew 5–7) and the Sermon on the Plain[1] (Luke 6:17–49) have remarkable similarities. Most of the material that appears in the SM is either included in the SP or appears elsewhere in Luke's Gospel. Material from the SM that has no parallel in Luke (Matt 5:33–37; 6:1–6,16–18; 7:6) had special importance to Matthew's Jewish Christian audience but was less applicable to Luke's primarily Gentile Christian audience.

Consequently several important figures in the early church, including Origen and Chrysostom, believed that the SM and the SP were two different accounts of the same sermon. Augustine, however, argued that the SM and the SP were two different sermons preached on two different occasions. His view became the dominant view of the church until the Protestant Reformation. John Calvin suggested that the SM was "a brief summary of the doctrine of Christ . . . collected out of his many and various discourses." He felt that Luke presented Jesus' teaching in a chronological format but that Matthew's arrangement was topical.

The interpretation that best accounts for all the data and appreciates the historical reliability of both Matthew and Luke suggests that the SM and the SP are two accounts of the same sermon. An excellent defense of this position was offered by John Broadus.[2] Broadus pointed to the following evidence in support of this position.

1. The SM and the SP begin and end exactly alike.
2. Almost all of the contents of the SP appear in the SM.
3. Both the SM and the SP are immediately followed by the account of Jesus' entrance into Capernaum and the healing of the centurion's servant.

---

[1] Hereafter SP.

[2] J. A. Broadus was one of the cofounders of the Southern Baptist Theological Seminary. His commentary on Matthew was the first by a Baptist in America. The name of this early series, An American Commentary on the New Testament, inspired the name of the series to which the present commentary belongs. For an excellent treatment of Broadus's contribution to biblical studies, see D. S. Dockery, "Mighty in the Scriptures: John A. Broadus and His Influence on A. T. Robertson and Southern Baptist Life," in *John A. Broadus: A Living Legacy*, ed. D. S. Dockery and R. G. Duke (Nashville: B&H Academic, 2008), 12–44.

Some commentators had objected that the SM and SP differed as to their place, time, circumstances, and content. Broadus pointed out that the description of the place from which Jesus preached the SM and the SP could be identical since the "level place" (*pedinos*) mentioned in Luke 6:17 could be a plain in a mountainous region or a flat piece of ground on the top or side of a mountain (Jer 21:13; Isa 13:2). The supposed differences in the time and circumstances of the SM and SP were mitigated by the recognition that Matthew's Gospel was probably topically arranged while Luke's Gospel was chronologically arranged. Although the SP lacked some important sections of the SM, those sections would have been of special interest to Matthew's Jewish Christian readers but less applicable to Luke's Gentile Christian readers. Although Matthew and Luke sometimes differ in detail in reporting the same saying of the sermon, this does not require the view that the SM and SP were two different sermons since many of the sayings of Jesus preserved in the Gospels are more along the lines of indirect quotations than direct quotations.[3]

Broadus defended the original unity of the SM/SP against Calvin's theory that Matthew collected isolated sayings of Jesus uttered on many different occasions and presented them as a single sermon. Such a view would undermine the historical reliability of Matthew's Gospel since "he does distinctly say that this discourse was delivered on a single occasion (comp. 5:1 and 8:1), and if the facts were otherwise his account of the matter would be definitely erroneous."[4]

Internal evidence from the SM itself further supports the view that the sermon was an original unit.[5] The material in the SM that is similar to material appearing outside of the SP in Luke's Gospel was likely preached on more than one occasion. That Jesus preached similar material on multiple occasions is evident from a comparison of Matt 5:31–32 and 19:8–9.

The question of the original unity of the SM is not merely a topic of meaningless scholarly speculation. One's opinion regarding the original unity of the SM has great exegetical implications. Interpreters

---

[3] J. A. Broadus, *The Gospel According to Matthew*, American Commentary, ed. Alva Hovey (Philadelphia: American Baptist Publication Society, 1886), 84. On this last point Broadus earlier commented, "As to the complete inspiration of the Scriptures, we must accept it as one of the facts of the case that the inspired writers not unfrequently [*sic*] report merely the substance of what was said, without aiming to give the exact words" (ibid., 58).

[4] Ibid., 83.

[5] See, e.g., the discussion of Matt 7:7–11.

who regard the SM as a collection of many isolated sayings are unable to rely on the context of the sayings to guide them in interpretation. Thus the meaning of the several important sayings in the SM would remain an enigma.[6] Interpreters who regard the SM as an original unit can interpret individual sayings in light of their context. This ability sheds enormous light on several important sayings.

[6] U. Luz writes, "I am going to permit myself not to interpret the logion in its Matthean context" (*Matthew: A Commentary*, Hermeneia [Minneapolis: Fortress, 2007], 1:356). He added that the logion "was never actually anchored in the Matthean context" and that the numerous interpretations of the saying by the church reflected "the erratic character of this logion, a logion that is not understandable in the Matthean context" (ibid.).

Chapter 3

THE STRUCTURE OF
THE SERMON ON THE MOUNT

The SM is carefully organized.[1] This is clear from the beginning of the SM, the Beatitudes. The first four beatitudes are alliterated. This alliteration serves to divide the eight beatitudes into two equal sections of four beatitudes each. Furthermore the promise, "because the kingdom of heaven is theirs" marks both the first and final beatitude and serves as an *inclusio*. This artistic structure prompts the interpreter to expect careful shaping of the remainder of the SM.

Ulrich Luz has argued that *inclusio* or literary bracketing is the key feature of the structure of the SM.[2] In his schema the SM is a series of enveloped inclusions. The first inclusion consists of 5:1–2 and 7:28–8:1, in which both sections of the frame include the words "crowds," "teaching," and "going up (or down) . . . mountain." The second inclusion consists of 5:3–16 (introduction) and 7:13–27 (conclusion), both of which include two occurrences of the phrase "kingdom of heaven." The third inclusion contains the introduction and conclusion to the main section of the sermon, 5:17–20 and 7:12, both of which refer to "the Law and the Prophets." The fourth inclusion contains the antitheses (5:21–48) and the section on possessions, judging, and asking (6:19–7:11), which have identical lengths, 56 lines in each in the Nestle-Aland Greek text. The fifth inclusion consists of 6:1–6 and 6:16–18, both of which refer to the righteousness of God. The sixth inclusion, 6:7–8 and 6:14–15, includes prayer words. This structure places the model prayer in the center.

Although several of the inclusions are convincing and will be used in the analysis of the structure below, several of the proposed inclusions seem forced. The sixth inclusion, for example, is doubtful. Although 6:14–15 is a brief commentary on a petition of the model prayer, its focus is the relationship of divine and human forgiveness rather than prayer itself. The appeal to the identical line length in the

---

[1] For a good introduction to recent proposals regarding the structure of the SM, see W. Carter, *What Are They Saying About Matthew's Sermon on the Mount?* (New York: Paulist, 1994), 35–55.

[2] Luz often refers to the inclusios as "rings" (e.g., *Matthew: A Commentary*, 1:172).

fourth inclusion is an even greater stretch.[3] Nevertheless Luz seems correct in his assertion that the model prayer is the center of the SM. This serves to highlight the importance of the prayer.

The Beatitudes serve as the introduction to the SM. The salt and light sayings in 5:13–16 have a similar form since both introductory statements begin with "You are the . . ." and end with a universal focus ("of the earth" and "of the world"). This section completes the introduction. The central section of the SM begins in 5:17 and extends to 7:12. The references to "the Law and the Prophets" at the beginning and end of the section serve as a literary bracket (*inclusio*) for the material. The material in 7:13–27 serves as a conclusion to the sermon.

The central section of the SM has several subdivisions. The so-called Six Antitheses (5:21–48) contrast Jesus' interpretation and application of the Law with that of contemporary Jewish teachers. The unity of this section is clear from the shared introduction: "You have heard that it was said to our ancestors . . . but I say to you" and abbreviated forms of the introduction.

The next subdivision (6:1–18) introduces and describes the proper Christian exercise of the three pillars of Judaism: almsgiving (6:2–4), prayer (6:5–15), and fasting (6:16–18). Another subdivision is devoted to a discussion of the disciple's relationship to money and material possessions and the anxiety that materialism often induces (6:19–34). Matthew 7:1–6 treats issues related to the proper judgment of others. Yet it is closely linked to the major sections of chap. 6 by shared references to hypocrisy.

Matthew 7:7–12 is tied to the preceding sections by the reference to the Law and the Prophets shared with 5:17. On the other hand 7:7–12 appears to be transitional and turns attention to the issue of kingdom entrance that will dominate 7:13–23. Matthew 7:7–12 stresses the ease with which one enters the kingdom. Matthew 7:13–14 balances the preceding paragraph by alerting hearers to the difficulty involved in entering the kingdom. Matthew 7:13–27 is tightly connected by a series of contrasts between two roads, two gates, two different plants yielding different kinds of fruit, two different confessions (one accompanied by good works and the other not), and two different kinds of hearers represented by two different builders.

[3] G. Stanton, *A Gospel for a New People: Studies in Matthew* (Edinburgh: Clark, 1992), 298.

The conclusion to the SM in 7:28–8:1 forms an *inclusio* with the introduction to the sermon in 5:1–2. Both texts mention the presence of the crowds and Jesus' activity of teaching. Matthew 5:1 describes His ascent of the mountain, and 8:1 describes His descent from the mountain.

This analysis of the structure may be expressed in the following outline:

I. Introduction (5:1–16)
   A. The Setting of the Sermon (5:1–2) [crowds, teaching, mountain]
   B. The Beatitudes (5:3–12)
   C. Salt and Light (5:13–16)
II. Body of the Sermon: Superior Righteousness (5:17–7:12)
   A. Demand for Superior Righteousness (5:17–20) [the Law and the Prophets]
   B. The Disciple's Obedience to the Law (5:21–5:48)
      1. Anger (5:21–26)
      2. Lust (5:27–30)
      3. Divorce (5:31–33)
      4. Dishonesty (5:34–37)
      5. Retaliation (5:38–42)
      6. Hatred (5:43–48)
   C. The Disciple's Avoidance of Hypocrisy in the Practice of the Pillars of Judaism (6:1–18)
      1. Introduction (6:1)
      2. Almsgiving (6:2–4)
      3. Prayer (6:5–15)
      4. Fasting (6:16–18)
   D. The Disciple's Priorities (6:19–34)
      1. Two Kinds of Treasure (6:19–21)
      2. Two Conditions of the Eye (6:22–23)
      3. Two Masters (6:24)
      4. The Result of Proper Priorities (6:25–34)
   E. The Disciple's Relationships (7:1–12)
      1. Relating to Brothers (7:1–5)
      2. Relating to Dogs and Pigs (7:6)
      3. Relating to the Father (7:7–12) [the Law and the Prophets]

F. The Conclusion (7:13–8:1)
  1. Two Roads and Gates (7:13–14)
  2. Two Trees and Fruits (7:15–20)
  3. Two Confessions (7:21–23)
  4. Two Hearers and Builders (7:24–27)
  5. The Response (7:28–8:1) [cp. 5:1–2: crowds, teaching, mountain]

Other important proposals for the structure of the SM have been offered. Michael Goulder has suggested that the eight Beatitudes in 5:3–10 are the key to the structure of the entire SM. Each beatitude is a summary statement or heading for each of the major sections of the sermon. The SM expounds each of the beatitudes in reverse order. Each exposition consists of three major parts, a well-known practice of the rabbis.[4]

Space does not permit a thorough critique of Goulder's proposal. However, a careful examination of his first proposed section raises serious doubts about his hypothesis. Goulder argued that the first section of the SM, 5:11–16, is a commentary on the eighth beatitude related to persecution. The commentary consisted of three sections: reward in heaven (5:11–12), salt of earth (5:13), and light of cosmos (5:14–16).

The connections between 5:11–12 and the final beatitude in 5:10 seem stronger than the suggested connection between other beatitudes and sections. However, three features of the SM make even this proposal tenuous. First, 5:13–16 makes no explicit reference to persecution.[5] Second, the structural parallels in 5:13 ("You are the salt of the earth") and 5:14 ("You are the light of the world") seem to demarcate 5:13–16 as belonging to a section distinct from 5:11–12. Third, the references to the Law and the Prophets in 5:17–20 and 7:12 seem to bracket the main body of the SM, but this separates the supposed commentary on the eighth beatitude from the commentary on all the other beatitudes. Similar problems plague the other major

---

[4] See especially the chart in M. Goulder, *Midrash and Lection in Matthew* (London: SPCK, 1974), 269.

[5] Jesus does warn that impure salt will be "trampled on by men" (Matt 5:13), but this is a reference to the abuse that one receives because of his hypocrisy rather than persecution "for righteousness" or "because of Me [Jesus]" as described in the final beatitude (5:10–11).

of the SM. Jesus and His faithful interpreter Matthew wanted and expected Christian disciples to exhibit the radical righteousness of the SM for the glory of the heavenly Father who produces such righteousness in His people.

Those who view the SM as an expression of impossible demands fail to interpret the sermon in light of the broad theological themes of Matthew's Gospel. These themes assure the reader that the disciples of Jesus have been divinely enabled to fulfill the teachings of the SM because (1) they have participated in the new exodus, (2) they have experienced the new creation, and (3) they are beneficiaries of the new covenant. These themes of the Gospel of Matthew demonstrate that Jesus sets His disciples free from their slavery to sin, recreates them, and places the Holy Spirit in them so that they are transformed from the inside out and live a new and different way.

The New Exodus: Jesus Is the Deliverer Who Will Lead God's People Out of Bondage to Sin

Matthew's Gospel presents Jesus as a figure like Moses by consciously highlighting parallels between the life of Jesus and the life of Moses.[1] The parallels first appear in Matthew's account of the circumstances surrounding Jesus' birth. An evil pagan king killed all the male infants in Bethlehem age two and under because he believed one of them was a threat to his kingdom. God intervened to protect Jesus supernaturally from this slaughter. The account immediately stirs reminiscence of a similar OT event. In Exodus 1, an evil pagan king ordered the slaughter of all male Israelite infants in Egypt because he feared that their growing numbers were a threat to his kingdom. God supernaturally protected one baby boy, a child named Moses. Matthew's Gospel reminds the reader that the events that surrounded Jesus' birth are similar to the events that surrounded Moses' birth in order to portray Jesus as a figure that is like Moses in a remarkable way.[2]

---

[1] This is not to suggest that Matthew imaginatively created material in order to portray Jesus as one like Moses. For a response to the claim that Matthew's Gospel is creative historiography, see C. Quarles, *Midrash Criticism: Introduction and Appraisal* (Lanham, MD: University Press of America, 1998). D. C. Allison Jr. correctly pointed out that typology could contribute to fictional narratives like 4 Ezra, but it could also be used to interpret historical facts. He mentioned Eusebius's use of a Moses typology to describe Constantine as an example (*The New Moses: A Matthean Typology* [Minneapolis: Fortress, 1993], 267).

[2] For a much more thorough treatment of Matthew's presentation of Jesus as the New Moses, see Allison, *The New Moses*, 137–270. The parallels between the circumstances of Jesus' birth

The parallels between Jesus and Moses are emphasized even more in Matt 2:20b. The words "Those seeking the life of the child are dead" are a clear and direct quotation of the Greek version (LXX) of Exod 4:19 with only minor changes that were necessary to adapt the statement to a new context.[3] The angel of the Lord took words originally spoken by God to and about Moses and applied them to Jesus in order to signal that Jesus would somehow be like Moses. Many of the parallels between Jesus and Moses are implicit rather than explicit. Nevertheless in 2:20 "the Moses typology of this chapter comes most visibly to the surface of the narrative."[4]

The parallels between Jesus and Moses are again prominent in the introduction to the SM. Jesus' ascent of a mountain to deliver His authoritative interpretation and application of God's law to His people is strangely reminiscent of Moses' ascent of Sinai to receive and deliver the law of God. The words "He went up on the mountain" in 5:1 are an exact verbal parallel to the description of Moses' ascending Mount Sinai in Exod 19:3. This particular construction appears only three times in the Greek OT, and all three occurrences describe Moses' ascent of Mount Sinai (Exod 19:3; 24:18; 34:4). When Matthew used this phrase to describe Jesus, many of his original Jewish readers who were steeped in the knowledge of the OT would have immediately recognized Jesus' similarity to Moses.[5]

Matthew used this construction "He went up the mountain" again in Matt 14:23 and 15:29. Interestingly both of these occurrences of the construction appear in the immediate context of narratives about Jesus' deeds that would also likely have recalled memories of the ministry of Moses. Matthew 14:23 introduces Jesus' miracle of walking on the water, which was reminiscent of the miraculous crossing of the sea in Exod 14:15–31. Similarly Matt 15:29 immediately precedes the miraculous feeding of the four thousand, which is reminiscent of the miracle of the manna in the wilderness.

---

and the circumstances of Moses' birth are even more pronounced when one consults the Moses traditions preserved in Josephus, Exod Rabb., the Talmud, and the Targum of *Pseudo Jonathan*.

[3] The only adaptations are Matthew's omission of πάντες and the replacement of σου with τοῦ παιδίου.

[4] R. T. France, *The Gospel of Matthew*, NICNT (Grand Rapids: Eerdmans, 2007), 90.

[5] Allison correctly noted, "At every juncture the book presupposes that the reader is bringing to its ubiquity of allusions an intimate knowledge of Judaica, knowledge without which one is reading commentary without text" (*The New Moses*, 270).

These parallels (and many others) between Jesus and Moses serve to identify Jesus as the fulfillment of Moses' prophecy in Deut 18:15–19. The prophecy promised the coming of "a prophet" who would speak with divine authority and would be "like Moses." NT texts such as John 6:14; 7:40; Acts 3:11–26; and 7:37 refer to this figure simply as "the Prophet" and identify Him as the Messiah.[6] This suggests that many of the Jews of this general period viewed Deut 18:15–19 as a messianic prophecy and expected the Messiah to be like Moses in numerous ways.

A later rabbinic tradition shows that this view persisted for nearly a millennium after the time of Jesus.

> R. Berekiah said in the name of R. Isaac: As the first redeemer [Moses] was, so shall the latter Redeemer [Messiah] be. What is stated of the former redeemer? "And Moses took his wife and his sons, and set them upon an ass" (Exod. 4:20). Similarly it will be with the latter Redeemer, as it is stated, "Lowly and riding upon an ass" (Zech. 9:9). As the former redeemer caused manna to descend, as it is stated, "Behold, I will cause to rain bread from heaven for you" (Exod 16:4), so will the latter Redeemer cause manna to descend, as it is stated, "May he be as rich as a cornfield in the land" (Ps 72:16). As the former redeemer made a well to rise (Num 21:17–18), so the latter Redeemer brings up water, as it is stated, "And a fountain shall come forth of the house of the Lord, and shall water the valley of Shittim" (Joel 4:18).[7]

Rabbinic tradition expected the Messiah to be a Redeemer, to be like Moses, and to repeat deeds associated with the ministry of Moses.

Thus Matthew's presentation of Jesus as the prophet like Moses fulfilled an important theological purpose. It identified Jesus both as the promised Messiah *and* as the Savior of His people in a vivid and memorable manner. Although modern Christians tend to think of Moses primarily as a lawgiver, to the ancient Jews he was far more. Moses was primarily remembered as a redeemer, a deliverer, and a savior. Presentation of Jesus as the new Moses thus emphasized His redemptive role.

Stephen, the first martyr of the Christian church, presented Jesus as the fulfillment of the prophet-like-Moses prophecy in his final sermon, the sermon that would cost him his life. Although his angry opponents cut his sermon short, the point of Stephen's message is clear:

---

[6] G. Friedrich, "προφήτης" *TDNT* 6 (1968): 845–48.

[7] *Qoh. Rab.* 1:9 (references are to the OT). This Midrash on Ecclesiastes dates to the first half of the ninth century. Thus one cannot automatically infer that the views contained in it are representative of Second-Temple Judaism.

Jesus, like Moses, was a rejected Redeemer and Deliverer. Stephen emphasized Moses' role as deliverer in Acts 7:25: "He assumed his brothers would understand that God would give them *deliverance* through him, but they did not understand."[8] And Stephen emphasized Moses' role as redeemer in v. 35: "This Moses, whom they rejected when they said, Who appointed you a ruler and a judge?—this one God sent as a ruler and a *redeemer* by means of the angel who appeared to him in the bush. This man led them out and performed wonders and signs in the land of Egypt, at the Red Sea, and in the desert for 40 years."[9]

Thus by showing that Jesus was a prophet like Moses, Matthew demonstrated that Jesus was more than a prophet or a miracle worker. He was one who would redeem and deliver His people. The Moses typology was a masterful manner in which to communicate Jesus' significance to Matthew's audience of Jewish Christians. Identifying someone with a well-known person can be a graphic way of describing him. For example an excited coach can watch one of the players on the college baseball team make a grand slam and say, "Wow, that student may become one of the greatest batters ever." Or he can watch the student knock the ball out of the park and say, "Wow, I believe that student is destined to become the next Mickey Mantle." The personal comparison more vividly and memorably describes the student's skill as an athlete. In a similar way, when Matthew portrayed Jesus as the next Moses or the new Moses, he offered a graphic description of Jesus' role as Redeemer, Deliverer, and Savior.

Moses rescued Israel from bondage to Pharaoh—their slavery in Egypt. Jesus would rescue His people from an even more frightening slavery, slavery to sin and Satan. Matthew 1:21 is recognized by most scholars as the programmatic statement of Matthew's Gospel, a statement that announces the primary theological agenda of the entire book: "You are to name Him Jesus [lit., Yeshua or Joshua], because He will save His people from their sins." Jewish readers would likely be struck by the fact that Jesus bore the name of Moses' immediate successor, the leader who took Moses' place after his death. The appeal to the etymological significance of the name and the promise "Jesus will save His people" served to confirm His identity as a redeemer like Moses. The angel added that Jesus would save His people "from

---

[8] Italics added.
[9] Italics added.

their sins." On the one hand this implied that Jesus would provide forgiveness of sins. Matthew 20:28 states that Jesus came "to give His life—a ransom for many." Nevertheless in 1:21 the angel promised far more than this. Jesus would not just save His people from the punishment that sins deserve. Jesus would "save His people from their sins." The Greek preposition translated "from" (*apo*) expresses the idea of removal or separation.[10] Jesus will save His people "away from" their sins. This is more than a promise of forgiveness. It seems to be a promise of deliverance from a life of sinfulness.[11]

The portrayal of Jesus as the new Moses is the key to understanding some of Matthew's more puzzling fulfillment citations that appear in the narrative of Jesus' birth and infancy. In Matt 2:15 Matthew quoted Hos 11:1: "Out of Egypt I called My son." In the context of Hosea, the "son" was the nation of Israel and the "call from Egypt" referred to the exodus when the enslaved Jews were set free from Pharaoh. At first it seems strange that Matthew would claim that this text was fulfilled by the holy family's journey to and from Egypt. However, when one recognizes Matthew's intention to present Jesus as the new Moses, the appeal to Israel's exodus makes perfect sense. As Luz has pointed out, Matthew used Hos 11:1 to show that "the exodus from Egypt is repeated and fulfilled in Jesus."[12] The appeal to the prophet Hosea shows that the reader "is to behold in Jesus' story the replay of another, that of the exodus from Egypt, a story whose hero is Moses."[13] In the next text (2:17–18) Matthew applied to Jesus a passage from Jer 31:15 about Israel's bondage (this time in Babylon), which was immediately followed by a promise of deliverance and restoration. Matthew appealed to OT texts about bondage and redemption, slavery and

---

[10] See "ἀπό," BDAG, 105, 1.b.

[11] D. A. Hagner shares this view since he describes the salvation Jesus provided as having "a much more profound, moral sense" (*Matthew 1–13*, WBC [Dallas: Word, 1993], 19). Davies and Allison share this view for they state, "Furthermore, Jesus' revelatory imperatives and abiding presence (18.20; 28:20) are salvific in so far as they encourage and enable believers to obtain the 'better righteousness' (5.20). Perhaps, then, Matthew thought that Jesus saved his people from their sins in a variety of ways" (W. D. Davies and D. C. Allison Jr., *A Critical and Exegetical Commentary on the Gospel According to Saint Matthew*, ICC [Edinburgh: Clark, 1988], 1:210).

[12] U. Luz, *Matthew: A Commentary*, Hermeneia (Minneapolis: Fortress, 2007), 1:121. For the view that Hosea intended Hos 11:1 to refer to the exodus as a metaphor for the Messianic future, see John H. Sailhamer, "Hosea 11:1 and Matthew 2:15," *WTJ* 63 (2001): 87–96; Michael B. Shepherd, *The Twelve Prophets in the New Testament* (New York: Peter Lang, 2011).

[13] Allison, *The New Moses*, 141.

deliverance to show that Jesus would be a deliverer who rescues God's people from the worst plight of all, sin and its serious consequences.

Through his motif in which he identified Jesus as the new Moses, Matthew beautifully and powerfully emphasized that Jesus came to lead His people on a new spiritual exodus, to rescue His people, to break the power of sin, and set its captives free. Jesus will lead His people out of spiritual bondage much as Moses led his people out of political bondage. Jesus will deliver His people from their slavery to sin much as Moses delivered his people from their slavery in Egypt. Jesus will lead His people into a spiritual promised land (Matt 5:5) much as Moses led his people to inherit the land of Canaan.

Augustine seems to have recognized that the SM was to be interpreted in light of the New Moses/New Exodus typology of the Gospel of Matthew. Augustine wrote that the SM was addressed to people whom Christ has "set free by his love."[14] More recently African-American believers understood well the connection between Jesus and Moses made prominent in Matthew's Gospel. The lyrics of their traditional spiritual exclaim:

> When Israel was in Egypt's land,
> Let My people go!
> Oppressed so hard they could not stand,
> Let My people go!

> *Refrain:*

> Go down, Moses,
> Way down in Egypt's land;
> Tell old Pharaoh
> To let My people go!

> No more shall they in bondage toil,
> Let My people go!
> Let them come out with Egypt's spoil,
> Let My people go!

> Oh, let us all from bondage flee,
> Let My people go!
> And let us all in Christ be free,
> Let My people go!

---

[14] Augustine, *Serm. Dom.* 1.1.2.

The righteousness described in the SM is an absolute impossibility for those who remain captive to Satan and are enslaved to sin. Yet Jesus' followers have been liberated from this slavery. The great Redeemer has cried, "Let My people go!" He has removed their shackles, killed their old harsh taskmaster, buried his body in the sand, crushed the power of their dark pharaoh with one plague after another, and led them to freedom across the parted sea. The SM describes the righteousness that will be exhibited by those who have experienced this emancipation from slavery to sin.

The New Creation: Jesus Bears the Power to Make His People New

John the Baptist, the forerunner of the Messiah, proclaimed that Jesus would radically transform His followers. John announced that the One coming after him was mightier than he. The coming Messiah would display His might by baptizing sinners, not with water but "with the Holy Spirit and fire" (Matt 3:11). The context of John's words demonstrates that baptism with fire was a reference to God's wrath which Jesus would pour out on unrepentant sinners.[15] Immediately before the reference to baptism with fire, John had announced that God would cut down every tree that does not bear good fruit and cast it into the fire (v. 10). Then John warned that the coming Messiah would separate the worthless chaff from the wheat and burn it in an inextinguishable fire (v. 12).

Just as the baptism of fire corresponds to the fate of chaff or trees that do not bear good fruit, so the baptism of the Holy Spirit relates to trees that do bear good fruit and wheat that is useful. This good fruit is the good deeds performed by the disciples in expression of their repentance (v. 8). The baptism of the Holy Spirit makes Jesus' followers useful to Him and ensures that they will bear the fruit of

[15] A number of commentators view baptism "with the Holy Spirit and with fire" as a hendiadys, a construction in which two ideas are linked with a coordinating conjunction although one is dependent on the other. See BDF, §442 (16). Thus Jesus' baptism would be a baptism "with the fire of the Holy Spirit." This view is defended by Davies and Allison (*A Critical and Exegetical Commentary on the Gospel According to Saint Matthew*, 1:316–17); and France (*The Gospel of Matthew*, 113–14). W. F. Albright and C. S. Mann argued this view earlier based on the use of the phrase "Holy Spirit and fire" in Qumran literature (*Matthew: Introduction, Translation, and Notes*, AB [Garden City, NY: Doubleday, 1971], 26–27). Although grammatically possible, the immediate context argues strongly against this view. See R. H. Gundry, *Matthew: A Commentary on His Literary and Theological Act* (Grand Rapids: Eerdmans, 1982), 49; Blomberg, *Matthew*, 80; and esp. Broadus, *The Gospel According to Matthew*, 50–52.

good works. The SM describes the righteousness that is the fruit of the Spirit whom Jesus imparts to His followers.

Jesus' own baptism by John clarifies the doctrine of the baptism of the Spirit by confirming that Jesus will baptize with the Spirit, and this baptism will result in a radical transformation of His disciples. At Jesus' baptism the Holy Spirit descended on Jesus "like a dove." The most plausible explanation for the association of the Spirit with a dove points to Genesis 1.[16] The activity of the Spirit in creation was described with the words, "And the Spirit of God was hovering over the surface of the waters" (Gen 1:2). The verb "hover" was the same verb used to describe a bird rapidly flapping its wings in order to remain in a stationary position in the air.[17] Since this verb was commonly associated with birds, Jewish rabbis sometimes portrayed the Holy Spirit as a bird. Later rabbinic writings associated the Spirit with the eagle. However, early rabbinic writings associated the Spirit with the dove. A fragment from the DSS describes the Spirit as "hovering" over the repentant, evidently based on Gen 1:2.[18] Thus the association of the Spirit with the dove at Jesus' baptism was most likely intended to be reminiscent of the Genesis 1 creation account. It served to mark Jesus' ministry as the beginning of a new creation.

The OT background is rich with theological significance. The allusions to Gen 1:2 hint that "the events of Gen 1 were being recapitulated or repeated in the Messiah's life: the eschatological creation had begun."[19] Jesus is endowed by the Spirit with the power of the "new creation." He will baptize sinners with the Spirit in order to make them new.

Matthew seems to have prepared his readers to recognize the significance of the theophany at Jesus' baptism in the first words of

---

[16] C. K. Barrett, *The Holy Spirit and the Gospel Tradition* (London: SPCK, 1947), 38–39; Davies and Allison, *A Critical and Exegetical Commentary on the Gospel According to Saint Matthew*, 1:334–35; Hagner, *Matthew 1–13*, 58; W. Lane, *The Gospel of Mark*, NICNT (Grand Rapids: Eerdmans, 1974), 56–57. Davies and Allison point out that the early church fathers, including Tertullian, Theodotus, Cyril of Jerusalem, and Didymus the Blind, relate Genesis 1 to the baptism of Jesus or of Christians (*A Critical and Exegetical Commentary on the Gospel According to Saint Matthew*, 1:334).

[17] The Hebrew verb used to describe the activity of the Spirit in creation is רָחַף.

[18] *b. Ḥag.* 15a (citing the late first-century rabbi Ben Zoma); *Tg. Cant.* 2.12. For the evidence from the DSSs, see D. C. Allison Jr., "The Baptism of Jesus and a New Dead Sea Scroll," *BAR* 18 (March/April 1992): 58–60.

[19] Davies and Allison, *A Critical and Exegetical Commentary on the Gospel According to Saint Matthew*, 1:334.

his Gospel. The Gospel opened with the title "the historical record of Jesus Christ." The Greek phrase (*biblos geneseōs*) literally means "book of origin" or "book of genesis." At first glance the phrase seems to be merely a title of Jesus' genealogy. Closer examination suggests otherwise.

The phrase was used in Gen 2:4 (LXX) as a title for the account of the origin of the heavens and earth: "This is the book of the origin of heaven and earth, when it happened, on the day in which God made the heaven and the earth."[20] The phrase appears again in Gen 5:1 as a title for the account of the origin of Adam: "This is the book of the origin of men, on the day when God made Adam, He made him according to the image of God."[21] These are the only two occurrences in the LXX of the clause "This is the book of the origin of . . ." Significantly both occurrences refer to creation rather than mere pro-creation, the first to the creation of the universe and the second to the creation of man. When the LXX introduces genealogies in Gen 6:9; 10:1; 11:10,27; 25:12,19; and 36:1,9, another construction is used.[22] This suggests that the title "book of origin" (*biblos geneseōs*) in Matt 1:1 is not merely the title for Jesus' genealogy but is also an introduction to the Gospel or a major portion of it that presents Jesus' ministry as an act of new creation.

Furthermore, the title of the First Book of Moses in the LXX is "Origin" or "Genesis" (*genesis*). The writings of Philo (20 BC–AD 50) show that this title was current in the early first century.[23] Davies and Allison have argued at length that Matthew's phrase was intended to call Genesis to the mind of his Jewish Christian readers.[24] As France observed:

> The first two words of Matthew's gospel are literally "book of genesis.". . . The effect on a Jewish reader is comparable to that of John's opening phrase, "in the beginning. . . ." The theme of the fulfillment of Scripture is signaled from the very start, and these opening words suggest that a new creation is now taking place.[25]

[20] The author's translation from the LXX.

[21] The author's translation from the LXX.

[22] Either αὗται δὲ αἱ γενέσεις or καὶ αὗται αἱ γενέσεις.

[23] Philo, *Poster. c.* 127; id, *Abr.* 1; id, *Aet. Mund.* 19. In the last passage Philo claimed that this title had been given to the book by Moses himself.

[24] Davies and Allison, *A Critical and Exegetical Commentary on the Gospel According to Saint Matthew,* 1:149–56.

[25] France, *The Gospel of Matthew,* 28.

The creation theme in the introduction to Matthew would have alerted Matthew's readers to expect connections to the creation account and would have prepared them to recognize the significance of the activity of the Holy Spirit in Jesus' baptism.

The apostle Paul probably derived his own teaching regarding the miracle of "new creation" from his own reflection on the meaning of Jesus' baptism. In 2 Cor 5:17 Paul exclaimed, "Therefore, if anyone is in Christ, he is a new creation; old things have passed away, and look, new things have come." Similarly in Gal 6:15 Paul wrote, "For both circumcision and uncircumcision mean nothing; what matters instead is a new creation." In Eph 2:10 Paul insisted that the believer is "His creation, created in Christ Jesus for good works, which God prepared ahead of time so that we should walk in them." Paul described the believer as a "new creation" because he recognized that Jesus imparted the Spirit to His disciples and the Spirit hovered over them just as He had done in Genesis 1 in order to continue His creative work and make God's people new.[26]

OT writers had longed for and promised the miracle of new creation. After his adultery with Bathsheba, King David had prayed and expressed his longing for transformation with the words, "God, create a clean heart for me and renew a steadfast spirit within me" (Ps 51:10). David's petition used the same verb for "create" that is employed to describe God's creative activity in Gen 1:1.[27] Ezekiel 36:26 announced the answer to David's prayer by using similar language to speak of the transformation of individuals that God would bring about through the new covenant: "I will give you a new heart and put a new spirit within you." These promises provide the theological framework necessary for understanding Jesus' description of His disciples as the "pure in heart" (Matt 5:8). The form of the Spirit at Jesus' baptism is thus a picturesque assurance that through the ministry of Jesus, God was answering David's prayer by creating new hearts in His people, renewing their spirits, making people new, radically transforming them so that they can live righteously and obediently.

---

[26] Paul's references to the restoration of the divine image in believers appear to be an extension of the new creation theme. See Rom 8:29; 1 Cor 15:49; 2 Cor 3:18; Col 3:10.

[27] See "בָּרָא," HALOT, 47.

The New Covenant: Jesus' Death Establishes a New Covenant in Which God's Law Is Written on the Hearts of His People

Perhaps most importantly, Jesus claimed that His death on the cross initiated a new covenant between God and His people. As Jesus instituted the Lord's Supper, He held up the cup, gave thanks for it, and offered it to His disciples. He declared, "This is My blood that establishes the covenant; it is shed for many for the forgiveness of sins" (Matt 26:28). Covenants between two parties were established and sealed with an act of sacrifice. God's covenant with Abraham provides an example. When God promised to give Abraham a son, multiply his descendants, and give him the land of promise, Abraham asked how he could know that God would keep this covenant. God had Abraham slaughter a heifer, a goat, and a ram and cut them in two. After night fell, a smoking firepot and a flaming torch appeared and passed between the split carcasses. The ritual showed that God Himself would be destroyed like the sacrifices if He should fail to keep His covenant with Abraham. This sacrifice sealed the covenant.

The OT expression for making a covenant is a Hebrew phrase that is literally "to cut a covenant." The making of a covenant required the slaughter, the "cutting," of a sacrificial animal. When Jesus spoke of "my blood [of] the covenant," He meant that His death was not only an atoning sacrifice. It was also the sacrifice that established and sealed a new covenant between God and His people.[28]

The new covenant was promised by God through the prophets in such passages as Jer 31:31–34 and Ezek 36:24–30. Jeremiah 31:31–34 promised:

> "Look, the days are coming"—this is the LORD's declaration—"when I will make a new covenant with the house of Israel and with the house of Judah. This one will not be like the covenant I made with their ancestors when I took them by the hand to bring them out of the land of Egypt—a covenant they broke even though I had married them"—the LORD's declaration. "Instead, this is the covenant I will make with the house of Israel after those days"—the LORD's declaration. "I will put My teaching within them and write it on their hearts. I will be their God, and they will be My people. No longer will one teach his neighbor or his brother, saying, 'Know the LORD,' for they

---

[28] The parallel in Luke 22:20 clarifies that Jesus' sacrifice established the new covenant. A few later manuscripts (A C D, etc.) also inserted the adjective "new" in Matt 26:28. The adjective is probably not original since it is absent from the earliest manuscripts such as p³⁷, p⁴⁵, ℵ, and B.

will all know Me, from the least to the greatest of them"—the LORD's declaration. "For I will forgive their wrongdoing and never again remember their
sin."

The old covenant was ineffective because it issued commands but did
not transform individuals and grant them the power to fulfill those
commands. The new covenant would involve the inner transformation of God's people. God would put His law in the minds of His
people and inscribe it on their hearts so that they would naturally
and spontaneously fulfill the law's righteous demands. The new covenant promised forgiveness of sins, but it also promised far more. God
would change His people from the inside out so that their character
resembled His own holy character and their lives would be pleasing
to Him.

Matthew alluded to Jeremiah's promise of the new covenant early
in his Gospel. Matthew 2:18 described Herod's slaughter of the male
infants of Bethlehem as a fulfillment of Jer 31:15: "A voice was heard
in Ramah, a lament with bitter weeping—Rachel weeping for her children, refusing to be comforted for her children because they are no
more."

These words were an eloquent description of Israel's plight during
the Babylonian exile. Although Rachel, matriarch of the nation Israel,
had long been dead, the prophet portrayed her as one who mourned
the destruction of the Israelites and their displacement from the land
of promise. Matthew recognized that Herod's slaughter of the infants
meant that Israel's exile continued to the time of the Messiah's coming. However, Matthew did not strip OT texts from their original context. Normally, when Matthew cited an OT passage, he intended for
his readers to recall the surrounding material as well. This appears to
be the case here. Immediately after the lament of Jer 31:15, the prophet launched into a series of glorious promises. He foretold the return
of Israel from exile (Jer 31:16–20), the repentance and restoration of
Israel (vv. 21–30), and finally the institution of the new covenant (vv.
31–34). By citing 31:15, Matthew raises the reader's anticipation of
the restoration and transformation of God's people, hopes that will
be fulfilled through Jesus' words at the Last Supper.[29] The allusion
to the promise of the new covenant at both the beginning and end of

---

[29] See Davies and Allison, *A Critical and Exegetical Commentary on the Gospel According to
Saint Matthew*, 1:267–69; and C. S. Keener, *The Gospel of Matthew: A Socio-Rhetorical Commentary* (Grand Rapids: Eerdmans, 2009), 111–12.

Jesus' life signals that He will bring about the fulfillment of the new covenant. The SM describes the law written on the believer's heart in fulfillment of the new covenant. The SM describes the righteousness that will naturally and spontaneously characterize the lives of His followers.

The amazing righteousness that Jesus produces in His disciples through the new exodus, new creation, and new covenant is also affirmed by some of Jesus' most important parables in Matthew. In the parable of the Soils (13:1–9,18–23), Jesus portrayed the believer as fertile earth on which the seed of His word has fallen. The seed produced a harvest of 100, 60, or 30 fold.

The fruit (v. 23) produced by the seed is likely a picture of the righteous deeds produced in the believer by Jesus' message since "fruit" in this Gospel frequently refers to deeds that exhibit one's true spiritual character (3:8,10; 7:16–20; 12:33; 21:19,34,43).[30] Hagner aptly commented that "the fruit is probably to be understood as the pattern of conduct described in the Sermon on the Mount (chaps. 5–7), i.e. the living out of the kingdom of God here and now (cf. 5:13–16; 21:43)."[31] The three quantities of fruit produced by the disciple are truly remarkable. A 7- to 15-fold harvest was considered a normal or good harvest. A 30-fold harvest was truly a bumper crop. A 60-fold harvest was double a bumper crop. A 100-fold harvest was more than triple a bumper crop.[32] The climax of the parable of the Soils thus demonstrates that Jesus will produce an amazing and miraculous harvest of good deeds in the lives of His followers. Nolland suggested that "the parable expresses Jesus' own relaxed confidence that God is working the renewal of his people through him (Jesus)."[33]

Similarly the parable of the Wheat and the Weeds (13:24–30,36–43) uses good seed to portray the "sons of the kingdom" (v. 38). These sons are described as the "righteous" who "will shine like the sun in their Father's kingdom" (v. 43). This promise evidently refers to the disciples' final glorification. The disciples will radiate the glory of God in a way that is strikingly similar to Jesus' own transfiguration (17:2)

[30] This assumes that the cursing of the fig tree is an enacted prophecy warning of the destruction of Jerusalem if the Jews did not bear righteous fruit.

[31] Hagner, Matthew 1–13, 380.

[32] See Keener, The Gospel of Matthew, 377–78.

[33] J. Nolland, The Gospel of Matthew: A Commentary on the Greek Text, NIGTC (Grand Rapids: Eerdmans, 2005), 528–30, esp. 530. See also Keener, The Gospel of Matthew, 376–78.

and an obvious fulfillment of the promise in Dan 12:3.[34] However, even before this final transformation while Jesus' disciples await the final harvest, He described them as both "good" and "righteous." This shows that Jesus' followers will experience radical transformation in this life which will be completed at the time of His return.

The Beatitudes express God's grace to undeserving and repentant sinners. God's gracious character is emphasized repeatedly later in the sermon as well (Matt 5:45; 7:7–11). The SM insists, however, that one must not disgrace divine grace by appealing to it as an excuse for a sinful lifestyle. True disciples will be characterized by a remarkable righteousness that exceeds even that of the scribes and Pharisees and fulfills even the least of God's commandments (5:17–20). Those who have become sons and daughters of the heavenly Father will resemble Him in their character and behavior (5:9,44–48; 6:7–12). As a result, personal holiness is an important indication of whether one who professes to follow Christ is truly His disciple (7:15–23). The disciples' righteousness is not a product of their self-effort. They express their repentance by hungering and thirsting for righteousness (5:6) and God graciously begins to fill them with that righteousness here and now and will finally and completely fill them with that righteousness when Christ returns and consummates His kingdom.

---

[34] Nolland, *The Gospel of Matthew*, 561–62; Keener, *The Gospel of Matthew*, 389–90; and Hagner, *Matthew 1–13*, 394.

Chapter 5

THE INTRODUCTION TO THE SERMON
ON THE MOUNT (MATT 5:1–16)

A. The Setting of the Sermon on the Mount
(Matt 5:1–2)

At first glance Matthew's introduction to the SM may appear mundane. A closer look demonstrates that the introduction is packed with theological significance. Matthew's introduction was clearly designed to do more than simply express the occasion and location of the sermon and Jesus' posture while He taught. Instead the introduction signals that the great Teacher is a fulfillment of one of the most important prophecies of the OT. Matthew often highlighted the fact that Jesus fulfilled the OT by using the fulfillment formula "now all this took place to fulfill what was spoken by the Lord through the prophet."[1] In 5:1–2 Matthew highlighted Jesus' fulfillment of the OT promises in a more subtle but equally powerful manner.

Jesus' ascent of a mountain to deliver His authoritative interpretation and application of God's law to His people is strongly reminiscent of Moses' ascent of Sinai to receive and deliver the law of God (Exod 19:3). See the section above, "Theological Framework for Interpreting the Sermon on the Mount—The New Exodus." Three details suggest that Matthew wanted his readers to notice this parallel. First, the words "He went up on the mountain" in Matt 5:1 constitute an exact verbal parallel to the description of Moses ascending Mount Sinai in Exod 19:3. This particular construction appears only three times in the entire Greek OT, and all three occurrences describe Moses' ascent of Mount Sinai (Exod 19:3; 24:18; 34:4).

Second, the definite article "the" may highlight the importance of the mountain and imply a comparison with Sinai.[2] The definite article

---

[1] See Matt 1:22; 2:15,17,23; 4:14; 8:17; 13:14,35; 21:4; 26:54,56; 27:9.

[2] In Greek grammar use of the definite article "the" with an object of a preposition is unnecessary even when the noun is definite. See A. T. Robertson, *Grammar of the Greek New Testament in Light of Historical Research* (Nashville: Broadman, 1934), 791; BDF, §255, 133–34; and Daniel Wallace, *Greek Grammar Beyond the Basics* (Grand Rapids: Zondervan, 1996), 247. The use of the definite article shows that Matthew had a particular mountain in mind. The article is not an

is best categorized as the article par excellence, which portrays an object as the best or most important of its kind. This hints that Matthew intended to compare this mountain with Sinai, the most important mountain of the OT.[3]

Third, many Jewish interpreters interpreted the Hebrew text of Deut 9:9 to mean that Moses sat on the mountain when he received the law. Although the Hebrew verb *yāšab* may mean "to remain or dwell," a common meaning of the verb in the Hebrew OT was "to sit," and references in the Talmud show that many rabbis took the verb in this sense.[4] The description of Jesus' posture on the mountain would thus constitute another parallel with Moses' reception of the law.

The reason Matthew highlighted these parallels is clear. The parallels between Jesus and Moses serve to identify Jesus as the "new Moses" and as the fulfillment of Moses' prophecy in Deut 18:15–19:

> The LORD your God will raise up for you a prophet like me from among your own brothers. You must listen to him. This is what you requested from the LORD your God at Horeb on the day of the assembly when you said, "Let us not continue to hear the voice of the LORD our God or see this great fire any longer, so that we will not die!" Then the LORD said to me, "They have spoken well. I will raise up for them a prophet like you from among their brothers. I will put My words in his mouth, and he will tell them everything I command him. I will hold accountable whoever does not listen to My words that he speaks in My name."

This prophecy in Deuteronomy 18 offers three descriptions of the one who would fulfill it. First, he would be an Israelite. Twice Moses described him as coming "from among your own/their brothers" (vv. 15,18). Second, he would speak with divine authority, and the people were obligated to obey whatever he said. Third, God told Moses that

"article of previous reference" since the only mountain previously mentioned in Matthew's Gospel was the mountain to which Satan carried Jesus during the temptation (Matt 4:8). The article is not "monadic" (pointing to one of a kind) since this mountain was not the only mountain in the region. The case for the article par excellence is weakened by Matthew's possible dependency on Mark 3:13, which has the definite article but does not seem to imply a Sinai typology.

[3] Contrast this view with T. L. Donaldson, *Jesus on the Mountain: A Study in Matthean Theology*, JSNTSS 8 (Sheffield: JSOT, 1985). Donaldson argues that the mountain motif in Matthew has reference primarily to Mount Zion. Matthew's point is that "those who gather to Jesus have come to the faithful Son (cf. Heb. 3:1–6) in whom all the hopes associated with Mount Zion and the heavenly Jerusalem have come to fulfillment" (ibid., 202). Donaldson suggests that while the "mountain" alludes to Zion primarily, it does not do so exclusively. He admitted that "Sinai typology is at work in Mt 5.1 in some fashion" even if it does not play a dominant role (ibid., 111–12).

[4] See *b. Meg* 21a and *b. Sotah* 49a.

the prophet would be "like you" (v. 18), and Moses told the people that the prophet would be "like me" (v. 15). Deuteronomy 34:10–12 listed two important features of Moses' unique prophetic ministry: Moses' intimate relationship with God and Moses' miracles. Jesus' life and ministry were also characterized by an intimate relationship with the Father and by numerous and amazing miracles.

The theological point made by comparing Jesus to Moses was quite profound—Jesus is the Savior of God's people. Although modern Christians think of Moses primarily as a lawgiver, to the ancient Jews he was far more. Moses was recognized first and foremost as a redeemer, deliverer, and savior.

By showing that Jesus is the prophet like Moses, Matthew demonstrated that Jesus is not only a prophet or a miracle worker. He is one who would redeem and deliver His people. Whereas Moses delivered Israel from their slavery in Egypt, Jesus would rescue God's people from their sins and from the punishment their sins deserved. Matthew 1:21 had already stressed that Jesus "will save His people from their sins." Later 20:28 said that He came "to give His life—a ransom for many." Matthew's presentation of Jesus as the prophet like Moses also demonstrates that He was chosen by the Father to save and redeem His people.

Matthew's Gospel clearly highlights parallels between Moses and Jesus in order to present Christ as the promised "prophet like Moses" (Deut 18:18; cp. Acts 3:22). Nevertheless, the Gospel shows that Jesus is more than One *like* Moses; He is One *greater* than Moses. Matthew's Gospel already emphasized that the Savior who came to rescue His people from the penalty their sins deserve was none other than "Immanuel," God with us (Matt 1:23). Although the introduction to the Sermon on the Mount presents Jesus as the new Moses, it also hints at Jesus' supremacy to Moses. Although Jesus insisted that neither the smallest letter or tiniest serif would be stricken from the Law "until heaven and earth pass away" (5:18), he later claimed: "Heaven and earth will pass away, but My words will never pass away." Jesus' teachings are clearly superior to the writings of Moses, and this implies that Jesus is greater than Moses (Heb 3:1–6).[5]

---

[5] D. E. Garland rightly cautioned that one should not emphasize the parallels between Jesus and Moses to the neglect of the differences. After examining four important differences between Jesus and Moses, he concluded, "While Matthew presents Jesus as Moses-like, he does not

Despite the Moses and Sinai typology in the introduction to the SM, one must not conclude that the SM constitutes a new law comparable to the Mosaic law. One major section of the SM is devoted to the proper interpretation and application of the law (Matt 5:17–48), but this hardly justifies categorizing the SM as a whole as "law." The SM is categorically different from the Mosaic law. Its precepts are the law written on the heart in fulfillment of the promise of the new covenant (Jer 31:33). It is a description of the righteousness that will characterize the followers of Jesus who have been transformed through the baptism of the Spirit and experienced new creation. "Law" is an apt label only if one remembers that this law is written not on tablets of stone but on the tablets of the human heart (Rom 8:1–4; 2 Cor 3:3).

Although "law" is not the best descriptor for the SM, neither is the term "gospel." Matthew probably shifted from use of the verb "preach" (*kērussō*) that described Jesus' evangelistic proclamation in Matt 4:17 and 23 to the verb "teach" (*didaskō*) in 5:2 to hint that the SM was not primarily about how one entered the kingdom. Rather, it was a description of the character and conduct of those who already belonged to the kingdom. The SM is not a call to repentance; it is a description of the expression and evidences of true repentance.

Although crowds were present when Jesus taught (5:1; 7:28), His primary audience was the disciples. The pronoun "them" in 5:2 almost certainly looks to the noun "disciples" as its antecedent. This confirms that the main purpose of the SM is discipleship rather than evangelism. Thus one may best categorize the SM as a description of the life of the true disciple.[6]

The Greek text says that Jesus "opened His mouth" and began to teach the disciples.[7] The phrase is a familiar Semitic idiom for making an important pronouncement (Job 3:1; 33:2; Ps 78:2; Dan 10:16). Since Matt 13:35 shows that Ps 78:2 was fulfilled through Jesus' teaching ministry, the use of the phrase here may be designed to stir remembrance of that psalm.[8]

---

depict him as a new Moses but as the Lord, the son of God" (*Reading Matthew: A Literary and Theological Commentary* [Macon, GA: Smyth and Helwys, 2001], 53).

[6] See F. V. Filson, *A Commentary on the Gospel According to St. Matthew* (1960; reprint, Peabody, MA: Hendrickson, 1987), 76.

[7] See the HCSB margin.

[8] Gundry claimed that the phrase "echoes 4:4: 'every word that comes out through the mouth of God' (so Matthew alone). Jesus is 'God with us' in the first gospel (1:23). When he opens his mouth, therefore, his disciples hear nothing less than the Word of God" (*Matthew*, 67).

B. The Beatitudes (Matt 5:3–12)

Jesus' sermon begins with eight pronouncements of blessing known as the Beatitudes. Since Matthew had just alerted his readers to Jesus' identity as the new Moses, he probably intended for his readers to interpret the Beatitudes against the backdrop of the most important pronouncement of blessing in the law of Moses. Moses' final blessing of Israel appears in Deut 33:29: "How happy you are, Israel! Who is like you, a people saved by the LORD? He is the shield that protects you, the sword you boast in. Your enemies will cringe before you, and you will tread on their backs." Israel's blessing had both a historical focus and a future focus. The words "saved by the LORD" referred to Israel's exodus from Egypt. The remainder of the blessing assured the Israelites of success in their conquest of the promised land.

Several evidences suggest that Matthew intended readers to interpret the Beatitudes against this backdrop. First, Matthew had just alerted his readers to Jesus' identity as the new Moses. Many Jewish-Christian readers would naturally think of the most important pronouncements of blessing in the law of Moses as they read the Beatitudes. Matthew did not introduce Jesus as the new Moses in the introduction to the sermon only to abandon the theme immediately afterward. Jesus' identity as the new Moses surfaces in the discussion of His view of the law (Matt 5:17–20) and in His authoritative interpretation of the law in the so-called antitheses (vv. 21–48). The Beatitudes are more likely a continuation of the new Moses theme than a temporary detour from the theme. Second, this blessing was prominent in the minds of first-century Jews since this blessing formed the final recorded words of Moses spoken before his death. Third, Matthew's Jewish readers would hear echoes of the OT themes of the exodus and the conquest in the promise that the meek would inherit the land (v. 5).

This background suggests that the Beatitudes are not mere expressions of ethical principles accompanied by rewards but are pronouncements of salvation that identify Jesus' disciples as the new Israel.[9] The new Moses is a spiritual deliverer rather than a political

Although Gundry's comments are theologically correct, it is doubtful that Matthew's use of the phrase in 5:2 pointed to 4:4 since a closer parallel exists elsewhere in his Gospel.

[9] The presentation of Jesus' disciples as the "new Israel" or "spiritual Israel" does not prohibit national Israel from having an important role in God's economy in the future. The apostle Paul described believers in Christ as spiritual Israelites (Rom 2:17–29; Gal 6:15–16) and beneficiaries

one, and his pronouncements and promises must be understood in a spiritual sense. Thus in the Beatitudes the new Moses pronounced the blessings of spiritual exodus (liberation from slavery to sin) and spiritual conquest (victory over spiritual enemies) to the new Israel.[10]

These observations have significant ramifications for the interpretation of the SM. The commandments of the SM are not to be viewed as laws that must be kept in order to achieve salvation or as requirements for becoming a child of God. Rather the commandments define the character and conduct of those whom God has already claimed as His children. They describe the holy life that necessarily results from genuine salvation. Jesus pronounced salvation on the disciples through the Beatitudes, then proclaimed the benefits of salvation in the ethical teaching that follows. Davies and Allison correctly observed:

> The beatitudes are first of all blessings, not requirements. So by opening the sermon on the mount they place it within the context of grace, and their function is very similar to the function of 4.23–5.2: just as healing comes before imperative, so does blessing come before demand. The precedence of grace could not be plainer. The hard commands of Mt 5–7 presuppose God's mercy and prior saving activity.[11]

Scholars disagree over the exact number and structure of the Beatitudes.[12] Nine pronouncements of blessing appear in Matt 5:3–12. However, verses 11 and 12 should be viewed as commentary on the eighth beatitude. Several factors suggest this eight-beatitude structure. First, the first and eighth beatitudes both offer the explanation "because the kingdom of heaven is theirs." The promise of the king-

---

of God's covenant with Abraham. On the other hand he also anticipated a time when national Israel will be restored (Rom 11:25–32).

[10] For an extensive discussion of this view with a comparison to alternative views see C. Quarles, "The Blessings of the New Moses: The Theological Purpose of the Matthean Beatitudes," in *Jesus as Israel's Messiah: Engaging the Work of N. T. Wright*, ed. R. Webb and M. Powell, Library of Historical Jesus Studies (London: Clark, forthcoming). Although a possible connection with Deuteronomy 28 cannot be completely ruled out, this is doubtful. Deuteronomy 28 (LXX) uses forms of εὐλογέω in the pronouncements. Matthew used μακάριος (blessed) rather than a form of εὐλογέω. Matthew had no reason to change verbs if he desired to point to a connection with Deuteronomy 28. Furthermore, in the LXX μακάριος never served as the translation of the Hebrew root ברך, the root meaning "bless," that appears frequently in Deuteronomy 28 anywhere in the LXX.

[11] Davies and Allison, *A Critical and Exegetical Commentary on the Gospel According to Saint Matthew*, 1:466.

[12] Davies and Allison count nine beatitudes and arrange these in three triads (ibid., 1:429–31). Betz counts ten (*The Sermon on the Mount*, 105–9). But he admits, "Most scholars in antiquity as well as today prefer eight beatitudes" (ibid., 108).

dom serves as a bracket (*inclusio*) that marks verses 3–10 as a single literary unit. Second, the first eight beatitudes have the same form: a terse pronouncement of blessing followed by a brief explanation, and 11–12 do not follow this pattern. Third, the first four beatitudes are closely linked to one another through alliteration. In the Greek text, the words identifying the poor, mourners, gentle, and hungry all begin with the Greek letter *pi* (π). If one sees eight beatitudes in the text, the alliteration serves to divide the Beatitudes into two equal halves.[13] Finally, verses 3–10 use third-person plural forms ("they" and "theirs") to refer to beneficiaries of the blessings, but 11–12 shift to second-person plural forms ("you" and "your").[14]

Early Christian interpreters were convinced that the number of beatitudes was not accidental but was purposeful, and they believed that numerical symbolism was involved. Many, including Gregory of Nyssa, Ambrose of Milan, and Augustine believed that the eight beatitudes depicted the ascent of the soul. One recent commentator has pointed out that eight was a number of perfection in Jewish numerology and that perfection is an important concept in the Sermon on the Mount (5:48).[15]

This hypothesis seems a bit too imaginative. The Gospel of Matthew does not appear to employ Jewish numerology anywhere else. Numbers are sometimes significant in Matthew. Matthew 1:17 is probably an instance of *gematria* in which numbers represent letters of the Hebrew alphabet.[16] Jesus probably selected 12 disciples to parallel the number of the tribes of Israel and demonstrate that His followers constitute the new true people of God. Nevertheless neither of these examples is a true parallel to the symbolic use of numbers that Betz has proposed here.

[13] See C. Michaelis, "Die Π-Alliteration der Subjektsworte der Ersten 4 Seligpreisungen in Mt. v 3–6 und ihre Bedeutung für den Aufbau der Seligpreisungen bei Mt, Lk und in Q," *NovT* 10 (1968): 148–61.

[14] These features lend support to the chiastic structure of the beatitudes proposed by N. J. McEleney, "The Beatitudes of the Sermon on the Mount/Plain," *CBQ* 43 (1981): 1–13, esp. 13; and D. Turner, "Whom Does God Approve? The Context, Structure, Purpose, and Exegesis of the Matthean Beatitudes," *CTR* 6 (1992): 29–42, esp. 34.

[15] Betz, *The Sermon on the Mount*, 105–6.

[16] The threefold repetition of the number 14 is probably an example of *gematria*. *Gematria* used the numerical value of letters of the alphabet to communicate a message. In Hebrew David's name consisted of three consonants, ד (*dālēt*), ו (*wāw*), and ד (*dālēt*), which had the numerical values 4, 6, 4, respectively. Thus the number 14, the sum of 4, 6, and 4, served as a symbol for David and the Davidic Messiah.

The Beatitudes (from the Latin *beatus*, meaning "happy" or "blessed") are pronouncements of divine blessing. The term "blessed" is *makarios*. The term describes those to whom Jesus spoke as privileged recipients of God's favor. Although some modern translations render *makarios* as "happy," this translation is misleading. Jesus was not referring to an emotion or feeling that is based on present circumstances, nor was he assuring that life will not be plagued with difficulties.[17] Later Jesus warned that His followers will face severe persecution that will impose great hardship on them. However, He insisted that persecuted believers whose lives are difficult can experience the joy that results from divine blessing.[18] Hagner expressed the sense of the term in this way: "Rather than happiness in its mundane sense, it refers to the deep inner joy of those who have long awaited the salvation promised by God and who now begin to experience its fulfillment."[19]

This joy results from divine blessing since the verbs in verses 4,6,7, and possibly 9 are "divine passives."[20] "They will be comforted," "they will be filled," "they will be shown mercy," and perhaps "they will be called" mean that God will comfort Jesus' followers, fill them, show mercy to them, and call them His sons. The fact that Jesus began the SM with such pronouncements of blessing on His disciples before placing demands on them is significant. This order suggests that the righteousness described in the sermon is a result of divine blessing rather than a requirement for divine blessing.

Matthew 5:3

The word translated "poor" is the Greek word *ptōchoi*. The adjective was derived from a verb that means "to cower" or "to bow down timidly" (*ptōssō*). It described the posture of a beggar as he held out his cup and pled for coins from the passersby. The adjective means "to be

---

[17] See France, *The Gospel of Matthew*, 160–61. France argued that μαράριος was not "theologically loaded" and that εὐλογητός was the term used to describe someone as "blessed (by God)." Nevertheless, εὐλογητός is typically used in the LXX and NT to ascribe praise to God, and the pronouncements of blessing using divine passives suggest that the term is theologically loaded in this context.

[18] Luz opposed the translation "happy" since it "sounds somewhat banal, and it obscures the eschatological character of the promises in the second clauses." He admitted "there is no ideal translation in German [or English]" (*Matthew: A Commentary*, 1:190).

[19] Hagner, *Matthew 1–13*, 91.

[20] See Wallace, *Greek Grammar Beyond the Basics*, 437.

destitute, beggarly." Beggars were often crippled or otherwise incapacitated and completely unable to provide an income for themselves.
Beggars lived in a state of absolute dependence on the graciousness
and generosity of others. "Poor in spirit" means "beggarly in spirit,"
and describes someone who is keenly aware that he is spiritually destitute and must rely entirely on the grace of God for salvation. In the
words of Robert A. Guelich, the poor in spirit are those who stand
"without pretense before God, stripped of all self-sufficiency, self-
security, and self-righteousness."[21]

The Lucan parallel to this beatitude does not include the phrase
"in spirit" but simply reads, "You who are poor are blessed, because
the kingdom of God is yours" (Luke 6:20). The Lucan form of the
beatitude is generally recognized as preserving the more original form
of the beatitude.[22] Some interpreters have claimed that by adding "in
spirit," Matthew spiritualized a statement that Jesus originally intended in a purely socioeconomic sense.[23] According to this interpretation, Jesus' original concern was the welfare of those who do not have
money to purchase the necessities of life.[24]

Although Jesus' concern for the poor should not be denied, Matthew's clarification here as well as his clarification in verse 6 is consistent with Jesus' teaching as a whole, the spiritual nature of His
kingdom (John 6:15; 18:36), and the use of the term "poor" in the OT.
In the OT, the "poor" are those who cry out to God for help, depend
entirely on God's grace to meet their needs, have a humble and con-
trite spirit, experience God's deliverance, and enjoy His undeserved
favor.[25] Psalm 86:1–5 beautifully illustrates this:

---

[21] Guelich, *The Sermon on the Mount*, 98.

[22] See J. M. Robinson, P. Hoffman, and J. S. Kloppenborg, *The Critical Edition of Q: Synopsis Including the Gospels of Matthew and Luke, Mark and Thomas with English, German, and French Translations of Q and Thomas*, Hermeneia (Minneapolis: Fortress, 2000), 46–47; Davies and Allison, *A Critical and Exegetical Commentary on the Gospel According to Saint Matthew*, 1:442; and Hagner, *Matthew 1–13*, 91. I. H. Marshall, on the other hand, pointed out that the phrase might well be original since the words "poor in spirit" were used to describe the DSS community in 1QM 14:7 (*The Gospel of Luke: A Commentary on the Greek Text*, NIGTC [Grand Rapids: Eerdmans, 1978], 250).

[23] Betz (*The Sermon on the Mount*, 115) credited K. Kautsky (*Der Ursprung des Christentums* [Stuttgart: Dietz, 1908], 345–47) for the "classic formulation" of this view.

[24] This appears to be the view of J. P. Meier in "Matthew 5:3–12," *Int* 44 (1990): 281–85, esp. 283.

[25] Pss 10:17; 34:6; 76:10; Prov 3:34; Isa 41:17–18; 57:15; 66:1–2. For more information on the OT usage, see Leonard J. Coppes, "עָנָה," in *TWOT*, 2:682–84.

> Listen, Lord, and answer me, for I am poor and needy. Protect my life, for I
> am faithful. You are my God; save Your servant who trusts in You. Be gracious
> to me, Lord, for I call to You all day long. Bring joy to Your servant's life, be-
> cause I turn to You, Lord. For You, Lord, are kind and ready to forgive, rich in
> faithful love to all who call on You.

Matthew's clarification kept his readers from misinterpreting the
"poor" as a mere socioeconomic category. His addition of "in spirit"
pointed his readers to the meaning of the adjective that Jesus originally intended.[26] As in the OT, so for Jesus and Matthew (and Luke),
the poor are godly people who trust God for their salvation, cry out
for His grace, and recognize His willingness to forgive.

The poor in spirit are spiritual paupers who recognize their spiritual bankruptcy, realize that there is nothing good in them that deserves God's love and forgiveness, and depend on God's grace alone
for their salvation. Stott aptly quoted the following hymn as a fitting
commentary on this beatitude:

> Nothing in my hand I bring,
> Simply to thy cross I cling;
> Naked, come to thee for dress;
> Helpless, look to thee for grace;
> Foul, I to the fountain fly;
> Wash me, Savior, or I die.[27]

To spiritual paupers who beg the gracious God for salvation, Jesus offers the promise of possessing God's kingdom. The kingdom in
the teaching of Jesus is commonly misunderstood and hotly debated.
Matthew's Gospel uses the word "kingdom" (*basileia*) to refer to the
"kingdom of heaven" (32 times), "kingdom of God" (five times), "the
kingdom" (five times), "your [God's] kingdom" (once), "your [Je-
sus'] kingdom" (once), "His [Son of Man's] kingdom" (twice), "kingdom of their [the righteous'] Father" (once), "kingdom of my Father"
(once), "the kingdom prepared before the foundation of the world"
(once).[28] These terms are synonymous and refer to the rule or reign
of God. Most scholars recognize that the kingdom of God was the

---

[26] Davies and Allison, *A Critical and Exegetical Commentary on the Gospel According to Saint
Matthew*, 1:444; D. Hill, *The Gospel of Matthew* (London: Oliphants, 1972), 110–11.

[27] Augustus M. Toplady, "Rock of Ages," quoted in J. R. W. Stott, *The Message of the Sermon
on the Mount (Matthew 5–7)* (Downers Grove, IL: InterVarsity, 1978), 39.

[28] Matthew used the word βασιλεία 54 times. The word also refers to human kingdoms in 4:8;
8:12 (?); 12:25; 24:7 (twice) and the kingdom of Satan in 12:26.

central theme of Jesus' preaching.[29] Jesus' teaching about the kingdom of God has a rich background in the OT and the Jewish literature of the Second Temple period.[30] Full exploration of this background is beyond the scope of the present work. However, a few brief comments are necessary.

The OT references to the kingdom that are most significant for understanding Jesus' teaching appear in the book of Daniel. Several lines of evidence support the Danielic background to Jesus' teaching about the kingdom. Most importantly, only in Daniel does the kingdom of God, the primary theme of Jesus' teaching, intersect with reference to the Son of Man, Jesus' favorite self-designation.

In Matt 26:64 Jesus exclaimed to the high priest during His trial: "In the future you will see the Son of Man seated at the right hand of the Power and coming on the clouds of heaven." The phrase "Son of Man" and the reference to "coming on the clouds of heaven" were clearly drawn from the vision recorded in Dan 7:13–14. In Daniel's vision the Son of Man approached the Ancient of Days and was granted a universal and eternal kingdom (v. 14): "He was given authority to rule, and glory, and a kingdom; so that those of every people, nation, and language should serve Him. His dominion is an everlasting dominion that will not pass away, and His kingdom is one that will not be destroyed."

Two of the descriptions of the kingdom in Matthew also allude to Daniel. The parable of the Mustard Seed (Matt 13:31–32) portrayed the kingdom as a "tree" in which "the birds of the sky come and nest in its branches." The description is an allusion to Dan 4:21–22, which portrayed the worldwide dominion of Nebuchadnezzar as an enormous tree "whose leaves were beautiful and its fruit abundant—and on it was food for all, under it the wild animals lived, and in its branches the birds of the air lived."[31] In Jesus' interpretation of the parable of the Wheat and the Weeds (Matt 13:24–30,37–43) He said that the "righteous will shine like the sun in their Father's kingdom" (v. 43). This is an allusion to Dan 12:2–3: "Many of those who sleep in the dust of the earth will awake, some to eternal life,

---

[29] J. D. G. Dunn, *Jesus Remembered*, vol. 1 of *Christianity in the Making* (Grand Rapids: Eerdmans, 2003), 387.

[30] See the thorough treatment in J. Pennington, *Heaven and Earth in the Gospel of Matthew* (Grand Rapids: Baker, 2007), 253–78.

[31] Matthew's words are especially close to Theodotian's version of Daniel (4:21).

and some to shame and eternal contempt. Those who are wise will shine like the bright expanse [of the heavens], and those who lead many to righteousness like the stars forever and ever."

A close relationship between Daniel and Matthew is clear from the more than 30 possible quotations, verbal parallels, and allusions to Daniel in Matthew.[32]

Twice Matthew explicitly associates the kingdom with the Son of Man. Matthew 13:41 says, "The Son of Man will send out His angels, and they will gather from His kingdom everything that causes sin and those guilty of lawlessness." Matthew 16:28 says, "There are some standing here who will not taste death until they see the Son of Man coming in His kingdom." These texts unmistakably show the influence of the Daniel 7 vision. Thus Daniel provides an important key for understanding the nature of the kingdom, particularly in the Gospel of Matthew.[33] This evidence has prompted several scholars to suggest that Daniel provides the primary background to the Gospel's teaching about the kingdom.[34]

The kingdom in the Daniel 7 vision has three primary characteristics. First, the kingdom belongs to God. The Ancient of Days grants to the One like a son of man the authority to rule over this kingdom. Second, the kingdom is universal not in the sense that it includes every single individual but in the sense that it includes "those of every people, nation, and language." Third, the kingdom is eternal. The dominion granted to the Son of Man is "an everlasting dominion that will not pass away, and His kingdom is one that will not be destroyed."

The third feature of the kingdom serves as a strong confirmation of the first feature. The description of the eternality of the kingdom echoes descriptions of the kingdom of God in Dan 2:44; 4:3,34; and 6:26. The interpretation of the vision shows that the people of God

---

[32] The appendix in NA27 lists 33 quotations, verbal parallels, and allusions in Matthew to Daniel. The appendix in UBS 4th rev. ed. lists two quotations and 19 verbal parallels and allusions in Matthew to Daniel.

[33] See also Matt 19:28 and 25:31 in which the Son of Man sits on His glorious throne.

[34] First suggested by G. Dalman, this point has also been defended by C. A. Evans, D. Wenham, and most recently by J. Pennington. The present author independently arrived at the same view. See G. Dalman, *The Words of Jesus*, trans. D. M. Kay (Edinburgh: Clark, 1902), 136; C. A. Evans, "Daniel in the New Testament: Visions of God's Kingdom," in *The Book of Daniel: Composition and Reception*, ed. J. J. Collins and P. W. Flint (Leiden: Brill, 2001), 2:490–527; D. Wenham, "The Kingdom of God and Daniel," *ExpTim* 98 (1987): 132; and J. Pennington, *Heaven and Earth in the Gospel of Matthew*, 285–93.

will reign with the Son of Man over this eternal kingdom: "But the holy ones of the Most High will receive the kingdom and possess it forever, yes, forever and ever" (Dan 7:18).[35] The allusion to Dan 4:12 in Matt 13:32 further emphasizes the universal nature of the kingdom.

The allusion to Dan 12:2 in the description of the kingdom in Matt 13:43 emphasizes the eschatological nature of the kingdom. The kingdom will come in its fullest sense after the resurrection of the dead when those who slept in the dust will awake to eternal life and will shine like the stars forever and ever. The allusion to bodily resurrection in the description of the kingdom shows that although the kingdom is eschatological, it is not ethereal. Matthew prefers the descriptor "kingdom of heaven," but he does not mean by this that the kingdom will not extend to the earth. He means rather that the kingdom is of divine origin and brings an end to sinful human dominions.[36]

Christ's message in this beatitude is that when individuals recognize their absolute inability to save themselves and cast themselves on Christ in total dependence on Him, He graciously reigns over them as King here and now and graciously promises them a part in His future kingdom. The two present-tense verbs used to describe the kingdom stand in sharp contrast to the future-tense verbs of the promises accompanying the rest of the beatitudes. The tension between the future promises and the present existence of the kingdom suggests that the kingdom has already been inaugurated even though it awaits consummation. The grammar thus confirms the "inaugurated eschatology" of the SM that was discussed in the "History of Interpretation" section of the Introduction.[37]

---

[35] Cf. Dan 7:27.

[36] Pennington has noted that this has two important implications for Matthew's readers. First, the heavenly nature of the kingdom discouraged Christians from seeking the violent overthrow of the Roman domination. Second, the language "critiques the ruling and oppressive Roman Empire and gives eschatological hope" (*Heaven and Earth in the Gospel of Matthew*, 324–30).

[37] D. A. Carson, "Matthew," in *Expositor's Bible Commentary*, vol. 8 (Grand Rapids: Zondervan, 1984), 132; France, *The Gospel of Matthew*, 164; Guelich, *The Sermon on the Mount*, 76–77; Hagner, *Matthew 1–13*, 92; D. L. Turner, *Matthew*, CBC (Carol Stream, IL: Tyndale House, 2005), 150. Others suggest that the tense is a proleptic or futuristic present. See Davies and Allison, *A Critical and Exegetical Commentary on the Gospel According to Saint Matthew*, 1:446; and Keener, *The Gospel of Matthew*, 166.

Excursus: Nature of the Kingdom in Matthew

Scholars debate whether the kingdom of heaven is internal or external and present or future.[38] A careful study of the concept of the kingdom of God in Matthew suggests that the kingdom is multifaceted and involves both internal, present, and external future aspects. This position has been called "inaugurated eschatology" or the "eschatology of biblical realism."[39]

First, the kingdom of God sometimes refers to the present reign of God over those who have submitted to the authority of the Messiah. As previously noted, the Beatitudes are bracketed by two statements that imply the kingdom of God is presently the possession of Jesus' disciples. Jesus blessed both the poor in spirit and those persecuted for righteousness with the words: "the kingdom of heaven is [estin; present tense] theirs."[40]

Even more dramatic is Matt 12:28: "If I drive out demons by the Spirit of God, then the kingdom of God has come to you."[41] Some of Jesus' teaching later in the SM implies that

[38] For an excellent introduction to these debates see C. Caragounis, "Kingdom of God/Heaven," in *DJG*, 417–30, esp. 420–24.

[39] The first category was suggested by G. Florovsky and A. M. Hunter. The latter category was suggested by G. E. Ladd.

[40] The expression could merely mean that the future kingdom belongs to Jesus' disciples. However, the majority of commentators see the statement as an expression of Jesus' view that the kingdom had in some sense already arrived.

[41] C. Caragounis has argued that the aorist-tense verb ἔφθασεν does not imply the presence of the kingdom. Instead the usage of the aorist tense here constitutes "a well-attested but little-known and generally misunderstood Greek idiom" in which the tense emphasizes "the certainty and immediacy of an action that properly belongs in the future by describing it as though it has already transpired" ("Kingdom of God/Heaven," in *DJG*, 417–30, esp. 423; and idem, "Kingdom of God, Son of Man and Jesus' Self-Understanding," *TynBul* 40 [1989]: 3–23, esp. 12–23). Wallace calls this usage the "proleptic aorist" and lists Matt 12:28 as a possible but debatable example (*Greek Grammar Beyond the Basics*, 564). J. Nolland points out that while a futuristic aorist is grammatically possible, "nothing in the verse or the immediate context offers any encouragement in this direction. On the contrary, the interest is in the nature of what has already happened or is happening" (*The Gospel of Matthew: A Commentary on the Greek Text*, NIGTC [Grand Rapids: Eerdmans, 2005], 501). Most commentators regard the use of the aorist here as an indication that the kingdom had in some sense already arrived through the ministry of Jesus. See Hagner, *Matthew 1–13*, 343; Davies and Allison, *A Critical and Exegetical Commentary on the Gospel According to Saint Matthew*, 2:340. The next statement seems to distinguish present and future aspects of the kingdom: "How can someone enter a strong man's house and steal his possessions unless he first (*prōton*) ties up the strong man? Then he can rob [lit. 'will rob,' future tense] his house." Many scholars have suggested that Jesus tied up the strong man (Satan) through His victory in the wilderness temptation and that His exorcisms reaped the results of that victory. The grammar seems to suggest that Jesus' exorcisms were a first step

the kingdom was a present possession of Jesus' disciples. In His discussion of anxiety over physical and material concerns, Jesus said, "Seek first the kingdom of God and His righteousness, and all these things will be provided for you" (6:33). This statement demonstrates that the kingdom is a present reality that should be presently sought after and that the rule of God through Christ over the disciples will result in present righteousness. When a disciple expresses submission to the rule of God through personal righteousness and views God's rule as his highest priority, God will meet the basic material and physical needs of his present life.[42]

Jesus described the kingdom as already present because He, the One through whom the Father would establish His rule over the earth, had come at last. He was already ruling over His disciples who had voluntarily submitted to His authority as King. Several of the sayings of Jesus in Matthew suggest that individuals enter the kingdom here and now through their submission to Jesus (19:14; 21:31).

Jesus' statements that depict the kingdom as a present reality demonstrate that His messianic rule was inaugurated during His earthly ministry. Scholars debate specifically when this inauguration occurred. Most tend to trace the inauguration to Jesus' death and resurrection. A survey of references to the kingdom in Matthew suggests that attempting to trace Jesus' inauguration to a single event is an oversimplification. Jesus' entire life from His birth to His resurrection consisted of multiple inaugural acts. The magi proclaimed Him King at His birth (2:2). The Father quoted Ps 2:7, a royal psalm composed for the coronation of the Davidic kings, in reference to Jesus at both His baptism and His transfiguration (Matt 3:17; 17:5). The crowds who cried, "Hosanna to the Son of David!"

---

toward a later and still future plundering of Satan's kingdom (Hagner, *Matthew 1–13*, 344). Jesus was binding Satan through the exorcisms, but His plundering of the strong man's house would await a later period.

[42] Cf. Davies and Allison, *A Critical and Exegetical Commentary on the Gospel According to Saint Matthew*, 1:660–61; M. J. Wilkins, *Matthew*, NIVAC (Grand Rapids: Zondervan, 2004), 299; Stott, *The Message of the Sermon on the Mount*, 170–73; and Hagner, *Matthew 1–13*, 165–66. Against Luz, *Matthew: A Commentary*, 1:344. For a discussion of the rabbinic view of present aspects of the kingdom of God, see E. Urbach, *The Sages: Their Concepts and Beliefs*, trans. I. Abrahams (Jerusalem: Magnes, 1987), 1:400–419.

in effect proclaimed Jesus to be king at the triumphal entry
(21:9). The inscription on the *titulus* at the top of Jesus' cross
announced His kingship (27:37). Jesus' famous pronouncement in Matt 28:18 exhibited His great authority as King over
heaven and earth. For this reason Jesus could speak of His
kingdom as a present reality throughout His ministry even
before His death and resurrection.

The apostle Paul, who wrote under the influence of Jesus'
teaching about the kingdom, sometimes described the kingdom of God as a present reality. The clearest example of this
is Col 1:13–14: "He has rescued us from the domain of darkness and transferred us into the kingdom of the Son He loves.
We have redemption, the forgiveness of sins." In this text believers are said to have entered the kingdom at conversion.
Romans 14:17; 1 Cor 4:20; and Col 4:11 may also refer to the
kingdom as a present reality for believers.

Other statements in the Gospel of Matthew emphasize the
nearness of the kingdom. The teaching of John the Baptist
(Matt 3:2), the teaching of Jesus (4:17), and the proclamation
of Jesus' disciples (10:7) all state that "the kingdom of heaven
has come near."

The nearness of the coming kingdom is also stressed in
16:28: "There are some standing here who will not taste death
until they see the Son of Man coming in His kingdom." Various scholars take this promise as a reference to Pentecost,
Jesus' resurrection, His crucifixion, or the end of the age (in
which case Jesus' promise failed).[43] Although solving this exegetical puzzle is difficult, Jesus' promise was most likely a reference to the transfiguration as a foreshadowing of the Second
Coming. Jesus described the Second Coming as the moment
when "the Son of Man is going to come with His angels in the

---

[43] For the view that the promise was fulfilled at Pentecost, see J. D. G. Dunn, "Spirit and
Kingdom," *ExpTim* 82 (1970): 40. For the view that the promise was fulfilled through the resurrection of Jesus, see F. F. Bruce, *The Message of the New Testament* (Grand Rapids: Eerdmans,
1972), 25–26; Davies and Allison, *A Critical and Exegetical Commentary on the Gospel According
to Saint Matthew*, 2:677–79. (Allison sees the resurrection as a foretaste or preview of the *parousia*.) For the view that the promise was fulfilled through the Second Coming, see A. Plummer,
An Exegetical Commentary on the Gospel According to St. Matthew (London: Elliot Stock, 1909),
236. For the view that the promise was fulfilled through the crucifixion, see Nolland, *The Gospel
of Matthew*, 695–96.

glory of His Father" (16:27). The transfiguration exhibited this amazing glory. When the glory cloud appeared over Jesus, a voice from the cloud said, "This is My beloved Son" (17:5). The language of sonship confirms that Jesus was displaying the glory of His Father. Furthermore the Father's utterance, as already noted, alludes to Psalm 2, a psalm celebrating the inauguration of Israel's king. This suggests that Jesus was "the Son of Man coming in His kingdom" as promised in Matt 16:28 and that the transfiguration was one episode in Jesus' inauguration as King.[44]

Many of the references to the kingdom in Matthew imply that the kingdom is still future. Matthew 5:20 insists that the disciple's extraordinary righteousness is a prerequisite for kingdom entrance. This seems to imply that entrance into the kingdom is associated with final judgment in which the deeds of all people are examined. This is confirmed by 7:22 in which kingdom entrance is associated with "that day," an apparent allusion to final judgment, in which true disciples are admitted into the kingdom but the wicked are turned away. Matthew 25:34 shows that although the kingdom was prepared by God from the foundation of the world, Christ's followers inherit the kingdom on the final day of judgment when the King separates the righteous from the wicked.[45] In 26:29 the kingdom is clearly still future and is associated with the great messianic feast.

Similarly several of the kingdom parables in Matthew stress the future dimension of the kingdom. The parables of the Wheat and the Weeds (13:24–30,36–43), the Net (13:47–50),

---

[44] The view that the transfiguration fulfilled the promise of Matt 16:28 was the dominant view in the early church. This view was held by Clement of Alexandria, Origen, Ephraem the Syrian, Hilary, Cyril of Jerusalem, Chrysostom, Augustine, and Cyril of Alexandria. See Davies and Allison, *A Critical and Exegetical Commentary on the Gospel According to Saint Matthew*, 2:677. Although Allison rejects this view here, he admits that this was the view of Mark on whose Gospel Matthew was likely dependent. Interestingly 2 Pet 1:16 used the word "coming" (*parousia*), a word often used for Jesus' eschatological coming, in association with a description of the transfiguration.

[45] This coheres well with Paul's discussions of the kingdom. When Paul spoke of inheriting the kingdom, the verb "inherit" (κληρονομέω) was always in the future tense and referred to reception of the eschatological kingdom after final glorification. See 1 Cor 6:9–10; 15:50; and Gal 5:19–21. Ephesians 5:5 uses a different construction that is identical in meaning ("have an inheritance;" ἔχει κληρονομίαν).

the Vineyard Workers (20:1–16), the Wedding Banquet (22:1–14), the Ten Virgins (25:1–13), the Talents (25:14–30), and the Sheep and the Goats (25:31–46) all associate the kingdom with final judgment. Thus, although God presently rules over His people through their voluntary submission to Jesus and a handful of texts in Matthew refer to this internal, present rule, the majority of references to the kingdom in Matthew appear to refer to God's eschatological rule through the triumphant Messiah.

The personal pronoun "theirs" (*autōn*) in the first beatitude is in an emphatic position in the Greek text.[46] This emphasis both highlights the unexpected nature of this blessing and implies that the blessing of the kingdom belongs only to the poor in spirit. One would not ordinarily expect the spiritually destitute to receive the promised kingdom. At the conclusion of the SM, Jesus noted that those who viewed themselves as spiritually privileged expected to enter the kingdom. Nevertheless, although they performed remarkable spiritual feats such as prophesying, casting out demons, and performing many miracles all in Jesus' name (7:22), Jesus would declare to them, "I never knew you! Depart from Me, you lawbreakers!" (7:23). In a great reversal that is characteristic of grace, the spiritually destitute, those who had no apparent claim to the kingdom, would be the very ones to possess it.[47]

This beatitude echoes themes from Isa 61:1, a text to which Matt 11:5 explicitly alludes. The text explains that the Messiah, the Servant of the Lord, will bring good news to the poor. The promise in Isaiah is likely the inspiration for the first beatitude.[48] In Luke 4:16–21, Jesus quoted this OT prophecy in the Nazareth synagogue and said, "Today as you listen, this Scripture has been fulfilled," meaning that He was the fulfillment of this prophecy. When Jesus pronounced blessing on the poor, that is, when He brought good news to the poor, He fulfilled the promise of Isaiah and manifested Himself as the Messiah of whom the prophet spoke. The hermeneutical and Christological

---

[46] Hagner, *Matthew 1–13*, 92.

[47] F. Hauck referred to the Beatitudes as "sacred paradoxes" because "the kingdom of God carries with it a reversal of all customary evaluations" ("μακάριος," *TDNT*, 4 [1967]:368). The shocking promise that the kingdom would be given to the poor in spirit is a powerful expression of divine grace.

[48] Hagner, *Matthew 1–13*, 91–92.

implications of the beatitude are profound. The beatitude not only defines the nature of discipleship and identifies qualifications for entering the kingdom. The beatitude also shows that Jesus regarded the Hebrew Scriptures as a testimony about Himself (Luke 24:27) and viewed Himself as the promised Messiah. The allusions to Isaiah 61 in the first few beatitudes support the Servant Christology that will become more prominent in Matt 8:17 and 12:17–21, which appeal respectively to Isa 53:4 and 42:1–4.

Matthew 5:4

Like the first beatitude, the second beatitude reverberates themes from Isaiah 61. Isaiah 61:1–3 says, "He has sent Me to heal the broken-hearted, . . . to comfort all who mourn, to provide for those who mourn in Zion; to give them a crown of beauty instead of ashes, festive oil instead of mourning, and splendid clothes instead of despair."[49] The context of Isaiah 61 portrays the "mourning" as an expression of sorrow over Israel's exile, which was a punishment for their sinful rebellion. This mourning was thus an expression of grief from those suffering the consequences of sin and constituted an attitude of repentance. The appeal to Isaiah 61 in the second beatitude thus implies that the mourning of which Jesus spoke was mourning for sin and its grievous consequences.[50]

The OT abounds with examples of this mourning for sin. Psalm 119:136 says, "My eyes pour out streams of tears because people do not follow Your instruction." Psalm 40:12 says, "My sins have overtaken me; I am unable to see. They are more than the hairs of my head, and my courage leaves me." Psalm 51:16–17 says, "You do not want a sacrifice, or I would give it; You are not pleased with a burnt offering. The sacrifice pleasing to God is a broken spirit. God, You will not despise a broken and humbled heart."

---

[49] The echoes of Isa 61:2 are unmistakable when one compares Matthew's Greek text to the LXX of Isa 61:2. The LXX says that the anointed one has come παρακαλέσαι πάντας τοὺς πενθοῦντας. Matthew's text shares the verb παρακαλέω as well as the participial form of πενθέω. Most scholars recognize that the second beatitude is an allusion to Isa 61:2. Hagner, for example, argued that the second beatitude was "an even more striking allusion to the words of Isa 61" than the first (ibid., 92).

[50] Luz recognized the allusion to Isaiah 61 but disregarded this background in his interpretation by stating that the mourning "includes all the sorrows of this eon that in the coming eon will be replaced with comfort" (Luz, *Matthew: A Commentary*, 1:194).

This mourning for sin expressed genuine contrition. The call to repentance was an essential element of the gospel of the kingdom in the teaching of Christ and John the Baptist in Matthew. Both had uttered the same message: "Repent, because the kingdom of heaven has come near!" (Matt 3:2; 4:17). Mourning showed the sincerity and intensity of this repentance. The word "mourn" that Jesus used in the beatitude often referred to the deep grief that one felt after the death of a dearly loved family member or friend.[51] This vivid term clearly refers to an intense remorse, not a superficial regret, over one's sinfulness and alienation from God. This is the same verb James used when he said,

> Draw near to God, and He will draw near to you. Cleanse your hands, sinners, and purify your hearts, double-minded people! Be miserable and mourn and weep. Your laughter must change to mourning and your joy to sorrow. Humble yourselves before the Lord, and He will exalt you. (Jas 4:8–10)

True repentance makes no excuses and offers no rationalizations. It grieves for sin from a broken heart.

Jesus promised that God will comfort the mourners and grant relief to those whose hearts are broken by their sin and their alienation from God. "Will be comforted" means that God will act to restore the broken relationship and bring the repentant mourner back into full fellowship with Himself. The sorrow of the sinner's exile from God will be replaced by the joy of His presence. The sinner's mourning for his sin will be replaced by praise to the God who saved him. One detects here another faint echo of Isaiah 61: "I greatly rejoice in the LORD, I exult in my God; for He has clothed me with the garments of salvation and wrapped me in a robe of righteousness" (61:10).

The ultimate fulfillment of this promise awaits Christ's disciples in the future. For that reason, although the promise of verses 3 and 10 was expressed using the present tense, this and the other beatitudes used future-tense verbs to identify the cause of the disciples' blessedness. The ultimate fulfillment of the promise "will be comforted" is stated in Rev 7:17: "And God will wipe away every tear from their eyes."[52]

---

[51] "πενθέω," BDAG, 795 defines the transitive use of the verb in this way: "to engage in mourning for one who is dead, ordinarily with traditional rites."

[52] Some ancient manuscripts and versions invert the order of the second and third beatitudes. Early scribes probably changed the order because they felt that the references to heaven in the first beatitude and earth in the third beatitude formed a natural "rhetorical antithesis" or

Matthew 5:5

The word "meek" (*praus*) is often defined by commentators as "gentle" or "self-controlled." However, the beatitude is best understood with an eye to the OT because its language has clear parallels there. The OT background shows that the meek are those who, like the poor in spirit, live in complete dependence on God and total submission to Him. The adjective translated "meek" occurs 16 times in the LXX. In all instances that have a corresponding Hebrew text, the word translates either *anaw* or *aniy*, the same terms that stand behind the LXX translation *ptōchos* ("poor") used in the first beatitude. The LXX translators evidently saw two important connotations of the Hebrew term: dependence and submission. *Ptōchos* (poor) emphasized the former and *praus* (meek) the latter. After a thorough study of the Hebrew OT use of "meek," F. Hauck and S. Schulz concluded that a meek person is "one who feels that he is a servant in relationship to God and who subjects himself to Him quietly and without resistance."[53]

The key to understanding the concept of meekness in the beatitude is Psalm 37. This psalm contains the closest OT parallel to the third beatitude.[54] Psalm 37:11 says, "The humble [meek] will inherit the land."[55] In context "meekness" seems to refer to one who seeks to live righteously even though it appears that the wicked prosper and the good suffer because he trusts God to deliver him from the wicked and to act justly in His judgment. The psalm describes the meek as those who "trust in the LORD" (vv. 3,5), "take delight in the LORD" (v. 4), "wait expectantly for" the Lord (v. 7), and "put their hope in the LORD" (v. 9). This dependence and trust is accompanied by obedience. The meek are described as those whose "way is upright" (v. 14),

---

because they saw a close connection between poverty in spirit and meekness. See B. Metzger, *Textual Commentary on the Greek New Testament* (Stuttgart: United Bible Societies, 1971), 12. Some question the authenticity of 5:4 and suggest that there were originally seven beatitudes (Betz, *The Sermon on the Mount*, 108).

[53] F. Hauck and S. Schulz, "πραΰς," in *TDNT*, 6 (1968): 647.

[54] 4Q171 (4QpPs 37) contains a running commentary from the Qumran community on Psalm 37. Contrary to Carson ("Matthew," 133), the commentary did not treat the psalm as messianic. The commentary did interpret the promise of Ps 37:11 eschatologically as a promise that would be fulfilled when there was no longer any wicked person on the earth. It also interpreted "meek" and "earth" in the manner suggested in the commentary below.

[55] Luz identified the beatitude as "a quotation from Psalm 36:11 LXX [37:11 in the English Bible]" (Luz, *Matthew: A Commentary*, 1:194). Psalm 36:11 (LXX) reads: οἱ δὲ πραεῖς κληρονομήσουσιν γῆν. . . . The direct parallels with Matt 5:5 are indicated by underlining: μακάριοι οἱ πραεῖς ὅτι αὐτοὶ κληρονομήσουσιν τὴν γῆν.

"righteous" (vv. 17,21,25,29,30,39), "blameless" (vv. 18,37). He has "the instruction of his God . . . in his heart" and "his steps do not falter" (v. 31). The word "meek" describes the disciples of Jesus as those who live in complete dependence on and submission to God. This interpretation fits the paradoxical nature of the earlier beatitudes; that is, the one who is subservient to God will be exalted as His heir.

This beatitude, like the first and second, may also have a connection with Isaiah 61. Isaiah 61 refers to inheriting the land (Isa 61:7) and the LXX uses the words "they will inherit the land," which are an exact verbal parallel to Matt 5:5b (*klēronomēsousin tēn gēn*).[56] If such an allusion were intended, this beatitude would further confirm Jesus' identity as the Servant of Isaiah 61 who brings good news to the poor and comforts the mourners and whose ministry enables the oppressed to inherit the land.

"Inherit the land" in the OT context refers to inheriting the promised land of Canaan. The mildly emphatic personal pronoun "they" seems to imply that the meek, and they only, will inherit the land. This implies that Jesus' followers who submit themselves to God constituted a new Israel that would inherit the land promised to Abraham.

Most English translations assume that the third beatitude promises more than residence in the land of Palestine and thus translate the Greek word *gē* as "earth" rather than "land." Some scholars have challenged this assumption. Nolland has argued that the beatitude specifically refers to the land of covenant promise on three grounds. First, Ps 37:11, to which Jesus clearly alluded in the beatitude, refers to the land of Israel. Second, Matt 4:25 focuses on the scope of the historic land of Israel in a way that implies its boundaries are of significance to Matthew's readers. Third, the interpretation of Ps 37:11 in the Dead Sea Scrolls also focuses on the holy land.[57]

Nolland is overly confident about the meaning of the land in the allusions to Ps 37:11 in 4Q171. The scroll fragments clearly interpret the psalm eschatologically. This eschatological interpretation

---

[56] Other than the previous allusions to Isaiah 61 in the Beatitudes, the only hint that that third beatitude may allude to Isa 61:7 (in addition to Ps 37:11) is Matthew's use of the definite article with γῆν which is absent in Ps 36:11 (LXX) but present in Isa 61:7. This feature suggested to Davies and Allison that "perhaps 5.5 should recall Isa 61.7 even though 5.5 clearly quotes Ps 37.11." Nevertheless these commentators noted that Matthew's definite article was supported by the Targum on Ps 37:11, thus making appeal to Isaiah unnecessary (*A Critical and Exegetical Commentary on the Gospel According to Saint Matthew*, 1:450–51).

[57] 4QpPsa 2:9–11; 3:9–11.

anticipates the complete extermination of all the wicked from the earth. Furthermore, the commentary speaks of "the ones who return from the wilderness, who will live a thousand generations in virtue" and promises, "To them and their descendants belongs all the heritage of Adam forever." Since the broken text of column 4 of the scroll interprets Ps 37:29 with reference to the thousand generations, the author probably equated the "earth" with "all the heritage of Adam." These features imply that the sectarians interpreted Ps 37:11 as referring to the "earth."[58] Thus recent translators of the scrolls prefer the translation "earth" to "land" in the commentary on Psalm 37 for good reason.[59]

Nolland is probably correct that Matt 4:25 describes the historic land of Israel as the focus of Jesus' ministry. Nevertheless, 5:5 makes no clear allusion to 4:25 and offers an eschatological promise rather than a description of the locale of Jesus' teaching and healing ministry. Other texts in Matthew are far more helpful for understanding the scope of land/earth ($g\bar{e}$) in the Gospel.

Although Ps 37:11 is about inheriting the land of covenant promise, Jesus was free to apply the text in new ways for His audience. The OT prophets had already begun to see the promise of the land as part of a still grander vision in which the entire earth, its fruits, and its treasures belonged to God's people (Isaiah 60). The NT continued and extended this approach. As France observed, "There is a general tendency in the NT to treat OT promises about 'the land' as finding fulfillment in nonterritorial ways, and such an orientation seems required here too."[60]

This does not mean that one should identify the promised land in this passage as heaven. Matthew typically distinguishes "earth" from heaven (5:18; 6:10; 11:25; 16:19; 18:18; 24:35: 28:18) in a way that precludes equating the two. The word "earth" is to be taken literally and not spiritualized. Nevertheless the use of the eschatological future in the Beatitudes reminds readers that Jesus was referring to the earth as it would stand after the eschaton. Thus, "inheriting the earth"

---

[58] L. R. Helyer suggested that the text moves from references to the land promised to Abraham to include the "whole earth" (*Exploring Jewish Literature of the Second Temple Period: A Guide for New Testament Students* [Downers Grove: InterVarsity, 2002], 234).

[59] See M. Wise, M. Abegg Jr., and E. Cook, *The Dead Sea Scrolls: A New Translation* (San Francisco: Harper, 2005), 248–52.

[60] France, *The Gospel of Matthew*, 166–67. See also W. D. Davies, *The Gospel and the Land* (Berkeley, CA: University of California, 1974), 366.

likely refers to possessing and living in a recreated earth over which Christ rules eternally.[61]

The immediate context supports this interpretation. Jesus used the word "earth" again in Matt 5:13, "You are the salt of the earth," words that are structurally identical to 5:14a, "You are the light of the world." The parallelism suggests that earth and world are synonymous. The use of "earth" in 5:13 would be confusing if "earth" in 5:5 merely referred to the land of Palestine. This suggests that inheriting the earth refers to possessing the entire earth. Matthew's vocabulary usage elsewhere in his Gospel confirms this view. Matthew used the term "earth" (gē) 43 times. When Matthew used the term to refer to a specific geographical location, he typically offered further qualification such as "land of Judah" or "land of Israel" (e.g., 2:6,20–21). He used the word without further qualification to refer to something other than soil in 5:13,18,35; 6:10,19; 9:6; 11:25; 12:42; 16:19; 18:18–19; 23:9; 24:30; 27:45. All these instances, with the possible exception of the last, refer to the entire earth rather than the promised land alone. The SM later refers to the earth in its eschatological state. Jesus taught His disciples to pray, "Your will be done on earth as it is in heaven" (6:10). The opposition between heaven and earth clearly implies that land/earth refers to the entire earth. The petition anticipates a time when God's plan for the earth itself will be fulfilled finally and completely. This is the blessed earth that Jesus' disciples will inherit. More explicitly, 19:28 anticipates the renewal (palingenesia) of the earth and assures Jesus' disciples that those who have left houses or farms will receive many times as much. Thus Jesus' disciples will inherit a recreated world, a world replete with material and physical as well as spiritual blessings.

Matthew 5:6

Hunger and thirst are metaphors for intense longing. The metaphors are not as meaningful to modern Westerners as they were to Jesus' first-century audience. Few modern Americans have ever experienced true hunger or thirst. Few first-century Jews had not. They were familiar with the powerful and even painful craving of the body for food

---

[61] Blomberg, Matthew, 99; Carson, "Matthew," 133–34; Davies and Allison, A Critical and Exegetical Commentary on the Gospel According to Saint Matthew, 1:450–51; Hagner, Matthew 1–13, 92; Luz, Matthew: A Commentary, 1:194–95.

and drink. They had suffered horrible deprivation because of poverty, famine, and siege.[62] Second Kings 6:25–29 describes a famine so severe that a donkey's head was sold for 80 shekels of silver, a fourth of a kab of dove's dung was sold for five shekels of silver, and mothers cannibalized their own sons. The ancients knew of hunger so intense that one would do or give anything to satisfy it. Thus hunger and thirst were powerful metaphors for the most intense cravings.

The OT used hunger and thirst not only to portray one's longing for the satisfaction of one's physical needs but also for one's deepest spiritual needs. The psalmist, for example, thirsted for God like a weary deer panted for streams of water (Ps 42:1–2). Jesus applied the imagery in a similar fashion. He could easily have described His disciples as those who want to be obedient or desire holiness, but such language simply was not powerful enough. The true disciple hungers and thirsts for righteousness. He longs to live a godly life as much as a starving man longs for his next piece of bread or a parched tongue yearns for a drop of water.

Scholars debate the precise meaning of the "righteousness" the disciple craves. Some scholars insist that the noun refers to "the justice associated with the coming of God's eschatological rule" rather than "personal righteousness."[63] These scholars see this sense as implied by the first three beatitudes. The poor, the grieving, and the downtrodden have all suffered injustice and long for God to vindicate them. This interpretation, however, seems to underemphasize the spiritual nature of the poor, the mourning, and the meek. Furthermore it overlooks the consistent use of the term "righteousness" in the SM. In 5:10,20; 6:1,33 (as in 3:15) righteousness refers clearly to personal righteousness.

Some have argued that the righteousness for which the disciple yearns is imputed righteousness, the righteousness of God or Christ that is transferred to the repentant and believing sinner so that he may be declared innocent in the eschatological judgment. This appears to be the view of G. Shrenk, who defined "righteousness" in 5:6 as "a right state before God" and "a pure gift from God." He further noted,

---

[62] L. Goppelt ("πεινάω," *TDNT*, 6 [1968]: 12–22, esp. 15) pointed out that the verb was normally used in the LXX to denote "persistent hunger" that resulted from famine, siege, or national or social distress.

[63] Hagner, *Matthew 1–13*, 93. See also Hunter, *A Pattern for Life*, 132; Keener, *The Gospel of Matthew*, 169–70; Nolland, *The Gospel of Matthew*, 202–3.

"The parallelism to the Pauline doctrine of justification is evident here, as at other points where the Gospel emphasizes the merciful salvation of sinners."[64] Similarly Rudolf Bultmann claimed that this beatitude referred to "those who long to have God pronounce the verdict 'righteous' as His decision over them in the judgment."[65] Although this view is theologically attractive to many, the preponderance of evidence precludes it from being a legitimate exegetical option. The term "righteousness" (*dikaiosunē*) simply is not used elsewhere in the Gospel of Matthew in the sense of imputed righteousness.[66] It is highly unlikely that "righteousness" refers to justification in the immediate context. For example Matt 5:10 pronounces a blessing on those who are persecuted for the sake of righteousness. To read "righteousness" as "justification" here would make little sense.

In the Gospel of Matthew, the term "righteousness" normally refers to actual personal righteousness that results from one's relationship with God, that is, the righteousness of sanctification rather than the righteousness of justification (Matt 1:19; 3:15; 5:10,20,45; 6:1,33; 9:13; 10:41; 13:17,43,49; 20:4; 21:32; 23:28–29,35; 25:37,46; 27:19).[67] This is especially clear in Matt 6:1, in which Jesus described righteousness not as something a disciple has but as something a disciple does or practices. Thus Jesus' disciples long to be literally and truly righteous, to both teach and practice even the least of the commandments, to be characterized by a righteousness that "surpasses that of the scribes and Pharisees" (5:19–20). They are grateful that God has forgiven them and accepted them as righteous though they are sinful, but they earnestly aspire for personal holiness. The present participles

---

[64] G. Shrenk, "δικαιοσύνη," *TDNT*, 2 (1964):192–210, esp. 198–99. Shrenk's view is difficult to classify. Despite the comments above, he classified Matthew's usage of the noun as "right conduct before God" and discouraged interpreting Matthew's use in the "forensically eschatological sense."

[65] R. Bultmann, *Theology of the New Testament* (London: SCM, 1952), 1:273.

[66] Even Luther rejected this interpretation and argued that hungering for righteousness described those "who strive to become pious with everything that they do." Melanchthon seems to have inspired the Protestant trend toward reading imputed righteousness into the beatitude. See Luz, *Matthew: A Commentary*, 1:195.

[67] Commentators who view δικαιοσύνη in this context as a reference to personal righteousness include Broadus, *The Gospel According to Matthew*, 90; Davies and Allison, *A Critical and Exegetical Commentary on the Gospel According to Saint Matthew*, 1:451–53; France, *The Gospel of Matthew*, 167–68; Hill, *The Gospel of Matthew*, 112; Luz, *Matthew: A Commentary*, 1:195; B. Przybylski, *Righteousness in Matthew and His World of Thought*, SNTSMS 41 (Cambridge: Cambridge University Press, 1980), 96–98. Carson ("Matthew," 134), Turner (*Matthew*, 151), and Wilkins (*Matthew*, 207) argue that righteousness includes both personal righteousness and social justice.

"hunger" and "thirst" imply that this spiritual yearning is a constant and perpetual longing that will not cease until the disciple fully possesses the righteous character God desires.

The words "they will be filled" are in the passive voice. The grammar clearly demonstrates that the righteousness for which Jesus' disciples aspire is not something that they achieve on their own. This verb, like those in Matt 5:4,6, and 7 (and possibly 9) is a divine passive that reverently describes an act of God. God, and God alone, imparts the righteousness for which the disciple hungers and thirsts. This promise is crucial to an understanding of the theology of the SM. Jesus made radical demands of His disciples in this sermon. He required them to have a righteousness that led them to keep the least of the commandments (v. 19) and that surpassed the righteousness of the scribes and Pharisees (v. 20). He even commanded them to "be perfect, therefore, as your heavenly Father is perfect" (v. 48). Such demands could easily degenerate into a false theology in which righteousness becomes a personal achievement. This, however, is foreign to the teachings of Jesus. The righteousness the SM demands is a divine gift graciously wrought in the heart and life of the Christian disciple by God Himself. If the disciple were personally responsible for his righteousness, he would deserve the glory for it. However, Jesus insisted that the good works of disciples bring glory to God (v. 6) since God is the source and author of them.

A tiny infant can hunger and thirst, but that infant is utterly incapable of satisfying those longings alone. Similarly, a believer can never satisfy his hunger or quench his thirst for righteousness. Only a gracious God who transforms mind, heart, character, and behavior can do so. The lifestyle described by the SM is not the product of mere human effort. It is the result of transforming grace.

The first two beatitudes (and possibly the third) contain echoes of Isaiah 61 and confirm Jesus' identity as the Servant whom God anointed with His Spirit. Echoes of Isaiah 61 appear in this beatitude as well. Isaiah 61:3 promised, "They will be called righteous trees, planted by the LORD to glorify Him." God's people will be spiritual trees that produce the fruit of righteousness. Isaiah 61:11 added, "For as the earth brings forth its growth, and as a garden enables what is sown to spring up, so the Lord GOD will cause righteousness and praise to spring up before all the nations" (see also Isa 60:21 and

62:1–2). This OT imagery dovetails perfectly with Jesus' use of agricultural images to describe the transformed behavior of the disciple
(Matt 7:15–20). God plants good spiritual trees whose righteous fruit
brings glory to the One who planted and tends the tree.

The use of the future tense in the beatitude implies that the disciple will not be fully blessed with righteousness until the consummation of the kingdom in the last days. However, because the kingdom
of God is already present (5:3,10), Jesus' followers have already begun
to receive and express God's righteousness here and now.

Matthew 5:7

Expressing mercy to others is essential to having a righteousness that
surpasses that of the scribes and Pharisees since Jesus frequently rep-
rimanded these religious leaders for lacking mercy (Matt 9:13; 12:7;
23:23). The merciful are those who relate to others with a forgiving
and compassionate spirit. Two key texts in Matthew serve as a guide
for understanding the nature of mercy: the teaching about acts of
compassion toward the poor (6:2–4) and the parable of the Unforgiving Servant (18:21–35). Each text emphasizes a crucial aspect of
Christian mercy.

This beatitude is a probable allusion to the Greek version of Prov
14:21: "Blessed is the one who has mercy on the poor."[68] The promise
"will be shown mercy" may have been drawn from Prov 17:5 (LXX).
The LXX contains a promise that is absent from the MT (and the English Bible): "but the one who has compassion will be shown mercy."[69]
Later references to expressions of mercy in the SM confirm this background. Matthew 6:2 refers to gifts offered to the poor, orphaned, and
widowed as an "act of mercy" (eleēmosunēn). Thus, the present beatitude relates to showing compassion to the needy through deeds of
kindness. Calvin emphasized this aspect of mercy in his exposition:
"They are blessed who are not only prepared to put up with their own
troubles, but also take on other peoples', to help them in distress,
freely to join them in their time of trial, and, as it were, to get right
into their situation, that they may gladly expend themselves on their
assistance."[70]

---

[68] LXX: ἐλεῶν δὲ πρωχοὺς μακαριστός. See Hagner, *Matthew 1–13*, 93.
[69] LXX: ὁ δὲ ἐπισπλαγχνιζόμενος ἐλεηθήσεται.
[70] Calvin, *A Harmony of the Gospels*, 1:171.

Mercy involves more than generous giving to the needy. It also involves forgiving others for their sins as an expression of gratitude to God for His gracious forgiveness. In the parable of the Unforgiving Servant, the servant failed to forgive because he failed to see the enormity of his own debt in comparison to the much smaller debt that another owed him. He viewed the debt that he owed his king as small and the debt that another servant owed him as great when he should have recognized that the debt he owed the king was enormous compared to the trifling debt that the other servant owed him. His perspective demonstrated his lack of genuine repentance and his complete selfishness.[71] The climax of the parable is the king's challenge, "Shouldn't you also have had mercy on your fellow slave, as I had mercy on you?" Mercy compels Jesus' disciples to offer others gracious forgiveness for their sins, just as God has forgiven their own sins.

Those who treat others mercifully will be treated mercifully by God. "Will be shown mercy" is yet another example of the divine passive that dominates the promises of the Beatitudes. Showing mercy does not earn mercy from God, but it does express the humble repentance that is essential to receiving divine mercy. The principle that emerges in this beatitude fits with a prominent theme of the SM. In the model prayer, Jesus emphasized that forgiving others was necessary if one is to receive divine forgiveness in eschatological judgment (6:12,14–15). He taught that disciples can expect forgiveness from God only as they express forgiveness to others. Still later in the SM, Jesus taught that people will be judged by God according to the same standard and in the same manner with which they judge others (7:2). Those who judge others harshly can expect to be judged harshly by God. Those who judge others mercifully can expect to be shown mercy by God.

Matthew 5:8

Some commentators have recently argued that the phrase "pure in heart" refers to "a heart of unmixed devotion to God." This view is based on the use of the term "pure in heart" in Ps 73:1 to refer to those "who recognize that God alone is their hope."[72] Nevertheless the emphasis in Psalm 73 is actually the faithful follower's determination

---

[71] Carson, "Matthew," 172.
[72] Keener, *The Gospel of Matthew*, 170.

to obey God despite the fact that the wicked seem to prosper in this life while the righteous suffer. Thus purity in heart in this psalm involves the determination to obey God with no thought of temporal reward because "I desire nothing on earth but You" (v. 25). Furthermore Psalm 73 is probably not the basis for this beatitude anyway, as will soon be seen.

Those who hold the view that "pure in heart" refers to unmixed devotion to God also appeal to Jas 4:8, in which the double-minded are urged to purify their hearts. One commentator suggests that James's statement "appears dependent on an early version of the Matthean Sermon on the Mount tradition."[73] However, the connections between Matt 5:8 and Jas 4:8 are not as strong as those between Matt 5:8 and Psalm 24. James, for example, used the verb *hagnizō* rather than *katharizō* to command purification of the heart. One would have expected the latter verb if James were deriving his statement from the phrase "pure (*katharoi*) in heart."

Psalm 24 serves as the likely OT background for the sixth beatitude. Psalm 24:4 states that the conditions for worshipping God in the holy place were having "clean hands" and a "pure heart" (LXX: "pure in heart"). Although other texts in the Greek OT refer to a pure heart, only Ps 24:4 describes an individual as "pure in heart."[74] Furthermore this psalm promises that the worshipper who is "pure in heart" will receive "blessing from the Lord" much as Jesus pronounced a blessing on the pure in heart in the beatitude. Finally, the psalm describes the "pure in heart" as those who "seek the face of the God of Jacob" (24:6). Several commentators rightly observe that Jesus' promise "will see God" is likely derived from this element of the psalm.[75] Thus Matt 5:8 is likely an allusion to this well-known text.[76]

In Psalm 24 the phrase "pure in heart" appears to describe a person as having moral integrity.[77] The psalm offered a description of the pure in heart: "who has not lifted up his soul to vanity or sworn

---

[73] Ibid. See also Hagner, *Matthew 1–13*, 94.

[74] In the LXX Gen 20:5–6 and Job 11:13; 33:3 refer to a καθαρά καρδία. Psalm 23:4 (LXX) refers to one who is καθαρὸς τῇ καρδίᾳ.

[75] Davies and Allison, *A Critical and Exegetical Commentary on the Gospel According to Saint Matthew*, 1:455–56; France, *The Gospel of Matthew*, 168.

[76] Cf. Davies and Allison, *A Critical and Exegetical Commentary on the Gospel According to Saint Matthew*, 1:455; France, *The Gospel of Matthew*, 168; and Nolland, *Matthew*, 204.

[77] P. Craigie, *Psalms 1–50*, WBC (Waco, TX: Word, 1983), 213. Craigie noted that the phrase also expressed moral integrity in Ugaritic texts (ibid., 210). Craigie also noted that Psalm 15 gives a more extensive description of the moral integrity in view in Psalm 24.

deceitfully to his neighbor" (LXX). The "pure in heart" refrain from idolatry and are characterized by honesty. Interestingly the description directly relates to two important themes in the SM. Matthew 5:33–37 prohibits deceitful oaths (cp. 23:16–22). Matthew 6:24 portrays materialism which was the focus of 6:19–23 as a form of idolatry, as serving Mammon rather than God. Similarly 6:32 argues that those who fret over food, drink, and clothing are exhibiting the priorities of idolaters.

Because first-century Judaism generally placed such a strong emphasis on ritual purity (15:1–9) and since Jesus instead emphasized the importance of internal purity (15:10–20), the phrase "pure in heart" likely emphasizes purity of the inner person.[78] Thus purity in heart is a sincere, authentic disposition that moves the disciple to pursue righteousness and compels him to live obediently. It is different from the hypocrisy of the Pharisees, who made a good show but lacked internal purity (23:25–28). Purity in heart is not a qualification for salvation; it is a result of salvation. Jesus had just stated that God will fill the one who hungers and thirsts for righteousness. Although final and complete fulfillment of the promise would be eschatological, the identification of Jesus' disciples as the "pure in heart" shows that dramatic, radical transformation is occurring already.

The OT clearly taught that no man can achieve purity of heart on his own. The sinner's heart is thoroughly evil, and the sinner is incapable of cleansing it himself. The first mention of the heart as the center of man's being in the OT appears in Gen 6:5: "The LORD saw that man's wickedness was widespread on the earth and that every scheme his mind [in Hb, "heart"] thought of was nothing but evil all the time." Genesis 8:21 added, "Man's inclination [lit., "the purpose of his heart"] is evil from his youth." The sinner's heart was corrupt due to his inherent depravity. This truth became even more pronounced in the writings of the Prophets (Isa 1:5; Jer 17:9). Proverbs 20:9 expresses man's inability to cleanse his own heart: "Who can say, 'I have kept my heart pure; I am cleansed from my sin'?"

The sinner must turn to God and seek purification of the heart from Him. Although Deut 10:16 urged God's people to circumcise their hearts, Deut 30:6 implies that only God can circumcise the heart:

---

[78] Cf. Davies and Allison, *A Critical and Exegetical Commentary on the Gospel According to Saint Matthew*, 1:456; France, *The Gospel of Matthew*, 168; Gundry, *Matthew*, 71; Turner, *Matthew*, 152.

"The LORD your God will circumcise your heart and the hearts of your descendants, and you will love Him with all your heart and all your soul so that you will live." Interestingly, in Ps 51:10 David prayed to God, "Create a clean heart for me."[79] "Create" (*bara'*) is a verb that consistently refers to an act of divine creation *ex nihilo*. David's prayer implied that nothing good resided in him and that if he were to have a pure heart, God would have to create it with His own supernatural power. The Prophets concurred that God must change the sinner's heart.[80]

Jesus' teaching in the Gospel of Matthew reflects these same convictions about man's depravity and the wickedness and impurity of the sinner's heart. In Matt 5:28 Jesus taught that lust arose from an impure heart. Matthew 12:34 describes the sinner's heart as the evil source of his evil words. In 15:8, Jesus warned that though the Jews honor God with their lips, their hearts were far from Him. Matthew 15:19–20 shows the wickedness of the sinner's heart: "For from the heart come evil thoughts, murders, adulteries, sexual immoralities, thefts, false testimonies, blasphemies. These are the things that defile a man." Matthew 19:8 describes the sinner's heart as hard. Other important texts in Matthew speak of the sinner's inner corruption, which is equivalent to the corruption of his heart (23:25–28). Christ knew well that if a man's or woman's heart was pure, it was only because God Himself had purified and cleansed it.

The description of Jesus' disciples as the "pure in heart" demonstrated that the new covenant was being fulfilled through Jesus' ministry (Jer 31:33; Ezek 11:19–20; 36:26). The new covenant promised not only forgiveness of sin but also inner transformation. God would write His law on His people's hearts so that their own hearts would compel them to live righteously. He would remove their heart of stone and give them a heart of flesh, a heart that would move God's people to "follow My statutes, keep My ordinances, and practice them" (Ezek 11:20). The new heart is linked with the indwelling Spirit who would cause God's people to follow His statutes and carefully observe His ordinances (36:27).[81] The new heart is the circumcised heart that was

[79] Author's translation. LXX (Ps 50:12): καρδίαν καθαρὰν κτίσον ἐν ἐμοί ὁ θεός

[80] See Jer 24:7 (cp. 4:14; 7:24; 9:26; 16:12; 17:9).

[81] In 1 and 2 Tim Paul comments on the concept of the pure heart. In 1 Tim 1:5 a pure heart, along with a good conscience and sincere faith, is the result of the gospel. In 2 Tim 2:22 believers are described as having a pure heart. This pure heart is the source of their Christian confession. Those who have a pure heart are characterized by righteousness, faith, love, and peace.

promised in Deut 30:6, a text that clearly anticipates the new covenant.[82] In light of the function of the heart in the Sermon on the Mount, purity in heart will express itself through an abandonment of lust (Matt 5:27–30) since lust is adultery of the heart, an abandonment of materialism (6:21) since treasuring worldly possessions shows that one's heart belongs to the world, and through having a piety that seeks to please God rather than impress others (6:1–18).

"Will see God" looks forward to that time when Jesus' disciples will behold God in all of His glory and majesty.[83] The words are not to be interpreted figuratively or mystically as if they referred to special insight into God's person and nature or to a visionary experience.[84] Nor should the promise be reduced to a sentimental level as if it referred to seeing God in the kindnesses of others. Although the early disciples saw God incarnate in the person of Jesus especially in events like the transfiguration, this promise like most of the others accompanying the Beatitudes anticipates eschatological fulfillment. In the new earth and the new heavens Jesus' disciples will literally see God.

OT figures longed for this great privilege. Moses came closest to experiencing it when he was placed in the cleft of the rock and allowed to behold the aftereffects of God's radiance. However, even Moses was warned, "No one can see my face and live." God's presence is surrounded by unapproachable light (1 Tim 6:16), a glory so great that sinners who attempt to look at it are destroyed by it. The new Moses promised His followers what even the old Moses could not experience. When believers are resurrected and glorified and every trace of sin is removed from them, they will have unhindered fellowship with God even to the extent of seeing Him. Those who "seek the face of the God of Jacob" (Ps 24:6) will see Him at last.

---

[82] See P. Craigie, *The Book of Deuteronomy*, NICOT (Grand Rapids: Eerdmans, 1976), 364; E. Merrill, *Deuteronomy*, NAC (Nashville: B&H, 1994), 387–89; J. Sailhamer, *The Meaning of the Pentateuch: Revelation, Composition, and Interpretation* (Downers Grove, IL: IVP Academic, 2009), 46–48; idem, *The Pentateuch as Narrative: A Biblical-Theological Commentary* (Grand Rapids: Zondervan, 1992), 473–74.

[83] Davies and Allison, *A Critical and Exegetical Commentary on the Gospel According to Saint Matthew*, 1:456.

[84] See the overview of the history of interpretation in Luz, *Matthew 1–7: A Commentary*, 196–97. Luz rightly warned against the tendency to interpret the Beatitudes as if they were already fulfilled in the present. He quipped, "The price paid for that interpretation was that the promises threatened to lose their concreteness and their world-encompassing character and to shrink to nothing more than the individual's personal salvation. That was not Matthew's opinion" (ibid., 201–2).

Matthew 5:9

Although the sense is rare in the OT, in the NT and rabbinic literature "peace" frequently means "the absence of strife."[85] This sense is clear in the Mishnah. *Aboth* 1:12 quotes Rabbi Hillel as teaching: "Be disciples of Aaron, loving peace and pursuing peace, loving people and drawing them near to the Torah." Peacemaking is the work of reconciling two alienated parties, of taking two enemies and bringing them into a relationship of unity and harmony.[86] Only two other NT texts refer to peacemaking: Col 1:20 and Jas 3:18. Colossians 1:20 explains that Jesus made peace between God and sinners through His death on the cross. Because of the clear relationship between the SM and the letter of James, Jas 3:13–4:1 is probably more helpful in understanding the nature of peacemaking in Matt 5:9.

> Who is wise and understanding among you? He should show his works by good conduct with wisdom's gentleness. But if you have bitter envy and selfish ambition in your heart, don't brag and deny the truth.
> Such wisdom does not come down from above but is earthly, unspiritual, demonic. For where envy and selfish ambition exist, there is disorder and every kind of evil. But the wisdom from above is first pure, then peace-loving, gentle, compliant, full of mercy and good fruits, without favoritism and hypocrisy. And the fruit of righteousness is sown in peace by those who cultivate peace. What is the source of the wars and the fights among you?

Since the surrounding context mentions conflict between James's readers several times ("bitter envy and selfish ambition," "disorder," "the wars and the fights"), "peacemaking" in James clearly refers to ending conflict between individuals, especially between oneself and others. In light of the echoes of the SM in James, the blessing on the "peacemakers" probably relates to those who seek to reconcile estranged individuals.

Consequently the seventh beatitude introduces a theme that will later rise to prominence in the SM. In Matt 5:21–26 Jesus commanded His disciples to interrupt the solemn act of temple sacrifice in order to seek reconciliation with a fellow disciple whom they had offended. He urged them to end legal conflicts quickly by agreeing to an

[85] W. Foerster, "εἰρήνη," in *TDNT* (1964), 2:400–417.
[86] Davies and Allison, *A Critical and Exegetical Commentary on the Gospel According to Saint Matthew*, 1:458; France, *The Gospel of Matthew*, 169; Hagner, *Matthew 1–13*, 94 (although Hagner's claim that the beatitude was aimed specifically at Jewish zealots is speculative; in the context of the SM the application seems to be broader); Luz, *Matthew 1–7: A Commentary*, 198.

out-of-court settlement. In verses 38–41 He commanded His disciples to refrain from retaliating against those who abused them. Under no circumstances were they to seek revenge. They were to diffuse the hostility of their Roman oppressors through loving submission that exceeded even an abusive soldier's harsh demands. Finally, He commanded His disciples to love their enemies and pray for, not against, their persecutors (vv. 43–48). The ministry of peacemaking involved putting an end to conflict by refusing to postpone apologies or restitution, refusing to seek revenge, humbly serving one's enemies, and having a love for others that is stronger than their hatred.

"Will be called sons of God" could be taken as teaching that others will recognize the disciple's unique relationship to God through his ministry of reconciliation. Nevertheless the other passive verbs in the Beatitudes are divine passives, and this is probably so here. Thus the sense is that God will call peacemakers His children. Since most of the promises that accompany the Beatitudes have an eschatological focus, this promise probably refers to eschatological judgment in which God will separate His children from His enemies. Jesus' disciples are already sons of God (v. 45). However, God will confirm His relationship to His children on judgment day.

The identification of Jesus' disciples as God's sons is an expression of the so-called replacement theology that is prominent in Matthew's Gospel. Jesus' disciples form the new spiritual Israel (see note 107). As suggested earlier, the very form of the Beatitudes probably recalls Moses' blessing for Israel in Deut 33:29 and thus identifies Jesus' disciples as the new Israel. As noted earlier, most scholars recognize that Jesus chose 12 disciples because of the corresponding number of the tribes of Israel in order to identify His disciples as the heirs of the Abrahamic covenant and the continuation of Israel's faithful remnant (10:2; 19:28). In Deut 14:1; 32:19; Isa 43:6; 45:11; and Hos 1:10, God identified Israelites as His sons.[87] Some Jews wrongly believed that all physical descendants of Abraham were true Jews who would receive the benefits promised to Abraham's seed (Genesis 15; Matt 3:9). Jesus insisted that those who followed Him would receive the fulfillment of these promises. Genesis 15:18–19 had promised the land to Abraham's descendants, and the third beatitude promised that Jesus' disciples would "inherit the earth" (Matt 5:5). The sixth beatitude

---

[87] See Betz, *The Sermon on the Mount*, 140–41.

reiterates the theme of the disciples' identification as the new Israel (see note 107). The pronoun "they" (*autoi*) in each beatitude is emphatic and serves to restrict the promises of the Beatitudes to Jesus' disciples alone. The meek are blessed because they and they alone will inherit the land/earth. The peacemakers are blessed because they and only they will be called sons of God. Thus individuals who are not characterized by the qualities listed in the Beatitudes are excluded by Jesus from Israel.

Peacemaking does not make one a child of God, but peacemaking is an essential expression of divine sonship. Sons of God will bear a resemblance to their heavenly Father, and the SM appeals to the character and behavior of God as a model that Jesus' disciples are to seek to emulate (vv. 44–45,48). Jesus' disciples will be recognized as God's children in eschatological judgment, not merely because they claim to be His children but because they resemble Him in their character and behavior.[88] Nothing expresses the Father's character more clearly than the ministry of reconciliation.

Matthew 5:10–12

Christ concluded the Beatitudes by pronouncing a blessing on those who suffer persecution because they exhibit the godly characteristics detailed in the Beatitudes. This beatitude has several important emphases. First, the beatitude assumes that persecution is an inevitable part of kingdom life. The particle "whenever" is used rather than "if" to highlight this assumption. As Paul taught, "All those who want to live a godly life in Christ Jesus will be persecuted" (2 Tim 3:12). Second, not all persecuted people are blessed but only those who are persecuted for manifesting Christlike character, that is, those persecuted for righteousness. Third, future reward will more than compensate for present sufferings.

Jesus had no doubt that His disciples would suffer both for their righteous character and for their devotion to Him. Although most versions translate the participle of verse 10 as if it were in the present tense ("those who are persecuted"), it is actually in the perfect tense ("those who have been persecuted"). The participles in verses 4,6,

---

[88] France correctly points out that the Semitic idiom "sons of" "often indicates those who share a certain character or status" (*Matthew*, 169). See Matt 8:12; 9:15 (HCSB marg.); 13:38; 23:31 for examples.

and 7 are in the present tense. The tense shift in verse 10 is clearly intentional and purposeful. Perhaps the grammar already anticipates verse 12, which refers to the cruel treatment of the OT prophets by the Jews. Perhaps it refers to acts of violence and injustice against the righteous previously mentioned in Matthew's Gospel, such as Herod's attempt to kill Jesus in His infancy or the arrest and imprisonment of John the Baptist. However, since the previous and following beatitudes refer to the disciples in Jesus' audience, the eighth beatitude may refer to incidents of persecution against Jesus' followers prior to the SM.[89] In any event persecution of righteous sufferers had already occurred, and it would continue to occur.[90]

Verse 11 also assumes the certainty of persecution. The verse used "when" (*hotan*) rather than "if" (*ei* or *eav*) since the persecution was sure to come.[91] Jesus spoke of persecution repeatedly in Matthew's Gospel (10:16–25,34–36; 21:34–36; 23:29–37) and warned that the persecution of His followers would intensify as the end approached (24:9–10).

Jesus mentioned two motives for the persecution of His disciples. First, they are persecuted "for righteousness." The godly character of Jesus' followers and the righteous conduct that SM describes serve as a silent indictment of the sinful lifestyles of others. Such righteousness incites resentment and inspires mistreatment. First Peter 3:14 alludes to the eighth beatitude, and 1 Pet 4:3–4 offers an explanation of the motive for persecution of the righteous: "For there has already been enough time spent in doing what the pagans choose to do: carrying on in unrestrained behavior, evil desires, drunkenness, orgies, carousing, and lawless idolatry. So they are surprised that you don't plunge with them into the same flood of wild living—and they slander you."

Jesus' followers strive for sexual purity, insist on absolute honesty, and practice self-control. Those who are sexually loose, dishonest,

---

[89] An allusion to previously unmentioned instances of persecution appears in Matt 10:25. The Gospel of Matthew mixes both topical and chronological arrangement, so some of the references to rejection of Jesus and accompanying persecution of His disciples later in the Gospel may have preceded the SM.

[90] Davies and Allison likewise note, "The perfect tense entails that persecution is a fact of the past and of the present" (*A Critical and Exegetical Commentary on the Gospel According to Saint Matthew*, 1:459). For other views of the perfect tense here, see Carson, "Matthew," 136.

[91] Matthew's Gospel used ὅταν 19 times. In every occurrence, although time of the action is contingent, the action is definite.

and unrestrained interpret the disciples' behavior as a condemnation of their own behavior. They often respond by pressuring the disciples to conform. If he or she refuses to conform, they may begin to mock and ridicule the disciples' commitment and character. Persecutors may even resort to more drastic measures. Although righteous behavior sometimes inspires the respect of others, it also often invites persecution. The corruption of the human heart and its love for sin (Matt 15:19) ensures that Jesus' disciples will be hated and hurt. The unbeliever's persecution of Jesus' followers is thus as natural and certain as a predator's attack on its prey (10:16).

Second, Jesus' followers suffer persecution "because of Me." Jesus Himself was a controversial figure. His claims and His teachings so stirred the rage of some of His hearers that they accused Him of being in league with Beelzebul, identified Him as Beelzebul, attempted to stone Him, and ultimately executed Him in the most brutal fashion. Jesus warned His disciples that they could expect similar treatment: "You will be hated by everyone because of My name. . . . If they called the head of the house 'Beelzebul,' how much more the members of his household!" (10:22,25). "Because of My name" is roughly equivalent to "because of Me" but implies more. Hagner recognized the construction as a "highly significant Christological element."[92] The phrase "because of My name" is likely an elliptical expression meaning "because of your confession of My name."[93] Since Jesus warned that many would come in His name and claim, "I am the Messiah" (24:5), the "name" to which Jesus referred in the Gospel is likely a Christological title.[94] Since Luke 6:22 uses the corresponding words "because of the Son of Man," the Son of Man title may have been the particular cause of offense. Jesus claimed this title in a clear allusion to Dan 7:13 in the confession of Matt 26:64. This title identified Jesus as a King of heavenly origin who will reign over a universal and eternal kingdom and who is worthy of worship by all the peoples of the earth. This claim was regarded as blasphemous by the high priest and led to Jesus' being sentenced to death by the Sanhedrin. The disciples' continuing affirmation of Jesus' heavenly origin and eternal kingship guaranteed ongoing Jewish opposition.

---

[92] Hagner, *Matthew 1–13*, 278.

[93] Nolland, *The Gospel of Matthew*, 426. This is preferable to the view that Jesus was referring to the name "Christian" since this label for Jesus' disciples was not in use during Jesus' ministry.

[94] See also France, *The Gospel of Matthew*, 902; Nolland, *The Gospel of Matthew*, 961–62.

This Christian claim remains scandalous today. Most moderns are willing to recognize Jesus as a good moral teacher, but insistence on the exclusive claims of Christianity, particularly the confession of Jesus as God, Savior, and King, remains offensive. Contemporary disciples must be willing to follow Christ faithfully and boldly affirm His identity despite the cost.

Jesus mentioned three different expressions of persecution that His disciples would experience. "They insult you" means that opponents of Christian righteousness and the gospel will disparage, mock, and verbally shame Jesus' disciples. The verb "insult" (*oneidisōsin*) appears later in Matthew to describe the insults hurled at Jesus while He suffered on the cross (27:39–44). The insults included mockery of Jesus' power to save, His identity as King of Israel, and His divine Sonship. Later persecutors used clever word plays, designed both to insult and to evoke a laugh, in their mockery of Jesus' claims. Jesus was recognized by early Christians as the "Son of a virgin" because of the virginal conception described in Luke 1 and Matthew 1. By rearranging the letters of the Greek word "virgin" (*parthenos*), later opponents of Christianity mocked Jesus as the son of a panther (*panthera*).[95]

Contemporary opponents of Jesus' disciples continue to ridicule Jesus' followers. Television sitcoms mention Jesus only as the basis of some irreverent or blasphemous joke and typically portray Christians as narrow-minded, naïve, or mentally ill. These are modern forms of the insults of which Jesus warned.

The word "persecute" in 5:11 means "to run after, pursue, or run out." Although the term could refer to any form of harassment, Matt 23:34 used this verb in a literal sense to describe persecutors chasing Jesus' disciples "from town to town." The verb thus may mean to pursue someone in hopes of apprehending him with the intention of either violently abusing him or turning him over to authorities for prosecution. The text associates such pursuit with killing, crucifying, and scourging Jesus' followers. Although violent persecution is rare in the United States, it is common in other parts of the world. By some estimates, more believers suffered martyrdom in the twentieth century than all previous centuries combined.[96]

---

[95] F. F. Bruce, *The New Testament Documents: Are They Reliable?* 5th ed. (Downers Grove, IL: InterVarsity, 1960), 101; J. Klausner, *Jesus of Nazareth* (London: Allen & Unwin, 1927), 23–24.

[96] Recent estimates suggest that 70 million Christians were martyred in the first two millennia of church history. Of these, some 45 million (approximately two-thirds) were martyred

Jesus' words "falsely say every kind of evil against you" mean that persecutors will slander His disciples and raise false accusations against them. During the first three centuries of church history, Christians were accused of cannibalism, incest, atheism, and general hatred of humanity.[97] Such accusations were gross distortions of actual Christian practices. The charge of cannibalism was probably related to the celebration of the Lord's Supper. The charge of incest was probably related to the early Christian practice of believing couples referring to their spouses as sisters and brothers. The charge of atheism was related to the Christian's rejection of the gods of the Roman pantheon. The charge of general hatred of humanity related to the Christians' refusal to follow society in its immoral practices. Some of these accusations were probably not merely confused interpretations of misunderstood Christian practices. They were likely deliberate distortions of the truth designed to defame believers.

Jesus commanded His disciples to respond to persecution with joy and gladness. "Be glad" (*chairete*) means to enjoy a state of happiness and well-being. "Rejoice" (*agalliasthe*) is similar in meaning but more intensive. The word speaks of being "overjoyed" or "extremely joyful."[98] Typically such intense joy was outwardly expressed either through words (Acts 2:26), tears, skipping, or jumping (Luke 1:44).

The imperatives are in the present tense and thus command continual joy and gladness. This joy is not a belated response to persecution that occurs after insults have ceased to sting or the nerves torn by the stripes on one's back have ceased to scream. This joy characterizes the disciple even as the insults are hurled and the scourge lacerates the flesh. Such immediate joy in the face of persecution characterized the apostles in Acts 5:40–41: "After they [the Sanhedrin] called in the apostles and had them flogged, they ordered them not to speak in the name of Jesus and released them. Then they went out from the presence of the Sanhedrin, rejoicing that they were counted worthy to be dishonored on behalf of the Name."

---

between 1900 and 2000. See A. Socci, *I nuovi perseguitati. Indagine sulla intolleranza anticristiana nel nuovo secolo del martirio* ("The New Persecuted: Inquiries into Anti-Christian Intolerance in the New Century of Martyrs") (Casale Monferrato: Piemme, 2002).

[97] Reference to accusations against Christians related to "Thyestean feasts and Oedipodean intercourse" (cannibalism and incest) appears in the Epistle of the Gallic Churches to Phrygia and Asia preserved in Eusebius, *Hist. Eccl.* 5:1. On the Christian's alleged "hatred of the human race," see Tacitus, *Ann.* 15.44.

[98] "ἀγαλλιάω," BDAG, 4.

The flogging administered by the Sanhedrin involved 39 lashes. The procedure for the flogging is described in the Mishnah in vivid detail. This torture was horrific and sometimes resulted in death. However, as the apostles walked out of the Sanhedrin meeting with their backs still raw and their rough garments rasping painfully against their bleeding flesh at their slightest movement, they rejoiced for having the honor of suffering for their Savior. Their behavior offers a powerful illustration of joy in the face of persecution. Jesus' command to be overjoyed leaves no room for martyr complexes that prompt the persecuted to wallow in self-pity. Joy and celebration are the disciples' response to suffering for Christ.

Jesus pronounced that the kingdom of heaven belongs to those who suffer for righteousness. In the Greek text "theirs" is shifted from its normal position at the end of the clause to the beginning of the clause. This placement gives the pronoun special emphasis. The nuance is that the kingdom belongs to righteous sufferers and to them alone. Those who compromise the teachings of Jesus in the SM in order to escape persecution are not true disciples and will not have a share in the kingdom because true disciples are willing to follow Jesus even at the cost of their very lives (Matt 16:24–25). The "kingdom of heaven" is the reign of God in the person of Jesus the Messiah. Righteous sufferers are subjects of God's rule through their submission to Jesus' authority. This kingdom has been inaugurated in the ministry of Jesus but will be consummated in the end times, bringing enormous blessing to Jesus' followers. Those who have been oppressed and persecuted will be exalted to a place of authority and privilege when the kingdom comes in all its fullness.

Both the first and the eighth beatitudes offer the promise that "the kingdom of heaven is theirs" (5:3,10). These two identical promises serve as brackets for the Beatitudes and mark them as a literary unity. This implies that poverty in spirit and righteous suffering and all the characteristics described in between are hallmarks of a single group, Jesus' followers. Disciples of Jesus manifest each of these characteristics and enjoy all the promised blessings.

Jesus also promised, "Your reward is great in heaven" (v. 12). The severity of the penalty suffered for faithfulness to Jesus will be offset by the enormity of the reward enjoyed in heaven. Jesus did not specify the nature of this reward. However, because of the divine reversals that appear in the Beatitudes (the poor will reign, the mourners will be comforted, the hungry will be filled, etc.), one expects the reward to involve the reversal of the persecutions suffered. Human insult will be replaced by divine commendation. Human rejection and harassment will be replaced by divine acceptance and favor. Earthly punishment will be replaced by eternal bliss. The eschatological reward will be so great that the earthly suffering will pale by comparison.

The disciples could be assured of heavenly reward for their sufferings because their righteous sufferings placed them in the company of the OT prophets, representatives of Israel's faithful and righteous remnant. Jewish leaders had rejected and vehemently persecuted the OT prophets (1 Kgs 18:4; 19:1–3; 2 Chr 36:16; Neh 9:26; Jer 20:10; 26:10–19; 36:1–38:28; Amos 7:10–12), and Jesus repeatedly denounced this persecution in Matthew's Gospel (Matt 21:34–36; 23:29–37; see also Acts 7:52). By treating Jesus' followers in the same way they had treated the prophets, Jewish persecutors would unwittingly bestow on them a prophet's honor. The prophets were not only spokesmen for God; they were also guardians of righteousness and models of faithfulness.[99] They were faithful Jews par excellence. Jesus' followers now stood in the line of the prophets.[100] Although Jesus here equated the disciples with the prophets, He later insisted that His disciples surpassed the prophets (Matt 11:9,11–15; 13:17) since they had seen and heard the fulfillments of the OT prophecies that the prophets had longed to see and hear.[101]

The introduction and form of the Beatitudes demarcate Jesus' disciples as the true Israel (see pp. 39–40, including note 10). The new Moses bestows on them the blessing that Moses had granted national Israel. Jesus explicated this identification even further by comparing His disciples to the prophets at the conclusion of the Beatitudes. The promise offered in 10:41 implies that many Jews recognized that the prophets would receive a special, enviable reward from God. The comparison to the prophets implies that since the disciples share the prophets' fate, they will also enjoy a prophet's reward. Followers of Jesus who suffer willingly for the cause of righteousness and for their devotion to Christ will enjoy the reward of an Elijah, Elisha, Isaiah, or Jeremiah. This is cause for the enormous joy that Jesus commanded.

---

[99] In Matt 10:41 "prophet" and "righteous person" are used interchangeably.

[100] France, *The Gospel of Matthew*, 173; Hagner, *Matthew 1–13*, 96.

[101] See Keener, *The Gospel of Matthew*, 171–72.

C. Salt and Light (Matt 5:13–16)

Although the transition from the Beatitudes to Jesus' commission to His disciples in Matt 5:13–16 seems abrupt, a close connection exists between the two sections. The Beatitudes ended with reference to the persecution that Jesus' disciples would suffer because of their righteousness. This section assures the disciples that not all people will react to their righteousness so negatively. Some will actually examine the disciples' righteous conduct and respond not with persecution but by glorifying the heavenly Father.

Matthew 5:13

Salt had at least 11 different uses in ancient times.[102] The Bible directly refers to several of these uses and assumes others.[103] Two verses refer to salt as a condiment for food that added flavor to a dish (Job 6:6; Col 4:6).[104] Some commentators assume that this was the function of salt to which Matt 5:13 refers since (a) this was the most common use of salt and (b) the clause "if the salt should lose its taste" strongly implies this view. On the other hand the assumption that the use of salt to flavor food was the primary use may be based more on modern practice than the evidence of ancient texts.[105] Furthermore the Greek text does not refer explicitly to the salt losing its taste. This translation actually has rather weak support (see below). Thus Broadus seems correct in his opinion: "Some bring in also the idea of salt as seasoning—that Christians are to save life from being stale and flat—but this seems strained, and little in harmony with the general tone of the discourse."[106]

Salt was also a preservative. Without refrigeration meat could quickly spoil. Spoilage was prevented by curing the meat with salt.

---

[102] See Davies and Allison, *A Critical and Exegetical Commentary on the Gospel According to Saint Matthew*, 1:472–73. J. Latham discusses at length the metaphorical use of the word "salt" in *The Religious Symbolism of Salt*, Théologie historique 64 (Paris: Beauchesne, 1982).

[103] In addition to canonical references, references to salt appear in Tob (S) 6:5 and Sir 39:26. Tobit refers to leftover fish being salted in order to preserve it. Sirach refers to salt as one of the basic necessities of life.

[104] Luz suggests that this is the function of salt to which Matt 5:13 refers "since seasoning is the most common use of salt" (*Matthew: A Commentary*, 206).

[105] Blomberg correctly argued that "given the amount of salt needed to preserve food without refrigeration, it is not likely that many ancient Jews considered salt primarily as enhancing taste" (*Matthew*, 102).

[106] Broadus, *The Gospel According to Matthew*, 95.

The salt killed the bacteria responsible for spoilage. The Bible does not directly describe salt as a preservative,[107] but this function seems to underlie the use of salt to symbolize what lasts or endures. The Bible mentions that a lasting covenant was made by eating bread and salt or salt alone (Num 18:19; 2 Chr 13:5). Because of the use of salt in sealing a lasting covenant, eating salt with someone was a sign of loyalty (Ezra 4:14; the words "have taken an oath of loyalty" are lit., "have eaten the salt of the palace"). Presumably salt came to symbolize what lasts because it was the instrument used to make perishables last.

The Bible frequently refers to salt as an agent of purification. Like snow and bleached wool (Isa 1:18), salt probably became a symbol for purity because of its white color. Salt was added to sacrifices both to symbolize the lasting nature of God's covenant with His people (Lev 2:13) and to purify the offering. Exodus 30:35 says that the incense offering was to be "seasoned with salt, pure and holy." The context suggests that salt was a symbol of purification. Ezekiel 16:4 refers to newborn children being washed with water and salted with salt. Evidently the water cleansed the child, and the salt purified it in a ritual sense. Salt also served as a purifying agent in 2 Kgs 2:21 in which Elisha threw salt into a contaminated spring and said, "This is what the Lord says, 'I have healed this water.'"[108]

Salt was capable of such a wide range of uses and symbolic meanings that some interpreters doubt that one can determine the particular use that Jesus had in mind here.[109] The majority of contemporary scholars suggest that no specific function of salt was in mind. Rather

---

[107] Early Christian teachers did appeal to this function of salt in their exhortations. For example Ignatius, writing sometime in the first three decades of the second century AD, urged believers to "be salted with him [Jesus Christ], so that none of you become rotten, for by your odor you will be examined" (*Magn.* 10). Salt preserved because of its antiseptic property. Thus the use of salt as a preservative that prevented putrefaction overlaps with the use of salt as a purifying agent.

[108] Because of its association with purity and holiness, some ancient Orientals believed that salt could drive away evil spirits. See F. Hauck, "ἅλας," *TDNT* (1964), 1:228–29.

[109] Davies and Allison concluded, "It is quite impossible to decide what one characteristic is to the fore in Mt 5.13" (*A Critical and Exegetical Commentary on the Gospel According to Saint Matthew*, 1:473). The authors add that the ambiguity should not trouble interpreters since Matthew's usage was likely "equivocal and multivocal" (ibid.). For a similar conclusion see Hagner, *Matthew 1–13*, 1:99. Hagner ultimately decided that "salt" is a metaphor for what is necessary to life, significant and important.

salt was mentioned merely as one of the necessities of life.[110] However, several clues suggest that the use of salt as a purifying agent is particularly in view in Matt 5:13. First, as the discussion above demonstrates, this was the most prevalent use of salt in the OT. Second, Jesus appears to have used the metaphor "salt" in this fashion elsewhere. In Mark 9:49 He said, "Everyone will be salted with fire." Jesus was comparing the persecution that His followers would endure to a refiner's fire that purifies precious metal by burning away the dross.[111] Thus, being salted with fire meant being purified or refined.

Third, this interpretation is most sensible in light of the clear parallelism between Matt 5:13 and 14. The statements, "You are the salt of the earth" and "You are the light of the world," are grammatically and structurally identical. Both statements begin with an emphatic use of the second-person plural pronoun followed by a present indicative second-person plural form of the verb "be." Furthermore the genitive modifiers "of the earth" and "of the world" seem to be synonymous.[112] This parallelism suggests that the metaphors "salt" and "light" have roughly the same sense. "You are the light of the world" means (a) that the disciples of Jesus will be characterized by righteousness and purity and (b) that their righteousness will move others to glorify God and seek to be transformed by Him in a similar way. Thus salt is also a likely metaphor for purity that has a transforming effect on others. Fourth, the preceding context emphasized the disciples' purity of heart (v. 8) and their longing for righteousness (v. 6), and this character and longing naturally prompt their mission as purifying agents. Thus, "You are the salt of the earth" means that Jesus' disciples are to seek to transform corrupt human societies.[113]

---

[110] Blomberg's caution is apropos: "One must avoid assuming that all possible uses of salt were in view here" (*Matthew*, 102).

[111] See J. Brooks, *Mark*, NAC (Nashville: Broadman, 1991), 153–54; W. L. Lane, *The Gospel According to Mark*, NICNT (Grand Rapids: Eerdmans, 1974), 349. A small group of scribes behind the Western text of Mark replaced "every sacrifice will be salted with fire" with "every sacrifice will be salted with salt," a clear allusion to Lev 2:13, which the scribes evidently saw as a key to the correct interpretation of the symbolic use of salt in this text. For an explanation of the probable history of transmission, see Metzger, *Textual Commentary on the Greek New Testament*, 102–3.

[112] For this reason both the NEB and REB translate 5:13, "You are the salt of the world."

[113] A few modern scholars support this view of the function of the salt metaphor in 5:13. Although Turner adopts Hagner's view, he seems to lean toward this view, noting "the purifying use of salt could be intended here given 5:8" (*Matthew*, 1:155). Hill noted, "In the ancient world salt symbolized that which purifies and gives flavour" (*The Gospel of Matthew*, 115).

The use of salt as a purifying agent overlaps somewhat with the use of salt as a preservative. Salt preserved because it first purified. As Broadus noted, "As salt preserves things from corruption and decay, so it is the office of Christians to preserve the mass of mankind from utter moral corruption and ruin."[114] Nevertheless the use of salt as a purifying agent is primary in 5:13 rather than the use of salt as a preservative. Jesus spoke elsewhere of the corruption of the world in its present state (John 12:31; 14:17,30; 15:18–19; 16:8,11,33; 17:14). He clearly did not want His disciples to preserve this corrupt world in its current condition. He wanted them to transform this corrupt world. Greek moralists also used salt to symbolize moral purity. Diogenes Laertius advised placing salt on a table in one's home "to remind us of what is right; for salt preserves whatever it finds, and it arises from the purest of sources."[115]

Jesus' disciples purify the world by living holy lives and proclaiming the gospel of the kingdom. The definite article that modifies the word "salt" is rich with significance. The article implies that Jesus' disciples are not merely a purifying agent for their corrupt world, that is, one purifying agent among many others. They are the one effective means of purifying their world.[116] This implication was reinforced by the emphatic use of the pronoun "you," which suggests, "You, and no one else, are the salt of the earth." Only Jesus' disciples are capable of transforming society.

Jesus did not explain how His disciples fulfill the role of purifying agents. However, His emphasis on His disciples' unique ability to purify the world suggests that they do so by means other than mere moral protest, political involvement, or social activism. Any person of any faith can engage in these activities. If these were the strategies for transforming society that Jesus had in mind, He could not have said that His disciples were "the," that is, "the one and only" salt of the earth. If Jesus' disciples alone are the salt, He must be urging them to

---

[114] Broadus, *The Gospel According to Matthew*, 95. L. Morris comes close to this view when he argued that Christians "act as a kind of moral antiseptic" (*The Gospel According to Matthew*, [Grand Rapids: Eerdmans, 1992], 104). See also W. C. Allen, *A Critical and Exegetical Commentary on the Gospel According to S. Matthew* (Edinburgh: Clark, 1912), 43; and Blomberg, *Matthew*, 102.

[115] Diogenes Laertius, 8.1.35, quoted in Nolland, *The Gospel of Matthew*, 212.

[116] The article is also regarded as "monadic" by Davies and Allison, *A Critical and Exegetical Commentary on the Gospel According to Saint Matthew*, 1:472.

undertake a unique ministry of moral transformation that only they can fulfill.

Only Jesus' disciples can purify society because only His disciples are characterized by the superior righteousness that the SM describes. According to verse 20 Jesus' disciples are characterized by a righteousness that exceeds that of the scribes and Pharisees, the noblest models of righteousness in first-century Judaism. Furthermore only Jesus' disciples can share the gospel of the kingdom which produces righteousness in those who repent and believe. Again the parallelism between verses 13 and 14 is important for the interpretation of verse 13. When read against its OT background, verse 14 is essentially a missionary mandate. The close relationship between the two parallel statements suggests that both verses highlight the disciples' responsibility to preach the gospel throughout the world.

Jesus warned that His followers can lose their ability to be agents of transformation if their lives are not pure. Although most modern translations refer to the salt "losing its taste," the verb translated in this fashion (*mōranthē*) does not mean "to lose flavor" anywhere else in all ancient literature.[117] The verb normally means "to become foolish, lose one's mind, or be mentally incapacitated." The verb seems to speak of losing effectiveness or becoming worthless rather than losing flavor. The idea is that salt which is impure cannot purify.[118] The puzzling use of the Greek verb here is likely a by-product of Greek translation of an originally Aramaic saying that involved a wordplay. In Hebrew and Aramaic, the root *tpl* can mean either "be foolish" (as suggested by some for Job 1:22; 24:12; Jer 23:13) or "be saltless, dull, insipid" (Job 6:6).[119] In the wordplay the "saltlessness" of the person referred allegorically to his "foolishness." Greek translators of the saying were forced to choose between the two senses since no Greek term had the same range of meanings. They appropriately chose the translation that expressed the allegorical significance of the imagery.

In Matthew's Gospel "foolishness" is not a judgment regarding a person's intellect. "Foolishness" is a moral and spiritual state. The foolish are those who disregard or ignore Jesus' teaching and refuse

---

[117] The related adjective μωρός was used to refer to taste (or the lack of it) in Dioscorides Pedanius, *Mat. med.* 4:19: ῥίζαι . . . γευσαμένῳ μωραί.

[118] Blomberg's translation "is defiled" renders the sense well in this context (*Matthew*, 102) even though the verb does not elsewhere have this meaning. Luz translated the verb literally, "when the salt becomes dumb" (*Matthew: A Commentary*, 1:203).

[119] See "תפל," HALOT, 393–94.

to obey it (Matt 7:26). Jesus' point is that those who hear but do not obey His message are like defiled salt that has lost its ability to be a purifying agent. Jesus' statement may be an indictment against the teachers addressed in 5:19–20. False teachers would defy the commandments of God's law and would also teach "people to do so" as well. When impurity characterized professing disciples, they would lose their ability to impact the world positively.

Believers are to purify the world, but they can do this only as they maintain their own purity. Corrupt salt that has lost its ability to purify is worthless. Impure salt that has lost its effectiveness cannot regain it. Jesus asked, "How can it be made salty?" (v. 13). Unfortunately Jesus' contemporaries did not have the ability to refine contaminated salt and remove its impurities. In the Talmud (b. Bek. 8b), Rabbi Joshua ben Hananiah (c. AD 90) asked, "If the salt starts to stink, with what shall one salt it?" He replied, "With the afterbirth of a mule." His audience recognized that mules were hybrids that were incapable of reproducing and thus never had an afterbirth. His reply made clear that it was impossible to purify salt that had become corrupt. On the basis of this statement, some scholars believe that reference to resalting salt was a "proverbial expression for something impossible."[120] Thus the implied answer to Jesus' question is, "It cannot be made salty again." Jesus seemed to be teaching that when those who claim to be His disciples fail to be pure, their potential for changing the world is permanently damaged and cannot be restored. Although divine forgiveness removes all the eternal consequences of sin, it does not eliminate the temporal consequences of sin. The hypocrisy of those who do not practice what they preach does lasting harm to one's Christian witness.

Jesus taught that professing disciples whose lives are characterized by impurity will not only have ineffective ministries, but also they will have counterproductive ministries. Salt that has lost its purity is good for nothing except to be "thrown out" and trampled by men. If concentrations of salt are strong enough in the soil, the salt acts as a herbicide that destroys the ability of the soil to produce.[121]

[120] Luz, *Matthew: A Commentary*, 1:206. The rabbinic statement ended with the question, "Can the salt even stink?" and the question seems to anticipate a negative response. This contrasts with Jesus' teaching in which it is assumed that salt can become corrupt.

[121] See Deut 29:23; Judg 9:45; Ps 107:34; Jer 17:6; Zeph 2:9. After the Romans defeated Carthage in the Second Punic War, they sowed their enemies' fields with salt. See Albright and Mann, *Matthew*, 54.

Thus bad salt had to be disposed of carefully to avoid ruining the soil. Luke 14:35 warned that ruined salt is useless either for the soil or for the manure pile. Ruined salt was worth less than dirt or manure because even they were useful as fertilizers that promoted the growth of plants.[122] But salt did not promote life; it destroyed life. The ancients used corrupt salt as gravel on beaten paths where grass could not grow anyway because of the heavy traffic.[123] The point is that salt that is too corrupt to have a purifying influence can have a destructive influence. Salt that has lost its purity has a herbicidal effect. Rather than purifying the lives of others, it destroys the potential for life.

When professing disciples lead impure lives, they invite the spite of even the corrupt world. Jesus did not describe pedestrians as merely walking on the worthless salt. Instead they "trample" (*katapateō*) it. This is the same verb used later in the SM to describe pigs trampling pearls with their hooves (7:6). The language implies that the world will abuse those who are like defiled salt, treating them with scorn and disgust. The final beatitudes show that those who claim to be Jesus' disciples are sometimes persecuted because their righteousness is a silent indictment of the sins of others. Sadly, those who claim to be Jesus' disciples but live sinfully may be persecuted because their hypocrisy is repulsive to those who have observed the inconsistency between their words and their actions.

Matthew 5:14–16

Although the general sense of Jesus' statement "You are the light of the world" is clear, determining the precise meaning of the words is difficult. A clear understanding of the words can only result from a thorough study of the OT background of the words, the use of the term "light" in first-century Judaism, and the use of the term in the Gospel of Matthew. Additional clues come from the placement of the statement in the context of the sermon.

---

[122] B. Malina and R. Rohrbaugh suggested that Jesus' words refer to adding salt to dung so that it would burn more efficiently in outdoor ovens (*Social Science Commentary on the Synoptic Gospels* [Minneapolis: Augsburg Fortress, 1992], 50). Contaminated salt could no longer fulfill this function. However, the connection between soil and dung in Luke 14:35 better supports the contrast between fertilizer and herbicide suggested above. Gundry offers no support for his theory that salt was mixed with manure to prevent fermentation (*Matthew*, 76).

[123] *m. 'Erub.* 10:14 shows that the priests scattered salt on the altar ramp to provide traction that would prevent them from slipping on the blood-drenched pavement.

The first clauses of verses 13 and 14 are examples of synonymous parallelism. Both clauses begin with "You are." The phrases "of
the earth" and "of the world" are equivalent, and both express the
universal focus of the disciples' mission. Since "earth" and "world"
are roughly synonymous, the roles defined in the terms of "salt" and
"light" are probably closely related. If "salt" designates the disciple's
role as a purifying agent, "light" probably refers to the task of establishing righteousness in the world. Furthermore "light" and "darkness" frequently refer to good and evil respectively in the OT, the
Dead Sea Scrolls, and the New Testament. Thus the description of
Jesus' disciples as the "light" highlights their acts of righteousness
(5:16; Rom 13:11–14) and the impact of this righteousness on the
world around them.

In the OT "light" symbolized revelation and instruction, the
law, hope, joy, righteousness, salvation, and the radiance of divine
presence.[124] Since echoes of Isaiah permeate the early chapters of
Matthew, a study of the symbolism of "light" in Isaiah is especially
informative. Throughout the prophecies of Isaiah, the shining light
is a metaphor of the Messiah and His people fulfilling the missionary
purpose of manifesting the glory of God among the nations. Matthew's previous use of the metaphor "light" in Matt 4:15–16 applied
Isa 9:1–2 to Jesus.[125] Jesus is the promised Light that blesses those
in darkness and gloom with hope, joy, deliverance, and salvation.
Interpreted against the background of this previous reference, "You
are the light" means that Jesus' disciples are to be extensions of the
Messiah's ministry by taking up His mission of bringing salvation to
the world.[126]

Isaiah 42:6 and 49:6 use similar language to describe the Servant
of the Lord: "I will appoint you to be a covenant for the people and a
light to the nations," and "I will also make you a light for the nations,
to be My salvation to the ends of the earth." Both texts describe the

---

[124] H. Conzelmann, "φῶς," TDNT (1974), 9:310–58; H. Wolf, "אוֹר," TWOT, 1:25–26 (§52).

[125] In Matthew's Gospel several of these usages of light appear. In 6:22 light seems to speak
of purity in contrast with darkness that symbolizes evil. In 17:2 light speaks of the radiance
of divine glory that Jesus manifested in the transfiguration. In 10:27 "light" means "out in the
open" or "in public." The many different uses of the metaphor in the Bible and even in this
single Gospel make it difficult to determine the sense here with real precision.

[126] Davies and Allison, A Critical and Exegetical Commentary on the Gospel According to Saint
Matthew, 1:474–75; France, The Gospel of Matthew, 175; Luz, Matthew: A Commentary, 1:207.

ministry of the Messiah.[127] Isaiah 60:1–3 may be especially important for understanding Matt 5:14 since the text is in close proximity to Isaiah 61, whose themes, as already noted, are prominent in the Beatitudes. "Arise, shine, for your light has come, and the glory of the LORD shines over you. For look, darkness covers the earth, and total darkness the peoples; but the LORD will shine over you, and His glory will appear over you."

Isaiah 60:1–3 was a promise given to Zion. The prophecy culminates in verse 21 in the promise, "All your people will be righteous; they will possess the land forever; they are the branch I planted, the work of My hands, so that I may be glorified." The allusion to righteousness that glorifies God in Matt 5:16 may be an echo of this OT text. Consequently the designation of Jesus' disciples as the "light of the world" identifies His disciples with Zion and marks them as the new Israel (see pp. 39–40, including note 10).

Ancient Jews saw Israel as this light to the nations. However, the words to Jesus' disciples include an emphatic "you," and the definite article "the" before "light" implies that Jesus' disciples alone are the true light of the world. They have thus supplanted national Israel as God's covenant people, a theme that is prominent in the Gospel of Matthew and has already been expressed in the Beatitudes.[128] In Isaiah 60 the light that shines in and over Zion is God's own glory. Similarly the light of Jesus' disciples derives from the heavenly Father. Furthermore in Isaiah 60 this glorious light attracts people from all the nations of the world to Zion to worship the one true God (Isa 60:3,5–6,8–16). The light of Jesus' disciples will likewise serve to draw unbelievers to God. In light of this rich OT background and the concluding remarks in Matt 5:14–16, "You are the light of the world" means (a) that the disciples of Jesus will be characterized by righteousness and purity and (b) that their righteousness will move others to glorify God and seek to be transformed by Him in a similar way.

---

[127] See F. Delitzsch, *Biblical Commentary on the Prophecies of Isaiah*, trans. J. Martin (Grand Rapids: Eerdmans, 1954), 2:179–80, 259–61. Luke 2:32 and the Targum on Isa 42:6 interpret the text in this fashion.

[128] Nolland expressed doubt that "the light of the world" was a definite allusion to Isaiah since Isaiah lacks the exact phrase and since a number of alternative backgrounds exist. Nolland argued that "at most the identity of the disciples as the light of the world may be linked with the other indications that have been noticed of the role of Israel being carried forward by the disciple band" (*The Gospel of Matthew*, 213–14).

Jesus clearly defined the arena in which His disciples are to shine. They are to be lights to the "world." This broad term demonstrates that Christ's disciples are to extend their mission not only among the Jews but among Gentiles as well. Isaiah 49:6 says, "I will also make you a light for the nations [i.e., Gentiles] to be My salvation to the ends of the earth." In Matt 4:16, where Jesus is described as the light, He is described as shining in Galilee of the Gentiles. Jesus insisted that His disciples recognize the entire world as their mission field. Jesus' statement thus anticipates the Great Commission that stands at the climax of Matthew's Gospel.[129]

Jesus insisted that the disciples' mission of shining in the world, extending salvation to the ends of the earth by proclaiming the gospel of the kingdom, and living transformed lives, is intrinsic to genuine discipleship.[130] In the illustration that appears in 5:14b, Jesus did not say that a city on a hill must not be hidden but that it cannot be hidden (lit., "is not able to be hidden" or "is not possible for it to be hidden").[131] In the same way it is impossible for a true disciple not to shine in the world. A disciple who does not glorify God and draw others to Him by exhibiting divine righteousness is like a light that does not shine, water that is not wet, or fire that is not hot. Since "shining" is identified as "doing good works" for the glory of the Father in verse 16, it is evident that true disciples will do good works and live in a way that exhibits their Father's holy character.

Verse 15 presents the nonsensical picture of someone lighting a lamp only to place a clay container over it. Hiding the light defeats the purpose of lighting the lamp. It results in a waste of oil and wick. It also threatens to extinguish the tiny flame. The illustration demonstrates that just as it is the purpose of a lamp to give light, so the purpose for

---

[129] Although the discussions of light in the DSS have some similarity with Jesus' portrayal of His disciples in the SM, a remarkable difference is apparent. The children of light do not hate the children of darkness as in the DSS (1QS 1:3) but seek to bring salvation to them.

[130] Similarly Chrysostom said, "For as that city can by no means be hidden, so it was impossible that what they preached should sink into silence and obscurity. Thus, since He had spoken of persecutions and calumnies, of plots and wars, for fear they might think that these would have power to stop their mouths; to encourage them, He saith, that so far from being hid, it should over-shine the whole world; and that on this very account they should be illustrious and renowned" (*Hom. Mat.* 15.11).

[131] Some interpreters beginning with von Rad have identified the city that cannot be hidden as the new Jerusalem. Although some OT and rabbinic texts may be cited in support of this interpretation, the reference to "a city" rather than "the city" suggests that Jesus was not referring to any particular city. See the discussion in Davies and Allison, *A Critical and Exegetical Commentary on the Gospel According to Saint Matthew*, 1:475.

which disciples exist is to express the glory of God through righteous living and bold witness. The placement of the lamp on the lampstand symbolizes the disciples' responsibility of maximizing their ministry, living in such a way as to shine their light the farthest and to impact the greatest number of people. The adjective "all" in verse 15 confirms again the universal scope of the disciples' mission. Just as a light shines for the benefit of all who are in the house, so His disciples are to extend salvation not just to some but to all.

Verse 16 states that the disciple shines by doing good works. These good works are the deeds, words, and attitudes described in the SM.[132] Jesus' teaching does not support the idea of a silent witness (10:7; 28:19–20). However, Jesus was emphatic that the mission of His disciples required more than words. It also required a righteous life that demonstrated God's willingness to grant righteousness to those who hunger and thirst for it.

According to Matt 5:10 some would view the disciple's righteousness as a silent indictment of their own conduct and would respond by persecuting the disciples. Verse 16 shows that others will recognize that the disciples' righteousness comes from God and will glorify God for the character of His people. The light of the disciple is not merely an annoying glare from which some hide their eyes. It is also a flickering blaze in the hearth that draws sinners from the dark and cold to bask in its warm light.

Jesus' words make clear that the disciples are not the authors of these good works but only the channel of them. God the Father is personally the source of the disciples' good deeds. If the disciples themselves were the authors of the good works they perform, they would receive praise for them. However, Jesus taught that the Father in heaven is the One who is to be praised for the disciples' good works. This implies that He is the true source of them. As stated in the Beatitudes, disciples hunger and thirst for righteousness, but it is God who fills them with righteousness. This truth must not be overlooked. Otherwise the SM could be viewed as describing impossible demands that God's people could never satisfy. On the contrary, the righteousness demanded by the SM is a divine gift that God imparts to those who follow Jesus. The righteousness described in the SM is not a requirement for salvation but is the result of true salvation.

[132] Luz, *Matthew: A Commentary*, 1:208.

Verse 16 shows that the disciples' righteousness is the result of their relationship with the Father. The implication is that just as human children resemble their biological parents, so Jesus' disciples resemble their heavenly Father. An earthly father is glorified for the achievements of his son if his son's abilities were inherited from or taught by his father. The heavenly Father is glorified for the good works of Jesus' followers because He gave them spiritual birth and made them heirs of His character and partakers of the divine nature. Several times in the SM Jesus urged His followers to emulate the character and behavior of their heavenly Father (Matt 5:44–45,48). Each of these references assumes the theology of the new birth and expects God's children to share the Father's character.[133]

The purpose of the disciples' "shining" is not to place themselves in the spotlight but to give glory to God. Although Jesus later discouraged His disciples from public acts of righteousness that were motivated by a desire for self-glory, He here encouraged disciples to perform public acts of righteousness in order to glorify God. This demonstrates that Jesus' concern in Matt 6:1–8 was not the location in which one performs acts of righteousness but the motivation by which one performs them. Some have wrongly concluded from the SM that, if at all possible, good works should be performed in private not in public. Here, however, disciples are clearly commanded to do good works before others. The issue is not one of audience but of purpose and motivation. Good works done for self-glory are wrong. Good works done for God's glory alone are truly righteous.

The desire to glorify God is the supreme motivation for the Christian life. The Westminster Catechism asks, "What is the chief end of man?" The answer is, "To glorify God and to enjoy Him forever." One of the great mottos of the Protestant Reformation was *soli Deo Gloria*, "to the glory of God alone." These emphases of the Reformation are strongly rooted in the teachings of Jesus.

---

[133] This observation dates to at least as early as Chrysostom, who commented on Matt 5:16: "And He said not 'God,' but 'your Father,' already sowing beforehand the seeds of that noble birth, which was about to be bestowed upon them" (*Hom. Mat.* 15.11).

Chapter 6

THE BODY OF THE SERMON: SUPERIOR RIGHTEOUSNESS (MATT 5:17–7:12)

The transition from the introduction to the SM to the actual body in the SM seems abrupt. Nevertheless the discussion in the body of the sermon flows naturally out of the preceding material. Jesus closed the introduction by referring to good works that prompt others to glorify the heavenly Father. The body of the SM then offers a detailed description of the righteous conduct and character that motivate others to praise God.

A. The Demand for Superior Righteousness (Matt 5:17–20)

Jesus said, "Don't assume that I came to destroy the Law or the Prophets." The grammatical form of the prohibition forbids the action as a whole and thus means "Do not even entertain this thought!" or "Do not let such a notion even enter your mind!"[1] Thus Jesus adamantly denied that He came to nullify the Law or Prophets.

The phrase "the Law and the Prophets" was a common designation for the Hebrew Scriptures.[2] Here Jesus referred to the Law *or* the Prophets rather than the Law *and* the Prophets. This probably implies that Jesus' opponents specifically accused Him of destroying the Law in particular. Jesus replied to this accusation by denying that He destroyed any portion of the Scriptures. His words meant "Do not think that I came to destroy the Law, or the Prophets either for that matter." The statement affirmed Jesus' fidelity to the entire OT.[3]

The accusation that Jesus destroyed the Law was likely motivated by Jesus' teaching regarding the Sabbath and ritual purity (Matt 12:1–8; 15:1–20).[4] This teaching scandalized many of the scribes and

---

[1] See Wallace, *Greek Grammar Beyond the Basics*, 723–24. BDF, 173–74 §337 refers to such uses as "categorical prohibitions."

[2] See Matt 7:12; 22:40; Luke 16:16; Acts 13:15; Rom 3:21.

[3] Scholars commonly assume that this logion was a creation of the early church composed to counter the charge of antinomianism that resulted from Paul's gospel. However, Carson is correct that while such issues later in the history of the church can explain the reason that the church preserved and transmitted the saying, it is explicable in Jesus' own setting. See Carson, "Matthew," 141.

[4] France, *The Gospel of Matthew*, 113.

Pharisees and appeared to them to be an outright rejection of the laws of Moses. Furthermore, in the so-called antitheses of 5:21–48, Jesus would strongly challenge popular Jewish interpretations of the OT. Although the antitheses are sometimes read as rebuttals of OT statements,[5] they actually affirm the inspiration and authority of the OT. The antitheses introduce OT quotations with the assertion, "It was said." The assertion is a divine passive which insists that the quotations of Scripture were actually spoken by God.[6] The implication of the divine passive is made explicit in 15:4 in which Jesus quoted the fifth commandment of the Decalogue but introduced the quotation with the words "God said." Nevertheless another element of the introduction to the antitheses, the phrase "you have heard," reminded Jesus' hearers that their knowledge of the contents of the Law had been mediated through the rabbis. This suggests that the antitheses are to be read as challenges to rabbinic interpretations of the Law rather than to the Law itself.

Unfortunately many of the Jewish teachers were not able to separate the authority of their errant interpretations of Scripture from the authority of the inerrant Scriptures. They gave their own confused interpretations of the Bible the same authority as the Bible. Thus when Jesus challenged their interpretation, it was, to their minds, the same as attacking the OT itself.

Jesus insisted that He came to fulfill the Law and the Prophets.[7] Interpreters disagree about precisely what Jesus meant by these words. Some believe that Jesus was claiming to have fulfilled the OT by obeying its commands perfectly.[8] Jesus certainly was characterized by perfect obedience, but the verb "fulfill" (*plēroō*) is associated with

---

[5] R. Schnackenburg claimed: "Jesus sets his understanding of the divine will in emphatic opposition to the literal meaning of the Decalogue" (*The Gospel of Matthew*, trans. R. Barr [Grand Rapids: Eerdmans, 2002], 55).

[6] See Luz, *Matthew: A Commentary*, 1:230; Wallace, *Greek Grammar Beyond the Basics*, 437–38. See also the discussion in Turner, *Matthew*, 162–63, n. 10.

[7] Some interpreters have suggested that the words "I came" (ἦλθον) imply Jesus' preexistence. This is unlikely since identical language was used to speak of the coming of John the Baptist (Matt 11:18). Nevertheless the language probably implies that Jesus was sent on a divine mission. See Carson, "Matthew," 142.

[8] Luz (*Matthew: A Commentary*, 1:217) admits the difficulty of interpreting the text but concludes, "We should most likely think that Jesus fulfilled the law through his obedience." Keener stated, "To 'fulfill' God's law was to 'confirm' it by obedience and demonstrating that one's teaching accorded with it" (*The Gospel of Matthew*, 177). Betz's view is similar to Keener's but stresses that "fulfill" refers to the recognition and implementation of Holy Scripture as legal authority (*The Sermon on the Mount*, 178).

obedience only once in this Gospel (3:15).[9] Thus, this interpretation is possible but doubtful.

Others believe that Jesus fulfilled the Law and the Prophets by faithfully interpreting the OT and explaining God's original purpose behind the Law.[10] Again, this is theologically true, and a rather strong contextual argument can be made for this view in light of Matt 5:21–48. However, the verb "fulfill" does not appear to bear this precise sense elsewhere either in Matthew or in other ancient Greek sources.[11]

Others argue that Jesus was describing Himself as the fulfillment of OT predictions.[12] This interpretation is supported by the best evidence. The verb "fulfill" (*pleroō*) appears 16 times in Matthew. Twelve of the occurrences (75 percent) definitely refer to the fulfillment of prophecy (Matt 1:22; 2:15,17,23; 4:14; 8:17; 12:17; 13:35; 21:4; 26:54,56; 27:9). Jesus' statement that the Law will not pass away until "all things are accomplished" (lit., "everything happens;" *ginomai*) also strongly suggests that the fulfillment of OT prophecies is in view. The verbs "fulfill" and "happen" are linked together in Matthew only in 1:22; 21:4; 26:54,56 in fulfillment formulas that demonstrate that Jesus fulfilled OT predictions. Furthermore, if keeping commandments were the topic of 5:17–18, one would have expected Matthew to use the verbs "do" (*poieō*), "keep" (*tēreō*), or "guard" (*phulassō*) as He did elsewhere when referring to obedience to commands (5:19; 7:24,26; 19:17,20).

Jesus' fulfillment of OT promises is one of Matthew's most prominent themes. Matthew cited the following OT texts as fulfilled through Christ:

1. Isaiah 7:14 (Matt 1:22–23) foretold that the Messiah would be born through a virgin.

---

[9] Unfortunately Matt 3:15 is the only text from Matthew cross-referenced by the UBS4 apparatus as a parallel to Matt 5:17. France has argued that even here the verb "fulfill" means to "bring about God's redemptive purpose through Jesus" (*The Gospel of Matthew*, 182).

[10] Broadus, *The Gospel According to Matthew*, 99–100; Hagner, *Matthew 1–13*, 106; Hill, *The Gospel of Matthew*, 117, 120; Filson, *A Commentary on the Gospel According to St. Matthew*, 83; F. L. Fisher, *The Sermon on the Mount* (Nashville: Broadman, 1976), 58–59; Nolland, *The Gospel of Matthew*, 218–19; Talbert, *Reading the Sermon on the Mount*, 60–61.

[11] Carson noted that this interpretation required an "extraordinary sense" for the verb πληρόω ("Matthew," 143).

[12] Carson, "Matthew," 143–44; Davies and Allison, *A Critical and Exegetical Commentary on the Gospel According to Saint Matthew*, 1:486–87 (Allison combines this view and the preceding one); France, *The Gospel of Matthew*, 182–83. See esp. the extensive discussion in Guelich, *The Sermon on the Mount*, 138–43.

2. Micah 5:2 (Matt 2:6) foretold that the Messiah would be born in Bethlehem.

3. Hosea 11:1 (Matt 2:15) foretold that the Messiah would be called out of Egypt.

4. Jeremiah 31:15 (Matt 2:18) foretold the slaughter of the infants.

5. Isaiah 40:3 (Matt 3:3) foretold that a prophet in the wilderness would prepare for the Lord's coming.

6. Isaiah 9:1–2 (Matt 4:14–16) foretold that the Messiah would come to Galilee of the Gentiles.

7. Isaiah 53:4 (Matt 8:17) foretold that the Messiah would take our sicknesses and carry our infirmities like a sacrificial lamb.

8. Micah 7:6 (Matt 10:35–36) foretold that the Messiah would turn family members against one another.

9. Isaiah 26:19; 29:18; 35:5; 42:18; and 61:1 (Matt 11:5; 15:31) foretold that the Messiah would give sight to the blind, cause the lame to walk, cause the deaf to hear, raise the dead, and preach good news to the poor.

10. Exodus 23:20 and Mal 3:1 (Matt 11:10) foretold that a messenger would precede the coming of the Messiah.

11. Isaiah 42:1–4 (Matt 12:18–21) predicted that the Messiah would not be loud or pretentious.

12. Isaiah 6:9 (Matt 13:14–15) predicted that the Messiah's teaching would be misunderstood.

13. Psalm 78:2 (Matt 13:35) predicted that the Messiah would teach in parables.

14. Isaiah 29:13 (Matt 15:8–9) foretold that God's people would rebel against Him and teach false things.

15. Malachi 4:5 (Matt 17:10–13) predicted that the coming of the Messiah would be preceded by the arrival of an Elijah-like figure.

16. Isaiah 62:11 and Zech 9:9 (Matt 21:5) predicted the Messiah's triumphal entry into Jerusalem.

17. Zechariah 13:7 (Matt 26:31) predicted that the Messiah's disciples would abandon Him.

18. Zechariah 11:13 (Matt 27:9) predicted that the Messiah would be betrayed for 30 pieces of silver.

19. Psalm 22:1–2,6–8,18 (Matt 27:35,43,46) foretold that people
     would gamble for the Messiah's garments, would mock Him,
     and that the Father would forsake Him during His suffering
     on the cross.

Interpreters who struggle to pinpoint one of the above views sometimes suggest that two or more of the views can be mingled together.
This is highly unlikely. Mingling the views would require the verb
"fulfill" to bear multiple senses at the same time. As Broadus argued,
"Such interpretation enfeebles the Scripture."[13] Apart from wordplays
or puns, speakers or writers seldom use language in this way.

A reasonable contextual argument can be made to support the
claim that Jesus fulfilled the Law in a way different from the way
He fulfilled the Prophets. With the exception of fulfillment no. 10
above, every OT text introduced by a fulfillment formula belongs to
the Prophets rather than the Law. The disjunctive "or" ("the Law *or*
the Prophets" rather than "the Law *and* the Prophets") might be taken
as additional confirmation of this view.[14] Thus one could affirm both
interpretations 2 and 3 mentioned above: Jesus explained the full implications of the Law and did all that the prophets promised.

Nevertheless the new Moses typology that permeates the initial
chapters of Matthew obviously relates Jesus' ministry to descriptions
of Moses in the Law and suggests that Jesus "fulfilled" the Law by
fulfilling the promise related to the prophet like Moses who was to
come (Deut 18:15–18). The prophetic function of the Law in Jesus'
teaching is particularly clear in Matt 11:13: "For all the Prophets and
the Law prophesied until John." Thus Jesus fulfills both the Law and
the Prophets in the same way. He is and does all that they predicted.

Jesus adamantly denied that even the minutest features of Scripture would pass away before the ordained time. This denial was expressed using a construction known as emphatic negation (*ou mē* with
a subjunctive verb) that precludes the possibility of an event. This
adamant denial was intensified by the use of "truly" (*amēn*), a word
that expresses "a strong affirmation of what is stated."[15] The "smallest

---

[13] Broadus, *The Gospel According to Matthew*, 99.

[14] Descriptions of the particle ἤ as "disjunctive" can be misleading. BDAG prefers to classify
the particle as "the marker of an alternative" and cites Matt 5:17 as an instance in which the
particle separates "related and similar terms, where one can take the place of the other or one
supplements the other." See "ἤ," BDAG, 432.

[15] "ἀμήν," in ibid., 53.

letter" is the Greek *iota*, which is almost certainly a translation of the Hebrew character *yod*. The *yod* is a tiny character that resembles the English apostrophe. The *yod* is the second letter (counting left to right) in the Hebrew word אלהים (*elohim*). The "stroke" (KJV: tittle; Gr: *keraia*, "horn") could refer to accents or breathing marks in Greek texts.[16] In a Semitic language the "stroke" could be a scribal ornament, a small letter, or a one-letter conjunction.[17] The HCSB is probably correct in interpreting Jesus' original reference as a "stroke of a letter," a serif that distinguishes letters that were nearly identical in appearance like *bêt* and *kāp*, *rêš* and *dālet*, and *hê* and *ḥêt*: ב כ, ד ר, ה ח. An English equivalent is the stroke that distinguishes "F" from "P," "P" from "R," and "R" from "B." The stroke can make a significant difference in the meaning of a text as the difference between "Fun," "Pun," "Run," and "Bun" demonstrates.[18] Similarly the presence or absence of this stroke of the pen in Hebrew texts could make an enormous difference in meaning. In Deut 6:4 deleting a single serif (changing אחד to אחר) would change the statement from "The Lord our God is one," to "The Lord our God is another." The change made inversely in Exod 34:14 would revise "Do not worship another God" to "Do not worship one God." Such changes would have such a drastic impact on the message of the Scriptures that Jewish teachers taught that it was impossible for even a single letter to pass from the law.[19]

Although the HCSB capitalizes "Law" in Matt 5:17, but not in verse 18, both uses of the noun *nomos* likely refer to the five books of Moses. Furthermore the "Law" in verse 18 is likely a shortened reference to the Law and Prophets mentioned in the preceding verse and thus refers to the entirety of the Hebrew Bible. Jesus did not intend to ascribe an accuracy, authority, or longevity to one section of the OT that He wished to deny to another. The use of the title "Law" (*nomos*) to designate the traditional Hebrew Scriptures clearly occurs in the Gospel of John. Although John frequently referred to the law of Moses

---

[16] "κεραία," in ibid., 540 (citing a Greek inscription that uses the word in this sense).

[17] Davies and Allison, *A Critical and Exegetical Commentary on the Gospel According to Saint Matthew*, 1:491.

[18] This illustration was borrowed from C. C. Ryrie, *Basic Theology* (Wheaton, IL: Victor, 1988), 88–89.

[19] *b. Sanh.* 107ab; *p. Sanh.* 2:6 *Gen. Rab.* 47:1; *Lev. Rab.* 19:2; *Num. Rab.* 18:21; *Song Rab.* 5:11. See the discussion in Keener, *The Gospel of Matthew*, 178. For other changes and their impact on the meaning of the OT, see Alfred Edersheim, *The Life and Times of Jesus the Messiah*, 3rd ed. (Mclean, VA: Macdonald, 1886), 1:537–38.

(1:17; 7:23; 8:5), John 10:34 quotes Ps 82:6 but ascribes the quotation to "your Law." Similarly John 15:25 quoted Ps 69:4 but ascribed the quotation to "their Law." Paul used the term "Law" in a similar way. Although Rom 3:21 refers to the OT as "the Law and the Prophets," in Rom 3:19 Paul ascribed a series of quotations from Psalms and the Prophets to "the Law." In 1 Cor 14:21 he ascribed a quotation from Isa 28:11–12 to "the Law." Matthew 5:18 appears to be an example of this same phenomenon.[20] The presence of the definite article ("the Law") supports this interpretation as does the reference to the more important matters of "the Law" in Matt 23:23. These matters include justice and mercy, which likely recall texts such as Isa 42:1–4 and Hos 6:6.[21]

The verb in verse 18 translated "pass" or "pass away" (*parerchomai*) means "to lose force" or "become invalid."[22] It is not a reference to an accidental omission of a letter or stroke in the process of copying a Hebrew manuscript, but to the loss of authority of the OT text. The verb "pass away" functions as a synonym in this context to the verb "destroy" (*kataluō*) in verse 17, which means "abolish, annul, or repeal" when used in reference to the Scriptures.[23] This terminology clearly demonstrates that inspiration, reliability, and especially enduring authority are the issue, not the transmission of the text.[24]

Jesus did establish two temporal limits on the enduring authority of the OT. First, even the tiniest detail of the Law would have abiding authority "until heaven and earth pass away." A number of texts suggest that heaven and earth will exist forever (Pss 72:5,17; 148:3–6; Jer 31:35–36; 33:20–21,25). Thus some interpreters regard this clause as an idiom for perpetuity: "until heaven and earth pass away (but of course they will not)."[25] In this view Jesus meant that the authority of the OT would endure for eternity. However, by using the singular form of the noun "heaven" (*ouranos*) rather than the plural, Matthew signaled that He was referring to the sky rather than to the abode of God. This implies that Matthew anticipated a day in which

---

[20] See "νόμος," BDAG, 678, which points to Matt 5:18 as an instance in which "law" refers to the Scriptures in general.

[21] See France, *The Gospel of Matthew*, 873.

[22] "παρέρχομαι," BDAG, 776.

[23] "καταλύω," in BDAG, 521–22 (definition 3).

[24] This is an important point. Some skeptics argue that differences in ancient Hebrew texts of the OT disprove Jesus' statement. However, those who raise such challenges misinterpret Jesus' statement.

[25] Luz, *Matthew: A Commentary*, 1:218.

the old earth will pass away and be replaced by a new creation since a reference to eternity would have been clearest if Matthew referred to God's eternal dwelling place. More importantly, in 24:35 Jesus said unambiguously, "Heaven and earth will pass away, but My words will never pass away." A comparison of the two statements shows that Jesus' words have an eternal authority and significance that the Law lacks. The supremacy of Jesus' words to the OT strongly implies that Jesus is far more than a prophet. If Jesus were anything less than fully God, His words would be blatant blasphemy.

Jesus' statement about the passing away of the sky and the earth can be harmonized with OT references to the eternal existence of the universe since Jesus was referring to the universe in its present state, before the present world order is destroyed and heaven and earth are recreated in the renewal of all things (19:28). The passing away of the sky and the earth will apparently occur at the time Jesus elsewhere described as the "end of the age," the point at which the present age ends and the coming age arrives (Matt 12:32; 13:39–40,49; 24:3,14; 28:20).[26] The end of the age is the time of Jesus' return and of eschatological judgment. Thus Jesus meant that the authority of the Law and the Prophets would end only at the demise of the present world and the beginning of the eschaton. The OT is of enduring significance and will not be out of date, passé, or useless so long as the universe remains in its present state.

The second temporal limit on the enduring authority of the Law was expressed in the clause "until all things are accomplished." A growing number of commentators insist that this refers to the fulfillment of the Law and the Prophets in Jesus' ministry, death, burial, and resurrection.[27] In this view, by fulfilling the testimony of the Law and the Prophets regarding the Messiah, Jesus restricted the application of certain elements of the Law. In the words of France, in this era of

---

[26] Carson, "Matthew," 145; Davies and Allison, *A Critical and Exegetical Commentary on the Gospel According to Saint Matthew,* 1:490; Guelich, *The Sermon on the Mount,* 144; Keener, *The Gospel of Matthew,* 178; Turner, *Matthew,* 163. For a similar view held by the rabbis, see *b. ʿAbod. Zar.* 9a; *b. Sanh.* 97a–b; *b. Nid.* 61b.

[27] Scholars who view the clause as a reference to Jesus' death and resurrection include J. Jeremias (*The Sermon on the Mount,* trans. N. Perrin [Philadelphia: Fortress, 1963], 24), Luz (*Matthew: A Commentary,* 1:218–19), and J. P. Meier (*Law and History in Matthew's Gospel: A Redactional Study of Mt 5:17–48,* AB [Rome: Biblical Institute, 1976], 30–35). In France's very carefully nuanced view, "it is with the coming of Jesus that this fulfillment has arrived" (*The Gospel of Matthew,* 185). France rejects attempts to be more specific, such as W. D. Davies's view that the cross was the point of fulfillment.

fulfillment, the jots and tittles of the law "serve not as simple rules of conduct but as pointers to a 'greater righteousness' which Jesus has brought into being and which supersedes the old type of lawkeeping." He explained:

> They [the Law and Prophets] remain the authoritative word of God. But their role will no longer be the same, now that what they pointed forward to has come, and it will be for Jesus' followers to discern in the light of his teaching and practice what is now the right way to apply those texts in the new situation which his coming has created. From now on it will be the authoritative teaching of Jesus which must govern his disciples' understanding and practical application of the law. Verses 21–48 will go on to show how this interpretation can no longer be merely at the level of the literal observance of regulations, but must operate at the deeper and more challenging level of discerning the will of God which underlies the legal rulings of the Torah.[28]

Similarly D. J. Moo has argued:

> If, however, verse 17 is taken as programmatic, then it is quite legitimate to conclude that verses 18–19 be taken as asserting the enduring validity and usefulness of the law, when seen in light of its fulfillment in Christ. The implication of this exegesis of Matt 5:17–19 is that the code of conduct applicable to life in the kingdom—and so, I would take it, to the church—is to be found essentially in Jesus' own teaching. The OT law is not to be abandoned. Indeed, it must continue to be taught (Matt 5:19)—but interpreted and applied in light of its fulfillment by Christ. In other words, it stands no longer as the *ultimate* standard of conduct for God's people, but must always be viewed through the lenses of Jesus' ministry and teaching.[29]

This view is theologically correct as a plethora of texts from Paul's letters demonstrates (Rom 7:1–6; 8:1–4; 10:4; Gal 2:15–21; 3:10–26). Nevertheless the view that "until all things are accomplished" relates exclusively to Jesus' ministry is problematic. The clause closely matches the reference in Matt 24:34 to the complex of events described in 24:3–28 (possibly 24:3–31). Thus the accomplishment of all things would include at least the destruction of the Jerusalem temple.[30] The reference to "all things" in 5:18 seems to include many more future events. The use of the near demonstrative pronoun in 24:34 shows

---

[28] France, *The Gospel of Matthew*, 183.

[29] D. J. Moo, "The Law of Moses or the Law of Christ," in *Continuity and Discontinuity: Perspectives on the Relationship Between the Old and New Testaments: Essays in Honor of S. Lewis Johnson, Jr.*, ed. J. S. Feinberg (Westchester, IL: Crossway, 1988), 203–18, esp. 206.

[30] France noted the connection between these two texts but regarded Jesus' coming (by which he seems to mean the first coming) as the point of fulfillment (*The Gospel of Matthew*, 185, esp. n.e 24).

that Jesus was referring to all the things about which He had just spoken. The clause in 5:18 lacks such a grammatical limitation and refers in context to all things foretold in the Law and the Prophets. This suggests that "all things" includes not only Jesus' ministry, death, and resurrection but also the dramatic events Jesus described in the Olivet Discourse including the destruction of Jerusalem, the great tribulation, the glorious coming of the Son of Man, and the gathering of the elect from the four winds.[31] Thus the clause "until all things are accomplished" is equivalent to "until heaven and earth pass away."

Garlington attempted to reconcile the recognition that Jesus and Matthew viewed the eschaton as the point of final fulfillment with the view that the law was abrogated through the ministry of Jesus. He argued that Matthew portrayed Jesus' death and resurrection as the new creation in which all things were accomplished. Matthew mentioned the darkness that covered the earth during Jesus' crucifixion (27:45) and the earthquake that preceded His resurrection (28:2) because these were the apocalyptic signs that signaled heaven and earth were passing away. Despite its appeal this theory is also unlikely. The Olivet Discourse did foretell that "the sun will be darkened, and the moon will not shed its light; the stars will fall from the sky, and the celestial powers will be shaken" (24:29).[32] Nevertheless one would have expected Matthew to have used an expression more similar to 24:29 to describe the darkness and earthquake if he intended to portray those events as the beginning of the eschaton and the abrogation of the Law. "Darkness came upon the whole land" (Matt 27:45) does not share a single common word with "the sun will be darkened" (Matt 24:29). The only semantic connection is the relationship between "darkness" (*skotos*) and "will be darkened" (*skotisthēsetai*). More importantly an earthquake is quite different from the celestial powers being shaken, especially since Jesus associated earthquakes with the beginning of woes (24:7–8) rather than with the new creation of the cosmos. The climactic words of the Gospel (28:20) indicate that the end of the age

---

[31] Commentators who view the clause as a reference to the coming eschatological era include Blomberg (*Matthew*, 104), Hagner (*Matthew 1–13*, 108), Keener (*The Gospel of Matthew*, 178), Gundry (*Matthew*, 80), and Wilkins (*Matthew*, 229).

[32] This prophecy with its apocalyptic language may have referred to the destruction of Jerusalem as Broadus (*The Gospel According to Matthew*, 489–91) and France (*The Gospel of Matthew*, 919–28) have argued. Nevertheless Broadus argued persuasively that the context demands that the destruction of Jerusalem relate typologically to the final parousia so that 24:29–31 "really points in some sense to both events."

is still future, even after Jesus' death and resurrection. This would be odd if Matthew intended to portray the end as already present. Matthew 19:28 associated the "Messianic Age" (lit., the renewal) with Jesus' earthly reign and the co-reign of the Twelve. Thus this interpretation must be dismissed as unlikely.

Jesus' point was that the authority and relevance of the OT would not wane until God fulfilled every promise and prediction in its pages. His purpose here was not to reconcile the abiding authority of the Law with every element of His teaching and practice or to explain the precise way in which the Law applies to His followers. Jesus' teaching in 5:21–48 provides a helpful illustration of the application of the Law and the Prophets to His disciples.

"Therefore" closely links 5:19 to the preceding discussion of OT Scripture and brings the discussion to its proper application. The enduring authority of the OT in even its tiniest details requires that Jesus' followers obey even the least of its commandments. The majority of commentators argue that the commandments refer to those of the OT Law.[33] Several details suggest this. First, the conjunction "therefore" links verse 19 to the immediately preceding discussion of OT authority. Second, the demonstrative pronoun "these" that identifies the commandments always points backward to preceding material rather than forward in anticipation of later material in this Gospel. Third, the distinction between the greatest and least commandments was frequently used by rabbis in discussion of the Law.[34]

Other scholars, however, argue that the commandments are the commands of the SM.[35] Several points may be made in support of this view. First, one might expect reference to "the" commandments rather than "these" commandments in a reference to OT commands. Second, the preceding discussion relates more to fulfillment of the OT prophecies than to OT commandments. Third, since Jesus' commandments are an extension of OT authority, the "therefore" is appropriate.

---

[33] Guelich, *The Sermon on the Mount*, 50–53; Davies and Allison, *A Critical and Exegetical Commentary on the Gospel According to Saint Matthew*, 1:496; Carson, "Matthew," 146; Keener, *The Gospel of Matthew*, 178–80; Hagner, *Matthew 1–13*, 108.

[34] See Keener, *Matthew*, 179.

[35] Chrysostom, *Hom. Matt.* 16:5 (Jesus "said this in behalf not of the ancient laws, but of those which He was proceeding to enact"); R. J. Banks, *Jesus and the Law in the Synoptic Tradition*, SNTSMS 28 (Cambridge: Cambridge University Press, 1975), 220–23; E. Lohmeyer, *Das Evangelium des Matthäus* (Gatlingen: Vanderhoeck and Reprecht, 1956), 110–12; and B. Schweizer, *The Good News According to Matthew* (Atlanta: John Knox, 1975), 108–9.

Fourth, obedience to Jesus' commands is prominent in the climax of the Gospel, the Great Commission of 28:18–20.

The two views are not mutually exclusive. Although the evidence favors the first view, "these commandments" refers to the commandments of the OT as interpreted by Jesus. Hagner rightly commented,

> What is being emphasized in this way are not the minutiae of the law that tended to captivate the Pharisees but simply a full faithfulness to the law *as it is expounded by Jesus.* Thus, the phrase "the least of these commandments" refers to the final and full meaning of the law, but taken up and interpreted by Jesus, as for example in the material that begins in v. 21.[36]

This seems confirmed by the fact that the reference to the Law and the Prophets in 7:12 forms an inclusio for the SM and suggests that everything between 5:17 and 7:12 relates to the Law and the Prophets.

The "least" commandments probably correspond to what the rabbis called the "light" as opposed to "weightier" commandments.[37] In the context of Jesus' teaching, these were the commandments Jesus viewed as less weighty such as the tithing of herbs (23:23–24) or purity regulations (23:25–26) in contrast with weightier demands like dispensing justice, showing mercy, and exercising faith (23:23).

"Will be called great" (5:19) refers to an eschatological divine pronouncement. Jesus is not saying that disciples who obey and teach the least of the commandments will be recognized by their peers as greatest in the kingdom but that God will recognize them as such on judgment day. The distinction between the least and the greatest in the kingdom implies that subjects of the kingdom will enjoy varying degrees of reward. These varying degrees of reward are further suggested by several other statements of Jesus in this Gospel such as 18:4 and the parable of the Talents (25:14–30).

The "scribes" (5:20) were highly trained experts in the interpretation and application of the Law. They normally began their training as children and continued their studies until formal ordination at age 40. The scribes were greatly respected by most Jews of the day. When scribes walked down the streets in their distinctive robes, others

---

[36] Hagner, *Matthew 1–13*, 108 (italics his).

[37] See *m. Ḥul* 12:5, which contrasts "unimportant" and "weightier" commandments. Keener cites later rabbinic discussions that compare the "greatest commandment" (honoring father and mother [Exod 20:12; Deut 5:16]) with the "least commandment" (commandment about the bird's nest [Deut 22:6–7]). See Keener, *The Gospel of Matthew*, 179; Luz, *Matthew: A Commentary*, 1:219.

would stand in their honor, greeting them with titles like "rabbi," "father," or "master."[38] Hosts typically offered the scribes the seat of honor at banquets (23:6).[39]

The "Pharisees" were members of a movement in Judaism that was committed to meticulous observance of the law. They particularly emphasized matters such as tithing, ritual purity, and Sabbath observance. Scribes and Pharisees belonged to two distinct groups. Serving as a scribe was a profession. The Pharisees, on the other hand, were a Jewish sect. Some scribes were Pharisees, and the Pharisees likely chose their leaders from among the scribes. The scribes and Pharisees shared in common a commitment to the study and observance of the law.

When Jesus demanded a righteousness that exceeds that of the scribes and Pharisees, He was not implying that the scribes and Pharisees were wicked lawbreakers who set a very low standard for conduct that could easily be surpassed. The scribes and Pharisees were recognized as those who scrupulously followed the OT commands and even added to the commands to "build a fence around the Torah" so that they would not creep toward disobedience or come close to transgression. When Jesus called for a righteousness that surpassed that of the scribes and Pharisees, His hearers would likely have gasped and wondered if it were possible to achieve such righteousness.

The righteousness required in 5:20 is not imputed righteousness, the perfection of Jesus transferred to the believer's account through justification (2 Cor 5:21).[40] The term "righteousness" and related words in Matthew consistently refer to a person's obedience to God's commands and conformity to His character expressed in personal behavior, speech, and attitudes.[41] This does not suggest that either Jesus or Matthew regarded kingdom entrance as a reward earned by good works. Instead, they recognized surpassing righteousness as the necessary evidence of one's identity as a true disciple. The righteousness Jesus demanded here is a gracious gift. It is the righteousness

---

[38] Matt 23:5,9; b. Qidd. 33a.

[39] For a good introduction to the scribes, see J. Jeremias, *Jerusalem in the Time of Jesus: An Investigation into Economic and Social Conditions During the New Testament Period* (Philadelphia: Fortress, 1969), 233–45; and A. J. Saldarini, "Scribes," in *ABD*, 5:1012–16.

[40] See the discussion on Matt 5:6 above.

[41] In Matthew the noun δικαιοσύνη appears seven times (3:15; 5:6,10,20; 6:1,33; 21:32). The adjective δίκαιος appears 17 times (1:19; 5:45; 9:13; 10:41 [three times]; 13:17,43,49; 20:4; 23:28–29,35 [twice]; 25:37,46; 27:19).

promised in the Beatitudes: Those who hunger and thirst for righteousness will be granted it by God. God Himself produces this righteousness in Jesus' disciples through the new exodus, new creation, and new covenant.[42]

The righteousness demanded by Jesus has several characteristics. First, Jesus literally spoke of a "righteousness that abounds more." The verb "abound" (*perisseuō*) often means "to be present in abundance."[43] Furthermore the word translated "more" is a comparative adjective that often means "more in number" or "relatively large in quantity."[44] Thus one recent commentator has argued that, although many commentaries focus on the qualitative difference between the righteousness of Jesus' disciples and that of the scribes and Pharisees, Jesus seems to have emphasized the quantitative difference instead. Thus the statement means, "If your righteousness is not present in a measurably higher quantity than that of the scribes and Pharisees, you will not enter the kingdom of heaven."[45]

Although this view is initially convincing, closer analysis reveals several serious problems in it. First, the verb *perisseuō* may mean "be outstanding, be prominent, excel," and it speaks to quality rather than mere quantity.[46] Second, the form of *polus* clearly demonstrates that it is functioning adverbially rather than adjectivally and thus may function qualitatively and mean "to a greater extent."[47] Third, if Matthew were referring to performing more deeds of righteousness than the scribes and Pharisees, one would have expected him to use the plural form of the term meaning "deeds of righteousness" (*dikaiosunē*) rather than the singular.[48]

These considerations suggest that the traditional qualitative interpretation of the statement is on target. The HCSB correctly translates

---

[42] See the section, "Theological Framework for the Interpretation of the SM."

[43] "περισσεύω," BDAG, 805.

[44] "πολύς," ibid., 848–49.

[45] Luz, *Matthew: A Commentary*, 1:221. Davies and Allison also favor a quantitative interpretation (*A Critical and Exegetical Commentary on the Gospel According to Saint Matthew*, 1:500).

[46] "περισσεύω," BDAG, 805.

[47] The adjectival use would require the nominative singular feminine form. The form here is nominative or accusative singular neuter. Accusative singular neuter forms of adjectives often function adverbially. When the accusative functions adverbially, it may mean "more, in greater measure, or to a greater degree" ("πολύς," BDAG, 848–49). BDAG lists Matt 5:20 as an example of this use. The last suggested translation seems related to the use of the adjective to express "being high on a scale of extent." In adverbial use the word becomes a close synonym of μᾶλλον.

[48] Although the plural form of δικαιοσύνη does not appear in the NT, it appears 13 times in the LXX.

the statement, "Unless your righteousness surpasses that of the scribes and Pharisees, you will never enter the kingdom of heaven." The Gospel of Matthew and the SM in particular offer several descriptions of this surpassing righteousness. First, superior righteousness focuses on the *spirit* of the law rather than merely the *letter* (15:1–6). Jesus' disciples would not interpret the law permissively, in a manner that sought loopholes which might permit behavior God clearly intended to prohibit or left optional behavior He clearly intended to command. Second, superior righteousness focuses on *internal* matters rather than merely *external* matters (15:10–20; 23:25–28). Jesus' disciples were more concerned about the moral purity of their hearts than about the ritual purity of their hands. Third, superior righteousness focused on more important matters of the law rather than minor points of the law (23:23). Jesus' disciples were more concerned about matters such as justice, mercy, and faith than about tithing the tiny herbs of their gardens. Fourth, superior righteousness focuses upon manifesting divine *character* rather than merely keeping divine *commands* (5:9,45, esp. 48). Jesus' disciples would not attain righteousness merely through efforts to keep God's commands. As His children, they would naturally and spontaneously exhibit the character of their Father and give Him glory through good works that reflected His holiness (5:16).

France rightly claimed, "Jesus is not talking about beating the scribes and Pharisees at their own game, but about a different level or concept of righteousness altogether."[49] Meier described this surpassing righteousness as "a radical interiorization, a total obedience to God, a complete self-giving to neighbor, that carries the ethical thrust of the Law to its God-willed conclusion, even when this means in some cases abrogating the letter of the Law."[50] Similarly Hagner described the surpassing righteousness as "a new and higher kind of righteousness that rests upon the presence of the eschatological kingdom he [Jesus] brings and finds its definition and content in his definitive and authoritative exposition of the law."[51]

Unless one is characterized by this surpassing righteousness, he "will never enter the kingdom of heaven" (v. 20). Although the kingdom of heaven can be viewed as a present possession of Jesus'

[49] France, *The Gospel of Matthew*, 189.
[50] Meier, *Law and History*, 110.
[51] Hagner, *Matthew 1–13*, 109.

disciples (vv. 3,10) because it had dawned through the ministry of Jesus (12:28), His disciples "enter" the kingdom on the day of judgment. This is particularly clear in the final section of the SM in which people seek to enter the kingdom on "that day," the day in which Jesus will serve as eschatological Judge and will condemn those who have defied God's law (7:21–23).[52] The surpassing righteousness demanded for kingdom entrance in no way earns admission into the kingdom. Nevertheless the true disciple of Jesus who is promised the kingdom is graciously granted by God the righteousness for which he hungers and thirsts (5:6), and his heart has been purified by God's transforming power (5:8). Thus Jesus appropriately spoke of God's gift of actual righteousness to the disciples as a prerequisite for kingdom entrance.

B. The Disciple's Obedience to the Law (Matt 5:21–48)

In the preceding section of the SM, Jesus demanded that His disciples obey the Law and the Prophets, and He required surpassing righteousness. The SM now proceeds by offering specific examples of this surpassing righteousness that characterizes true disciples.

Interpreting the Antitheses

Matthew 5:21 begins a section of the SM generally known as the "Six Antitheses." The title, however, is somewhat misleading since it seems to imply that Jesus opposed the OT in some way.[53] Some scholars have viewed the Antitheses as attacks on the law or as enunciations of Jesus' nullification of at least certain aspects of the law.[54] However, this

[52] "Entering the kingdom" is mentioned in Matt 5:20; 7:21; 18:3; 19:23–24; 23:13. Of these references all use either the future indicative or the subjunctive to describe kingdom entrance. Matthew 23:13 uses the present tense and could refer to entering the kingdom through salvation now. See Carson, "Matthew," 478; Davies and Allison, *A Critical and Exegetical Commentary on the Gospel According to Saint Matthew*, 3:287; Nolland, *Matthew*, 933. However, J. A. Gibbs claims that even 23:13 refers to final salvation at the consummation of the age (*Matthew 1:1–11:1*, Concordia Commentary [St. Louis: Concordia, 2006], 266). This is possible if the verb translated "go in" is a gnomic present. In Matt 25:34 the day of judgment is the occasion when Jesus' disciples will "inherit the kingdom."

[53] Betz seems correct that the title "antitheses" was first applied to this section of the SM by the heretic Marcion (*The Sermon on the Mount*, 200–201). For a view similar to that adopted here, see Turner, "Antitheses or Contrasts," *Matthew*, 165–66.

[54] R. Bultmann, *Jesus and the Word*, trans. L. P. Smith and E. H. Lantero (New York: Charles Scribner's Sons, 1958), 89–90; Luz, *Matthew: A Commentary*, 1:228–30; G. Strecker, "Die Antitheses der Bergpredigt (Mt 5:21–48 par)," ZNW 69 (1978):71. This position is most often affirmed

view is plagued by some overwhelming problems.[55] In 5:17–20 Jesus strongly and clearly insisted that He came to fulfill the law down to the tiniest detail rather than to nullify it. Furthermore, if Jesus' teaching were truly antithetical to the OT law, one would expect, "You have heard that it was said to the ancients, Do not murder," however, I say to you, 'Commit murder!'" Clearly Jesus' teaching is not antithetical to the law in this sense. The introductory formula used in each of the six so-called antitheses actually affirms the inspiration of the OT. The words "it was said" (Matt 5:21,27,31,33,38,43) are another example of Matthew's use of the divine passive. The form of the verb reminds readers that the Law (15:4) and the Prophets (1:22–23; 2:15,17,23, etc.) record the Word of God spoken through human agents. The form implies that the OT quotations in 5:21–48 are the very words of God. This nuance fits well with 15:4, in which Jesus quoted the fifth commandment and introduced the quotation with the words "God said."

Jesus' teaching is, however, sometimes antithetical to the interpretation of the Law as expounded by the scribes and Pharisees in the synagogue.[56] "You have heard that it was said" implies that the disciples of Jesus had not had the opportunity to study the OT for themselves but were largely dependent on the teaching of the scribes for their knowledge of the Scriptures.[57] Unfortunately the interpretations of the Law that the scribes espoused were often misguided. Matthew 15:1–6 shows that they sometimes "revoked God's word" (v. 6) because of their traditions. In Matthew 23 Jesus repeatedly criticized the scribes and Pharisees for trying to guide others when they were spiritually blind (23:16–17,19,24,26). Their mishandling of the law is especially clear in the "Sixth Antithesis" (5:43) in which the

---

for Matt 5:38–42. See W. Barclay, *The Gospel of Matthew*, rev. ed. (Philadelphia: Westminster John Knox, 1975), 133; Meier, *Law and History*, 157 (who describes Matt 5:38–42 as "the clearest and least disputable case of annulment in the antitheses"); and F. Thielman, *The Law and the New Testament: The Question of Continuity* (New York: Crossroad, 1999), 49–60.

[55] E. Boring has helpfully suggested that these passages be labeled "hypertheses" or "epitheses." See his "The Gospel of Matthew," in *New Interpreter's Bible* (Nashville: Abingdon, 1994), 8:188.

[56] Hagner, *Matthew 1–13*, 111.

[57] Davies and Allison approve this view (*A Critical and Exegetical Commentary on the Gospel According to Saint Matthew*, 1:510–11), but it is affirmed by Hagner (*Matthew 1–13*, 115), who cites Strack and Billerbeck's view that "you have heard" was equivalent to "you have received as tradition" (see H. L. Strack and P. Billerbeck, *Kommentar zum Neuen Testament aus Talmud und Midr* [Munich: Beck, 1961]).

command "Love your neighbor," a reference to Lev 19:18, is accompanied by the command, "Hate your enemy." The latter command has no clear parallel in the OT and appears to be an inference drawn from the previous command using confused principles of interpretation. Jesus' teaching clearly challenged the command to hate one's enemy, a product of rabbinic interpretation, but He affirmed the OT imperative. The antitheses thus contrast Jesus' ethical demands with those of the OT law *as interpreted by the scribes.*

Jesus' teaching and His interpretation of the OT transcend the literal demands of the law. He surpassed the law by insisting that one should avoid sinful attitudes as well as sinful actions (5:21–30), by showing that the absence of absolute prohibition of an action in the law does not necessarily imply divine approval (vv. 31–37), and by showing that the behavior of His followers is to be guided by God's own character rather than merely by His commands (vv. 43–48). Jesus comes closest to challenging the OT in verses 33–37, in which He prohibited all oaths despite the fact that the OT allowed them. However, the OT did not require individuals to take oaths. It merely insisted that those who made an oath were obligated to fulfill it. The legislation regarding oaths is thus provisionary.[58] It takes oaths for granted and then creates restrictions for them. Jesus probably regarded the legislation concerning the taking of oaths much as He viewed the legislation related to divorce. Such legislation was permitted because of hardness of heart (19:8). However, Jesus taught that a pure heart had replaced the hard heart of His disciples (5:8; Ezek 36:25–27). Thus permissive legislation was no longer needed.[59]

Jesus emphasized His own authority to interpret the law with the words "but I tell you." The pronoun "I" is emphatic and contrasts Jesus' authority with that of other Jewish teachers. Jesus' audience could not ignore the unusual authority with which He taught. This feature of the SM in part prompted the reaction noted at the conclusion of the sermon: "The crowds were astonished at His teaching, because He was teaching them like one who had authority, and not like their scribes" (Matt 7:28–29).

---

[58] See Davies and Allison, *A Critical and Exegetical Commentary on the Gospel According to Saint Matthew*, 1:507.

[59] For a good discussion of the major interpretive approaches to the antitheses, see ibid., 1:505–9.

Another contrast is equally important for understanding the antitheses. Jesus contrasted the recipients of the law, "It was said to our
ancestors," with His disciples, "I tell *you*."[60] The Greek word translated "ancestors" (*archaios*) literally means "people of ancient times."[61]
The contrast between "people of ancient times" and Jesus' disciples
emphasizes that they belong to two different eras. The contrast is
reminiscent of the promise of the new covenant in Jer 31:31–34. The
translation "ancestors" in the HCSB insightfully highlights the connection between the two texts: "'Look, the days are coming'—this is
the LORD's declaration—'when I will make a new covenant with the
house of Israel and with the house of Judah. This one will not be like
the covenant I made with their ancestors" (vv. 31–32).

The term "people of ancient times" is probably the Greek equivalent of a Hebrew term used both in rabbinic literature and the Dead
Sea Scrolls to refer to the Sinai generation.[62] This was the generation
that the new covenant promise identified as the recipients of the old
covenant: "The covenant I made with their ancestors when I took
them by the hand to bring them out of the land of Egypt" (v. 32). Thus
the phrases "to the ancients" and "to you" distinguish two groups of
people belonging to two important eras of salvation history.[63]

As I argued in the introduction, references to the new covenant
bracket the Gospel of Matthew, thereby demonstrating that the new
covenant provides the theological foundation necessary for understanding the message of the Gospel. The Beatitudes also alluded to the
new covenant (Ezek 36:24–30) with their description of Jesus' disciples as the "pure in heart" (Matt 5:8). This faint allusion to the new
covenant in the repeated introductory formula of 5:21–48 reminds
the reader that Jesus' sermon was describing the law inscribed by God
on the disciples' hearts in fulfillment of the new covenant promise.
The repetition of the statement suggests that the new covenant is the
key to the surpassing righteousness the SM describes.

[60] Few scholars have explored the significance of this contrast. Betz is a rare exception. He
suggested that the contrast between the ancients and Jesus' hearers implied "that the inadequate
doctrine has passed through many hands before it has reached the present hearers" (*The Sermon
on the Mount*, 208).

[61] "ἀρχαῖος," BDAG, 137.

[62] Luz, *Matthew: A Commentary*, 1:230, esp. n. 34.

[63] A similar observation was made by Guelich: "It may also be legitimate to see a deliberate
contrast between the giving of the Law to the generation of old—namely, God's people Israel—
and Jesus' address to you in the present eschatological moment of his audience" (*The Sermon
on the Mount*, 179–80). See also Allison's essay on "Jesus and the Torah," in *New Moses*, 182–90.

The complete introductory formula, "You have heard that it was said to our ancestors," introduces the first and fourth antitheses (vv. 21,33) and serves to divide the six antitheses into two triads. The abbreviated formula, "You have heard that it was said," introduces the second, fifth, and sixth antitheses (vv. 27,38,43). The even shorter formula, "It was also said," introduces the third antithesis (v. 31). Even when the introductory formula is abbreviated, the sense is the same.[64]

Anger (Matt 5:21–26)

For the meaning of the introductory formula, see the preceding section "Interpreting the Antitheses." Jesus quoted from Exod 20:13 and Deut 5:17, "Do not murder." The HCSB offers a better translation than the KJV's "Thou shalt not kill" since many modern readers wrongly interpret the archaic rendering as forbidding capital punishment, just war, or even the killing of animals, acts specifically commanded by God in the OT.

Jesus added a summary of OT teachings regarding the penalty for murder: "Whoever murders will be subject to judgment." Those who murder were to stand trial, and if found guilty, they were to be sentenced to death (Exod 21:12; Lev 24:17; Num 35:12; Deut 17:8–13). This "judgment" is apparently a criminal judgment in a human court of law or the Sanhedrin (Matt 5:22). Jesus then explicated the original implications of the murder commandment and showed that it prohibited not only murderous actions but also a murderous attitude, a violent temperament. He insisted that ethics of His kingdom exceeded the standards of the OT law, so that even a murderous attitude was deserving of the penalty prescribed for murder.

Despite popular interpretation, Jesus did not mean by this that all anger is wrong. In the face of injustice and evil, it can be very right to be angry. Jesus' description of wrongful anger has several specific characteristics.

The term used for "anger" (*orgizō*) here is a very intense term. Elsewhere in Matthew's Gospel, the term is used only of anger that is a prelude to destructive behavior. In 18:34 the word describes the anger of a king at a servant's hypocrisy that prompts him to send the

---

[64] France (*The Gospel of Matthew*, 195) commented on the various forms of the introduction: "There is no discernible difference in intention: the full formula, one introduced in v. 21, does not need to be repeated in order to make the same point."

servant to jail to be tortured. In 22:7 the word describes the rage of a king against those who murdered his servants. In his fury he sent his troops to destroy the murderers and burn down their city.

The verb is never used to describe the anger of Jesus. However, a related noun is used to describe God's fury against sin, which will destroy the wicked in the last days. This word does not refer to minor frustration or irritation with someone but to intense fury, seething rage.

Ancient writers distinguished the term "wrath" (*orgē*, the noun form related to the verb *orgizō*) from another similar term for anger (*thumos*). Origen said, "*Thumos* differs from *orgē* in that *thumos* is anger rising in vapor and burning up, while *orgē* is a yearning for revenge."[65] Jerome said, "*Thumos* is incipient anger and displeasure fermenting in the mind; *orgē* however, when *thumos* has subsided, is that which longs for revenge and desires to injure the one thought to have caused harm."[66] The Stoic Diogenes Laertius defined *orgē* as "a desire for revenge on the person who seems to have caused injury wrongfully."[67] Gregory Nazianzus wrote that "*thumos* is the sudden boiling of the mind, *orgē* is enduring *thumos*."[68] Theodoret argued that when *thumos* and *orgē* occur together, "Through *thumos* is revealed suddeness, and through *orgē* continuation."[69] Dio Cassius described the explosive temper of Emperor Tiberius by saying, "He became violent (*orgizeto*) at what barely aroused his anger (*ethumouto*)."[70]

Several of the writers quoted above suggested that the term used by Christ implies enduring anger as well as destructive rage. Even if this were not insinuated by the definition of the verb, it is certainly implied by the grammatical form. The present participle is progressive in nature. It describes an abiding, continuing, or habitual anger that characterizes a person. This is confirmed in verse 25 in which Jesus said that His disciples are to agree with adversaries quickly, without delay, not harboring their anger but seeking to resolve it at first opportunity.[71]

---

[65] Origen, *Selec. Ps.* 2.5 (Trench).
[66] Jerome, *Comm. Eph.* 4.31 (Trench).
[67] Diogenes Laertius, 7.113 (Trench).
[68] Gregory of Nazianzus, *Carm.* 2.34.43–44 (Trench).
[69] Theodoret, *Comm. Ps.* 69.24 (Trench).
[70] Cassius Dio, *Vit. Tib.* (Trench).
[71] The oldest manuscripts of the Gospel of Matthew presently in existence, p[64] (AD 200), Sinaiticus (fourth century), and Vaticanus (fourth century) do not include the phrase "without

Jesus especially prohibited anger that is expressed at a brother. In this address to Christian disciples the word "brother" clearly speaks of a fellow disciple.[72] The SM previously described God as the heavenly Father of Jesus' disciples (vv. 9,16). Hence disciples are spiritual siblings with one another. While disciples have a responsibility to treat all people, not just spiritual brothers, kindly (vv. 43–48), Christ placed a special emphasis on treating fellow believers with grace and compassion. The same emphasis recurs in 25:40, in which judgment is based on one's treatment of "one of the least of these brothers of Mine." The heavenly Father has a unique love for His own children. Because of that love, He considers abuse of a Christian brother with special seriousness. Earthly fathers do the same. A good father does not like to see any child bully other children. But if someone bullies his own son or daughter, he is especially angered. Because Jesus' disciples are children of God by faith, God views their abuse and mistreatment of one another as a more grievous offense. A similar emphasis appears in Paul's teaching: "Therefore, as we have opportunity, we must work for the good of all, especially for those who belong to the household of faith" (Gal 6:10).

Throughout Matt 5:22 the anger Jesus prohibited escalates and is met with an increasingly harsher penalty. The anger progresses from emotion to verbal expression, to more hateful verbal expression. "Fool" (*hraka*) means empty-headed and is comparable to the modern terms "idiot" and "dimwit." The word insults the intelligence of the person who is the target of one's anger and shames him as "dumb" or "stupid." "Moron" (HCSB) translates the Greek term *mōros* from which the modern word "moron" is derived.

Many commentators insist that *hraka* and *mōros* are synonyms, and neither is worse than the other.[73] However, an examination of the use of *mōros* in Matthew's Gospel shows that it is far more severe

a cause" (εἰκῇ, 5:22). Apparently it was added in the second century by some who felt Jesus' words were too harsh. The scribe who added the phrase apparently failed to see the force of the present participle and feared that without further qualification readers might see Jesus' teaching as forbidding all anger, something He clearly did not intend to do. While Jesus was not addressing the motive of anger here, the scribal addition reminds readers that becoming angry for the wrong reason is sinful whether or not the anger is harbored or leads to destructive behavior.

[72] France, *The Gospel of Matthew*, 200; Guelich, *The Sermon on the Mount*, 189. Nolland argues that "brother" reflects "Jewish usage and points to shared membership in the community of the historic people of God" (*The Gospel of Matthew*, 230).

[73] France, *The Gospel of Matthew*, 200–201; Nolland, *The Gospel of Matthew*, 230.

than merely calling someone an idiot.[74] The word is used in Matt 7:26; 23:17; 25:2–3,8 to describe those who do not truly belong to the kingdom. Calling a brother "moron" was essentially calling him unregenerate and unsaved and consigning him to hell.[75]

Christ demonstrated the escalating severity of each category of anger by the different penalties of which they were worthy. Mere anger was worthy of prosecution in a regular local court, the local Sanhedrin that consisted of a 23-member counsel. Calling a brother "idiot" was worthy of trial before the greater Sanhedrin, the Jews' supreme court, which consisted of seventy-one members.[76] Disputing a brother's salvation out of personal anger was worthy of trial before God. This capital crime was not punishable merely by death; it was a crime punishable by eternal torment. Such hatred was the natural prelude to the act of murder itself.

The phrase translated "hellfire" in the HCSB is literally "the gehenna of fire" or "fiery gehenna."[77] Jesus frequently used the familiar term "hell" (geenna) to refer to this place of punishment (5:22,29–30; 10:28; 18:9; 23:15,23). Originally the term referred to the "valley of Hinnom." This valley in south Jerusalem was infamous for the human sacrifices to Moloch that were offered there during the reigns of Ahaz and Mannaseh (2 Kgs 16:3; 21:6). The prophet Jeremiah had proclaimed God's judgment over the area. He threatened that the valley would become known as "the Valley of Slaughter," where birds would feed on the exposed corpses of those struck down by enemy swords (Jer 7:32–33; 19:6–8). This was apparently the place on the outskirts of Jerusalem described in Isa 66:24: "As they leave, they will see the dead bodies of the men who have rebelled against Me; for their worm will never die, their fire will never go out, and they will be a horror to all mankind."

These descriptions were applied to Gehenna by later Jewish and Christian writers who used this imagery to portray the eternal punishment of the wicked. As early as the second century BC, 1 Enoch

---

[74] Filson, *A Commentary on the Gospel According to St. Matthew*, 85; Gundry, *Matthew*, 84–85; Jeremias, *New Testament Theology: The Proclamation of Jesus*, trans. J. Bowden (New York: Scribner's, 1971), 149.

[75] Also the word μωρέ here may possibly be a transliteration of a Hebrew or Aram word that means "rebel" or "heretic." This would reinforce the meaning the Matthean usage demands.

[76] *m. Sanh.* 1:6.

[77] For an excellent treatment of the background of the term see Jeremias, "γέεννα," *TDNT* (1964), 1:657–58.

described the place of eternal punishment as an "accursed valley" at the foot of a holy mountain (27:1–5), a "valley, deep and burning with fire" where the wicked are kept in heavy iron fetters (54:1–6).

Jesus described Gehenna as a "blazing furnace where there will be weeping and gnashing of teeth" (Matt 13:42,50). In Matt 18:8–9 He used the phrases "eternal fire" and "hellfire" (lit., "gehenna of fire") interchangeably. He also drew the description of the place of eternal punishment as a place "where their worm does not die, and the fire is not quenched" (Mark 9:44,46,48) from the apparent description of Gehenna in Isa 66:24.

To Jesus' listeners the threat of such severe punishments for mere feelings and insults probably seemed so extreme that it bordered on the ridiculous. Nevertheless Jesus used these extreme examples to demonstrate that the standards of the kingdom far exceed those of ordinary people. He wanted to be abundantly clear that God is not concerned merely with external acts but with the condition of the heart.

The conjunction "so" (*oun*) in Matt 5:23 shows that verses 23–26 give practical implications of Jesus' teaching in verses 21–22. This suggests that the following examples prohibit an abiding anger that prevents a person from making restitution or paying for damages in either a personal or a legal dispute.

"Offering your gift on the altar" (v. 23) refers to presenting a sacrifice in the Jerusalem temple. The sacrifice was probably a sin offering through which a faithful Jew sought atonement for sins. As the offerer reflected on his guilt and his need for forgiveness, he remembered that his brother had something against him. In context, "something against you" refers not to some unreasonable grudge but to a legitimate grievance. The offerer had truly wronged another person and his conscience reminded him of the offense when he presented his sacrifice.[78]

Worship, especially placing an offering on the altar in the Jerusalem temple, was a solemn act. The duties of worship were simply not to be interrupted except in the most extenuating circumstances. Nevertheless Jesus taught that temple worship and the presentation of an offering should be interrupted by the urgent need to seek reconciliation with a brother. When Jesus spoke of interrupting the act of

---

[78] This is contrary to Turner (*Matthew*, 169), but Davies and Allison support it (*A Critical and Exegetical Commentary on the Gospel According to Saint Matthew*, 1:517).

sacrifice, His hearers must have been shocked. Most of Jesus' hearers were from Galilee, and their disputes with others would be centered there as well. Jesus' teaching would require them to bind the legs of the sacrificial animal and leave it at the base of the altar in the Jerusalem temple, travel the approximately 80 miles back to Galilee to seek reconciliation and offer restitution to an offended brother, then travel the same 80 miles back to Jerusalem to complete the sacrificial ritual![79]

Although Jesus' teaching seemed radical, it had precedence both in the OT and in the teachings of the rabbis. The OT taught that before a worshipper offered sacrifice for a sin against someone else, he should first make restitution with that person (Lev 6:1–7; Num 5:5–8). The rabbis later added that the atoning sacrifice had no value for the sinner if restitution had not been made first (*m. Yoma* 8:9). Against this background Jesus' point was that it is meaningless to offer sacrifices and weep before the altar, pleading for divine forgiveness, when one is unwilling to express repentance to persons against whom he has sinned and take practical steps to make things right with them. Divine forgiveness demands repentance. Repentance is sincere only when restitution is made and reconciliation is sought. Thus Jesus' disciples must deal with their abiding anger and make sure that it does not prevent them from seeking forgiveness from those they have wronged.

Jesus also expressed the urgency of dealing with one's anger and seeking reconciliation through a scene from the legal world. The illustration has much in common with the preceding one. Although the previous illustration treated the relationship between two fellow disciples, this illustration is broader, treating relationships between a disciple and any person he has harmed.

As in the preceding illustration, the disciple is guilty of actually wronging another person. The offense is evidently a serious one, for if the case goes to trial, the defendant will be arrested and imprisoned. He will not be released until the "last penny" that is due the plaintiff is paid. This presumption of guilt is an important point. Some have interpreted this text as if it required Jesus' followers to meet the demands of plaintiffs even in frivolous lawsuits. Such an interpretation ignores the context of Jesus' statement and reduces His teaching to an impractical and impossible demand.

[79] France, *The Gospel of Matthew*, 203.

When two individuals are involved in a legal dispute, it is wisest
for the guilty party to seek an out-of-court settlement before the trial
begins. Generally the earlier the reconciliation, the lighter the cost
of the dispute. The longer the defendant postpones settlement, the
more costly it becomes. If his bitterness prevents him from seeking a
settlement and he battles his opponent in the court, his penalty may
become unbearable.

The general principle taught by the legal illustration is that the
earlier an offender makes restitution and seeks reconciliation, the better. One should settle things before the anger escalates, before words
are uttered that cannot be taken back, or before wounds are inflicted
that are painful and slow to heal. Paul expressed a similar truth in Eph
4:26: "Be angry and do not sin [cp. Ps 4:4]. Don't let the sun go down
on your anger."

Augustine viewed the illustration in Matt 5:25–26 as an allegory
in which God is the enemy with whom reconciliation is needed, Jesus
is the judge, angels are represented by the officer, hell is the prison,
and complete judgment for every sin is the last penny to be paid.[80] A
number of leading modern commentators adopt variations of Augustine's allegorical interpretation.[81] Several considerations support this
view. Luke 12:57–59 parallels Matt 5:25–26. The Lukan parallel appears in the context of an eschatological discussion (Luke 12:54–56)
and immediately before Jesus' teaching about the urgency of repentance (13:1–5). Furthermore some interpreters see the "judgment" in
Matt 5:22a as eschatological and the Sanhedrin as a reference to the
heavenly court. Thus the Matthean context may also provide clues
suggesting an eschatological interpretation. Finally, the words "I assure you" (lit., "Amen! I say to you") have been regarded as confirming the use of the illustration as an eschatological parable since both
"Amen" and "I say to you" frequently appear in eschatological contexts in Matthew.[82]

On the other hand significant differences in word order, grammar, and vocabulary exist between Luke 12:57–59 and Matt 5:25–26,
which raise serious doubts that Luke and Matthew were referring to

[80] Augustine, *Serm. Dom.* 1.29–31.
[81] Luz, *Matthew: A Commentary*, 1:241; Nolland, *The Gospel of Matthew*, 233–34. See the
important qualifications to this view in Blomberg, *Matthew*, 108.
[82] Luz, *Matthew: A Commentary*, 1:241. Luz views the phrase "on the way" as a reference to
the period of time leading up to final judgment during which one may repent and seek to be
reconciled to God.

the same teaching.[83] More likely, Jesus used a similar illustration in two different contexts in His preaching ministry, and Matthew and Luke have each preserved a different form of the illustration.[84] Furthermore, although the preceding context in Matthew does discuss eschatological judgment and implies the need to prepare for it, the emphasis in the context is the need to seek reconciliation with other people as a means of preparing for the judgment of God. Thus the literal interpretation of Matt 5:25–26 that views the "adversary" as a human being whom one has sinned against better suits the preceding context.[85] Finally, although "Amen" and "I say to you" often appear in eschatological contexts in Matthew, approximately one-third of the instances of "Amen" and the large majority of instances of "I say to you" occur in noneschatological contexts.[86] Thus, this text is a straightforward legal illustration that urges disciples to seek reconciliation with offended parties as soon as possible. No allegorical meaning should be sought.[87]

Adultery (Matt 5:27–30)

The introductory formula here varies from the introductory formula in verse 21 only by the omission of "to our ancestors." Readers should not attempt to distinguish the meaning of this construction from the one used previously. This is simply an abbreviated formula that implies the more complete form.[88] For the meaning of the introductory formula, see the section "Interpreting the Antitheses."

The words "you have heard" may imply that Jesus is challenging rabbinic teaching that had diluted the demand of the commandment. Some ancient interpreters, like some modern interpreters, interpreted texts like Deut 22:22 permissively. They argued, for example, that adultery was a sexual act with the wife of one's neighbor, that is, the

---

[83] The only verbatim agreements in the Greek text are ἐν τῇ ὁδῷ . . . καὶ ὁ κριτής . . . εἰς φυλακὴν in v. 25 and λέγω σοι, οὐ μὴ ἐξέλθῃς ἐκεῖθεν, ἕως . . . ἀποδῷς (ἔσχατον) in v. 26.

[84] Carson, "Matthew," 150.

[85] Although Keener has argued extensively that the Sanhedrin of 5:22 is the heavenly court ("Matthew 5:22 and the Heavenly Court," ExpTim 99 [1987]:46), he did not affirm the allegorical interpretation (The Gospel of Matthew, 185).

[86] Luz (Matthew: A Commentary, 1:241) notes that ἀμὴν occurs 31 times in Matthew and lists nine eschatological uses. He lists 13 eschatological uses of λέγω out of 61 total occurrences.

[87] See Broadus, The Gospel According to Matthew, 106 (who cites in his favor Chrysostom, Jerome, Zwingli, and Calvin); Carson, "Matthew," 150; and Hagner, Matthew 1–13, 118.

[88] See the discussion of Matt 5:21.

wife of a fellow Israelite. Thus a sexual act with the wife of a Gentile would not technically constitute an act of adultery.[89]

Jesus' hearers were familiar with the seventh commandment, "Do not commit adultery" (Exod 20:14; Deut 5:18). Adultery involves a married man or woman having sexual relationships with someone other than his or her spouse.[90] Adultery was punishable by death according to OT law (Deut 22:22; Lev 20:10).

Jews of the time of Christ continued to view adultery as a serious offense. The Mishnah devotes one entire tractate to the test of bitter water that was used to confirm the guilt or vindicate a suspected adulteress as described in Num 5:11–31.[91] Jesus taught that adultery did not require actual copulation; even a lustful look constituted adultery of the heart. This teaching had some precedent in Judaism. Job 31:9–12 seems to forbid lustful thoughts and plans and to equate these with adulterous acts. Later rabbis interpreted the command along the lines of Jesus' interpretation. One rabbi cited Job 24:15 to prove that "he who regards a woman with lustful intention is as one who cohabits with her."[92] Another rabbi taught, "He who commits adultery with his eyes is also called an adulterer."[93]

---

[89] See F. Hauck, "μοιχεύω," TDNT (1967), 4:731, n. 7, who cites Strack and Billerbeck, Kommentar zum Neuen Testament aus Talmud und Medrasch, 1.295 and Sipra Lev. 10. Jesus' contemporaries had taken steps to reduce the number of accusations of adultery made by suspicious husbands. Rabbinic law said that a suspected adulteress could not be subjected to the test of bitter water (Num 5:11–31) unless the husband had first warned her of his jealousy and suspicion and commanded her to avoid contact with the suspected partner in the presence of two witnesses (m. Soṭah 1:1–2).

[90] Hauck, "μοιχεύω," 4:730 stated, "Adultery is possible only if there is carnal intercourse between a married man and a married or betrothed Israelitess, Dt. 22:22ff.; Lv. 20:10. Adultery is the violation of the marriage of another, Gn. 39:10 ff. Hence a man is not under obligation to avoid all non-marital intercourse (πορνεία). Unconditional fidelity is demanded only of the woman, who in marriage becomes the possession of her husband." Hauck's definition of adultery is simply incorrect, even as the texts that he cites demonstrate. Hauck's definition implies that it would be permissible for a single man to have relationships with another man's wife. However, Deut 22:22 never defines the marital state of the adulterer. Genesis 39:10–20 shows that Joseph, though apparently single, regarded relationships with Potiphar's wife as a heinous act (Gen 39:9). Adultery did not require that both the male and female partners were married. The Pentateuch does not explicitly describe sexual activity between a married man and a single woman as adulterous. However, later OT texts apply the law as prohibiting all extramarital sexual activity (Prov 2:16–23; chaps. 5 and 7; and esp. Mal 2:13–15).

[91] m. Soṭah.

[92] See Pesiq. Rab. 24 (124b); b. Ḥal. 1; and b. Yoma 29a. For other examples, see Betz, Sermon on the Mount, 234–35; France, The Gospel of Matthew, 204; and Luz, Matthew: A Commentary, 244–45.

[93] Lev. Rab. 23 (123b).

Jesus offered a specific description of the lustful look that constitutes adultery of the heart. The look is not a fleeting glance that trig-
gers a sexual thought that is then quickly dismissed from the mind.
The look is a lingering look. The present participle could be translated "everyone who keeps on looking." This is a sensual stare, a lustful
gawking. This has important ramifications for the application of Jesus'
teaching.[94] He did not intend that men or women hide their eyes from
any beautiful or handsome member of the opposite sex, nor did He
teach that it is wrong to admire someone's appearance. The lustful
look locks eyes on another person and uses him or her to fuel one's
sexual imagination.

The lustful look is specifically intended to stir one's own sexual
desire. The phrase "to lust for her" expresses the purpose of the look.
Some recent commentators have disputed the interpretation implied
by the HCSB (and most other modern translations) by arguing that
the man's lustful look is designed to stir the desire of the female object
of the look rather than his own desire. Thus the look is a flirtatious
look that expresses the man's attraction to the woman and signals
his willingness to engage with her in sexual sin. This alternative interpretation is possible given the ambiguity of the grammar used in
Matt 5:28. The accusative pronoun "her" may serve as the direct object of the infinitive meaning "lust for," but it could function like the
subject of the infinitive instead (in which case it would be translated
"she"—"so that she lusts for him").[95] Two major arguments have been
used to support this interpretation. First, verbs of desire like "lust"
(*epithumeō*) normally take their direct object in the genitive case.
No precedent exists for the accusative serving as the direct object of
verbs like *epithumeō*.[96] Second, if Jesus intended to speak of the man's
desire for the woman, the pronoun "her" would be unnecessary. Jesus

---

[94] See especially the excellent treatment of this issue in G. Stassen and D. Gushee, *Kingdom
Ethics: Following Jesus in Contemporary Context* (Downers Grove, IL: InterVarsity, 2003), 295–98.

[95] This alternative interpretation was suggested by K. Haaker ("Der Rechtsatz Jesu zum
Thema Ehebruch," *BZ* 21 [1977]: 113–16) and was later suggested or adopted by commentators such as Blomberg (*Matthew*, 109); Carson ("Matthew," 152); and Turner (*Matthew*, 170).

[96] Carson wrote, "The expression πρὸς τὸ ἐπιθυμῆσαι αὐτὴν (*pros to epithymēsai autēn*) could
mean 'so as to lust after her,' whether with telic or ecbatic force (cf. BDF, par. 402 [5]), her presumably the former. If so, it is the only place where this kind of verb uses the accusative: *autēs*
(gen.) rather than *autēn* is expected (cf. BDF, par. 171 [1]). The accusative *autēn* more probably
therefore functions as the accusative of reference (i.e., the quasi-subject) of the infinitive (as in
the equivalent construction in Luke 18:1) to generate the translation 'so that she lusts'" ("Matthew," 152).

could simply have said, "Everyone who looks at a woman in order to lust." Thus the presence of the pronoun implies the alternative interpretation.[97]

The first argument is fallacious. Although verbs of desire normally take their objects in the genitive case, Matthew departed from this norm. He already used the accusative case to mark the direct object of a verb of desire earlier in the SM (v. 6). Matthew 5:28 is another example of this distinct style.[98] More importantly, in the LXX the verb *epithumeō* ("to desire, covet, lust") often takes its object in the accusative case. In fact Matthew's use of the accusative object is likely derived from the use of accusative objects with the verb *epithumeō* in the tenth commandment: "Do not covet your neighbor's wife" (Exod 20:17; Deut 5:21).[99] Matthew recognized that Jesus was interpreting the seventh commandment in light of the tenth commandment and thus adopted both the vocabulary and grammar of Exod 20:17.

The second argument is also unpersuasive. Since the LXX used the verb *epithumeō* to speak of coveting objects as well as lusting after a person, the presence of the pronoun "her" is not redundant. The personal pronoun "her" is not necessary after the verb "commit adultery" either, since the verb *moicheuō* is sometimes used without a direct object (Luke 16:18 [twice]; Rom 2:22). Yet Matthew repeated the pronoun that had appeared just two words earlier in the sentence. This suggests that the presence of the pronouns is a product of Matthew's precision and his quest for clarity as a writer. It does not imply a particular usage of the accusative case. Thus the traditional interpretation is to be preferred. Matthew described ogling that is the basis for a man's sexual fantasy.

The person who gawks at a woman lustfully "has already committed adultery with her in his heart" (Matt 5:28). The heart is the locus in which sin originates. Jesus would later explicitly teach that "from the heart come evil thoughts . . . adulteries, sexual immoralities. . . . These are the things that defile a man" (15:19–20). Jesus' disciples have been granted "pure hearts" (5:8), new hearts that prompt righteousness rather than inspire defilement. Adultery in the heart is inconsistent with the dramatic change that Christ has made in the heart of His disciples.

---

[97] Carson, "Matthew," 151.
[98] This was previously noted in BDF, par. 171.
[99] οὐκ ἐπιθυμήσεις τὴν γυναῖκα τοῦ πλησίον σου.

One should not conclude from the description of lust as "adultery in the heart" that the physical act of adultery is no worse than a lustful look. Contrary to popular opinion, all sins are not equal (John 19:11). Earlier Christ used increasingly severe punishments to express the escalating wickedness of the angry attitude, angry word, hateful word, and murderous act. The same gradation applies here. A lustful attitude is adultery of the heart, but an adulterous act compounds one's guilt and is obviously more heinous.

The principle Jesus taught has many important applications in the modern world. Jesus' teaching urges disciples to guard their eyes and hearts carefully from lust, fantasizing, and any other thought or act that might lead to acts of sexual sin. His teaching prompts believers to avoid pornography and to fight to protect others from it, knowing that feeding one's soul on these sexual images is no substitute for sinful sexual acts, but leads to more sinful sexual acts.[100]

Matthew 5:29–30 is startling, and multiple interpretations have been proposed that seek to blunt its force. In the effort to make sense of Jesus' words, interpreters must not forget that His words were intended to shock His audience. The thought of gouging out one's eye and cutting off one's arm is grotesque and disturbing, but readers must not reach too quickly for any and every interpretation of the text that might weaken Jesus' warning or undermine its candid portrayal of the serious consequences of sin.

Although loss of the hand and eye would seem drastic enough, Jesus specified the "right eye" and the "right hand." The right hand typically had greater strength, dexterity, and purity. The right hand was used to greet others, bestow blessings, and establish legal agreements.[101] Thus the loss of the right hand or right eye could portray the ultimate sacrifice (Ps 137:5).

Some readers have taken Jesus' words literally and have mutilated their bodies in their effort to conquer sinful longings. This text was one of two passages (the other being Matt 19:12) that prompted Origen (c. 185–254), the famous church father from Alexandria, Egypt, to combat his lust by rolling naked over sharp briars. When this effort

---

[100] Article XV of the Baptist Faith and Message, "The Christian and the Social Order," appropriately says, "In the spirit of Christ, Christians should oppose racism, every form of greed, selfishness, and vice, and all forms of sexual immorality, including adultery, homosexuality, and pornography."

[101] W. Grundman, "δεξιός," *TDNT* (1964), 2:37–40.

did not succeed in taming his desires, he ultimately castrated himself. Origen later regretted the drastic measure that he had taken in youthful zeal and concluded that he had misinterpreted Jesus' teaching.[102]

Contrary to Origen's early view, the immediately preceding context makes clear that the true culprit behind the sin of adultery is neither the eye nor the hand but the heart. If one severs the right hand, he may still sin with the left. Even if one amputates every limb of the body and removes each nonvital organ, he will not eradicate sin.

Others have viewed the passage as metaphorical. Several of the early church fathers appealed to texts like 1 Cor 12:12–30 and argued that the "eye" and "hand" represented different members of the body of Christ, the church. They suggested that the gouging out of the eye and cutting off of the hand referred to the process of church discipline.[103] Although this initially sounds like an inappropriate imposition of Pauline imagery on the teaching of Jesus, later references in Matthew suggest that Jesus also may have referred to persons who cause the spiritual downfall of others as members of the body that should be amputated. In Matt 18:7–9 Jesus warned:

> Woe to the world because of offenses. For offenses must come, but woe to that man by whom the offense comes. If your hand or foot causes your downfall, cut it off and throw it away. It is better for you to enter life maimed or lame, than to have two hands or two feet and be thrown into the eternal fire. And if your eye causes your downfall, gouge it out and throw it away. It is better for you to enter life with one eye, rather than to have two eyes and be thrown into hellfire!

Only a few verses later, Jesus clearly outlined the process of church discipline (18:15–20). Nevertheless this metaphorical interpretation

---

[102] See P. Schaff, *History of the Christian Church* (Grand Rapids: Eerdmans, 1910) 2:788; Eusebius, *Hist. Eccl.* 6.8. This practice became so prevalent that the first of the 20 Canons of Nicea addressed it: "If any one in sickness has been subjected by physicians to a surgical operation, or if he has been castrated by barbarians, let him remain among the clergy; but, if any one in sound health has castrated himself, it behooves that such an one, if [already] enrolled among the clergy, should cease [from his ministry], and that from henceforth no such person should be promoted. But, as it is evident that this is said of those who willfully do the thing and presume to castrate themselves, so if any have been made eunuchs by barbarians, or by their masters, and should otherwise be found worthy, such men the Canon admits to the clergy."

[103] By the time Origen wrote his commentary on Matthew, of which fragments have been preserved to the present day, he had embraced a metaphorical interpretation of Matt 5:29–30 in which the "hand" and "eye" refer to members of the body of Christ, the church, and the gouging out and cutting off refer to church discipline (*Comm. Mt.* 13.24). Chrysostom, *Hom. Mat.*, 17.3 interpreted the hand and eye as persons who lead believers into sin including friends and family members. Origen also affirmed this view as a possible interpretation (*Hom. Mt.* 17.3).

seems far more appropriate for the saying in 18:8–9 than for the saying in 5:29–30. The eye in verse 29 seems to be the instrument of the
look in verse 28 and thus a literal eye. The reference to the "right" eye
and "right" hand do not comport with the metaphorical interpretation. Furthermore, if Jesus were speaking metaphorically, one would
expect him to refer to "the eye" and "the hand" (as Paul did in 1 Cor
12) rather than "your eye" and "your hand."

In a variation of the metaphorical view above, the eye and hand
symbolize the lustful look and thoughts described in Matt 5:28 that
must be abandoned. This symbolism is supported by discussions
among Jewish teachers regarding the interpretation of Deut 25:11–12
that called for a woman's hand to be severed from her body. When
Philo, a contemporary of Jesus, discussed this text, he suggested that
the text should be interpreted figuratively (*sumbolikōs*):

> Very naturally, therefore, the law commands that the executioner should cut
> off the hand of the woman which has laid hold of what it should not, speak-
> ing figuratively, and intimating not that the body shall be mutilated, being
> deprived of its most important part, but rather that it is proper to extirpate all
> the ungodly reasonings of the soul.[104]

He later insisted on this interpretation based on principles of justice.[105]

The rabbis used references to dismemberment metaphorically as
well. In a discussion of hygienic practices important for the preven-
tion of maladies of the eye, Rabbi Muna declared that the unwashed
hand that touched the eye, nose, mouth, ear, and so forth should "be
cut off" since such touching promotes infections that cause blindness, deafness, and painful sores.[106] In this context the reference to
dismemberment is either a metaphor for cursing or an example of
hyperbole since severing a hand could be far more dangerous to one's
health than the maladies that poor hygiene produced. First-century
moralists from the Gentile world used similar hyperbole. Seneca
wrote, "If any vice rend your heart, cast it away from you; and if you
cannot be rid of it any other way, pluck out your heart also."[107]

Based on the above evidence, most scholars today view Jesus'
statement as hyperbole, that is, as extreme speech that was not intended to be taken literally. The hyperbole functions to teach that any

[104] Philo, *Spec. Laws* 3.179.
[105] Ibid., 3.180–82.
[106] *b. Šabb.* 108b.
[107] Seneca, *Ep. Lucil* 51.13.

sacrifice necessary to pursue sexual purity is worthwhile since the consequences of sexual sin are so frightening.[108]

Despite the enormous popularity of this view, however, not all rabbinic references to dismemberment constitute examples of symbolism or hyperbole. Some references are clearly literal. For example, the Mishnah taught that it was commendable for women to use their hands to examine themselves frequently to ensure that they had not begun to menstruate. However, if men used their hand to examine themselves, the hand should be "cut off."[109] In the Talmud rabbis debated whether the reference to the cutting off of the hand should be interpreted literally or as a symbolic reference to "execration," the cursing of the hand. In the ensuing debate the case was decided in the favor of a literal interpretation.[110] During the debate one of the rabbis mentioned that Rabbi Huna ordered that the hand of a man who often struck others be severed from his body.

In light of this and other evidence, several commentators have argued that Jesus' statement must be interpreted literally.[111] Furthermore Jesus' statement makes perfect sense at a literal level. If one must choose between the loss of an eye or hand and suffering eternally in hell, dismemberment is the obvious choice! Nevertheless it is critical to note that, although the illustration is *literal*, it is also *hypothetical*. Jesus began the illustrations with the clauses "if your right eye causes you to sin" and "if your right hand causes you to sin."

---

[108] Betz, *The Sermon on the Mount*, 238–39; Blomberg, *Matthew*, 109; Calvin, *A Harmony of the Gospels*, 1:189; Davies and Allison, *A Critical and Exegetical Commentary on the Gospel According to Saint Matthew*, 1:524–25; France, *The Gospel of Matthew*, 205; Guelich, *The Sermon on the Mount*, 196–97; Hagner, *Matthew 1–13*, 120–21; Luz, *Matthew: A Commentary*, 1:246–48; Schnackenburg, *The Gospel of Matthew*, 56; Turner, *Matthew*, 170–71; and Wilkins, *Matthew*, 245.

[109] *m. Nid.* 2:1.

[110] *b. Nid.* 13b. Against Betz, *The Sermon on the Mount*, 239. Nolland correctly observed: "Rabbinic opinion favors a literal understanding of the Mishnah, though there is no evidence of actual implementation of this judgment" (*The Gospel of Matthew*, 239). This gemara contains one of the closest rabbinic parallels to Jesus' statement: "R. Tarfon said, 'If his hand touched the membrum let his hand be cut off upon his belly.' 'But,' they said to him, 'would not his belly be split?' 'It is preferable,' he replied, 'that his belly shall be split rather than that he should go down into the pit of destruction.'" For a detailed discussion of this passage from the Talmud and its possible relationship to Matt 5:29–30, see W. Deming, "Mark 9:42–10:12, Matthew 5:27–32, and B Nid 13b : A First-Century Discussion of Male Sexuality," *NTS* 36 (1990): 130–41.

[111] Broadus, *The Gospel According to Matthew*, 109–10; Gundry, *Matthew*, 88–89; and Stählin, "ἐκκόπτω," in *TDNT* (1965), 3:859–60. Stählin viewed the dismemberment as "self-punishment" rather than as a preventive to sin.

Two features of these clauses are very important. First, the verb translated "causes you to sin" often means "to cause to be brought to a downfall," normally a spiritual or moral downfall.[112] The present tense of the verb may have a progressive nuance, that is, "if your eye keeps on causing your spiritual downfall." In this context the downfall (or at least its consequences) is identified in the explanation in verses 29b and 30b—the casting of the whole body into hell. Certainly any sacrifice, no matter how radical—even the loss of cherished limbs of the body—is warranted to avoid such a downfall.

Second, the clauses are conditional. Jesus used the construction known as a first-class conditional statement, which assumes the reality of the condition for the sake of argument. The nuance of the construction is "if—and let's assume for the sake of argument that this is true, then . . . ."[113] Although some interpreters treat the condition as an assertion of reality, sometimes even translating it "since," the condition is a contingency.[114] The only means of determining whether the contingency in a first-class condition is real or unreal is to examine the context. The context of Matt 5:29–30 strongly suggests that the condition is unreal.[115]

The immediately preceding context makes clear that the true culprit behind the sin of adultery is neither the eye nor the hand but the heart. Even though the eye was the instrument of the lustful look, the act of adultery occurred "in the heart." Jesus stated this even more clearly in Matt 15:19, "From the heart come . . . adulteries." Matthew assumed that his readers would discern that dismemberment would not prevent sin since the hand and eye were not the source of sin.[116] Broadus correctly observed:

---

[112] "σκανδαλίζω," BDAG, 926.

[113] Wallace, *Greek Grammar Beyond the Basics*, 690–92.

[114] This is clear from the numerous examples of first-class conditional constructions in which the condition is actually contrary to fact. Matthew's Gospel has several of these. Matthew 12:27, "If I drive out demons by Beelzebul," is clearly a condition that is untrue. Similarly, Matt 17:4 and 26:39 (cp. 26:42) use a positive form of the first-class conditional construction to express an unreal contingency.

[115] Wallace lists Matt 5:29–30 among examples of first-class conditional statements in which the protasis is contrary to fact (*Greek Grammar Beyond the Basics*, 691). BDF §372 lists Matt 5:29–30 as an example of the "encroachment of εἰ on the sphere of ἐάν" apparently on the basis of the usage of the latter particle in Mark 9:43,45,47. According to this opinion, the reality of the condition in Matt 5:29–30 would be left entirely open.

[116] Many Jews of Jesus' time were already aware that amputation, even castration, was ineffective in preventing sin. Sirach 20:4 referred to a eunuch who longed to take a girl's virginity.

Thus the idea is, if thy right eye causes thee to sin. The expression is obviously designed to teach a general lesson by "assuming an extreme case," a
method quite "characteristic of our Lord's teachings" (see Alexander, and
comp. on v. 24 and v. 39). He is not presenting this as an actual case, or one
likely to occur; but "if it should occur, if the only alternative presented to a
man were habitual transgression or the loss of his most valuable members,"
then he ought to "choose mutilation rather than a life of sin; and that choice
includes all minor cases, as the whole includes the part, and as the greater
comprehends the less."[117]

Avoiding spiritual downfall is worthy of any sacrifice, no matter how
great.

In summary, although Jesus' reference to amputating one's limbs
is literal, Jesus' point was hypothetical. Even if one removes the right
hand, he may still sin with the left. Even if one amputates every limb
of the body and removes each nonvital organ, he will be vulnerable
to temptation. The key to sexual purity is to seek a circumcised heart
(Deut 10:16; 30:6), a heart on which God's holy law is etched (Jer
31:31–34), a new heart (Ezek 36:24–27), a heart that is pure (Matt
5:8). Only God may grant such a heart in fulfillment of His new covenant promise, the promise that forms the theological foundation for
the radical demands of the SM.[118]

The text has a number of very important theological implications.
First, Jesus' teaching demonstrates that a lifestyle of sexual sin leads to
spiritual downfall, and its consequences will be eternal punishment.
Although contemporary culture now views sexual sin very casually
because of its rampancy, Jesus insisted that such sin was terribly dangerous and urged others to repent and abandon such lifestyles immediately. Any sacrifice necessary to avoid a life of sin is appropriate.
Second, the reference to the "whole body" being "thrown into hell"
clearly implies that the wicked will be resurrected and suffer hell's
punishments in a physical body.[119]

Similarly, Sir 30:20 referred to a eunuch who held a young woman and sighed with longing. For
similar references, see Keener, *The Gospel of Matthew*, 188.

[117] Broadus, *The Gospel According to Matthew*, 110. Davies and Allison note that Col 3:5,
"Put to death the members which are upon the earth" is immediately followed by reference to
fornication, impurity, and evil desire and may be dependent on the tradition of Jesus' *skandalon*
sayings (*A Critical and Exegetical Commentary on the Gospel According to Saint Matthew*, 1:523).

[118] See "Theological Framework for Interpreting the SM" in this text.

[119] See Gundry, *Matthew*, 89; id., "*Sōma*," in *Biblical Theology*, SNTSMS 29 (Cambridge: Cambridge University Press, 1976), 24. Against France, *The Gospel of Matthew*, 206. On the meaning
of "hell" see the discussion on Matt 5:23.

Divorce (Matt 5:31–32)

For an explanation of Jesus' introduction formula, "It was also said," see the section "Interpreting the Antitheses." Jesus' discussion of adultery led naturally to a discussion of divorce for two reasons. First, Jesus taught that sexual immorality constitutes biblical grounds for divorce. Second, Jesus taught that divorce and remarriage without biblical grounds constitutes adultery.

Jesus introduced His discussion of divorce and remarriage by quoting a loose paraphrase of Deut 24:1. The text made provisions for divorce and laid down restrictions related to divorce. The text specified only one legitimate ground for divorce, "something improper" (lit. "a matter of indecency"). Although the word translated "improper" often means "nakedness," other uses show that "something improper" was not necessarily related to a sexual act. The same Hebrew phrase was used in Deut 23:14 (HB v. 15) to refer to failure to send a soldier with a bodily emission outside of the camp or exposure of one's body in the camp while defecating. Such shameful acts might prompt God to abandon the camp: "He must not see anything improper among you or He will turn away from you."

The ambiguity of the phrase "anything improper" led to a significant debate over the correct interpretation among the rabbis. The school of Hillel interpreted the phrase very permissively as including anything that displeased one's husband. The school of Shammai and Jesus interpreted "anything improper" as a reference to sexual sin.

By the time of the composition of the Mishnah (AD 200), most rabbis seem to have embraced the view of Hillel. The Mishnah specified numerous and ridiculous grounds for divorce that made the covenant of marriage meaningless.

The Mishnah stated that a man could divorce his wife if she were barren (*m. Yebam.* 6:6; *m. Giṭ.* 4:8), if she became a deaf mute (*m. Yebam.* 14:1), or if she had epilepsy, tetanus, warts, or leprosy. *Mishnah Ketubbot* 5:5 insisted that a man could divorce his wife if she failed to perform certain services in the home. Each day she was required to grind flour, bake bread, wash clothes, cook food, nurse the children, make the beds, and weave with wool. If she brought one servant into the marriage, she did not have to grind, bake, or wash. If she brought a second servant into the marriage, she did not have to nurse the children or cook. If she brought a third servant into the home, she did not have to make up the bed or work in wool. If she brought four servants into the home, she could sit in a chair all day long and not lift a finger. However, if her husband considered her lazy, he still had the prerogative to divorce her.

Rabbinic law also stated that certain physical defects in the wife were so offensive that they were legitimate grounds for divorce. The general principle was that any physical defect or blemish that was serious enough to disqualify a man from the priesthood was sufficiently repulsive to serve as a ground for divorce (see *m. Ketub.* 7:7; *m. Qidd.* 2:5; and *m. Bek.* 7). Consequently a man could divorce his wife if she had a head that was wedge shaped, turnip shaped, or hammer shaped, or if her head was otherwise malformed such as "sunk in" or "flat at the back." He could divorce his wife if she had poor posture or if she had thinning hair. He could divorce her if she had no eyebrows, only one eyebrow, or bushy eyebrows. He could divorce her if she had a pug nose. The condition of her eyes was particularly important. If she had eyes too high or too low, if she were cross-eyed, had no eyelashes, had eyes of two different colors, watery eyes, or eyes big as a calf or small like a goose, any of these justified divorce. The man could divorce his wife if her nose were too big or too little, her ears too little or too floppy, if she had an overbite or underbite, missing teeth, a poor figure, a swollen belly, a protruding navel, oversized or damaged sexual organs, a dark complexion, bony ankles or knees, swollen feet, if she were bowlegged, suffered from swelling of the big toe, if her heel had protrusions, if the sole of her foot was as wide as that of a goose, or if she were ambidextrous.

According to *m. Ketub.* 7:1, a man could divorce his wife if she ate something he had forbidden her to eat, if she visited the home of her parents, or if, against her husband's wishes, the in-laws moved into the same city to be near their daughter. The husband had the right to divorce his wife if she broke the laws of Moses or if she transgressed Jewish custom by going outdoors with her hair unbound, spun cloth in the street, or spoke to any man other than her husband. She would also be divorced if she cursed her husband's parents or yelled at her husband so loud that her voice could be heard outside the house. A man could divorce his wife if she had a bad reputation (*m. Giṭ.* 4:8), if she burned his supper, or if he simply found someone that he thought was prettier (*m. Giṭ.* 9:10).

Not offering sexual relations frequently enough was also grounds for divorce, and the law specifically expressed appropriate expectations regarding this matter. The wife had to satisfy her husband every day if he had the time, twice a week if he were a day laborer, every 30 days if he were a camel driver, and every six months if he were a sailor (*m. Ketub.* 5:6).

Clearly, many Jews in the first century believed that couples could divorce for any reason. This view is implied in the Pharisees' question in Matt 19:3: "Is it lawful for a man to divorce his wife on any grounds?" Josephus' statement that divorce was permitted "for any causes whatsoever" also confirms this view.[120]

Some modern interpreters have challenged the view of Deut 24:1 embraced by Shammai and by Jesus. They argue that indecent sexual behavior could not have been a ground for divorce since many forms of indecent sexual behavior including adultery, bestiality, and homosexuality were punished by execution. However, some offenses less heinous than those leading to capital punishment were serious enough to make divorce justifiable under the law. These might include indecent sexual behavior that did not result in actual copulation.[121]

The description of a formal divorce process in Deut 24:1 that includes a written certificate of divorce served to prevent a husband from flippantly and casually severing relations with his wife. Many interpreters suggest further that Deut 24:2–4 presents a second marriage as analogous to an adulterous relationship that "defiled" the woman and made her returning to her first husband "detestable to the Lord."[122] Nevertheless rather than challenging the legitimacy of the second marriage, the law may have been designed to prevent hypocrisy on the part of the first husband. If he claimed to divorce her on grounds of sexual activity with another, then chose to remarry her after her sexual union with a second husband, the grounds of divorce originally claimed would seem like a fabrication contrived to justify a divorce without any legitimate grounds. Thus the law may have been designed to protect the wife from frivolous divorce and slanderous challenges to the wife's character.

---

[120] Josephus (*Ant.* 4.8.23 §253). Philo also affirmed this view (*Spec. Leg.* 3.5 §330–31).

[121] C. F. Keil and F. Delitzsch, *Biblical Commentary on the Old Testament: The Pentateuch*, trans. J. Martin (Grand Rapids: Eerdmans, 1956), 3:417.

[122] E. Merrill, *Deuteronomy*, NAC (Nashville: B&H, 1994), 318; P. Craigie, *The Book of Deuteronomy*, NICOT (Grand Rapids: Eerdmans, 1976), 305.

Although Jesus quoted a free summary of Deut 24:1 in His antithesis, the evidence suggests that He was countering rabbinic interpretations of the law rather than the law itself. Two details of the paraphrase support this conclusion. First, the paraphrase did not express the one ground for divorce given in Deut 24:1. Second, the paraphrase changed the discussion of divorce into a command to divorce.[123] This suggests that the authors of the paraphrase required their hearers to divorce under some circumstances. Jesus challenged this interpretation of Deut 24:1 more explicitly in Matt 19:7–8. There the Pharisees replied to Jesus' teaching regarding the permanency of marriage with the retort, "Why then . . . did Moses *command* us . . . to send her away?" Jesus countered, "Moses *permitted* you to divorce your wives." Although the distinction between command and permission is not as clear in Matthew 5, the distinction is nonetheless present. Since the first element of the other five antitheses is consistently a command, the allusion to Deut 24:1 is probably to be viewed as a command rather than an offer of permission. Jesus, by contrast, rephrased Deut 24:1 in such a way as to make divorce permissible given the proper circumstances but not mandatory even in these circumstances.[124]

Jesus challenged the common rabbinic interpretation of the text in Deuteronomy by identifying frivolous divorce as a heinous sin and defining remarriage after a frivolous divorce as adultery. Jesus taught, "Everyone who divorces his wife, except in the case of sexual immorality, causes her to commit adultery" (Matt 5:32). Jesus taught that no divorce certificate could dissolve the enduring covenant of marriage in God's eyes when divorce was sought on trivial grounds. Despite the certificate of divorce, those who had promised "till death do us part" remained married in God's eyes until death or an actual dissolution of the one-flesh relationship through the spouse's union with a paramour or a partner in a second marriage.

Some interpreters have argued that Jesus' teaching is a critique of a patriarchal society in which divorced women found it necessary to

[123] Both the rabbis and the Qumran community commanded divorce in some circumstances, particularly after the spouse was discovered to have committed adultery. See M. Bockmuehl, "Matthew 5.32; 19.9 in the Light of Pre-rabbinic Halakhah," *NTS* 35 (1989): 291–95. Hermas also required divorce if a spouse committed adultery and did not repent since otherwise "he becomes responsible for her sin and an accomplice in her adultery" (Herm. *Mand.* 4.1.5).

[124] In his discussion of Deut 24:1–4, Merrill observed, "The legislation here neither commands nor condones divorce in general but only regulates its practice for ancient Israel" (*Deuteronomy*, 316).

work as prostitutes or live as the mistress of another married man and be supported at his expense in order to survive. In this view Jesus' concern was not with divorce and remarriage but with the oppression of women. Jesus' teaching does assume that most divorced women had no choice but to remarry since he says that the divorcing husband *makes* or *causes* (*poieō*) her to commit adultery. Jesus' teaching also assumes that men rather than women had the prerogative to seek divorce. This was true in Jewish society, although women in the Roman world could seek divorce (Mark 10:12). However, Jesus' concern in this text is not so much the status of women in first-century Jewish society as the sanctity of marriage. He was not chiding society for failing to grant employment opportunities to women. He was insisting that a mere divorce certificate alone does not dissolve a marriage. If Jesus were merely combating patriarchal societal structures, he would have scolded the divorcing husband for forcing the wife into adultery. However, Jesus implicated not only the divorced wife but also the husband who married her after the divorce in the adulterous act. Furthermore in Matt 19:9, the husband who divorces his wife without proper grounds and then remarries is also labeled an adulterer. The parallel text in Mark adds that a woman who divorces her husband and marries someone else likewise commits adultery (Mark 10:12).[125] All this implies that Jesus' concern was not so much the employment rights of women as the perpetuity of the marriage covenant in the eyes of God. Remarriage after frivolous divorce constituted an adulterous act because the original marriage was not dissolved when God deemed the grounds invalid.[126]

Several commentators have described Matt 5:32 as an example of "rhetorical overstatement" or "hyperbole" comparable to the supposed hyperbole in verse 40.[127] However, the statement makes good sense when taken literally. A literal sense seems to follow from the theological argument that Jesus offered in 19:4–9. Furthermore Jesus'

---

[125] Luz correctly observed that this creates serious problems for the claim that Jesus intended only to address the needs of the disadvantaged woman since "the prohibition against marrying a divorced woman is in no way in the interest of the disadvantaged woman" (*Matthew: A Commentary*, 1:251–52).

[126] Davies and Allison, *A Critical and Exegetical Commentary on the Gospel According to Saint Matthew*, 1:532.

[127] Keener, *The Gospel of Matthew*, 190; R. Stein, "'Is It Lawful for a Man to Divorce His Wife?'" *JETS* 22 (1978): 119; idem, "Divorce," in *Dictionary of Jesus and the Gospels*, ed. J. B. Green, S. McKnight, and I. H. Marshall (Downers Grove, IL: InterVarsity, 1992), 198.

disciples seem to have interpreted His statement in 19:9 literally since their retort was, "If the relationship of a man with his wife is like this, it's better not to marry!" The disciples recognized that Jesus was insisting that marriage was a permanent commitment that one should not enter lightly and that one could not evade except in the most extenuating circumstances.

Jesus interpreted the ground for divorce in Deut 24:1 far more narrowly than most of His contemporaries. Jesus equated divorce and remarriage with adultery "except in a case of sexual immorality" thus establishing sexual sin as the one appropriate ground for divorce. Some interpreters argue that even sexual immorality does not justify divorce since the so-called "exception clauses" are actually inclusive rather than exclusive.[128] This requires Matt 5:32 to be translated, "Everyone who divorces his wife, including in a case of sexual immorality, causes her to commit adultery." However, this interpretation tortures the Greek grammar of the exception clauses both here and in 19:9. The adverb *parektos* appears only two other times in the NT. It appears in Acts 26:29 ("except for these chains") and in 2 Cor 11:28 ("apart from what I leave unmentioned," author's translation), and in both cases is clearly exceptional rather than inclusive.[129] Thus the exception clause clearly expresses the legitimate ground for pursuing a divorce.[130]

"Sexual immorality" (*porneia*) is sometimes translated as "fornication" or "marital unfaithfulness" and interpreted as referring not to adultery but to premarital sexual sin of the bride which is discovered on the wedding night through the ritual of the tokens of virginity.[131] Other interpreters suggest that *porneia* refers to incestuous marriages described in Leviticus 18.[132] However, the noun is much broader in

[128] This view was argued by B. Vawter, "Divorce Clauses in Matthew 5:32 and 19:9," *CBQ* 16 (1954): 155–67, esp. 163–65. It has been adopted by few scholars (see R. J. Banks, *Jesus and the Law in the Synoptic Tradition*, SNTSM 28 [Cambridge: Cambridge University Press, 1975], 156–57). Vawter later abandoned the position ("Divorce and the New Testament," *CBQ* 39 [1977]: 528–48, esp. 534–35). See the discussion and rejection of this view in Carson, "Matthew," 414–15. Luz correctly observed that attempts to revise the exceptional sense of the clause "have today just about disappeared from the discussion, because the philological finding is unambiguous" (*Matthew: A Commentary*, 1:304).

[129] "παρεκτός," BDAG, 784.

[130] See A. Guenther, "The Exception Phrases: Except πορνεία, Including πορνεία or Excluding πορνεία? (Matthew 5:32; 19:9)," *TynBul* 53 (2002): 83–96.

[131] Abel Isaksson, *Marriage and Ministry in the New Temple* (Lund: Gleerup, 1965), 116–52.

[132] B. Witherington, "Matt. 5.2 and 19.9—Exception or Exceptional Situation," *NTS* 31 (1985): 571–76.

meaning than this, and in other NT usages it includes premarital sex, adultery, sex with prostitutes, and general sexual immorality. Others suggest that "sexual immorality" specifically means "adultery."[133] This has been disputed since Greek has a more specific term for adultery (*moicheia*). Jesus used the word group referring to adultery repeatedly in Matthew 5 so it was readily available to Him here. Furthermore 15:19 distinguishes between *porneia* and *moicheia* as expressions of a corrupt heart and thus implies that they are not perfect synonyms. Nevertheless Greek writers sometimes used the former term to specify adultery on the part of a woman and the latter term to specify adultery on the part of a man.[134] Thus the term *porneia* can refer specifically to an adulterous act. The evidence best supports the view that *porneia* involved sexual relationships with anyone other than the husband during betrothal or after marriage.[135] Blomberg correctly observed: "Πορνεία should therefore be translated as 'adultery,' possibly including but not limited to related sexual sins such as incest, homosexuality, prostitution, molestation, or indecent exposure. This is its typical semantic range."[136]

Perhaps the clearest clues for defining *porneia* in this context arise from a consideration of the meaning of Deut 24:1 it its original context. Eugene Merrill sought to define the ground for divorce in Deut 24:1:

> The major difficulty in the passage at hand is that the point of contention is described not explicitly as adultery but as *'erwat dābār* ("something indecent about her"; lit., "the nakedness of a thing"). The noun *'erwa* bears the meaning of both "nakedness" or "pudenda" (i.e., the sexual organs), meanings no doubt to be combined here to suggest the improper uncovering of the private parts. Clearly this circumlocution is to be understood as a euphemism that may or may not include adultery (cf. Lev 18:6–18; 20:11,17,20–21; Ezek 22:10; 23:29; Hos 2:10), but not in this case.[137]

---

[133] The word πορνεία clearly refers to adultery in Sir 23:23; Herm. *Mand.* 4.1.5; *T. Jos.* 3:8. In these texts the word refers specifically to the adulterous act of the female, a sense that applies well in Matt 5:32.

[134] J. Bauer, "Bemerkungen zu den matthäischen Unzuchtsklauseln (Mt 5,32; 19,9)," *Begegnung mit dem Wort: Festschrift für Heinrich Zimmermann*, ed. Josef Zmijewski and Ernst Nellessen (Bonn: Hanstein, 1980), 23–33; Davies and Allison, *A Critical and Exegetical Commentary on the Gospel According to Saint Matthew*, 1:531; France, *The Gospel of Matthew*, 209, n. 107.

[135] D. Janzen, "The Meaning of PORNEIA in Matthew 5.32 and 19.9: An Approach from the Study of Ancient Near Eastern Culture," *JSNT* 80 (2000): 66–80; D. C. Allison Jr., "Divorce, Celibacy, and Joseph (Matthew 1:18–25 and 19:1–12)," *JSNT* 49 (1993): 1–10.

[136] C. Blomberg, "Marriage, Divorce, Remarriage, and Celibacy: An Exegesis of Matthew 19:3–12," *TJ* 2 (1990): 161–96, esp. 177.

[137] Merrill, *Deuteronomy*, 317.

Most commentators on Deuteronomy regard the ground for divorce in Deut 24:1 as something that falls short of the actual act of adultery since adultery was normally punished by death and would automatically terminate the marriage (Deut 22:22).[138] Nevertheless Merrill seems correct in his assertion that it is difficult to limit the phrase to anything less than adultery in this context and that the phrase is "broad enough to include adultery but not synonymous with it."[139] Matthew probably used the term *porneia* in a broad sense as well to include adultery but also serious sexual transgressions that fell short of actual copulation outside of wedlock.

Matthew's Greek term *porneia* refers to sexual sin in general and means sexual sin that constitutes legitimate grounds for divorce. It constitutes a legitimate ground for divorce because it dissolves the one-flesh relationship of marriage like no legal document can. When the adulteress unites her body with that of another man, she has become one with him in a way that destroys her previous one-flesh union.[140]

One could argue that the exception only means that when a spouse divorces an adulteress, he does not make her an adulteress because she already is one. Matthew 19:9 argues against this. This text says that if a man divorces a wife except for *porneia* and he remarries, he thereby commits adultery. His point is that a certificate of divorce cannot of itself dissolve the one-flesh relationship of husband and wife so that remarriage after divorce without biblical grounds constitutes adultery.

The early church often interpreted Jesus' words as allowing for (sometimes even requiring) divorce in the case of adultery but prohibiting all remarriage.[141] Most modern Roman Catholic and a few modern-day Protestant commentators also affirm this view.[142] Luz has

---

[138] S. R. Driver, *A Critical and Exegetical Commentary on Deuteronomy*, ICC (Edinburgh: Clark, 1902), 271. Craigie suggested the unlikely view that the matter of indecency was a physical defect such as infertility (*Deuteronomy*, 305).

[139] Merrill, *Deuteronomy*, 317, n. 220.

[140] Paul used language from Gen 2:24 to describe sexual union with a prostitute.

[141] See Herm. *Mand.* 4.1.7–10 (although the argument is based on the possibility that the spouse may repent, thereby requiring remarriage to the original spouse, rather than an appeal to Jesus' teaching); Justin, *Apol.* 1.15; Clement of Alexandria, *Strom.* 2.23.

[142] For an evangelical argument for this position, see D. Warden, "The Words of Jesus on Divorce," *RQ* 39 (1997): 141–53; and W. Heth, "Divorce and Remarriage: The Search for an Evangelical Hermeneutic," *TJ* 16 (1995): 63–100. Heth later abandoned this position. See his "Jesus on Divorce: How My Mind Has Changed," *SBJT* 6 (2002): 4–29.

argued that Jesus expanded the OT prohibition against marrying one's own divorced wife to a prohibition against marrying any divorced woman without exception.[143] This interpretation is highly unlikely. In the first-century Jewish world, divorce carried with it the prerogative of marriage to another. *Mishna Giṭṭin* 9:3 shows that the text of the writ of divorce read, "Lo, you are permitted to any man." Attempts to place restrictions on the possibility of remarriage nullified the certificate of divorce (*m. Giṭ.* 9:1–2). In the absence of any clear prohibition on remarriage, the approval of the divorce should be deemed approval for remarriage as well. Those who view Jesus' teaching as prohibiting remarriage entirely typically view the exception clause as an insertion that distorted Jesus' original intention.[144]

The other Gospels do not include Matthew's exception clause. Matthew apparently made explicit an exception that was merely implicit in Mark's Gospel. Two suggestions have been made for Matthew's inclusion of the exception clause. First, Matthew may have included the exception in order to defend Joseph's original plan to divorce Mary when he assumed that she had been unfaithful to her betrothal. Joseph serves as a model to Jesus' disciples by tempering righteousness with kindness and compassion. If Joseph's original intention to seek a divorce had been unjustified, it would have been a stain on his otherwise exemplary conduct.[145]

Second, Matthew may have included the exception clause to justify God's "divorce" of national Israel because of its spiritual adultery. Several statements in Matthew's Gospel warn of God's rejection of Israel. The cleansing of the temple (21:12–13), the cursing of the fig tree (vv. 18–22), the parable of the Wicked Tenants (vv. 33–46), the denunciations of the scribes and Pharisees (chap. 23), the woe pronounced over Jerusalem (23:37–38), and the prophecy of the destruction of Jerusalem (24:1–2) all anticipate God's abandonment of unrepentant Israel. Matthew may have wished to justify God's rejection of Israel to the Jewish Christians in his audience by showing that just as the marriage covenant could be destroyed by infidelity, thereby making it permissible for a husband to divorce his wife, so also Israel's

---

[143] Luz, *Matthew: A Commentary*, 1:256.

[144] See, e.g., J. P. Meier, *Law and Love*, Marginal Jew 4 (New Haven, CT: Yale University Press, 2009), 104–28.

[145] Davies and Allison, *A Critical and Exegetical Commentary on the Gospel According to Saint Matthew*, 1:531.

spiritual adultery fully justified God's abandonment or "divorce" of His covenant people, His "bride." In a probable allusion to Deut 32:5, Jesus later portrayed national Israel as "an evil and adulterous generation" (Matt 12:39; 16:4). This spiritual state provided legitimate grounds for God's judgment of Israel and His shift in focus to a new spiritual Israel, composed of followers of Jesus Christ and including people from Gentile backgrounds (see note 107).

Some Christian groups have argued from Jesus' teaching that a divorced person who marries anyone other than the original spouse lives in a perpetual state of adultery. Couples in which at least one of the spouses was previously divorced are sometimes banned from church membership since adultery is grounds both for church discipline and exclusion. This interpretation and application of Jesus' teaching is driven by a compelling logic. However, it appears that the first act of adultery within the new marriage dissolves the one-flesh union of the original marriage so that the new marriage is initially but not perpetually adulterous. Thus remarriage without biblical grounds is sinful, even adulterous, but the marriage does not remain so. The present-tense verbs in the proposition are not progressive presents implying a perpetual state of adultery. Rather they are "gnomic presents" that state an abiding general principle. This is confirmed by the shift from the present verb "make" (*poiei*) to the aorist infinitive "commit adultery" (*moicheuthēnai*). Consequently, although the church should discourage divorcees who did not have appropriate biblical grounds for their divorce from marrying another person, it should not challenge the legitimacy of the second marriage after it is consummated. As Blomberg wisely urged, "Divorced Christians who have remarried should not commit the sin of a second divorce to try to resume relations with a previous spouse (see again Deut 24:1–4) but should begin afresh to observe God's standards by remaining faithful to their current partners."[146]

---

[146] Blomberg, *Matthew*, 111. Blomberg made his argument on different grounds. He followed W. F. Luck in arguing that the "adultery" that followed divorce without appropriate grounds was metaphorical, "infidelity to the lifelong, covenantal nature of marriage (cf. the characteristic Old Testament use of 'adultery' to refer to breaking one's commitments to God—e.g., Hos 2:4; Jer 5:7; Ezek 16:32)." See Blomberg, "Marriage, Divorce," 174–75. More likely, "adultery" refers to a sexual act and Jesus assumed the remarriage of the wife. Otherwise, when a husband chose to divorce an innocent wife, the wife would be considered an "adulteress" even if she remained unmarried because of her faithfulness to her vows.

Jesus clearly expected divorce to be a rarity among His followers. Jesus explained in Matt 19:8 that Moses permitted divorce "because of the hardness of your hearts." However, Jesus' followers are categorically different from those for whom provision for divorce was made. The contrast between "it was said to the ancients" and "I say to you" reminds Jesus' disciples that they belong to the era of the new covenant rather than the old covenant. In the new covenant God has taken away the "heart of stone," the "hard heart," and given His people a "heart of flesh" (Ezek 36:26). This new heart gives Jesus' followers an ability to remain faithful to their marital vows in a way and to a degree that others cannot. Blomberg commented:

> Many writers have appealed to this σκληροκαρδία as a possible ground for divorce under the new covenant as well. If God was gracious enough to permit less than his ideal in the age of law, surely he would be at least as compassionate in the age of grace! Unfortunately, this argument completely inverts the logic of Jesus' ethic. Jesus' commands consistently establish a greater standard of righteousness than the law required (Matt 5:20). Grace comes into play because God concurrently offers a greater empowerment to enable one better to perform his more demanding will (11:28–30). By saying in this verse, "from the beginning it was not so," Jesus insists that God did not originally intend for hard-heartedness to be an excuse for divorce. Now in the age of the new covenant, therefore, Christians may no longer appeal to hard-heartedness as grounds for dissolving a marriage.[147]

Ancient commentators also recognized the dramatic impact that the transformation wrought by Christ in the heart of the disciple had on the institution of marriage. In his discussion of Jesus' teaching on divorce, Chrysostom commented, "For he that is meek, and a peacemaker, and poor in spirit, and merciful, how shall he cast out his wife? He that is used to reconcile others, how shall he be at variance with her that is his own?"[148]

Dishonesty (Matt 5:33–37)

The entire introductory formula used in verse 21 appears again here, and this structure serves to divide the six antitheses into two major sections consisting of three units. "You heard that it was said" reminds the original hearers that the interpretation of the law had been mediated to them through the teachers of the Jewish synagogue. The divine passive

---

[147] Blomberg, "Marriage, Divorce," 171.
[148] Chrysostom, *Hom. Mt.* 17.4.

verb "it was said" reminded them of the divine inspiration of the OT law. The contrast of what was said "to the ancients" and "but I say to you" implies that the OT law belonged to an old era, a previous period, and that Jesus' disciples belonged to a new era with a new covenant. Although different vocabulary is employed by Jesus, the contrast echoes Jer 31:31–34, which described the old covenant as one that God "made with their ancestors" and described the new covenant as one that God would make with His people "after those days." This new covenant was inaugurated through the coming of the Messiah and produced righteousness in the people of God that transcended the old covenant. The new era demands a new ethic, and the new ethic surpasses the ethic of the Mosaic law. For a more extensive discussion of the introductory formula, see the section "Interpreting the Antitheses."

Unlike the direct quotations of the OT in Matt 5:21 and 27, the words "you must not break your oath, but you must keep your oaths to the Lord" are not direct quotations of the OT. Instead, this seems to be a rabbinic paraphrase of texts like Lev 19:12; Num 30:3; and Deut 23:21–23. The rabbinic paraphrase that appears later in Matt 5:43 clearly distorts the OT text and teaches the opposite of what the law intended. One must be open to the possibility of some distortion of the OT intent here also. The first element of the command "You must not break your oath" literally means "Do not commit perjury" or "Do not lie under oath."[149] The command does not necessarily prohibit all forms of deceit and leaves a legal loophole by not prohibiting deception when one is not under oath. The following clause begins with the adversative conjunction "but" (*de*), which contrasts the action commanded in the second clause with the action prohibited in the first clause. The second clause interprets the first but states the principle in a positive way.[150] The rabbinic paraphrase "you must keep your oaths *to the Lord*" also seems to contain a loophole that might allow dishonesty to others. The Greek text places the words "to the Lord" in an emphatic position, which suggests that the rabbis taught that one was to be honest in commitments made to God and especially to Him but not necessarily to others unless God had been invoked in the

---

[149] The Gk. verb ἐπιορκέω (*epiorkeō*) appears twice in the LXX but only in the apocryphal books (1 Esd 1:48 and Wis 14:28; see also *Did.* 2:3). The more important occurrence is 1 Esd 1:48 in which the verb describes Zedekiah's breaking of his oath not to rebel against Nebuchadnezzar, an oath that he swore in the name of the Lord to the Babylonian ruler.

[150] So also Betz, *The Sermon on the Mount*, 265.

oath.[151] In the second clause the use of the word "oaths" rather than "vows" suggests an oath made to another individual in the name of God rather than to God Himself. However, the paraphrase calls for one to pay back to the Lord one's oaths. The implication is that since oaths were sworn before God, they constituted an obligation to Him as well as to the individual. Fulfilling the promise to the individual thus involved satisfying a divine obligation.[152] An oath to an individual became a vow to God when God's name was invoked.

The final words on honesty in the OT are Zech 8:16–17: "These are the things you must do: Speak truth to one another (lit., 'to one's neighbor' [LXX]) . . . and do not love perjury, for I hate all this," and Mal 3:5, "I [Yahweh] will come to you in judgment, and I will be ready to witness against . . . those who swear falsely." However, some first-century rabbis emphasized only the importance of speaking the truth to God and downplayed the importance of absolute honesty in all communication. They thought that they had a special obligation to keep promises made *to God* specifically but could break promises made to others when it was convenient.

Jesus challenged the rabbinic interpretation of the law with His familiar words, "But I say to you." As before, the formula contrasts Jesus' authority as a teacher/prophet with that of the rabbis and contrasts Jesus' disciples with the ancients as those who belong to a new spiritual era. Jesus' command, "Don't take an oath at all," serves to

---

[151] In general vows (εὐχή) are promises made to God. Oaths (ὅρκος) are promises or assertions made to another human being which invite a divine curse if the promise is broken or the truth is not being told. Oddly the rabbinic paraphrase spoke of paying to God what one promised by oath when one would have expected the text to speak of paying to God what one had vowed (the awkwardness of the construction has been noted also by Davies and Allison, *A Critical and Exegetical Commentary on the Gospel According to Saint Matthew*, 1.534; and Guelich, *The Sermon on the Mount*, 212–13). The Gk. text of Matt 5:33b, ἀποδώσεις δὲ τῷ κυρίῳ τοὺς ὅρκους σου, is very similar to Ps 50:14 (49:14, LXX), καὶ ἀπόδος τῷ ὑψίστῳ τὰς εὐχάς σου. The differences are that "the Lord" has been substituted for "Most High" and "oaths" has been substituted for "vows." The adaptations of the psalm seem to have been intentional. Perhaps the rabbis were teaching that one was obligated to be faithful to God but not necessarily to other persons. Guelich suggests that Matt 5:33a pertains to an "assertive oath" while v. 33b pertains to a promissory oath which is roughly synonymous with a vow (*The Sermon on the Mount*, 214). Davies and Allison rejected Guelich's interpretation arguing, "This subtlety does not illumine the text" (*A Critical and Exegetical Commentary on the Gospel According to Saint Matthew*, 1:534). For more information on the nature of vows in Judaism, see D. Garlington, "Oath-taking in the Community of the New Age (Matthew 5:33–37)," *TJ* 16 (1995): 139–70.

[152] Betz, *The Sermon on the Mount*, 265; and Strecker, *The Sermon on the Mount*, 77–78. See also Hagner, *Matthew 1–13*, 1:126. Hagner translated the rabbinic paraphrase, "You shall fulfill your oaths as to the Lord." However, Hagner offered no justification for his insertion of the word "as."

undermine the legal loopholes in the Jewish system of oath-taking and requires consistent truthfulness that does not require oaths at all.[153] Jesus' disciples are to be characterized by such integrity that an oath is not necessary to make their words credible.

Many scholars have insisted that at least here in the antitheses, Jesus actually opposed the clear teaching of the law. The law clearly commanded the use of oaths, yet Jesus renounced the use of oaths.[154] Evangelical scholars sometimes argue that this has positive Christological implications: Jesus' authority is greater than that of the OT law itself.[155] However, the Christological implications of this view are not entirely positive since this interpretation may bring Matt 5:33–37 into direct contradiction with Jesus' express claim in verses 17–20.[156] In fact Jesus' prohibition of oaths in no way contradicts the law since Deut 23:22 said, "But if you refrain from making a vow, it will not be counted against you as sin."

Jesus continued by prohibiting oath formulas that were intentionally deceptive, that is, that gave others the impression that a binding oath had been taken when the speaker himself did not regard the oath as binding and felt he was under no obligation to speak truthfully. Jesus more directly addressed this dishonest practice in 23:16–22, and His teaching there serves as helpful commentary on this text:

> Woe to you, blind guides, who say, "Whoever takes an oath by the sanctuary, it means nothing. But whoever takes an oath by the gold of the sanctuary is bound by his oath." Blind fools! For which is greater, the gold or the sanctuary that sanctified the gold? Also, "Whoever takes an oath by the altar, it means nothing. But whoever takes an oath by the gift that is on it is bound by his oath." Blind people! For which is greater, the gift or the altar that

[153] For a detailed defense of the authenticity of this saying, see A. Iko, "The Question of the Authenticity of Jesus' Ban on Swearing (Matthew 5:33–37)," *JSNT* 43 (1991): 5–13.

[154] France claimed, "Since the OT law not only provided for but in some cases demanded such elaborating oaths (e.g., Num 5:19–22), there is a *prima facie* case to be made that Jesus is here opposing the intention of one aspect of the law" (*The Gospel of Matthew*, 213). France also identified v. 34 as one of the points in the SM in which Jesus left "the regulations themselves at best irrelevant and apparently even obsolete."

[155] See, for example, ibid., 213.

[156] See the introduction to the so-called "antitheses." Davies and Allison have correctly argued that "we cannot think that he [the evangelist] believed the teachings of 5.21–48 to contradict the Torah. In other words, in Matthew's eyes the tension between Jesus' teaching and the Mosaic commandments was much less than in the eyes of many modern scholars" (*A Critical and Exegetical Commentary on the Gospel According to Saint Matthew*, 1:492). In his carefully nuanced view, France sees no real contradiction with 5:17–20 since "the Torah . . . is not God's last word to his people, but is in a sense provisional, looking forward to a time of fulfillment through the Messiah" (*The Gospel of Matthew*, 183).

sanctifies the gift? Therefore, the one who takes an oath by the altar takes an oath by it and by everything on it. The one who takes an oath by the sanctuary takes an oath by it and by Him who dwells in it. And the one who takes an oath by heaven takes an oath by God's throne and by Him who sits on it.

Jesus' rebuke demonstrates that the rabbis had developed a system of oaths in which people could evade the obligation to be honest through carefully crafted oath formulas. According to the rabbis oaths were deemed valid and legally binding only when they invoked the name of the Lord. However, in the first century Jewish law allowed only the high priest performing the atoning rituals of the Day of Atonement in the holy of holies or the priests of Jerusalem who pronounced the priestly blessing of Num 6:24–26 to utter the divine name. First-century Jews viewed all other utterances of the divine name as blasphemy.[157] Thus when one took an oath, substitutions for the divine name had to be used.[158] In the complicated rulings of the rabbis, however, only certain substitutions were valid and made the oath binding. Valid substitutions, called *kinnuyim*, included "Alephdalet" (the first two letters of the Hebrew name *Adonai*), "Yod-He" (the first two letters of the name *Yahweh* or Jehovah), "Shaddai," "Sabaoth," "the Merciful and Gracious," "Him that is longsuffering and of great kindness" or any substituted name that involved a description of God's unique character (*m. Šebu.* 4:13).

According to rabbinic ruling none of the oath formulas Jesus listed in verse 34 included approved substitutions for God's name.[159] The objects mentioned in the oath formulas were not closely enough associated with God to serve as valid substitutions for the unutterable name of God in oath formulas. Therefore, oaths that utilized these formulas were considered nonbinding oaths in Jewish law. Breaking such oaths did not constitute an act of taking the Lord's name in vain or misusing the divine name (Exod 20:7). For example *m. Šebu.* 4:13 stated, "If a man said, I adjure, command or bind you, they are liable. But if he said, 'By heaven and by earth,' they are exempt." Later the rabbi Maimonides argued,

---

[157] *m. Yoma* 3:8; 6:2; *m. Sota* 7:8.

[158] See Keener, *The Gospel of Matthew*, 194; and G. Vermes, *The Religion of Jesus the Jew* (Minneapolis: Augsburg Fortress, 1993), 34–35.

[159] Other ancient Jews disagreed with the rabbinic rulings, however. Philo, e.g., argued that vows by heaven and earth were valid and binding (*Spec. Leg.* 2.2–5).

If any swear by heaven, by earth, by the sun, etc., although the mind of the
swearer be under these words to swear by Him who created them, yet this is
not an oath. Or if any swear by some of the prophets, or by some of the books
of the Scripture, although the sense of the swearer be to swear by Him that
sent that prophet or that gave that book, nevertheless this is not an oath.[160]

Similarly *m. Ned.* 1:3 insists that an oath sworn "by Jerusalem" was
nonbinding. Later Jewish commentary on this legal principle argued
that a vow made "by" Jerusalem was nonbinding but a vow made "toward" Jerusalem was binding (*t. Ned.* 1.2.3). Evidently by facing Jerusalem, the abode of God, when making the vow, one indicated that
one was making a vow to God. *Mishna Sanhedrin* 3:2 states, "If a man
must take an oath before his fellow, and his fellow said to him, 'Vow
to me by the life of thy head,' R. Meir says, 'He may retract.' But the
Sages say, 'He cannot retract.'" In this illustration a man commanded
a person to make an oath using the formula "by the head." Evidently
he wished to retract this command and require another oath formula
instead because of some perceived loophole in the oath formula. This
seems confirmed by the teaching of Jesus in Matt 23:16–22.[161] These
examples suggest that Jesus prohibited oath-taking among His disciples because oath-taking often degenerates into a thin veneer of technical honesty that masks deception.

Jesus argued that these objects were so closely associated with
God that to swear by them was to swear by Him. Heaven is God's
throne from which He reigns as heavenly King. The earth is the stool
beneath the throne on which the heavenly King rests His feet (Isa
66:1; Acts 7:49). Jerusalem is the city of the great King. Jesus' use of
royal language such as "throne" and "footstool" to portray God as a
King (Matt 5:34–35) suggests that the great King is not a reference to
David or even the Messiah but to God Himself.[162] Furthermore Jesus'

[160] Maimonides, *Mishneh Torah, Sefer Hafla'ah, Shevuot* 12, *hal.* 3. Translation from J. Lightfoot, *A Commentary on the New Testament from the Talmud and Hebraica* (reprint, Peabody, MA:
Hendrickson, 1989), 2:127.
[161] Other interesting rabbinic texts dealing with invalid oaths include *b. Ned.* 14b, "He who
vows by the Torah has said nothing; but he who vows by what is written in it, his words count."
[162] One must be cautious about driving a wedge between God and the Messiah. Matthew
25:34 uses the title "the king" to describe Jesus as eschatological King who sits on a glorious
throne and judges the nations. A comparison of the two texts shows that Jesus regarded Himself
as divine heavenly King, which clearly asserts Jesus' deity. This text is thus important for understanding the nature of the "kingdom of God" or "kingdom of heaven" which was the central
theme of Jesus' teaching. The "kingdom of God/heaven" is the reign of God in the person of
Jesus. See the discussion above on the nature of the kingdom.

words are an allusion to Ps 48:2, which refers to Jerusalem as the city of the great King. In that text "the city of the great King" parallels "the city of our God" from the preceding verse.[163]

Jesus also prohibited certain oaths because many oath formulas were blasphemous in that they somehow usurped the authority of God. When a person swore by a particular object, he was saying, "May such and such be destroyed if I break my word to you." Thus, when a person swore by heaven and by earth, he was saying, "May heaven and earth be destroyed if I do not keep my word." However, heaven and earth belong to God and only He has the authority to choose to destroy them. Such oaths are comparable to a modern colloquialism that refers to someone "promising the moon." The oath would fail to persuade because everyone knows that the moon does not belong to an individual and is not his to give. To take an oath "by heaven and earth" blasphemously usurps God's position as Lord of heaven and earth.

Someone might object that while some oaths are blasphemous, an oath sworn by the head is not blasphemous, for surely a person has authority over his own head. Nevertheless Jesus disputed even this claim. An oath sworn "by my head" means, "May I be decapitated if I do not keep my word."[164] This seems confirmed by *m. Sanh.* 3:2, in which vows are made "by the life of my head." This would be similar to the modern American oath, "Cross my heart, hope to die, stick a needle in my eye." This is an oath saying, "May my eye be tortured and I be killed if I do not keep my promise." Likewise, swearing by one's head implied that the person has authority over his own life, whether he lives or dies. Jesus insisted that God has absolute authority over our heads, and this is determined by the fact that He alone has creative power over the head. Jesus argued that His disciples must not swear by the head "because you cannot make a single hair white or black." A person cannot make his or her hair grow a different color. God can. The changing hair color in Jesus' illustration is probably because of the aging process.[165] The typical Jew in Jesus' audience had

---

[163] Against D. Duling, "'[Do not Swear . . .] by Jerusalem Because It Is the City of the Great King' (Matt 5:35)," *JBL* 110 (1991): 291–309. Duling argued that "the Great King" was Herod Agrippa I, thereby ruling out the authenticity of the saying.

[164] See also Broadus, *The Gospel According to Matthew*, 116.

[165] Davies and Allison, *A Critical and Exegetical Commentary on the Gospel According to Saint Matthew*, 1:537; Keener, *The Gospel of Matthew*, 194–95. See also Prov 16:31 in which the LXX translated the Hebrew word שׂיבה ("gray-headed") as γῆρας ("old age"). Similarly Prov 20:29

black hair in early adulthood, but his hair turned white as he aged. A young man cannot make his hair grow gray, nor can an old man make his hair grow black (or grow back for that matter!). Try as he might to discover the fountain of youth, even modern man cannot reverse the aging process. A person's inability to make white hair grow dark again demonstrates that he does not have authority over his head. A person's inability to reverse the aging process shows that he or she does not have authority over his or her physical life. Thus to swear by one's head is to usurp God's position as the authority over human life and death. Such oaths are an act of blasphemy. The moral principle on which Jesus based His argument has enormous implications for the Christian understanding of the value of life. Taking human life is a divine prerogative. Without biblical justification (capital punishment, just war, and acts of self-defense), taking another human life is both murderous and blasphemous. Human life must be valued not only because that life is sacred and bears the stamp of the divine image but also because only the Author of life has the prerogative to take human life. This principle influences the Christian view of suicide, abortion, euthanasia, stem-cell research, and human medical experimentation.

Jesus concluded by commanding, "But let your word 'yes' be 'yes,' and your 'no' be 'no'" (Matt 5:37).[166] The words of Jesus' disciples must be consistent with the truth. They must not deny what is in fact true (saying "no" when they should say "yes") or affirm what they know to be untrue (saying "yes" when they should say "no"). Jesus wants His disciples to be people of such integrity that they will be trusted without making an oath. Taking an oath can imply that one is committing himself to a higher standard of honesty than is normal for him. But if one's life is committed to consistent honesty in every statement, insinuation, and implication, oath-taking becomes unnecessary.

Other first-century Jews were concerned by the deceptive abuses of the complex distinctions between oath formulas. According to Josephus,[167] the Essenes avoided oaths except for the oath one took

translates the Hebrew word using πολιά ("old age," a derivative of the Greek word meaning "gray").

[166] Strong evidence exists in support of the view that this saying was widely known in the early church. See D. Wenham, "2 Corinthians 1:17,18: Echo of a Dominical Logion," *NovT* 28 (1986): 271–79.

[167] Josephus, *J.W.* 2.8.6 §135; id., *Ant.* 15.10.4 §§370–71.

when joining the sect.[168] Thus, one could trust the word of the Essene even more than the oath of an ordinary man.[169] Similarly Philo, writing under the influence of Greek moralists and philosophers, stated,

> To swear not at all is the best course and most profitable to life, well-suited to a rational nature which has been taught to speak the truth so well on each occasion that its words are regarded as oaths; to swear truly is only, as people say, a "second-best voyage," for the mere fact of his swearing casts suspicion on the trustworthiness of the man.[170]

Jesus' teaching was more radical than that of His contemporaries since He did not merely advise His followers to refrain from oaths; He commanded them to do so. Furthermore Jesus taught that anything beyond these simple statements of truth was "from the evil one" (v. 37). The Greek words translated "from the evil one" may also be translated "from evil." The text may merely characterize deceptive oaths as influenced by the general principle of evil. Nevertheless in light of the same language used in the model prayer (6:13), this is probably a reference to Satan, as the HCSB translation suggests. Satan is the father of lies (John 8:44), the master of subtlety who can tell half-truths with persuasive power and whose deception led to humanity's downfall (Gen 3:1–7). All acts of deception display Satan's deceptive influence.[171]

Does this mean that oaths are absolutely forbidden under all circumstances? Some Quakers and many Anabaptists forbid the use of any oaths even in a court of law. Although this effort to follow completely Jesus' teaching is commendable, it does not seem that Jesus intended to prohibit all oaths in all circumstances.[172] First, the oath formulas that Jesus' condemned were formulas used in ordinary speech, not the formula employed in court.[173] Second, Jesus Himself testified under oath in Matt 26:63–64. Although He did not voluntarily use an oath, He was placed under oath by the adjuration of the high priest. When placed under oath, He did not refuse to speak; He spoke boldly and truthfully. Those who affirm Jesus' moral perfection recognize that His life was fully consistent with His own moral

---

[168] Josephus, *J.W.* 2.8.7 §§139–42.

[169] Ibid., 2.8.6 §135.

[170] Philo, *Decal.* 84 (F. H. Colson).

[171] For an interesting treatment of the evil nature of oaths that traces the use of oaths through the rest of Matthew, see J. A. Brant, "Infelicitous Oaths in the Gospel of Matthew," *JSNT* 63 (1996): 3–20.

[172] This was recognized by Augustine, *Serm. mont.*, 1.17.51.

[173] Jeremias, *New Testament Theology*, 220.

teaching and that His example serves as the best commentary on His teaching. Since modern legal systems like the ancient Jewish legal system require oaths in certain situations such as testimony in court or in depositions, and since the oath formula utilized in courts today is not inherently blasphemous, legal testimony under oath is not a breech of Jesus' commandment.

Third, even apart from legal settings Jesus ("truly, truly I say to you") and Paul often used special formulas to emphasize the truthfulness of a statement (Rom 1:9; 9:1; 2 Cor 1:23; 11:31; Gal 1:20; Phil 1:8; 1 Thess 2:5; 1 Tim 2:7). However, Paul's practice seems fully consistent with the spirit of Jesus' teaching. Paul did not use a complex system of oath formulas to mask deception, nor did He utilize oath formulas that usurped God's authority or devalued truthfulness in ordinary speech. Furthermore not all oath-taking implies one's dishonesty when not under oath since in very important matters even God may swear an oath (Gen 9:9–11; Ps 16:10 [cp. Acts 2:27–31]; Ezek 33:11; Gen 22:17 [cp. Heb 6:13–18]) even though "it is impossible for God to lie" (Heb 6:18).

In summary Jesus prohibited the use of misleading oaths, but he did not intend to prohibit all use of oaths. Oaths in court, marital vows, oaths of office, and the use of other oaths on solemn occasions to emphasize one's truthfulness comport both with biblical teaching and Christian practice.

Although some groups seem to have pressed Jesus' words too far, others have wrongly dismissed them by relegating Jesus' command to the "old dispensation" or by arguing that they are an appropriate ethic for the millennial kingdom but are impractical for the present time. Jesus' earliest interpreters clearly regarded His command as applicable to disciples in the present. James, the brother of Jesus, commanded the readers of his letter, "Don't brag and deny the truth" (Jas 3:14). He also stressed, "Now above all, my brothers, do not swear, either by heaven or by earth or with any other oath. Your 'yes' must be 'yes,' and your 'no' must be 'no,' so that you won't fall under judgment" (5:12).

Since James was applying Jesus' teaching after His death and resurrection, it cannot be relegated to an old dispensation. Furthermore, although James wrote these words at least two millennia before Jesus' return, he still saw this ethic as authoritative for the present and not merely the future.

Retaliation (Matt 5:38–42)

For a discussion of the introductory formula "You have heard," see the section "Interpreting the Antitheses." Verse 38 directly quotes portions of the law of retribution, also known as the *lex talionis*, that appears in Exod 21:23–25; Lev 24:17–21; and Deut 19:21.[174] Exodus 21:22–25 describes the sentence for accidentally causing personal injury. The law states that fines have to be paid for personal injuries "according to judicial assessment" and then defines the judicial assessment in terms of the *lex talionis*. This implies that the *lex talionis* was a guide to the courts in their judgments and was not intended to guide individuals in exacting revenge.

That Lev 24:20 refers to legal guidelines for the Jewish courts is less clear. However, the discussion follows on the heels of a description of the punishment for blasphemy in which the "whole community" carried out the sentence for the crime. This suggests that the *lex talionis* was intended to guide the community in seeking justice rather prompt individuals to pursue revenge.

Deuteronomy 19:21 applies the *lex talionis* to false witnesses who lie under oath during a trial, falsely accusing an innocent person. The law stated that the false witness was to suffer the same penalty that the wrongly accused person would have suffered if the false testimony had been believed and the innocent person had been condemned. The discussion concluded, "You must not show pity; life for life, eye for eye, tooth for tooth, hand for hand, and foot for foot."[175]

This evidence suggests that the *lex talionis* was intended to prevent the court from being unjustly lenient ("you must not show pity") or unduly harsh in its sentences. The court should not, for example,

---

[174] Many commentators have pointed out that the Code of Hammurabi utilized the *lex talionis* long before the time of Moses. However, they sometimes fail to mention that the Code of Hammurabi applied the principle differently. The *lex talionis* applied only if the social standing of the perpetrator and the victim were equal. Much lesser penalties applied if the victim was inferior to the perpetrator. The Mosaic law, however, applied the principle indiscriminately.

[175] Guelich argued convincingly that Jesus had Deuteronomy 19:16 particularly in mind in His citation of the *lex talionis*. First, the Deuteronomy text was focused on the problem of the false witness who lies under oath, thus forming a connection with the preceding antithesis in the SM (Matt 5:33–37). Second, the Deuteronomy text had significant verbal parallels with Matt 5:39. Deuteronomy 19:18 used the verb ἀνθίστημι to describe the act of accusing one's brother, thus paralleling the use of the same verb in Matt 5:39. Deuteronomy 19:19–20 used τὸν πονηρὸν to speak of the evil that needed to be purged from the congregation of Israel, and Matt 5:39 used the same substantive to identify the opponent of the disciples. Guelich seems to misinterpret Jesus' teaching here though by depending more on Deuteronomy 19 than the context of the statement in the SM to guide his understanding of Matt 5:39a (*The Sermon on the Mount*, 220).

cut off the hand of a beggar for stealing a loaf of bread. The court should exercise a form of justice, however, in which the sentence was appropriate to the crime. Knowledge that the perpetrator of a crime would suffer to the same degree that he caused his victims to suffer would be a powerful deterrent to crime.

Some ancient Jews interpreted the *lex talionis* literally. Around AD 90, Rabbi Eliezer ben Hyrcanus argued that "eye for eye" meant "actual eye for eye" (*b. B. Qam.* 84a). Philo also argued for the literal application of the law.[176] However, Josephus argued that monetary value could be assigned to the destroyed member and monetary compensation could be made in place of the perpetrator's loss of limb if the victim so agreed.[177]

No evidence suggests that Jesus intended to contradict the *lex talionis* of the Mosaic law.[178] Jesus had clearly stated earlier that He did not intend to destroy the Law and the Prophets. In both the preceding and following antitheses, Jesus opposed rabbinic interpretation of the Law rather than the Law itself. Here Jesus opposed the interpretation of the Law that, in this case, distorted the principle of the *lex talionis* by using it to justify personal acts of vengeance. Perhaps in this case, though, the misapplication of the Law was a product of popular rather than rabbinic interpretation, paralleling the confused application of the principle by those who seek to justify acts of personal vengeance today. Clearly the *lex talionis* was not intended to justify revenge.

---

[176] Philo, *Spec. Leg.*, 3.181–204.

[177] Josephus, *Ant.* 4.8.35 §280. See also *b. Ketub.* 32ab.

[178] Although Betz states, "Present New Testament scholarship is in virtual agreement that vs 39a contradicts vs 38b, saying that the SM opposes the Torah with its own command, disavowing retaliation and vengeance, and advocating submission to the evildoer" (*The Sermon on the Mount*, 281), he personally concluded, "The meaning of the controversial command μὴ ἀντιστῆναι ('Do not retaliate') is not to recommend an attitude of resignation and defeatism concerning evil or a principled self-surrender to all kinds of villains. Rather, what is commanded is not non-violence in general but desistance from retaliation in specific instances. The difference is that such desistance is in effect a positive method of fighting evil and helping justice prevail. This method corresponds to the 'intent' of the *ius talionis* and is thus an adequate way to fulfill the Torah prescription" (ibid., 284). Davies and Allison are correct to see that 5.38–42 involves a contradiction between the OT and the NT. While in the Pentateuch the *lex talionis* belongs to the judiciary process, this is not the sphere of application in Matthew. Jesus, to repeat, does not overthrow the principle of equivalent compensation on an institutional level—that question is just not addressed—but declares it illegitimate for his followers to apply it to their private disputes." They later added, "Unlike many modern scholars, our author would never have affirmed that Jesus' words 'overthrow' or 'contradict' the Torah" (*A Critical and Exegetical Commentary on the Gospel According to Saint Matthew*, 1:542). See also Gundry, *Matthew*, 94.

Revenge was explicitly prohibited by Lev 19:18: "Do not take revenge or bear a grudge against members of your community, but love your neighbor as yourself."

Scholars debate the meaning of every element of the command, "Don't resist an evildoer." The sense of the verb "resist" (*anthistēmi*) is particularly important for an understanding of this passage. Unfortunately, the verb is capable of several different meanings. The verb generally means "to oppose someone or something in some way." Most of the uses in the OT refer to violent opposition, particularly armed conflict.[179] Several interpreters view Jesus' prohibition of resistance as a prohibition of judicial action in which a victim defends his rights in a court of law. Guelich argued that the presence of the Greek term translated "resist" in Deut 19:18, the passage from which Jesus apparently drew the *lex talionis*, requires Jesus' usage of the term to match that of the OT passage. Thus "resist" means "prosecute in a court of law."[180]

To the contrary, the words "the evil" also appear in both texts but mean one thing in the SM and something else in Deut 19:19-20. The HCSB, along with the NASB, NIV, NLT, and NRSV, recognizes that the text in Deuteronomy refers to an evil act, but in Matt 5:39a the term refers to an evil person. Also the distinction in the meaning of *ho ponēros* ("the evil") demonstrates that *anthistēmi* does not necessarily have the same meaning in both texts. Furthermore only eight out of 85 occurrences of the verb mean "to prosecute" or "to challenge legally."[181] Since the illustrations that Jesus offered in Matt 5:39b-41 relate to both violent actions and legal challenges, it seems unwarranted to narrow the sense of the verb to either violent action

[179] Josephus used the verb to speak of enemies at war (*Ag. Ap.* 2:23). The NT occurrences refer mostly to verbal protest (Luke 21:15; Acts 6:10; 13:8; Gal 2:11; 2 Tim 3:8). However, nearly as often, the verb describes the believer's opposition to Satan (Eph 6:13; Jas 4:7; 1 Pet 5:9). Ephesians 6:13 uses the imagery of warfare to describe this opposition.

[180] Guelich, *The Sermon on the Mount*, 220. See also Daube, *New Testament and Rabbinic Judaism*, 259. Daube translated the verb "do not prosecute the wicked man." Davies and Allison entertain this possibility (*A Critical and Exegetical Commentary on the Gospel According to Saint Matthew*, 1:543). For a detailed defense of the view, see S. Currie, "Matthew 5:39a—Resistance or Protest," *HTR* 57 (1964): 140–45. Blomberg notes that the verb was often used in legal contexts and suggests that the verb should be interpreted in this way here. He sees Jesus' prohibition as a parallel to the 1 Cor 6:7 prohibition of taking a fellow believer to court (*Matthew*, 113). It is unlikely, however, that either Jesus or Matthew would refer to a believer as "an evil person." In Matt 7:11 the adjective "evil" seems to apply to sinful humanity in general as opposed to holy Deity rather than to Jesus' disciples specifically. Describing Jesus' disciples as "evil" would be inconsistent with the hunger for righteousness and purity of heart attributed to Jesus' disciples earlier in the sermon (5:6,8).

[181] Deut 19:18; Job 9:19; 41:11; Isa 3:9; 50:8; 59:12; Jer 49:19; and 50:44.

or legal procedures. Apparently Jesus had both in mind. The broader
translation in the HCSB is a good one. The verb refers to all retaliatory
actions, violent, verbal, or legal.[182]

Jesus' words prohibit His disciples from viewing any person as
a personal enemy. Jesus' followers must regard all people, even evil
people, as "neighbors" and relate to them lovingly rather than hate-
fully. Jesus' followers are to endure abuses graciously and to refuse to
seek revenge. The intent of the prohibition becomes especially clear
through a comparison with the Lucan parallel (Luke 6:27–36) and in
light of Paul's commentary on the text in Rom 12:9–21 and 1 Thess
5:15.

"Evil" may refer to evil as a principle, a specific evil deed, an evil
person, or even the ultimate evil figure, Satan himself (Matt 5:37,45;
6:13; 13:19). Most interpreters recognize the adjective here as a reference to an evil person.[183] Although "the evil one" refers to Satan
repeatedly in Matthew's Gospel (Matt 5:37; 6:13; 13:19), the NT repeatedly commands Jesus' followers to resist Satan (Eph 6:13; Jas
4:7; 1 Pet 5:9). The NT also commands believers to "detest evil" and
"conquer evil" (Rom 12:9,21). Furthermore in the immediate context
the adjective refers to evil people whom God graciously blesses (Matt
5:45) and whom Jesus' followers must graciously bless. Thus Jesus
prohibited His followers from seeking vengeance against an evil person who mistreats them through an act of violence, a legal challenge,
or political oppression.

Some interpreters have argued that the word translated "the evildoer" (tō ponērō) means "in an evil manner" or "by evil means." Clar-
ence Jordan writes:

> The Greek for evil can mean either "by evil means" or "the evil person." Ei-
> ther translation is equally good according to Greek grammar; the decision
> must come from the context. The context is that Jesus repeatedly confronts

---

[182] Some scholars fail to see that the prohibition relates specifically to acts of personal retaliation and wrongly assume that the text demands complete nonresistance. However, some admit
that such a radical view only results in Jesus' teaching being ignored (G. Mavrodes, "The Hard-
est Verses in the Bible," *RJ* 36 [1986]: 12–14).

[183] Davies and Allison, *A Critical and Exegetical Commentary on the Gospel According to Saint
Matthew*, 1:543; and France, *The Gospel of Matthew*, 220. Luz takes the adjective as "neutral," a
reference to "evil" rather than an "evil person" based on Matthew's normal usage (*Matthew: A
Commentary*, 1:276). However this is unlikely in this context. The three illustrations that follow
all show that persons are in view. Hagner sees the adjective as a reference to an evil deed since it
possesses the definite article (*Matthew 1–13*, 1:131).

evil, but never by evil means, and never by means of revengeful violence. Therefore, the context favors the instrumental "do not resist by evil means."[184]

Although the dative case can be used in Greek to specify the means by which an action is performed, this usage is unlikely here. With the verb "resist" (*anthistēmi*) writers consistently used the dative case to mark the direct object. Thus one naturally expects the dative substantive here to indicate the person or object opposed. Since the dative marks the direct object of this particular verb, writers tended to indicate means through the use of prepositional phrases rather than bare datives in order to avoid confusion.[185] Although the verb appears 86 times in the LXX, not once does an accompanying dative noun indicate the means of resistance. Thus the translation "evildoer" in the HCSB is correct.

Jesus first applied this general ethical principle to the disciple's response to a violent insult. A slap on the right cheek was particularly painful and insulting. Since most first-century Jews were right-handed and thus would strike with their right hand, a slap on the right cheek was a back-handed slap. A back-handed slap was more painful and injurious than being slapped with the open palm. This type of slap was particularly insulting to the victim's honor, and the rabbis taught that it deserved a fine double the normal amount.[186] Some conclude from this that Jesus referred to a slap that was far more insulting than injurious.[187] This conclusion is unsupported by the evidence. Matthew's word "slap" (*hrapizō*) is the same used when soldiers blindfolded Jesus, spat in His face, beat Him with their fists, slapped Him, and then said, "Prophesy to us, Messiah! Who hit You?" (26:67–68).[188] Furthermore the parallel in Luke 6:29 used the term

---

[184] C. Jordan, *The Substance of Faith and Other Cotton Patch Sermons*, ed. Dallas Lee (New York: Association, 1972), 69, quoted in Stassen and Gushee, *Kingdom Ethics*, 138. Hagner argued that τῷ πονηρῷ refers to the evil deed against which disciples are not to retaliate (*Matthew 1–13*, 130–31).

[185] Wisdom 10:16 indicated the means of retaliation or resistance with the preposition ἐν. First Maccabees 6.4 indicates the means of resistance with the preposition εἰς. First Peter 5:9 indicated the means of resistance using the nominative case (and an implied participle).

[186] "If he slapped him he must pay him 200 zuz. If he struck him with the back of his hand he must pay him 400 zuz. If he tore his ear, plucked his hair, spat and his spittle touched him, or pulled his cloak from off him, or loosed a woman's hair in the street, he must pay 400 zuz. This is the general rule: all is in accordance with a person's honour," *m. B. Kam.* 8:6 (Danby).

[187] France, *The Gospel of Matthew*, 220.

[188] D. C. Allison Jr. appealed to verbal links between this text of Isa 50:6–9 to suggest that Matthew wanted his readers to reflect on how Jesus fulfilled His own teaching in the passion

tuptō which means "to strike a blow," "to assault," or even "to wound" and clearly describes a violent act causing pain and possible injury. The verb "slap" in both Matt 5:39 and 26:67 is a derivative of the Greek word for "rod" and originally meant "to strike with a rod or club." Although the verb was consistently used in the NT of slapping with an empty hand, the earlier history of the word implies that the slap was injurious as well as insulting.

Jesus commanded His followers to respond to the slap on the right cheek by exposing the other (left) cheek. This willingness to endure further insult and abuse shows the strength of the disciple's resolve not to retaliate. Jesus Himself was the perfect model of this gracious response to the abuses of others. He was mocked, spat on, beaten with sticks, slapped, scourged, and nailed to a cross. Nevertheless He endured this all without retaliation and even with forgiveness on His lips. Never is the disciple more like the Savior than when he responds to abuses graciously and without retaliation.

Having said this, several qualifications are necessary. First, Jesus' command prohibits acts of retaliation and revenge inspired by anger and resentment, not defensive or evasive action necessary to protect oneself or others from serious harm. Jesus was no hypocrite who taught one thing but practiced something entirely different. He lived by His own teaching so consistently that His example provides the best commentary on how to apply His teaching. From the example of Jesus Himself, "turning the cheek" is to be understood as a figure for enduring abuse without seeking revenge. John 18:22–23 shows that when Jesus was slapped, rather than suffering silently or inviting further abuse, He protested the injustice of the beating.[189] Rather than responding with quiet absolute pacifism, Jesus defended Himself verbally. He repeatedly withdrew from particular areas in order to avoid being a victim of violence (Mark 9:30–31; Luke 4:30; John 7:1,10; 10:39). Evasive action and nonretaliatory acts of self-defense were consistent with Jesus' teaching. Calvin aptly commented,

> The law is not confined to outward works, as long as you read it with intel-
> ligence. I grant that Christ holds back our hands from revenge, just as much

("Anticipating the Passion: The Literary Reach of Matthew 26:47–27:56," *CBQ* 56 [1994]: 701–14, esp. 703–5).
    [189] Similarly in Acts 23:3 when the high priest ordered Paul to be struck, he protested, "God is going to strike you, you whitewashed wall! You are sitting there judging me according to the law, and in violation of the law are you ordering me to be struck?"

as our minds, but where a man may, without taking revenge, protect himself and his own from injuries, Christ's words do not stop him from peaceably and non-violently deflecting the force as it runs onto him.[190]

Second, the blow Jesus commanded His disciples to endure graciously was painful and insulting but not likely to cause permanent harm or be life-threatening. Jesus could have chosen many forms of attack to illustrate His point. Of significance is the fact that He did not say, "If someone strikes you with a sword on the right cheek," or "If someone pierces you with a spear on the right side . . ." or "If someone pummels your nose with his fist . . ." The *lex talionis* quoted in Matt 5:38 related to the loss of an eye or tooth. In light of that preceding context, it is surely significant that Jesus did not say, "If someone gouges out your right eye, offer them the other also," or "If someone knocks out one of your right teeth, offer them the left."[191] The shift from a discussion of acts that have the potential to kill or maim to a discussion of a mere slap is intentional and significant. The shift implies that a person may do what is necessary to defend himself in the case of a life-threatening or potentially dangerous attack.

Matthew may have purposefully adapted an originally simpler version of this statement, like the statement in Luke 6:29, in order to prevent his readers from affirming a form of pacifism that prohibits defending one's life or warding off serious personal injury. In Matthew's form of the saying, one first suffers a more severe blow (a backhanded slap on the right cheek) and then braces for a less severe blow (a slap with the open palm on the left cheek). The disciple's gracious response seems to defuse the conflict so that the second anticipated blow is milder than the first. Matthew's clarification of Jesus' teaching seems intended to demonstrate that if an attack is escalating, another course of action may be necessary.

The principle of love and other declarations of Scripture require further qualifications. Turning the other cheek does not preclude prosecuting those who have harmed someone if the legal action is properly motivated. Victims of violent crimes should press charges against the one who assaulted them. This is necessary for the public good in order to prevent others from being victimized. Still the victim must seek to purge his or her heart of malice and quench the longing

[190] Calvin, *A Harmony of the Gospels*, 1:194.
[191] As Nolland said, "We do not seem to be operating at the level of the kind of permanent damage envisaged in the texts alluded to in v. 38" (*The Gospel of Matthew*, 258).

for a vendetta. Later Matthew 18 and 1 Corinthians 5 show that the most loving response to sinful behavior is to hold a person accountable for that behavior.[192]

After describing the disciples' response to violent insult, Jesus now described the appropriate response to a legal attack. Matthew described the opponent as one who "wants to sue" rather than one who has already brought suit to court. In the Lucan parallel (Luke 6:29) the opponent is already in the process of taking the disciple's property (*tou airontos sou to himation*). The presence of the verb "wants" in Matt 5:40 suggests that Matthew saw a connection between this text and verses 25–26 in which Jesus commanded His disciples to seek reconciliation with a legal opponent quickly before the case actually went before the judges since the judges were certain to respond with a harsh sentence. In that scenario the disciple had truly wronged the accuser. That seems to be the case here as well.[193]

Other evidence supports the view that the suit was legitimate. Frivolous legal suits were probably rare in the first-century Jewish world. According to the Mishnah, cases concerning property, including cases related to loans, inheritances, sales, and boundary disputes, were to be decided by a committee of three. The three judges were not professional judges but were peers of the disputants. Each of the two disputants chose one committee member and the two disputants had to agree together on the third. The third judge, whom both disputants recognized as honorable, fair, and wise, could break a tie between the other two committee members. Relatives, friends, and enemies were ineligible to serve as a judge. After hearing witnesses, the appointed judges decided how legally and fairly to settle the dispute. The judges delivered their verdict as a group and were required to conceal the specific results of the vote, that is, who voted pro or con (*m. Sanh.* 3). Frivolous suits were not likely to succeed under these conditions. So Jesus was describing a situation in which an opponent was planning a legitimate suit that would likely result in acquiring the disciple's inner garment.

---

[192] For an argument for the consistency of Jesus' teaching with the *lex talionis*, just war, and judicial retribution, see D. Charles, "'Do Not Suppose that I Have Come': The Ethic of the Sermon on the Mount Reconsidered," *SwJT* 46 (2004): 47–70. For the view that each of Jesus' illustrations commanded forms of nonviolent protest, see W. Wink, "Beyond Just War and Pacifism: Jesus' Nonviolent Way," *RevExp* 89 (1992): 197–214.

[193] Nolland stated, "We have no reason to doubt that the indebtedness implied is genuine: the plaintiff has a good case" (*The Gospel of Matthew*, 259).

Ordinarily a defendant in such a suit would be angry that he was forced to turn property over to the one who brought the suit. He would give what the judges required him to give and nothing more. Jesus, however, commanded His disciples to seek reconciliation with their opponent by going beyond what the law required in order to make amends with the plaintiff.

Jewish law permitted an opponent to sue for possession of an individual's inner garment. The "shirt" (*chitōna*) was a long or half-sleeved tunic that extended to the ankles and was made of either wool or linen. These garments could be quite valuable and were frequently used for bartering or making payments in the ancient world. The "coat" (*himation*) was an outer robe or wrap. It was both the most visible and most essential piece of clothing. The garment was necessary for warmth and also served as a blanket under which the poor slept. Because of its value and necessity, it often served as a pledge. However, the OT twice states that the coat cannot be kept as a pledge overnight (Exod 22:26–27; Deut 24:12–13). Based on these OT texts, Jewish law insisted that the coat was exempt from seizure by the courts (*m. B. Qam.* 8:6). Jesus thus commanded His disciples to make amends with an opponent at law by paying more than the court required, even to the point of yielding what the law protected.

Many commentators argue that Jesus' command is clear hyperbole, intentional exaggeration for the sake of making a point.[194] They argue that Jesus could not possibly have expected His disciples to fulfill His command literally since doing so would leave the disciple without either inner or outer garment. Surely Jesus did not approve of public nudity![195]

Despite the popularity of this interpretation, the evidence for hyperbole here is not as strong as many imply. First, many ancient people, including OT Jews, had more than one suit of clothes (Gen 24:53; 27:15; 35:2; 41:14; 45:22; Lev 6:11; Josh 9:5,13; 1 Sam 28:8; 2 Sam 12:20; 2 Kgs 7:15; Ezek 16:16; Jas 5:2). Many ancient Jews had various outfits suited for particular occasions such as mourning garments and festal garments (2 Sam 14:2; 2 Kgs 5:22; Isa 52:1). Second,

---

[194] Davies and Allison, *A Critical and Exegetical Commentary on the Gospel According to Saint Matthew*, 1:545; Luz, *Matthew: A Commentary*, 1:272; Nolland, *The Gospel of Matthew*, 259.

[195] Davies and Allison quipped: "The literal observance of Mt 5.40 would land one in prison for exposure" (*A Critical and Exegetical Commentary on the Gospel According to Saint Matthew*, 1:545). Keener called the example "a shockingly graphic, almost humorous, illustration" (*The Gospel of Matthew*, 198).

even if an individual had only one outfit of clothes, some rabbis argued that the garments could be seized and replaced with garments of lesser value in order to fulfill legal obligations.[196] Fulfilling Jesus' command would not necessarily leave His disciples unclothed. At worst, it would leave them poorly clothed. Thus the command should not be dismissed as mere hyperbole.

The command teaches that rather than retaliating against an opponent, Jesus' disciples should pay what is fair and would be required by the court plus an additional amount that seeks to make amends for mistakes and earns the respect of the opponent. Jesus' teaching seems to assume something like the following scenario. A disciple was overdue on a debt for ten denarii and his creditor planned to sue him for his shirt even though it was worth only eight denarii since the debtor's more valuable coat was protected from seizure. The disciple should forfeit the right to retain his coat and wear less expensive garments in order to relate to his creditor fairly and in a manner that prompted reconciliation.

Jesus also urged His disciples to refuse to retaliate against abuse of authority. Because the Roman government could not supply all the resources needed for its troops, Roman soldiers often requisitioned necessary supplies or seized beasts of burden from the local residents.[197] They also had the legal authority to force residents of subjugated lands to perform menial tasks. Matthew 27:32 provides an example of this by mentioning that Simon of Cyrene was "compelled" (angareuō) to carry Jesus' cross after Jesus' loss of blood so weakened Him that He crumbled beneath its weight. Requisition of supplies and labor by the Roman soldiers sometimes exceeded the bounds of the law. A letter written in AD 19 by Germanicus, the adopted son of Tiberius, scolded subordinates for unnecessarily requisitioning boats, animals, and residences for Germanicus's tour of Egypt. Germanicus ordered that money be paid those inconvenienced by legitimate requisitions

[196] b. B. Meṣiʿa. 113b stated, "R. Ishmael and R. Akiba: For we learnt: If one was a debtor for a thousand zuz, and wore a robe a hundred manehs in value, he is stripped thereof and robed with a garment that is fitting for him. But therein a Tanna taught with the authority of R. Ishmael and R. Akiba: All Israel are worthy of that robe." The text suggests that before the time of Ishmael and Akiba, creditors were permitted to exchange garments with debtors in order to diminish the debt. This would probably have been the policy during Jesus' lifetime.

[197] For references to primary and secondary sources, see Keener, The Gospel of Matthew, 199–200. See Digest 50.4.18.4; 50.5.10.2–3; 50.5.11; Theodosius, Cod. Theod. 8; and Sall. Jug. 75.4. Epictetus, Diss. 4.1.79 and m. B. Meṣiʿa 6.3 seem to imply that the army was not obligated to return beasts of burden and they were permanently lost to the owner.

and insisted that "the forcible seizure of beasts of burden as they are encountered traversing the city is hereby forbidden, for that is nothing but an act of self-evident robbery."[198] Ordinary soldiers lacked the authority to requisition property or compel labor and were specifically prohibited from doing so in order to prevent abuse of local residents. Some emperors insisted that they alone were authorized to require requisitions or compulsory service. However, requisition was exercised by soldiers so freely that the emperor's own beasts of burden had to wear bronze tags identifying them as Caesar's property and thus not subject to impressments.[199] Abuses of this privilege not only grieved subjugated peoples but also irritated the Roman senate.[200]

Requisitioning and impressment predated the Roman rule. Josephus mentioned that the Syrians under Demetrius II requisitioned the Jews' beasts of burden.[201] The Romans, however, exceeded the Syrian practice by forcing oppressed people to serve as beasts of burden. Such oppressive measures must have been reminiscent of Israel's bondage in Egypt and were deeply resented especially on Israel's soil. The Palestinian Talmud speaks of Romans forcing Jews to carry burdens on the Sabbath, an offense not only to their dignity but also to their consciences, during the oppressive rule of the Emperor Hadrian (AD 117–138).[202]

The word "mile" which Jesus used here was originally a Latin term meaning "one thousand paces." The use of the Latin term is a clue that Jesus had the much-resented Roman practice of compulsion in mind. Although it is commonly assumed that a Roman soldier could compel a person to carry a burden for only one mile, no ancient texts support that theory. The written warrants that were given to the soldiers by a superior to authorize impressments designated the distance a beast of burden or labor could be forced to travel. Warrants probably limited impressments to a distance of one mile in order to prevent the resentment of the subjugated people from boiling up into full rebellion. Soldiers who forced labor without proper authorization

[198] N. Lewis, *Life in Egypt under Roman Rule* (Oxford: Oxford University Press, 1985), 173.
[199] For the full text of one of these bronze tags recently discovered in Egypt, see ibid.
[200] See Livy 43.7.11; 43.8.1–10; Apuleius, *Metam.* 9.39.
[201] Josephus, *Ant.* 13.52.
[202] p. Ḥag. 2:1. See S. R. Llewelyn, *New Documents Illustrating Early Christianity*, vol. 7 of *A Review of the Greek Inscriptions and Papyri Published in 1982–83* (Sydney, NSW: Macquarie University, 1994), 85–87, for a list of rabbinic texts and measures taken to curtail abuse of the Roman system.

may have limited the impressment to one mile for more pragmatic reasons. An impressed person was probably forced to carry a heavy load that quickly exhausted him after one mile or so and required the soldier to find a different bearer.

Jesus commanded His disciples to exceed the distance commanded or expected by the soldier. The disciple would carry the soldier's pack or crate out of obligation for the first mile. He should carry it the second mile out of compassion and a humble desire to serve.

Jesus' words provide a powerful example of the disciples' refusal to retaliate. Many of Jesus' contemporaries were furious at the Romans, and Palestine was on the brink of rebellion. When Rome turned Judea into a province ruled by a procurator and Roman troops in AD 6, Judas the Galilean led a brief resistance movement. Judas's descendants, known as the *sicarii*, would continue to resist Roman rule. The sicarii became stealthy urban terrorists who would assassinate Roman officials in a crowd and quickly slip away unnoticed. By the early 60s the sicarii made the streets of Jerusalem wet with Roman blood and stirred the revolt that would lead to the destruction of Jerusalem in AD 70. Even during the time of Christ, the oppressive leadership of Pontius Pilate incited several popular insurrections.[203] Although many voices were calling for the blood of the Roman oppressors, Jesus commanded His disciples to serve those oppressors lovingly and patiently.

Jesus then applied the principle "Do not retaliate" to His disciples' acts of charity. "Give to the one who asks you, and don't turn away from the one who wants to borrow from you" (5:41). The OT and other ancient Jewish literature abound with commands to assist the poor (Exod 22:25; Lev 25:36–37; Deut 15:7–11; Prov 28:27; Sir 4:1–10; 29:1–2; Tob 4:7; *T. Job* 9:1–12:4; *T. Zeb.* 7:2; Luke 6:30).

Jesus' original readers would have recognized that the person who approached the disciple with a request had needs that were legitimate and probably desperate. Leviticus 25:35 commanded charitable giving "if your brother becomes destitute and cannot sustain himself among you." The person who asked for a gift or loan in Matt 5:42 was presumably destitute as well. Most who made requests for financial help did so out of legitimate need. It was deemed so shameful to beg that some Jews preferred death to begging.[204]

---

[203] See D. Rhoads, "Zealots," in *ABD*, 6:1047.
[204] See Keener, *The Gospel of Matthew*, 201, n. 120.

Neither the OT nor the NT required Jesus' followers to finan-cially support the slothful, lazy, or those who waste their resources irresponsibly. Paul, who was familiar with the contents of the SM, rebuked those who expected to live on the church's charitable gifts without working at all. In 1 Thess 5:15 he summarized the content of the fifth and sixth antitheses of the SM immediately after a command to "warn those who are irresponsible" (v. 14). He later instructed the same Christian fellowship: "If anyone isn't willing to work, he should not eat" (2 Thess 3:10). Qualifications such as this make it unlikely that Jesus was commanding indiscriminate charitable giving to those who had no need and wished to live luxuriously at another's expense.

These observations are very important. Many interpreters assume that Jesus demanded that His followers "surrender one's possessions to whoever requests them."[205] They then argue that the teaching must be "rhetorical overstatement" since true obedience to this com-mand would "leave the giver a beggar."[206] However, when interpret-ed in its context, Jesus' teaching, though difficult, is not completely impractical.

The primary point of Matt 5:42 is that charitable giving should not be a means of rewarding those who flatter the giver or of retaliat-ing against those who have harmed him. Many commentators argue that this verse is unrelated to the preceding verses and has nothing to do with the command not to retaliate.[207] However, no compelling rea-son exists for disjointing this verse from its context.[208] At least some Jewish teachers argued that one should grant charitable gifts only to the godly and righteous, not to sinners or to enemies who might use the gifts to gain an advantage over the giver. For example, a Pharisee writing from Jerusalem in the second century BC advised:

> Give to the devout, but do not help the sinner. Do good to the humble, but
> do not give to the ungodly; hold back their bread, and do not give it to them,
> for by means of it they might subdue you; then you will receive twice as
> much evil for all the good you have done to them. For the Most High also
> hates sinners and will inflict punishment on the ungodly. Give to the one who
> is good, but do not help the sinner. (Sir 12:1–7, NRSV)

[205] Ibid., 201.

[206] Ibid.

[207] Davies and Allison suggest that the saying "was originally no doubt isolated. It does not really fit its present context well, which is about revenge and love of enemies" (*A Critical and Exegetical Commentary on the Gospel According to Saint Matthew*, 1:547).

[208] Broadus, *The Gospel According to Matthew*, 120.

The Jewish teacher argued that if one gave bread to an enemy, the act of charity might only empower the enemy to overcome the giver. Thus one was exempt from the laws of charity when an enemy was in need.

The next two verses in this quotation show that enemies delighted in kicking their opponents when they were down. "A friend is not known in prosperity, nor is an enemy hidden in adversity. One's enemies are friendly when one prospers, but in adversity even one's friend disappears" (Sir 12:8–9).

The warning that an enemy was not hidden in adversity means that enemies might retaliate against their foes in a passive-aggressive manner rather than an active one. Rather than attacking their opponent, they might simply wait until he was in trouble or in need and then callously refuse help. "You want help from me?" they might ask sarcastically. "You have got to be kidding."

Although withholding aid from an enemy was acceptable and even wise in the minds of some Jewish ethicists, Jesus condemned even passive-aggressive expressions of retaliation. He insisted that His disciples should view an enemy's adversity, not as an opportunity to rub salt in his wounds or kick him while he is down but to express love and generosity. Paul taught the same principle in Rom 12:20 through an appeal to Prov 25:21–22: "If your enemy is hungry, give him food to eat, and if he is thirsty, give him water to drink."

Hate (Matt 5:43–48)

For a discussion of the introductory formula, see the section "Interpreting the Antitheses." This commentary argued earlier that the so-called antitheses contrast Jesus' teaching, not with the OT itself, but with rabbinic or popular interpretations that distorted the OT message. Never is this more obvious than with this antithesis. The words "Love your neighbor" (v. 43) are thoroughly biblical. These words are a verbatim quotation of Leviticus 19:18 from the LXX. But the quotation did not include the phrase "as yourself." This subtle revision transformed a command about *how* God's people are to love into a command focusing on *whom* they are to love.[209] The command "hate your enemy" simply does not appear anywhere in the OT.[210] Evidently

[209] Nolland, *The Gospel of Matthew*, 264.
[210] The closest parallels in the Pentateuch are Deut 7:2; 20:16; 23:4,7; 30:7.

some of Jesus' contemporaries argued that the command to focus one's love specifically on his neighbor also implied the inverse, that is, one was to hate all who were not his neighbor.[211] The grammar of the Greek expression "hate your enemy" mimics that of the OT commands and suggests that some Jewish teachers viewed the inverse of the divine command as having the same authority as the divine command itself.[212]

This interpretation seems to have been affirmed by the Essenes of the Qumran community. The Community Rule from the Dead Sea Scrolls repeatedly commands members of the community to "hate the children of darkness" (1QS 1.3–4; 9.16,21–22). Josephus also mentioned that the Essenes were required to take "an oath that causes one to shudder" which consisted of a vow to "always hate the wicked and assist the righteous."[213] Some later Jewish interpreters agreed with the Essene interpretation.

Although the term "enemy" is broad enough to refer to any hostile or estranged person,[214] most Jews probably applied this statement primarily at a national level.[215] The specific reference to "Gentiles" greeting only their brothers (fellow Gentiles) seems to imply that the national sense of enemy was at least partially in mind here. Thus neighbors were fellow Jews and enemies were Gentiles.

The medieval scholar Maimonides commented on Lev 19:18 by saying, "He is thy neighbor if he is good, but not if he is wicked, as it is written (Prov. 8:13), the fear of the Lord is to hate evil."[216] He also interpreted this and similar commands in nationalistic terms. Maimonides argued that although Jews should not seek to kill Gentiles with whom Israel was not at war, they should not intervene to save the life of a Gentile:

[211] For several theories regarding the origin of the command, see M. Smith, "Hate Your Enemy," *HTR* 45 (1952): 71–73.

[212] The words "love your neighbor" (ἀγαπήσεις τὸν πλησίον σου) are a verbatim quotation of the LXX of Deut 19:18, which uses the imperatival future rather than an imperative. The command "hate your enemy" (μισήσεις τὸν ἐχθρόν σου) imitates the LXX by using the imperatival future rather than the imperative form that Jesus typically used to express His own commands (Matt 5:44). This grammatical form made the command sound scriptural much like echoing King James grammar ("thou shalt not") might give a biblical ring to a command or prohibition today.

[213] Josephus, *J.W.* 2.8.7 §139.

[214] Nolland, *The Gospel of Matthew*, 264.

[215] Davies and Allison, *A Critical and Exegetical Commentary on the Gospel According to Saint Matthew*, 1: 550; France, *The Gospel of Matthew*, 223–24; Hagner, *Matthew 1–13*, 134.

[216] Quoted in Smith, "Hate Your Enemy," 72.

But as to the Gentiles, with whom we have no war, and likewise to the shepherds of smaller cattle, and others of that sort, they do not so plot their death;
but it is forbidden them to deliver them from death if they are in danger of it.
For instance, "A Jew sees one of them fallen into the sea; let him by no means
lift him out thence: for it is written, 'Thou shalt not rise up against the blood
of thy neighbor;' but this is not thy neighbor."[217]

The tendency of many of the ancient Jews to love only fellow Jews was
noticed by Roman writers. Tacitus and Juvenal both inferred from the
behavior of Jews that they had observed that hatred of non-Jews was
an essential part of the Jewish religion.[218]

The argument that Maimonides cites applies the same narrow and
exclusive definition of the word "neighbor" to interpret Lev 19:18
that many of Jesus' contemporaries likely applied. Jesus was correct
to reject this interpretation for it clearly departs from the intention of
the OT text. First, although Lev 19:18 addresses one's obligation to
love his neighbor, the reference to the neighbor was motivated by the
concerns of the immediate context which discussed the relationships
between members of the congregation of Israel (Lev 19:9–19) rather
than a desire to restrict the love commandment to one's neighbor.
Leviticus 19:11 says, "You must not steal. You must not act decep-
tively or lie to one another." However, this did not mean that Israelites
were only obligated to be honest with other Israelites since Exodus
20 gives similar commands without any restrictions. Similarly, Lev
19:15 says, "You must not act unjustly when rendering judgment. Do
not be partial to the poor or give preference to the rich; judge your
neighbor fairly." However, this did not mean that non-Israelites were
to be unfairly treated by the courts simply because they were poor.
This would clearly contradict Lev 19:10 which says that remnants of
a harvest were to be left in the fields and vineyards "for the poor and
the foreign resident" and demonstrates divine compassion for Jews
and non-Jews alike.

Second, Leviticus 19 explicitly applies the love command to foreigners as well as native-born Israelites. Leviticus 19:33–34 states,
"When a foreigner lives with you in your land, you must not op-
press him. You must regard the foreigner who lives with you as the

---

[217] Maimonides, *Mishneh Torah, Rotseah uShmirat Nefesh*, 4 hal. 11 (J. Lightfoot, *A Commentary on the New Testament from the Talmud and Hebraica* [Grand Rapids: Baker, 1979], 3:107).
[218] Tacitus, *Hist.* 5.5; Juvenal, *Sat.* 14.102.

native-born among you. You are to love him as yourself, for you were foreigners in the land of Egypt; I am the LORD your God."

The words, "You are to love him as yourself," closely parallel Lev 19:18 and show that God expected his people to love indiscriminately, to focus their love both on their neighbors (fellow Jews) and foreigners (non-Jews).[219]

Third, other OT texts specifically command God's people to express love for their enemies. "If you come across your enemy's stray ox or donkey, you must return it to him. If you see the donkey of someone who hates you lying helpless under its load, and you want to refrain from helping it, you must help with it" (Exod 23:4–5). Stott observed that this command was virtually identical to the instruction regarding a brother's ox or donkey in Deut 22:1–4. The similarity between the commands shows that God intends for His people to show the same love to both friend and foe.[220]

Fourth, even if hearers might restrict the commandment to one's neighbor, Jesus argued that the word *neighbor* had been too narrowly defined by His contemporaries. Although many first-century Jews recognized only other Israelites with whom they were in good relations as neighbors, Jesus argued that even hated Samaritans were also one's neighbors (Luke 10:27–37).

Jesus countered the popular rabbinic interpretation of Lev 19:18 by saying, "But I tell you, love your enemies" (Matt 5:44).[221] The command "love" is a present imperative which, in this context, demands either a continuous or habitual action. Thus Jesus' disciples are to keep on loving their enemies. They are to love them with an undying love that does not wane or grow cold in the face of their enemies' abuses.

In the context of the SM, the "enemy" is not merely an individual with whom the disciple has a personality conflict or a citizen of another country with which he is at war. The enemy is rather the one who persecutes the Christian disciple as an expression of his hatred for the Christian's faith and his God.[222] This motivation was made

---

[219] Many of the rabbis argued that this passage applied only to Jewish proselytes. See Strack and Billerbeck, *Kommentar zum Neuen Testament aus Talmud and Midrasch*, 3.280.

[220] Stott, *The Message of the Sermon on the Mount*, 116.

[221] For the views of how one should relate to an enemy in antiquity, see M. Reiser, "Love of Enemies in the Context of Antiquity," *NTS* 47 (2001): 411–27.

[222] See Davies and Allison, *A Critical and Exegetical Commentary on the Gospel According to Saint Matthew*, 1:551. Luz (*Matthew: A Commentary*, 286) correctly notes that this command

clear by Christ in 5:11 when He spoke of those who persecute His disciples "because of Me." This enemy is further described in verse 45 as an "evil" and an "unrighteous" person. The enemy is one who is diametrically opposed to all that the disciple believes, stands for, and holds precious: his faith, his moral convictions, and his Lord.

One way in which the disciple can express love to his enemy is by praying for his persecutors. Many of Jesus' contemporaries made frequent mention of their enemies in their prayers. But rather than praying for them, they prayed against them. Their prayers were imprecatory prayers that called on God to curse the enemy, not bless him. Some such prayers appear in the OT itself. "May my adversaries be disgraced and destroyed; may those who seek my harm be covered with disgrace and humiliation" (Ps 71:13). "Add guilt to their guilt; do not let them share in Your righteousness. Let them be erased from the book of life and not be recorded with the righteous" (Ps 69:27–28).

The parallel to Jesus' command in Luke 6:27–28 says, "Love your enemies, do good to those who hate you, bless those who curse you, pray for those who mistreat you." Jesus called for His disciples to bless rather than curse their enemies. Paul was likely referring to Jesus' teaching here when he wrote in Rom 12:14, "Bless those who persecute you; bless and curse not."[223]

The substantival participle translated "those who persecute you" is in the present tense. Present participles typically emphasize the continuous nature of the action. Present participles also describe an action that is contemporaneous with the main verb.[224] The present participle thus portrays the disciple's prayer and the persecutor's mistreatment as simultaneous. Jesus did not command His disciples to pray blessing on their persecutors long after their wounds were healed, their pain forgotten. He commanded His disciples to pray blessing on their persecutors even as the scourge lacerated their flesh, even as they carried their crosses, and even as nails were pounded through

includes "even the most extreme kind of enmity" since in the examples in the Lucan parallel the animosity escalates from one that is merely internal ("hate"), to verbal expression ("curse"), to active expression ("abuse").

[223] Davies and Allison rightly conclude from the widespread call to love one's enemies in early Christian writings that the content of Matt 5:44 is "one of the most cited and influential dominical words in early Christian literature" (*A Critical and Exegetical Commentary on the Gospel According to Saint Matthew*, 1:551).

[224] This is often true with adjectival and substantival participles as well as adverbial participles.

their hands and feet. What Jesus commanded here far exceeds what He commanded in the previous antithesis. The previous antithesis prohibited Jesus' disciples from retaliating vengefully against an evil person. In this antithesis Jesus turned from the negative to the positive and commanded His disciples to love their enemies. Rather than responding to abuse passively, Jesus' disciples are to do so actively, not merely avoiding aggression but expressing compassion.

Jesus did not command this response to persecution for pragmatic reasons. He did not teach, for example, that loving one's enemy would transform the enemy into a friend, though it may. He did not teach that His disciples should pray for their persecutors because love defuses hate, though it may. Jesus' disciples were to love their enemies "so that you may be sons of your Father in heaven" (Matt 5:45). Jesus commanded His disciples to love their enemies because this is the kind of love that characterizes God. Jesus' disciples are sons and daughters of God who should resemble their Father in their character and conduct. The words "so that" (*hopōs*) cannot be construed as expressing the ground or cause of Jesus' command, that is, "Love your enemies . . . because you are sons of your Father in heaven." Instead the words "so that" clearly introduce the purpose of the command.[225] The verb "be" (*ginomai*) can express a process of change and transformation ("become") or simply refer to a state of being. In this instance the verb probably has the nuance of change and transformation.[226]

Jesus' concern in this text was not with the status of sonship but with the characteristics of sonship.[227] Jesus recognized that just as the son of an earthly father will resemble his father in many ways—his appearance, his mannerisms, his gait, and so forth—so the children of God will resemble their heavenly Father in their character and behavior. The Talmud stated, "When you behave as sons, you are sons."[228] Jesus' point was that love for one's enemies exhibits the divine character and identifies Jesus' disciples as sons and daughters of God. Nolland captured the essence of Jesus' teaching well:

---

[225] "ὅπως," BDAG, 718.

[226] "γίνομαι," BDAG, 196–98 (def. 5) suggests that in this context the verb means "to experience a change in nature and so indicate entry into a new condition, *become someth[ing]*."

[227] See Guelich, *The Sermon on the Mount*, 230. France noted that the status of sonship was implied already in the title "your Father who is in heaven." Thus the thought is not "that such behavior will by itself make the disciples into God's children" but that "it will be the proper outworking of that relationship and demonstrate its legitimacy" (*The Gospel of Matthew*, 226).

[228] *b. Qidd.* 36a.

Where 5:9 promised divine acknowledgment as sons, here the link with the example of God is best respected by taking the thrust of the text to be: "By loving enemies you will be acting in the proper family manner (like father, like son)." Marked by this family likeness, one's actions will be good works that "glorify your Father in heaven" (5:16).[229]

Although God shows special favor to His own spiritual children (Matt 7:9–11), He lavishes grace and kindness on all His creatures. In arguing this, Jesus appealed to God's sovereignty over nature and His providence. "He causes his sun to rise" (5:45) portrays God as the master of the cosmos who orders the orbit of the planets and the rotation of the earth on its axis.

The statement should not be read as indicating that Jesus held a geocentric view of the universe, that is, that the sun orbits around the earth. This is clearly "phenomenological" language in which events are described according to their appearance. Even in this scientific age when most know well that the earth orbits around the sun, it is still common to speak of the sun rising or setting since from a human vantage point the sun seems to rise above the horizon and descend below the horizon.

What is important is that Jesus clearly saw God as in control of the dawning of the sun. He even calls the sun "His sun" to indicate that the stars and planets all belong to their Creator and are subject to His command. The conviction that God is in control of the cosmos, particularly the rising of the sun, appears in OT texts like Ps 104:19–23:

> He made the moon to mark the seasons; the sun knows when to set. You bring darkness, and it becomes night, when all the forest animals stir. The young lions roar for their prey and seek their food from God. The sun rises; they go back and lie down in their dens. Man goes out to his work and to his labor until evening.

This doctrine also surfaces in texts like Job 38:12–41. The rising of the sun was part of natural revelation. The sun's consistent appearance on the horizon every morning over the heads of the good and the evil demonstrates that God is gracious and kind to His enemies as well as His friends.[230] Paul and the OT agree that certain aspects of

---

[229] Nolland, *The Gospel of Matthew*, 268. Similarly Broadus appealed to Eph 5:1 to argue that "one element and proof of sonship is resemblance" (*The Gospel According to Matthew*, 122). Davies and Allison identify a number of Jewish parallels to this statement (*A Critical and Exegetical Commentary on the Gospel According to Saint Matthew*, 1:555).

[230] Texts like Job 18:5–6 and 38:15 speak of light being denied to the wicked. However, even in these figurative references, the light of the sun is not described as darkened.

God's character and nature are manifested through natural or general revelation (Ps 19:1–6; Rom 1:19–20).

This indiscriminate divine love for both the good and the evil does have its limits. Later Jesus based His comments in Matt 24:29 on Isa 13:10; Ezek 32:7; Joel 2:10,31; and 3:15 to warn that the sun will not shine perpetually on the wicked. The sun will be darkened by God, and the moon will not give its light. God will pour His wrath out on the unrepentant wicked. One must carefully distinguish the common grace that God lavishes on all people now indiscriminately with the saving grace that only repentant followers of Jesus receive.

Jesus also reminded His disciples that God causes the rain to fall "on the righteous and the unrighteous" (Matt 5:45). Although modern readers may be tempted to see a dark and rainy day as an indication of divine disfavor, ancient peoples associated rain with divine blessing.[231] Before irrigation and electric water pumps, farmers depended on frequent rains to water their crops and ensure an abundant harvest (Isa 30:23). Without rain, the crops would wither and people would go hungry. God's people knew that God sent the rain (Gen 2:5; Deut 28:12; 1 Kgs 18:1; Job 5:10; 37:6; Ps 147:8; Jer 5:24; Zech 10:1). God occasionally withheld rain from His people as a measure of discipline and in order to move them to repentance (Deut 11:14,17; 28:23–24; 1 Kgs 8:35–36; Isa 5:6; Amos 4:7). First Kings 17 records that rain did not fall in Israel for an entire three-year period because of Israel's idolatry. Although God withheld rain to discipline Israel, He did not withhold rain from other wicked nations.[232] Furthermore, when the rain fell, it fell on the crops of both the righteous Israelite and his wicked neighbor. The rain that blessed the crops was thus a powerful picture of the kindness that God showed indiscriminately to His friends and enemies alike.[233] Thus when Jesus' disciples show love to their enemies, they are acting as God acts. They are emulating

---

[231] On the other hand rain on certain occasions, like harvest day in which rain ruined the harvest before it could be gathered, was recognized as a sign of God's disfavor. See 1 Sam 12:17–18.

[232] However, Zech 14:17–18 warned that God would withhold rain from pagan nations that refused to worship God in His holy temple in Jerusalem in the last days.

[233] Other Jewish teachers also pointed out that God's kindness to the evil is seen in His blessings like rain. See b. Taʿan. 7a; and Mek. on Exod 18:12. Pesiq. Rab. 48.4 says, "In all your life have you ever seen rain come down upon the field of So-and-So who is righteous, but not upon the adjacent field of So-and-so who is wicked? Of course the sun shines upon those in Israel who are righteous, but it also shines upon those who are wicked."

the behavior of the Almighty. They are identifying themselves as sons of the heavenly Father by their resemblance to their spiritual Father.

Later theologians would refer to the ideal of emulating God's example as the *imitatio Dei*, the imitation of God. Paul, John, and Peter all refer to this principle as a means of righteousness (Eph 5:1–2; 1 Pet 1:13–25; 1 John 4:7–12). In each of these texts, the emphasis is on imitating God by loving as He loves.[234]

Jesus taught that loving only those who express love in return cheapens and degrades Christian love (Matt 5:46). This kind of sentiment is not true love but is actually self-serving pragmatism. Jesus challenged this poor substitute for true love on two counts. First, this so-called love was not deserving of any reward in eschatological judgment. Perhaps the statement already anticipates the teaching of Matt 6:1–2 in which those who express Christian virtues with hidden agendas and out of selfish motives will receive no reward beyond their own temporary pleasure. Second, this so-called love was characteristic of the collectors of tolls and taxes who were infamous in first-century Judaism. Tax collectors were despised as traitors and thieves who were ritually defiled. Tax collectors had allied themselves with the hated Romans who imposed a heavy tax burden on the people of Galilee and Perea. Tax collectors were not salaried employees of the Roman government. Instead they received a modest commission, but by elevating already astronomical tax rates, they could increase their takings. The people called them "licensed robbers." The Babylonian Talmud listed service as a tax collector or publican among the most despised trades.[235] The mere entrance of a tax collector into a Jewish home left the entire home in a state of uncleanness.[236] Anything they touched was deemed defiled.[237] Jewish law said that a Jew could not handle money from a tax collector's chest. Law forbad even a beggar to receive money from a tax collector's wallet.[238] Tax collectors were expelled from Pharisaic communities. Tax collectors could never serve as a judge and their testimony was invalid in court. Jewish law

[234] Davies and Allison note, "Apparently there is embedded in Mt 5, Eph 5, 1 Pet 1, and 1 Jn 4 a paraenetic pattern common to early Christian moral teaching: as God's children, imitate him in his love. Presumably the pattern derives from the teaching of Jesus" (*A Critical and Exegetical Commentary on the Gospel According to Saint Matthew*, 1:554).

[235] *b. Sanh.* 25b.
[236] *m. Tehar.* 7:6.
[237] *m. Ḥag.* 3:6.
[238] *m. B. Qam.* 10:1.

gave them no more rights than a Gentile slave. Thus by comparing self-serving love for others to the love of a tax collector Jesus was giving a stinging rebuke. Righteous Jews wanted to think that they had nothing in common with tax collectors.[239]

Self-serving love was particularly characteristic of tax collectors since they had betrayed their own subjected people and befriended the hated Roman oppressors for the sake of their personal financial gain. The love and loyalty of the tax collector was for sale to the highest bidder. Their love was inspired by schemes to get ahead. But the love God displays and that Christian disciples are to emulate is unconditional, selfless, and sacrificial.

Jesus also urged His disciples to be different from those who greeted only their brothers.[240] Ancient greetings in both the Jewish and Gentile worlds typically expressed some kind of blessing. The Hebrew greeting *shalom* wished the peace that results from divine favor on the one being greeted. The greeting essentially meant, "May it be well with you." Some Jews were evidently hesitant to pronounce such greetings to their enemies in fear that they might thereby ensure their enemies' prosperity and success. The rabbis debated at length whether Jews should greet Gentiles, and they concluded that greetings could be offered to Gentiles "in the interests of peace" (*m. Giṭ.* 5.9).[241] The Greek greeting *chairein* meant "joy be to you." Thus Gentiles sometimes refused to greet those whom they deemed unworthy, perhaps particularly Jews.[242] Jesus asked, "If you greet only your brothers, what are you doing out of the ordinary?" (5:47). The words "out of the ordinary" (*perisson*) mean "extraordinary, remarkable" or "excellent, surpassing the normal standard."[243] The word is the adjectival form of the verb "surpass" (*perisseuse*) in verse 20, which Jesus

---

[239] See *m. Sanh.* 3.3; *t. B. Meṣiʿa* 8.26 and Luke 3:12–13. See also Jeremias, *Jerusalem in the Time of Jesus*, 310–12.

[240] "Brothers" in this context may mean either "fellow Jews" or perhaps "fellow disciples."

[241] *m. Abot* 4:14 urged, "Be first in greeting every creature." Similarly *b. Ber.* 17a said of Rabbi Johannan ben Zakkai, "No man ever gave him greeting first, even a heathen in the street."

[242] On anti-Semitism in the ancient world, see J. J. Collins, "Antisemitism in Antiquity? The Case of Alexandria," in *Ancient Judaism in Its Hellenistic Context*, ed. C. Bakhos (Boston: Brill, 2005), 9–29; L. Feldman, "Antisemitism in the Ancient World," *History and Hate: The Dimensions of Antisemitism*, ed. D. Berger (Philadelphia: Jewish Publication Society, 1986), 15–42; P. Hughes, "The Jewish Problem in the Ancient World," *EvQ* 12 (1940): 247–74; D. Rokéah, "Tacitus and Ancient Antisemitism," *REJ* 154 (1995): 281–94; and Z. Yavetz, "Judeophobia in Classical Antiquity: A Different Approach," *JJS* 44 (1993): 1–22.

[243] "περισσός," BDAG, 805.

used to urge His disciples to have a righteousness that surpasses that of even the scribes and Pharisees.[244] They are to live lives of extraordinary righteousness. Jesus did not condemn withholding a greeting from an enemy because such behavior was deemed socially unacceptable in ancient culture. On the contrary, such shunning was common, ordinary human behavior, but it was just this that made the behavior unworthy of the disciple. Theirs was to be no ordinary, common righteousness. Theirs was to be a remarkable, surpassing, even miraculous righteousness. Only this degree of righteousness would display their resemblance to their heavenly Father and inspire others to glorify their Father in heaven (v. 16).

As discussed earlier, in texts such as Deut 14:1; 32:5,19; Isa 43:6; 45:11; and Hos 1:10, God identified Israelites as His sons. Jesus taught, however, that the true sons of God, and thus the true Israel (see note 107), were those who lived in likeness to God. When Jesus argued that many in His audience lived more like Gentiles did than as God did, He was challenging their claim to be true Israelites by showing that their behavior was more pagan than divine.

Jesus drew the antitheses to a close with a summarizing conclusion. Verse 48 is most closely tied to the final antithesis (Matt 5:43–47). This is true not only because the conclusion immediately follows the final antithesis but also because verse 48 alludes to Lev 19:2 and uses it to interpret Lev 19:18, which Jesus quoted in Matt 5:43. Jesus' point is that Leviticus 19 opened with a call to pursue God's own holy character. Since loving only one's neighbors was normal pagan behavior but foreign to God's character, rabbinic interpretations of Lev 19:18 that sought to justify hatred of one's enemies were obviously incorrect. On the other hand the structure of the antitheses and the references to extraordinary behavior at the beginning and end of the antitheses (Matt 5:20,47) so closely unite this entire section that the conclusion appropriately sums up the entirety of verses 21–47.

Despite efforts to dilute the sense of the adjective "perfect" (*teleioi*), the word in this context clearly does not mean "mature." It is a reference to moral perfection.[245] Jesus defined this moral perfection as matching God's own perfect character. Verse 48 combines Lev 19:2

---

[244] See comments on Matt 5:20.

[245] So also Davies and Allison, *A Critical and Exegetical Commentary on the Gospel According to Saint Matthew*, 1:561; France, *The Gospel of Matthew*, 228; and Luz, *Matthew: A Commentary*, 289–90.

("Be holy because I, the LORD your God, am holy") and Deut 18:13 ("You must be blameless [*teleios*] before the LORD your God").[246] Love for others, including one's enemies, is the essence of divine perfection and the key to true righteousness.

This truth has already surfaced in Matthew's Gospel. Joseph did not want Mary to suffer the humiliation of a public divorce because he was "a righteous man" (Matt 1:19). Many first-century Jews might have objected that if Joseph were truly righteous, he would seek a public divorce and expose Mary to the shame that her alleged sin deserved. However, Matt 1:19 introduces the reader to a different kind of righteousness, a righteousness that is more than mere fidelity to the law, a righteousness that has love, mercy, and kindness at its heart. The same theme surfaces on the two different occasions (9:13; 12:7) in which Jesus quoted Hos 6:6, "I desire loyalty and not sacrifice." The theme surfaces in the emphasis on forgiving others both in the SM (Matt 6:12,14–15) and later in the parable of the Unforgiving Servant (Matt 18:21–35). It climaxes with Jesus' insistence that love is the essence of the Law and the Prophets (22:34–40). Paul agreed that love is the key to true righteousness and leads to the fulfillment of the law. He likely drew this truth from Jesus' teaching (Rom 13:8,10; Gal 5:14).

The future indicative verb "be" in Matt 5:48 may express a promise for the future: "you will be perfect."[247] As in the Beatitudes, this promise may anticipate the consummation of the kingdom when Jesus' disciples will be "filled with righteousness" (v. 6) and "will see God" (v. 8). However, the LXX frequently used the future indicative to express divine commands with great solemnity. The OT commands in Matt 5:21,27, and 43 all use future indicative verbs. Furthermore, verse 48 is itself an echo of OT commands that use the future indicative. Thus the verse should be read as a command. One should not read this command to be perfect as a frustrating demand for the impossible that is irrelevant for modern-day disciples. The ethic of Jesus' kingdom is full perfection. Believers should strive for this ideal with the conviction that, as children of God, they are heirs

---

[246] The LXX used the adjective τέλειος for "blameless" in Deut 18:13.

[247] W. Carter mentioned that the grammar permits v. 48 to be read as a command, a social-ethical consequence, or an eschatological promise. He preferred to see the text as richly multivalent and affirmed all three views ("Love Your Enemies," *Word and World* 28 [2008]: 13–21, esp. 21).

of His character and will resemble Him. The emphatic "you" in verse 48 reminds believers that they have a power to pursue perfection that others lack.[248] They should strive for this perfection armed with the awareness that righteousness is a divine gift that God graciously imparts as His people crave it (v. 6). They should also remember that while Christ's kingdom has already been inaugurated, its consummation awaits His glorious return. Although Jesus' disciples are progressively and increasingly characterized by divine righteousness here and now, their transformation will not be completed until the kingdom is consummated.

C. The Disciple's Avoidance of Hypocrisy in the Practice of the Pillars of Judaism (Matt 6:1–18)

Introduction (Matt 6:1)

Jesus began this section of His sermon by stating the guiding principle that He will apply to three different acts of righteousness: "Be careful not to practice your righteousness in front of people, to be seen by them." The verb "be careful" (*prosechete*) is a present imperative that commands constant vigilance. The grammatical form implies that the disciple must continually and consciously avoid making a show of acts of righteousness since the temptation to seek personal aggrandizement is ever present.

Although some interpret the text as if Jesus' concern was with the location in which one performed acts of righteousness, Jesus' greater concern was actually the motive for which His disciples perform their deeds of righteousness. Jesus did not challenge acts of righteousness simply because they were done "in front of people." Jesus had already urged His disciples to let their light shine before people "so that they may see your good works and give glory to your Father in heaven" (5:16). Matthew 6:1 and 5:16 are closely related since both refer to performing good works "before men" or "in front of people," both using the construction *emprosthen tōn anthrōpōn* followed immediately by a purpose clause.[249] The two verses contrast two very different

---

[248] See the section "Theological Framework for the Interpretation of the Sermon on the Mount" in the introduction.

[249] Matthew 5:16 uses ὅπως followed by the subjunctive. Matthew 6:1 uses πρός with the articular infinitive.

motivations for good works: a desire to give glory to God and a desire to gain glory for oneself.[250] As discussed earlier, one gives glory to a father for the actions of his child either when the child inherited the ability to perform the action or when he learned from his father the skills necessary for the action. Jesus' teaching implies the doctrine of the new birth, through which the disciples receive the Father's character and behave as the Father behaves. Disciples who perform public acts of righteousness to be seen by people are seeking human applause for themselves rather than glory for God. Their actions and motives imply that they are responsible for their personal acts of righteousness and deserve all the credit for them. Their behavior is an implicit denial that their actions are a product of divine grace. Their behavior betrays not only their own selfishness but also their ignorance of the nature and source of righteousness in the new covenant.[251]

Jesus did not merely command His disciples to do the right thing; He commanded them to do the right thing for the right reason. An action is not truly righteous unless it has the proper motivation. The motivation for every truly righteous act is a desire to glorify God and to please Him. Jesus urged His followers to resist the drive to glorify themselves. Humility and sincerity are absolutely necessary if a person is to receive the applause of heaven and receive God's rewards for his good deeds.

Jesus warned that those who view acts of righteousness as an opportunity to call attention to themselves and to seek human applause for their personal piety "will have no reward from your Father in heaven" (6:1). The word "reward" (*misthon*) may indicate remuneration for work done, that is, a wage (20:8). It may also describe recompense or recognition by God for praiseworthy action or character (5:46).[252] The positive references to divine reward or recompense have prompted some interpreters to see Jesus' teaching in the SM as

---

[250] *m. Abot* 6:11 says, "Whatsoever the Holy One, blessed is he, created in his world, he created it only for his glory, as it is written, 'Everything that is called by my name and that I have created, I have formed it, yea, I have made it.'"

[251] France suggests that Matthew intended to distinguish two types of actions as well as two different motives. "Good works" refers to the godly lifestyle and holy character of the disciples which must be exhibited publicly. "Righteousness" refers specifically to religious duties that are best performed privately (*The Gospel of Matthew*, 234). Although the term "righteousness" in Matt 6:1 does refer contextually to the three pillars of Judaism, almsgiving, prayer, and fasting, it is doubtful that Matthew intended to limit the term to these. In every other occurrence of the term in Matthew, it refers to the good works that exhibit godly character.

[252] "μισθός," BDAG, 653.

incompatible with Paul's doctrine of grace, which insists that man's just reward is death and that eternal life may be received only as a divine gift (Rom 6:23).[253] Nevertheless, as argued at length earlier, the supposed contradictions between the teachings of Jesus and Paul are a product of confused readings of Paul's or Jesus' teachings (or both). Although Jesus did frequently speak in the SM of rewards for righteousness, He insisted that this righteousness is a divine gift (Matt 5:6) for which His disciples might hunger and thirst but which they were incapable of producing on their own. Thus in the theology of the SM God graciously transforms the heart of Jesus' disciples, imparts (not merely imputes) true righteousness to them, and then rewards them for that righteousness. Those who argue that Paul would object have misinterpreted Paul. Paul likewise insisted that God imparts as well as imputes righteousness to the believer (Rom 8:3–4; 1 Cor 6:9–11; Gal 5:16–26; 6:15; Eph 2:10; 4:20–32; Col 3:1–11). He also freely spoke of rewards given for righteous conduct and faithful ministry (1 Cor 3:8,14; 9:17–18). He used the imagery of sowing and reaping to teach the same concept (Gal 6:7–10). Both Jesus and Paul taught that God grants righteousness to the believer and then rewards the believer for that righteousness. Furthermore in Matt 19:29; 25:21,23; and especially 20:1–16, the reward God grants is disproportionate-ly greater than one deserves, thus clearly demonstrating that divine judgment will not consist of a strict merit system. Jesus' later teaching in the Gospel of Matthew strongly emphasizes God's goodness rather than human merit as the basis for the disciple's reward.[254] Neither Jesus, Matthew, nor Paul saw teaching regarding rewards for personal righteousness as conflicting with the gospel of grace.

Although many translations refer to the reward in 6:1 as "from your Father in heaven," the preposition *para* does not mean "from" elsewhere in the NT in this particular grammatical construction.[255] In

---

[253] See especially H. Windisch, *The Meaning of the Sermon on the Mount: A Contribution to the Historical Understanding of the Gospels and to the Problem of Their True Exegesis*, trans. S. M. Gilmour (Philadelphia: Westminster, 1951), 62–93. The term for "wages" in Rom 6:23 is ὀψώνιον which speaks of "pay, wages, or compensation." The term is a synonym for μισθός. However, although Paul used ὀψώνιον to refer to the financial support given to Christian leaders (1 Cor 9:7; 2 Cor 11:8), he did not use the term to describe heavenly reward.

[254] Guelich, *The Sermon on the Mount*, 277.

[255] When παρά appears with a genitive object, it may mean "from." However, here the object is in the dative case. The preposition with the dative case is not used elsewhere in the NT to mark the source of a gift or reward. See "παρά," BDAG, 756–58 for the range of possible meanings.

this particular construction the preposition may serve as a marker of proximity, in which case the phrase would mean that the reward is "with the Father," that is, a reward in heaven. In this case the preposition would confirm that the future tense "will have" is an eschatological future and thus emphasizes that Jesus was referring to eschatological reward rather than present, temporal reward.[256]

On the other hand the preposition could serve as a "marker of one whose viewpoint is relevant," in which case the phrase would mean that the person who performs acts of righteousness for human applause merits no reward in God's sight, in God's view, or in God's judgment. Choosing between these two senses is no easy task. The majority of commentators support the first option. A survey of the other five uses of the preposition *para* with a dative object in Matthew yields no firm conclusion. In 8:10, the preposition associates a characteristic or quality with a person. In 19:26 (twice), the preposition serves as a marker of personal reference. In 22:25 and 28:15, the preposition serves as a marker of proximity and means "among." Enough variety exists in the Gospel to make any of the meanings possible. In the context of 6:1 the second possible meaning seems more likely.[257] The reference to "reward" introduces a judgment scenario. In contexts referring to judgment the sense "in the sight of" or "in the judgment of" predominates. This construction was used by Paul in Rom 2:13 to speak of those who are "righteous before God" in the sense of being declared righteous in final judgment. The issue in Matt 6:1 is the criterion used by God in eschatological judgment to determine whether one's "righteousness" is truly righteous.

Thus Jesus was reminding His disciples that God and human beings sometimes have two different perspectives on the actions people perform. What may seem laudable from a human vantage point may be despicable from a divine perspective. What may seem insignificant from a human point of view may be worthy of a reward from a heavenly perspective. Thus Jesus' disciples must decide whether they will perform acts of righteousness for the pleasure of the human or heavenly audience, whether they wish to please God or to impress others.

---

[256] Broadus, *The Gospel According to Matthew*, 126; and Nolland, *The Epistle of Matthew*, 274. This was the sense suggested for this text in BDAG.

[257] Betz, *The Sermon on the Mount*, 332; A. T. Robertson, *Word Pictures in the New Testament* (New York: Harper, 1930), 1:50 ("as he looks at it"). Although Guelich does not explicitly discuss the preposition, his comments suggest that he also interpreted it in this fashion (*The Sermon on the Mount*, 276–77).

Jesus continued by applying the general principle of verse 1 to three different acts of piety: almsgiving, prayer, and fasting. These three religious acts are sometimes referred to as the "pillars of Judaism." In some branches of Judaism, such as the Judaism of the Diaspora, the Essenes, and even some Pharisaic groups, these acts of righteousness began to replace temple sacrifice as the means of atonement for sins. For example Tob 4:10, a text from the Diaspora, states, "Almsgiving delivers from death and keeps you from going into the Darkness." Tobit 12:8–9 adds, "Prayer with fasting is good, but better than both is almsgiving with righteousness. . . . For almsgiving saves from death and purges away every sin." Sirach 3:30, a text written by a Pharisee shortly before the time of Christ, states, "As water extinguishes a blazing fire, so almsgiving atones for sin."[258]

By contrast, although Jesus taught that these acts, if properly motivated, would be rewarded by God, He made no hint that they were the means by which sin is forgiven. In Jesus' teaching, forgiveness of sin is never a reward for good behavior. Good works cannot compensate for sins or make up for them in any way. However, good works do result in greater reward for those who follow Jesus. The NT teaches that there are degrees of reward in heaven and that those whose lives are characterized by the superior righteousness of the SM will enjoy the greatest eternal blessings (5:19).

Almsgiving (Matt 6:2–4)

Jesus assumed that His disciples would give to the poor. He did not say, "if you give" but "whenever you give." He clearly saw compassionate giving as a responsibility of all disciples. This charitable giving supported childless widows, orphans, and the handicapped. When nations had no government-sponsored social assistance programs, the needy depended greatly on the gifts of the more fortunate.

Jesus forbade His disciples to "sound a trumpet" when they gave to the poor. Sounding a trumpet may simply be a vivid metaphor for calling attention to one's act of charity. In some ancient texts "sound a trumpet" meant "to advertise" or "to call attention to oneself with fanfare." However, the reference could be literal rather than metaphorical. Two explanations are possible. First, the offering chests

---

[258] For a more in-depth treatment of the issue, see C. Quarles, "The New Perspective and Means of Atonement in Jewish Literature of the Second Temple Period," *CTR* 2 (2005): 39–58.

in the temple were called "shofar chests" or "trumpet chests" since the mouths of the coffers were trumpet-shaped, wide at the top and narrow at the entrance into the chest, in order to facilitate giving the offering and in order to prevent theft from the offering chest.[259] Sounding the trumpet, then, might be a reference to tossing coins noisily into the trumpet-shaped coffer and thereby calling attention to one's generosity.[260] Second, trumpets were sounded on fast days when alms were requested. It is possible that large gifts were recognized by a blast of the trumpet.[261] Although no record of such a practice exists, large gifts were rewarded in other ways. When a significant contribution was made, the giver was honored with an invitation to sit among the rabbis.[262] The most likely option is probably the first.

Jesus referred to hypocrites "sounding the trumpet" in both "synagogues" and "streets." Shofar chests were used in both the temple and in local synagogues, but no evidence suggests that they were also used in the streets.[263] However, this poses no problem to this interpretation if the originally literal practice of noisy contributions to the shofar chest came to serve as a metaphor for calling attention to one's charity in other ways.

Jesus said that the giver blew his trumpet "to be applauded by people" (lit., "so that they might be glorified by the people"). With these words Jesus made the true motive of the giver clear. He did not give out of a desire to meet the needs of the poor, nor did He give out of pity for the underprivileged. Instead he gave out of a desire for self-aggrandizement. What was intended to be a selfless act was perverted into a completely selfish act.

---

[259] See *m. Šeqal.* 2:1; 6:1,5.

[260] This view was first suggested by McEleney and later adopted by Davies and Allison (*A Critical and Exegetical Commentary on the Gospel According to Saint Matthew*, 1:579). Earlier scholars such as G. Klein and S. T. Lachs proposed that the person responsible for translating the Aram Matthew into Greek read a reference to the shofar chests and mistranslated it as the verb "to trumpet." However, Davies and Allison are correct in their objection that "speculation about a mistranslation should be countenanced only if the text as it stands is problematic, which is not true of Mt 6.2" (ibid.).

[261] See P. Bonnard, *L'Évangile selon Saint Matthieu* (Paris: Neuchatel, Delachaux & Niestlé, 1963), 78; and D. Hill, *The Gospel of Matthew*, NCB (London: Oliphants, 1978), 133.

[262] G. Friedrich, "σαλπίζω," in *TDNT* 7 (1971):71–88.

[263] The word "streets" refers to the narrow alleys (ῥύμαις) where beggars sat and pled for alms. Beggars probably preferred these alleys to broad streets since the narrowness of the alley made it more difficult for passersby to avoid them.

Jesus said such conduct is hypocritical. The word *hupocritēs* originally referred to a play-actor who performed on the stage of the Greek or Roman theater.[264] The verbal form of the word was frequently used in Jewish writings in the time between the writing of the OT and NT to speak of the act of "pretending."[265] Many ancient play-actors aspired to be celebrities adored by the masses. They lived for the thrill of standing ovations and the prizes and awards sometimes presented for excellent dramatic performances. The hypocrites to whom Jesus referred were spiritual play-actors who pretended to have a piety that they did not actually possess in order to inspire the applause of a human audience.

In Matt 15:7–9 Jesus appealed to Isa 29:13 to describe hypocrisy: "Hypocrites! Isaiah prophesied correctly about you when he said: These people honor Me with their lips, but their heart is far from Me. They worship Me in vain, teaching as doctrines the commands of men." This suggests that hypocrisy involves pretended devotion to God, empty worship, and the substitution of human authority for divine authority.

Jesus warned that if a giver gives in hopes of receiving recognition from others for his gift, he will receive that recognition but no greater reward. "They've got their reward!" (Matt 6:2) means that they have already received their full reward and can expect no other reward. The verb *epechousin* means "to receive in full what is due." The verb was originally a technical term for providing a receipt marked "paid in full."[266] The point is that if a person seeks human applause through acts of piety, that applause will be his entire reward. The account is then closed and no further reward is due. He who seeks such earthly rewards for righteousness forfeits heavenly rewards for those righteous deeds. So Jesus then urged His followers to take any measure necessary to ensure that acts of righteousness were driven by the proper motivation.

---

[264] See Keener (*The Gospel of Matthew*, 206), who cites Aristotle, *Poet.* 18.19, 1456a; Diod. Sic. *Bib. Hist.* 37.12.1; Herodian 3.8.9.

[265] 2 Macc 5:25; 6:21,24; 4 Macc 6:15,17; Sir 1:29; 32:15; 33:2; *Pss. Sol.* 4:20,22. In the LXX of Job 34:30 and 36:13 the noun ὑποκριτής simply means "godless one" and serves as the translation of the Hebrew אָדָם חָנֵף and חַנְפֵי־לֵב. For a thorough treatment of the word's history and many nuances, see Wilkins, "ὑποκριτής," *TDNT* 8 (1972): 559–71.

[266] "ἀπέχω," BDAG, 102.

"Don't let your left hand know what your right hand is doing" (v. 3) figuratively prohibits a person from pridefully celebrating his own personal acts of righteousness. The two hands are obviously different members of the same body, and the image of keeping one's acts of goodness secret even from oneself is a hyperbole meaning that the disciple must not give so that he can pat himself on the back or applaud his own goodness.[267] If a disciple should refuse to seek to be self-complimentary, how much more should he avoid seeking to be a spiritual celebrity in the eyes of others.

Jesus' disciples could be sure that their actions were not motivated by a desire for human accolades if they performed their acts of righteousness in secrecy without the knowledge of other people. If one gives compassionately and humbly, motivated only by his concern for the needs of others and his desire to glorify God, he will receive a heavenly and eternal reward for his act: "Your Father who sees in secret will reward you" (v. 4). Because God is omnipresent, no act is hidden from Him. He sees acts of righteousness that no one else can see. The references to "Father" rather than to "God" in both verses 1 and 4 are intentional and probably allude to the fact that just as a child seeks the approval of his parents above all others, so the approval of the heavenly Father will matter more to the child of God than the approval of other people. The identity of the disciple as a child of God is apparent in his desire to please the heavenly Father and hear his words of approval.

Prayer (Matt 6:5–15)

Just as Jesus assumed that His followers would give to the poor, He also assumed that they would pray. By using "whenever" (*hotan*) rather than "if" (*ean*), Jesus expressed this expectation clearly. For Jesus, a prayerless disciple was inconceivable. True disciples prayed.

The word "whenever" may also express Jesus' rejection of fixed times for prayer that sometimes reduced prayer to an empty ritual.[268]

---

[267] The view that Jesus' teaching is hyperbole can be traced to Chrysostom, *Hom. Matt.* 19.2: "He hath put the thing hyperbolically. As thus: 'If it can be,' saith He, 'for thyself not to know it, let this be the object of thine endeavor; that, if it were possible, it may be concealed from the very hands that minister.'"

[268] This is based on the slight distinction between ὅτε with the indicative and ὅταν with the subjunctive. Although BDAG argues that ὅταν pertains to an action that is "conditional, possible, and, in many instances, repeated" and often approaches the meaning of ἐάν, it is the timing of the action rather than the occurrence of the action that is normally conditional in Matthean

Jewish tradition required a rigorous daily spiritual program of faithful Jews. This spiritual program could degenerate into a mere formality that the worshipper participated in mindlessly.

First-century Jews were expected to recite the *Shemà* (Deut 6:4–9) twice each day. The *Shemà* was to be recited each morning before sunrise and in the evening before midnight (*m. Ber.* 1.1–2). According to the school of Shammai, the morning *Shemà* was recited while standing and the evening *Shemà* while reclining, since Exodus 6 spoke of reciting the *Shemà* while one reclined and rose up. The recitation of the *Shemà* was accompanied by particular benedictions inserted before and after the *Shemà* in a prescribed order. In the evening recitation, a reflection on the exodus was also included.[269]

Prayers were offered at the beginning and end of each meal (*m. Ber.* 3.4). Different mealtime prayers were prescribed depending on the menu, with one prayer for fruit, another for vegetables, another for bread, another for unripe fruit, sour wine, or locusts. Rabbis debated the amount of food necessary to require a mealtime prayer. The consensus was that if the food amounted to the size of an olive, the prayer was mandatory. At the close of each Sabbath, three prayers were offered: one for the lamp, one for the spices, and another for the *Habdalah* (ceremony marking the end of the Sabbath).

Particular prayers were also prescribed for such occasions as approaching the site of a miracle, seeing a shooting star, experiencing an earthquake, a clap of thunder, or a flash of lightning. A particular prayer was prescribed when one saw mountains, hills, seas, rivers, and deserts. One prayer was prescribed for the reception of good news, another for bad news. Particular prayers were prescribed for building a home or the purchase of new cooking vessels. Two different prayers were to be offered when one entered a town, then another two when one left the town.

---

use. Twelve times Matthew used ὅτε only with the aorist indicative to describe events that had already occurred (7:28; 9:25; 11:1; 12:3; 13:26,48,53; 19:1; 21:1,34; 26:1; 27:31). And 19 times Matthew used ὅταν with the subjunctive to describe future events that will occur but at an undesignated time (5:11; 6:2,5,6,16; **9:15**; 10:19,23; 12:43; 13:32; 15:2; **19:28**; **21:40**; 23:15; 24:15,32–33; **25:31**; **26:29**). References in bold identify texts that illustrate well that the timing of the event is unspecified but that the event is still certain. Since Matthew did not use ὅτε to refer to future events that will occur at a specified time, one cannot be certain that the construction in Mt 6:2,5–6 is a challenge to programmed almsgiving, prayer, or fasting.

[269] See *m. Ber.* 1. This tractate, whose title means "Benedictions," is the first tractate of the Mishnah. It is the Mishnah's most comprehensive discussion of Jewish prayer.

Jews were also expected to pray the *Tefillah* or "Eighteen Benedictions" three times each day, in the morning (anytime up to midday), the afternoon (anytime up to sunset but most commonly at the time of the afternoon sacrifice), and the evening.[270] The law prescribed an additional *Tefillah* that could be said at any time of the day. The additional *Tefillah* was normally recited corporately by the congregation that met for prayer daily in the synagogue.

Some rabbis insisted that the Eighteen Benedictions needed to be prayed verbatim and by rote. Others, like Rabbi Eliezer, argued, "He that makes his prayer a fixed task, his prayer is no supplication" (*m. Ber.* 4.3–5.1). Similarly Rabbi Simeon taught, "Be heedful in the reciting of the *Shemà* and in the *Tefillah*; and when thou prayest make not thy prayer a fixed form, but a plea for mercies and supplications before God" (*m. ʾAbot* 2.13). The prayer was to be given while facing Jerusalem and while the heart was focused on the holy of holies. Some rabbis insisted that absolutely nothing should be allowed to interrupt the *Tefillah*. The one praying should not stop his benediction even if he were greeted by the king or a snake coiled around his leg.

First-century Jews appreciated fervency in prayer. During periods of corporate fasting, they would invite an old man, well-versed in prayer, who had children and whose cupboard was empty to lead in the prayer "so that he might be wholehearted in the prayer" (*m. Taʿan.* 2.2).

Although Jesus was devoted to prayer (Mark 1:35; Luke 5:16; 11:1), His prayers were not memorized recitations given at the whim of the clock. His prayers were intensely personal, often spontaneous, and an expression of His deep communion with His Father.

"You must not be like the hypocrites" (Matt 6:5) uses the imperatival future. This grammatical form normally expresses commands that are particularly solemn, universal, and timeless.[271] Since this was the grammatical form used for commands and prohibitions in the LXX, most NT uses involve OT quotations. The use of the imperatival future in this verse is one of only a few that do not involve an appeal to the OT. This grammatical form was probably intended to highlight the contrast between this prohibition and the command in 5:48 since

---

[270] See Dan 6:10; Acts 3:1; 10:3,30; *t. Ber.* 3:6; *m. Sukk* 5:5; and *m. Tamid* 7:5. Under the influence of the Jewish practice, *Did.* 8:3 commanded believers to pray the model prayer three times each day.

[271] See Wallace, *Greek Grammar Beyond the Basics*, 718–19.

both use "be" (*esesthe*) and "like" or "as" (*hōs*). The grammatical form is a reminder that Jesus' disciples are to be like their heavenly Father, and that leaves no room for being like hypocrites.

Jesus described the "hypocrites" as those who "love to pray standing in the synagogues and on the street corners to be seen by people" (6:5). That a person loves to pray is certainly commendable if he or she loves prayer for the privilege of expressing devotion and gratitude to God and the privilege of entrusting his or her burdens to the Almighty. However, the hypocrite loves prayer for an entirely different reason. Prayer is an opportunity to parade one's alleged piety before the eyes of others.

Many modern translations treat the perfect participle (*estōtes*) as if it were a present infinitive (to stand and pray).[272] Others treat the participle as a participle but ignore its perfect tense.[273] However, the tense of the participle is significant.[274] Perfect participles describe action that is antecedent to or prior to the action of the main verb, in this case, the verb "love." Hence the idea is that hypocrites love to pray "*after* they have stood in the synagogues and on the street corners." The implication is that they do not love to pray otherwise. They love prayer only when they pray in the posture and in the location in which they may call the most attention to themselves. The word order confirms this subtle implication. The Greek text placed the words "after standing in the synagogues and on the street corners" between the verb "love" and the infinitive "to pray." This places the reference to posture and location in a position of emphasis and highlights the hypocrite's real concern, which is to "be seen by people."

First-century Jews normally prayed in a standing position.[275] One knelt in prayer or prostrated in prayer only on very solemn occasions or during times of trouble (1 Kgs 8:54; Ezra 9:5; Mark 14:32–35; Acts 20:36; 21:5). Kneeling or prostrating oneself exhibited too much humility to be comfortable for the hypocrite. He wished only to stand in prayer so that he might be seen by more people and his voice might

---

[272] See ESV, NASB, and NRSV.

[273] See HCSB and NIV.

[274] Other commentators have suggested that the perfect tense may imply a lengthy prayer (Guelich, *The Sermon on the Mount*, 281 and Davies and Allison, *A Critical and Exegetical Commentary on the Gospel According to Saint Matthew*, 1:585). Although this does not seem to be a proper explanation of the grammar of the participle "standing," the present tense of the infinitive "to pray" probably does imply a prolonged prayer, that is, "they love to keep on praying."

[275] Both the Pharisee and the publican stood while praying (Luke 18:9–13).

carry to greater distances. Hagner shows the intention of the hypocrites by translating the participle "standing" as "positioning themselves conspicuously."[276]

The hypocrite loved prayer in two locations in particular, in synagogues and on street corners. Synagogue prayers were typically led
by the "messenger of the congregation" who prayed standing before
the ark containing the synagogue scrolls.[277] The privilege of leading
in synagogue prayer was no doubt a coveted privilege. Receiving this
privilege showed that the person was esteemed by the religious community and regarded as devoted to God.[278]

Hypocrites also love to pray "on the street corners." The Greek text
states that they loved to pray "on the corners of the broad streets." The
word "broad streets" (plateiōn) stands in stark contrast to the narrow
alleys (hrumais) where beggars pled for money (Matt 6:2).[279] These
were major thoroughfares that were heavily trafficked. The hypocrite
preferred these street corners to other locations for the same reasons
that prostitutes did and modern advertisers do. By praying on the
corners at intersections of these major streets, the hypocrite could
ensure that he would be seen by the greatest numbers of people in a
given period of time. Jewish custom did dictate that one should pray
wherever he happened to be at the time of the daily prayers. However,
Jesus recognized that it was no coincidence that many of His contemporaries just happened to be in this precise location so often when the
trumpet calling God's people to prayer sounded.[280]

Again the word hypocrite was the word used to describe a play-
actor who performed a role on a stage for the entertainment of an
audience. The hypocrites whom Jesus scorned were people who put
on a show of religiosity in order to impress others. An example of

---

[276] Hagner, Matthew 1–13, 141. France criticized that translation but admitted that the context indicates that intention (The Gospel of Matthew, 239, n. 41).

[277] See G. F. Moore, Judaism in the First Centuries of the Christian Era: The Age of the Tannaim
(Cambridge: Harvard University Press, 1954), 1:291–96.

[278] France suggests that συναγωγή simply refers to an assembly or gathering of people because
of its connection with the streets (The Gospel of Matthew, 238). However, this would be unusual
for Matthew, who always used the term elsewhere to refer to the synagogue (4:23; 6:2; 9:35;
10:17; 12:9; 13:54; 23:6,34). Although the term is connected to a reference to streets in 6:2,
France acknowledges that it refers to the synagogue in that context.

[279] The word πλατειῶν is actually the feminine genitive plural form of the adjective πλατύς
meaning "broad, wide." The noun ὁδός," a feminine noun meaning "road," was assumed.

[280] Trumpets were blown at the time of the afternoon sacrifice to call faithful Jews to interrupt their activities for the second prayer of the day. See Sir 50:16; m. Sukk. 5:5; m. Tamid 7:5.

this hypocrisy was the prayer uttered with great drama and pretended passion while standing in the street corner or in the synagogue. Jesus warned that those who pervert prayer into a dramatic performance to impress a human audience will receive no heavenly reward for their prayers. "They've got their reward!" (v. 5) means that they have already received their full reward and can expect no other.[281]

Jesus taught that disciples could ensure that they prayed with proper motives by faithfully praying in private. Jesus urged His followers to pray in their "private room" (v. 6). The word "room" (*tameion*) refers to any room inside a building that did not have doors or windows to the outside. Such rooms included storerooms where valuables were kept (Luke 12:24),[282] the private chambers of high-ranking government officials (Gen 43:30), bedrooms (Exod 8:3), and even hidden rooms to which threatened kings might escape.[283] This "private room" was the place where one went when he did not wish to be overheard (Luke 12:3). Closing the door granted the one who prayed even more privacy.

Jesus instructed His followers to pray to their Father. The hypocrite prayed for a human audience; the true disciple prays for the heavenly audience. By referring to God as the disciple's Father, Jesus reminded His disciples of their intimate relationship to God, which guarantees that their prayers will be heard (Matt 7:9–11).

Jesus specifically described the Father as "the one who is in secret," that is, the secret place (6:6). Because God is omnipresent, prayer need not be offered in the temple, the synagogue, or on the street corner to be effective. The God who resided in the temple resides in the storeroom, bedroom, and inner chamber as well. He is ever present, and His disciples can encounter that presence through humble supplication in the most obscure locations. The God who is in the secret place will hear prayers offered in the private place, and He will reward His followers for their faithfulness in prayer and the pure motives behind their prayers.

Jesus' teaching was not intended to prohibit all public prayer. As with His teaching regarding gifts to the poor, Jesus' concern was motivation not location. Both Jesus and His disciples prayed publicly, but their public prayers were an expression of their private devotion

---

[281] See comments on Matt 6:2.
[282] Josephus, *J.W.* 2.2.2 §17.
[283] Josephus, *Ant.* 8.15.4 §410.

to God. The fact that the model prayer addresses "our Father" rather than "my Father" shows that Jesus approved of public and corporate prayer. Jesus was insisting that prayer to God must not degenerate into an oration in which the prayer becomes more concerned about the human audience than the heavenly audience. Public prayers that do not issue from a consistent private prayer life or that easily shift from talking to God to talking about God are probably hypocritical and misdirected. Jesus preferred that His disciples not pray publicly if public prayer tended to make them forget the true purpose and focus of prayer. Prayers offered to impress people are idolatry masquerading as piety for they address prayer to human beings instead of God, who is the one and only proper focus of prayer.

Since people have a natural tendency to want to impress others, Jesus urged His disciples to pray privately on a consistent basis. This ensures that their prayers are true communion with God and that they are not distracted by the critical ears of other people. Private prayer allows the disciple to bare his soul and to be completely honest and open with God without fear of what others might think. The prayer closet is a place where prayers can consistently be transparent, authentic, and intimate communication with God.

After prohibiting hypocritical prayer, Jesus then set forth guidelines for the practice of prayer. First, when His disciples pray, they must not "babble" like Gentiles (v. 7). The precise meaning of the verb "babble" (*battalogeō*) is difficult to determine. The word occurs only here in the NT and appears only a few times elsewhere in literature not influenced by Matthew's usage. Scholars have proposed three different etymologies that suggest meanings such as "speak thoughtlessly," "speak futilely," or "stammer."[284] The evidence best supports the last of these options. A similar Greek verb *battarizō* meant "to stammer, stutter." The prefix *batta* appears to be onomatopoetic, that is, the pronunciation of the word imitates the sound that it describes (e.g., "buzz"). Since such babbling or stammering especially characterized Gentile prayers, it may refer to meaningless magical gibberish that appears in Greek magical papyri.[285] Like the familiar "abracadabra,"

---

[284] For detailed discussion, see G. Delling, "βατταλογέω," in *TDNT* 1 (1964):597; and Davies and Allison, *A Critical and Exegetical Commentary on the Gospel According to Saint Matthew,* 1:588.

[285] See Betz, *The Sermon on the Mount,* 364–65; Hagner, *Matthew 1–13,* 147; Davies and Allison, *A Critical and Exegetical Commentary on the Gospel According to Saint Matthew,* 1.588.

these formulas called *voces magicae* were nonsensical combinations of sounds that were believed to have special power.[286] Many ancient magical texts show that Jews sometimes embraced these magical practices.[287] Several ancient sources describe communications from pagan gods through their oracles as unintelligible babble.[288] Perhaps the babbling to which Jesus referred involved Gentiles attempting to communicate with their gods in the language of the deities.

Several texts speak of a similar phenomenon in Judaism. For example, *T. Job* 48–50 refers to humans attempting to communicate in three angelic languages, the languages spoken in heaven in the presence of God. When interpreted against this background, "Do not babble" likely means that Jesus' disciples should not seek to use a mystical language to communicate with God. They should pray to Him in their own everyday language. Although many modern Christians address God in an ecstatic "prayer language," the practice has no root in the teaching or example of Jesus. Jesus seems to have viewed such practices in paganism as inappropriate for His disciples.

Jesus warned that these pagan prayer practices were influenced by the notion that "they'll be heard for their many words" (v. 7). The notion is merely illusory since it is something they only "imagine." The verb translated "imagine" (*dokeō*) simply means "to think" or "suppose" in most contexts and does not necessarily mean that the subjective opinion is false. However, in this context the translation "imagine" is appropriate. Jesus has already indicated that the Gentile practice should be rejected by His disciples, and this implies that the assumptions underlying the practice are wrong. The verb "be heard"

---

[286] See C. Arnold, "Magical Papyri," in *Dictionary of New Testament Background*, ed. C. A. Brans (Downers Grove, IL: InterVarsity, 2000), 668.

[287] Ibid., 669.

[288] Lucan, *Civil War* 5.165–224; Strabo, *Geog.* 9.3.5; Plato, *Phaed.* 244B-C. M. Chambers offered this summary of the practice of the oracle at Delphi: "Delphi was also the site of the famous oracle that Greeks consulted for advice on every sort of problem; this too is a symbol of growing Panhellenism. The god Apollo supposedly spoke through the mouth of a peasant girl whom the priests chose as the oracle. After first intoxicating herself by chewing laurel leaves, thus supposedly infusing herself with the presence of the god, she would babble in a state of frenzy. Two priests would present questions to her and then report her replies to the person seeking advice. The reply was often deliberately ambiguous; the duty of interpreting it rested with the inquirer. Delphi managed, as an exception, to blend religion with political importance. Many Greek states consulted the oracle before making war or sending out colonies and repaid the oracle with luxurious offerings. Though never more than a small village, Delphi was adorned with treasure houses built by the various Greek states to house their gifts, and many individuals also dedicated offerings to the god" (*The Western Experience*, 44).

(*eisakousthēsontai*) is an intensive form of the verb "to hear," which means "to listen, heed, and respond."[289] The implication is not that the Gentiles thought their prayers were not heard if they prayed wrongly but rather that the prayer might be ignored. In order to get God's attention and to guarantee His response, many Gentiles assumed that prayer had to include the strings of gibberish and be very long.[290] The prayers often piled up one flattering title of the deity on top of another in hopes of manipulating the god to act. The prayers sometimes sought to coerce the gods by reminding them of favors owed to the one praying or with threats to deny the god's power if he failed to act.[291] Even some pagan critics like Seneca complained that the verbose prayers of the Gentiles were "fatiguing the gods."[292] France's characterization of those who prayed like Gentiles is apt: "Instead of trusting a Father to fulfill their needs, they think they must badger a reluctant Deity into taking notice of them."[293]

Some rabbis seem to have believed that lengthy, verbose prayer guaranteed a divine response. The Talmud states, "He who multiplies prayer will be heard."[294] On the other hand, many other Jewish teachers, no doubt in response to superstitious practices of their contemporaries, argued otherwise. Ecclesiastes 5:2 urged, "Do not be hasty to speak, and do not be impulsive to make a speech before God. God is in heaven and you are on earth, so let your words be few." During the time of Isaiah, God warned His people that He would ignore their prayers because of their sins: "When you lift up your hands in prayer, I will refuse to look at you; even if you offer countless prayers, I will not listen" (Isa 1:15). Between the time of the OT and NT, Sirach wrote, "God is in heaven and you upon earth; therefore let your words be few" (Sir 5:2) and "Do not repeat yourself when you pray" (Sir 7:14). The consensus among the rabbis was that prayer should be both simple and short.[295]

---

[289] "εἰσακούω," BDAG, 293.

[290] For an OT example, see the behavior of the priests of Baal and Elijah's mockery in 1 Kgs 18:26–29.

[291] For a thorough discussion of Gentile attempts to coerce the gods and for a rich bibliography, see Keener, *The Gospel of Matthew*, 213.

[292] Seneca, *Ep. Mor.* 31:5.

[293] France, *The Gospel of Matthew*, 240.

[294] *y. Ber.* 4.7b.

[295] *Mek.* on Exod 15:25; 2 Bar 48:26; *b. Ber.* 61a.

Jesus rejected the view that prayer was an attempt to manipulate God and that lengthy prayers filled with gibberish and memorized formulas could coerce God to act. As the model prayer and Jesus' Gethsemane prayer show, Jesus viewed prayer as the petitioner surrendering to the divine will, not bending the divine will. True prayer pleaded for God's will to be done on earth just as it is in heaven. As Jesus prayed in Gethsemane, "Not as I will, but as You will" (26:39).

"Don't be like them" (6:8) reminds Jesus' hearers that they are to seek to be like their heavenly Father rather than like pagan idolaters. Referring to God as "your Father" reminded Jesus' disciples that they had an intimate relationship with God, which makes efforts to gain His hearing completely unnecessary. God is attentive to the needs of His children far more than human fathers are attentive to the needs of theirs (7:9–11). Unlike pagan gods who were ignorant of the situations their worshippers faced, the God of Jesus knows every single need of His children before they express it. Isaiah 65:24 expressed the conviction that God was working to meet the needs of His people even before they uttered their petitions: "Even before they call, I will answer; while they are still speaking, I will hear." Just as Jesus appealed to God's omnipresence to assure His disciples that God hears the prayer offered in the "secret place" (Matt 6:6), so He now appealed to God's omniscience to assure them that God is not ignorant of their needs: "Your Father knows the things you need before you ask Him." The verbose prayers of the Gentiles implied that their gods lacked this comprehensive knowledge. When Jesus' hearers adopted their practices, it implied that their god was more like the gods of the idol worshippers than the true God of heaven.

Matthew 6:9–15

After Jesus told His disciples how they were not to pray, He offered a positive model for prayer. "Therefore" shows that the model prayer expresses the conclusion of Jesus' previous teaching regarding prayer. The prayer is a direct contrast to the verbosity, self-centeredness, and poor view of God reflected in the praying that Jesus rejected in verses 5–8.[296]

---

[296] This is also suggested by the use of the mildly emphatic pronoun "you" (ὑμεῖς). The emphatic use of the pronoun sharply distinguishes the way Jesus and His disciples pray from the way idolaters and hypocrites pray.

The adverb "like this" (*houtōs*) shows that Jesus' prayer is a model to be emulated rather than a script to be recited. Jesus did not say "pray this (*touto*)" but "pray like this." The model prayer expresses the attitudes and concerns that should guide the prayers of Jesus' disciples. Mindlessly reciting the prayer is a futile exercise more like the babbling of the idolaters than the cry of Jesus' followers. The present tense of the imperative verb "pray" indicates that Jesus' followers should pray often and habitually in accord with this model. The insertion of the word "should" in the HCSB probably softens Jesus' command too much. Jesus commanded His disciples to pray, and so failure to pray is an act of disobedience to the Savior.

Jesus instructed His followers to address God as "Our Father." The address is full of significance. Jesus referred to God as Father 43 times in Matthew. Thirty-eight of the occurrences are accompanied by a personal pronoun. Jesus referred to God as "your Father" when speaking to the disciples, "my Father" when referring to His own unique relationship to God, "their Father" when speaking about the righteous as sons of the kingdom, and "his Father" when speaking in the third person about the Son of Man. Personal pronouns are absent only in the prayer of 11:25–26, in which Jesus addressed God directly as Father and in 11:27; 24:36; and 28:19 in combination with references to Himself as "the Son."[297] The use of personal pronouns with "Father" in Matthew shows that Jesus did not view God as the Father of all people in general. Instead, God is the Father of Jesus' followers exclusively.[298]

This exclusive relationship of Jesus' followers to God is even more explicit elsewhere in Matthew. Jesus taught that "no one knows the Father except the Son and anyone to whom the Son desires to reveal Him" (11:27). Jesus insisted that the true children of God can be identified by their resemblance to their Father (5:9,44–45). Because

---

[297] The noun πατήρ is used 19 times in Matthew with second-person pronouns (ὑμῶν/σοῦ) to refer to God: 5:16,45,48; 6:1,4,6 (twice), 8,14–15,18 (twice), 26,32; 7:11; 10:20,29; 18:14; 23:9. It appears 16 times with the first-person singular pronoun μοῦ: 7:21; 10:32–33; 11:27; 12:50; 15:13; 16:17; 18:10,19,35; 20:23; 25:34; 26:29,39,42,53. It occurs once with the third-person plural pronoun αὐτῶν (in 13:43), and once with the third-person singular pronoun αὐτοῦ (in 16:27). The noun appears without pronouns only in 11:25,26,27 (twice); 24:36; and 28:19.

[298] Against Betz, *The Sermon on the Mount*, 386–89. See also R. Brown, "The Pater Noster as an Eschatological Prayer," *TS* 22 (1961): 175–208, esp. 182–84; Davies and Allison, *A Critical and Exegetical Commentary on the Gospel According to Saint Matthew*, 1:601; France, *The Gospel of Matthew*, 245.

of this exclusive relationship to God, Jesus' followers can be confident that He is attentive to their prayers. Even wicked earthly fathers desire to give good gifts to their children. How much more does the heavenly Father give good things to His children who make their requests to Him (7:9–11)! The address of the prayer to the heavenly Father thus reminds Jesus' followers of God's graciousness toward His children.

The use of the first-person plural pronoun "our" (hēmōn) rather than the first-person singular pronoun "my" shows that Jesus expected His disciples to pray together as a group.[299] This is confirmed by the use of seven additional first-person plural pronouns in the second half of the prayer (vv. 11–13). Thus Jesus' teaching in 6:5–6 should not be interpreted as a prohibition of corporate prayer. Matthew 6:5–6 is more concerned with the motivation for one's prayers than one's location. Jesus loathed the spiritual showmanship of those who prayed in order to call attention to themselves. However, He also recognized that public prayers could be accompanied by genuine humility and focused on the heavenly audience rather than the human audience. Jesus' appreciation for corporate prayer was later demonstrated powerfully by His decision to involve the inner circle of disciples, Peter, James, and John, in His own pleas to the Father in Gethsemane (26:36–46). Although human pride can easily corrupt public prayer, the weakness of the flesh and the tendency to sleep when we ought to pray may be best thwarted through mutual encouragement in corporate prayer.

The petitions of the model prayer are among some of the most difficult verses in the entire SM. The petitions have traditionally been interpreted as focusing on the present needs of the disciple. Thus the first petition seeks to glorify the name of God through personal obedience. The second and third petitions seek to submit to God's rule so that God's will may be perfectly fulfilled in the disciple's lives here and now. However, in the second half of the twentieth century several scholars suggested that the petitions of the model prayer are specifically eschatological in focus.[300] The petitions of the prayer are concerned with last things, particularly the revelation of God's glory on the Day of the Lord, the ushering in of God's eternal reign, forgiveness

---

[299] R. T. France, *Matthew*, TNTC (Grand Rapids: Eerdmans, 1985), 133.

[300] See esp. Jeremias, *New Testament Theology*, 193–203; and Brown, "The Pater Noster as an Eschatological Prayer," 175–208.

at the final judgment, and protection during the time of tribulation that immediately precedes the end. The difficulties in choosing between these two schemes of interpretation led one prominent commentator to exclaim, "A decision concerning the issue under review is, in our judgment, exceedingly hard to render, and there is no room for certainty."[301] This commentary will proceed by introducing the interpretation of each of the petitions affirmed by the traditional and eschatological schemes and then examining the strengths and weaknesses of the interpretive schemes for the individual petitions.

"Your name be honored as holy."   In the traditional interpretation, this petition is a prayer "not only to reverence and honor God, but also to glorify him by obedience to his commands, and thus prepare for the coming kingdom."[302] The petition is normally seen as having a strong ethical dimension. The OT provides a basis for this interpretation. Honoring God's name as holy is the opposite of profaning God's name. Some 14 times the OT refers to God's people profaning God's name by their wicked deeds (Lev 18:21; 19:12; 20:3; 21:6; 22:2,32; Ps 74:7; Jer 34:16; Ezek 36:20; 39:7; 43:7–8; Amos 2:7).[303] Thus when Jesus' followers pray that God's name may be honored as holy, they are committing themselves to glorify God's name through their good works (Matt 5:16). Dietrich Bonhoeffer summarized the petition in this way: "May God protect his holy gospel from being obscured and profaned by false doctrine and unholiness of living, and may he ever make known his holy name to the disciples in Jesus Christ."[304]

Two OT texts specifically refer to honoring God's name as holy: Isa 29:22–23 and Ezek 36:22–23.[305] Those who favor the traditional

---

[301] Davies and Allison, *A Critical and Exegetical Commentary on the Gospel According to Saint Matthew*, 1:594. Allison concluded, "We are inclined to agree with those who see the Lord's Prayer as thoroughly eschatological" (ibid.). Scholars who accept some form of the traditional view include Dietrich Bonhoeffer, John Calvin, Martin Luther, Ulrich Luz, Leon Morris, Rudolf Schnackenburg, and Michael Wilkins. Most scholars whose interpretation of the prayer is traditional recognize that the second petition is eschatological. Scholars who see the prayer as thoroughly eschatological include Dale Allison, Raymond Brown, and Joachim Jeremias. Scholars who fuse the two views include R. T. France, Robert Guelich, Robert Gundry (who argues that Jesus emphasized the future aspects of the kingdom but that Matthew's application emphasized present aspects), David Hill, Craig Keener, and Ben Witherington.

[302] Hill, *The Gospel of Matthew*, 136.

[303] *T. Naph.* 8:4 says, "God shall be glorified among the Gentiles through you, but through him that does not that which is good, God shall be dishonored."

[304] Bonhoeffer, *The Cost of Discipleship*, 166.

[305] These texts from the LXX combine ἁγιάζω and ὄνομα in reference to God's name in a manner similar to Matt 6:9.

view of the first petition of the model prayer, typically see its meaning as deeply influenced by Isa 29:22–23. Those who favor the eschatological view see a closer connection between the petition and Ezek 36:22–23. Isaiah 29:22–23 says,

> Therefore, the LORD who redeemed Abraham says this about the house of Jacob: Jacob will no longer be ashamed and his face will no longer be pale. For when he sees his children, the work of My hands within his nation, they will honor My name, they will honor the Holy One of Jacob and stand in awe of the God of Israel.

The text seems to refer to the restoration of Israel after the exile and uses language similar to Matt 6:9. This text could be taken as supporting the traditional interpretation with its focus on the ethic of Christian disciples since the preceding context (vv. 19–21) focuses on the moral purification of God's people:

> The humble will have joy after joy in the LORD, and the poor people will rejoice in the Holy One of Israel. For the ruthless one will vanish, the scorner will disappear, and all those who lie in wait with evil intent will be killed— those who, with their speech, accuse a person of wrongdoing, who set a trap at the gate for the mediator, and without cause deprive the righteous of justice.

In light of this content, God's people may honor God's name as holy through their moral purity and their deeds of righteousness and justice.

Interpreters who affirm the eschatological view argue that good reasons exist for doubting that Isaiah 29 provides the background for Jesus' petition. Most importantly, they claim Isaiah 29 and Matthew 6 are distinct in that Isaiah referred to God's children honoring His name, but the model prayer seems to refer to God Himself honoring His name as holy.[306] They suggest that Ezek 36:22–23 constitutes a closer parallel:

> "This is what the Lord GOD says: It is not for your sake that I will act, house of Israel, but for My holy name, which you profaned among the nations where you went. I will honor the holiness of My great name, which has been

---

[306] This assumes that the passive verb in Matt 6:9 is a "divine passive," a reverent reference to the activity of God. One might argue that a divine passive is to be expected in a prayer since prayer, by its very nature, calls on God to act. See Davies and Allison, *A Critical and Exegetical Commentary on the Gospel According to Saint Matthew*, 1:602. Early church fathers like Augustine and Cyril of Jerusalem took the petition as a reference to the hallowing of God's name by His people.

profaned among the nations—the name you have profaned among them. The
nations will know that I am Yahweh"—the declaration of the Lord GOD—
"when I demonstrate My holiness through you in their sight."

The following verses (24–38) describe in detail how God will
honor the holiness of His name: He will restore Israel, cleanse His
people, place His Spirit in them so that they at last keep His commands, and bless the soil of Israel with amazing fruitfulness.

If Jesus intended an allusion to Ezekiel in His first petition, His
prayer might be interpreted as a plea for Israel's restoration.[307] Raymond Brown has argued that the closest NT parallel also supports this
interpretation:

> The most revealing text in this regard is found at the end of Jesus' public min-
> istry (John 12:28). Feeling that His hour is at hand—the culminating hour
> of return to the Father in passion, death, resurrection, and ascension—Jesus
> cries out, "Father, glorify your name." . . . The answer comes back from the
> Father: "I have glorified it and will glorify it again." We should notice the past
> and future tenses. The past (aorist) tense seems to cover the glorification of
> the divine name through Jesus' earthly work; the future seems to cover the
> glorification that will be effected in Jesus' return to the Father and the send-
> ing of the Spirit (see John 16:14). Thus, the ultimate sanctification of the
> divine name is still to come: the glorification accomplished by the Spirit will
> include the guidance of the Church toward the last times and the final strug-
> gle with Satan (as the whole of 1 John makes clear, especially chap. 5).[308]

Brown concluded that the honoring of the divine name consists in
the final coming of God's kingdom and the completion of His divine
plan as intimated in the second and third petitions. He noted, "Only
the last days will see that vindication of the holiness of God's name
promised by Ezekiel to the new Israel."[309]

An examination of the relationship between the model prayer and
other ancient Jewish prayers may shed some light on the meaning of
the petition. The model prayer is similar to a standard Jewish prayer
called the *Kaddish*. The *Kaddish* eventually developed into a synagogue prayer that was recited antiphonally and later in unison while

[307] Some interpreters have gone so far as to suggest that the entire model prayer is based on
Ezekiel 36. In this view the first petition was drawn from Ezek 36:23; the second from Ezek
36:24; the third from Ezek 36:28; the fourth from Ezek 36:29–30; the fifth from Ezek 36:31,33;
and the sixth from Ezek 36:26,29. However, because of the lack of verbal connections between
the petitions and their alleged sources, this seems rather far-fetched. Possibly the first petition
bears some allusion to Ezek 36:23, but as will be seen, even this is doubtful.
[308] Brown, "The Pater Noster as an Eschatological Prayer," 187.
[309] Ibid.

entering the synagogue and in response to the reading of Scripture in the synagogue.[310] Joachim Jeremias has offered the following as the earliest probable form of the prayer: "Exalted and hallowed be his great name in the world which he created according to his will. May he let his kingdom rule in your lifetime and in your days and in the lifetime of the whole house of Israel, speedily and soon. And to this, say: amen."[311]

Like the model prayer, the *Kaddish* prays for the hallowing of God's name, the coming of the kingdom, and mentions God's will.[312] Most scholars infer from these connections that Jesus' prayer was an adaptation of the ancient *Kaddish*.[313] One cannot prove that the *Kaddish* existed during the time of Jesus since it does not appear in any of the extant Jewish literature from this period. However, many scholars date the prayer to the period before AD 70 because of its similarity to temple liturgy and the lack of any reference to the fall of Jerusalem.[314] The petitions of Jesus' prayer are much shorter than those of the *Kaddish*, and that brevity presents the greatest challenge to a precise interpretation of the petitions. However, Jesus' disciples would likely have immediately recognized the connection between Jesus' prayer and the *Kaddish* and would have interpreted the first two petitions especially in light of the familiar Jewish prayer. If so, the *Kaddish* rather than the allusions to honoring God's name as holy in Isaiah and Ezekiel provide the primary reference point for the interpretation of these petitions.

The first petition of the *Kaddish* was probably drawn from a number of different doxologies in the OT. The petition appears to be a

---

[310] D. Blumenthal, "Observations and Reflections on the History and Meanings of the Kaddish," *Judaism* 50 (2001): 35–51, esp. 38–40. See also Leon Wieseltier, *Kaddish* (New York: Knopf, 1998).

[311] J. Jeremias, *The Prayers of Jesus* (Philadelphia: Fortress, 1964), 98.

[312] Luz quoted another Jewish prayer that says, "Hallowed be your name among us before the eyes of all living things; let his reign be obvious and visible over us quickly and soon" (*Matthew 1–7*, 317, n. 79).

[313] See Jeremias, *The Prayers of Jesus*, 98; Luz, *Matthew 1–7*, 317; Keener, *The Gospel of Matthew*, 215–26. The connection between the prayers is sometimes noted without a clear suggestion of dependence. See France, *The Gospel of Matthew*, 134; Hagner, *Matthew 1–13*, 147.

[314] Luz, *Matthew 1–7*, 317. France stated confidently that the "Aramaic Qaddish prayer . . . was already in regular synagogue use by the time of Jesus" (*The Gospel of Matthew*, 243). On the other hand, B. Graubard and R. Byargeon have challenged assumptions regarding the antiquity of the *Kaddish* ("The Qaddish Prayer," in *The Lord's Prayer and Jewish Liturgy*, ed. J. J. Petuchowski and M. Brocke [New York: Seabury, 1978]); R. Byargeon, "Echoes of Wisdom in the Lord's Prayer (Matt 6:9–13)," *JETS* 41 (1998): 353–65, esp. 354–57.

paraphrase of Job 1:21; Ps 113:2; and Dan 2:20. None of these texts has a particularly eschatological focus. They each speak primarily of glorifying the name of God here and now. This is especially clear in Ps 113:2 in which the exclamation, "Let the name of the Lᴏʀᴅ be praised both now and forever," is followed by the words, "From the rising of the sun to its setting, let the name of the Lᴏʀᴅ be praised" (v. 3). The *Kaddish* likewise focuses primarily on presently glorifying the name of God: "Exalted and hallowed be his great name in the world which he created according to his will." If the focus were eschatological, the petition would likely have read, "Exalted and hallowed be his great name in the world which is to come."[315]

Thus Jesus' disciples would likely have understood the first petition of the model prayer as a petition that God would receive the glory that He deserves from His people here and now.[316] This involved praising the name of God with one's lips from the heart. It also involved glorifying God through righteous deeds (Matt 5:16). These righteous deeds are especially the righteous acts and attitude that are prescribed in the SM. Jesus' ministry resulted in God's being glorified (9:8; 15:31). The lives of His disciples must pursue this same goal.

The traditional and primarily ethical interpretation of the petition seems to be confirmed by the conclusion of the SM. Interestingly 7:21–23 combines reference to activities done in the Lord's name with references to doing the Lord's will and entering the kingdom. Thus the primary features of the first three petitions of the model prayer recur in the conclusion to the SM. There false disciples do important works in the Lord's name but dishonor Him by their disobedient lifestyles. They fail to hallow the name of the Lord because of their lawless acts. Those who pray the model prayer are thus asking that God enable them to live as true disciples who honor the Lord's name through holy living.

---

[315] See, e.g., *m. Sanh.* 10:1–4, which uses the phrase "world to come" no less than ten times. Nolland correctly observes, "Attempts to read the first petition of the Qaddish as itself eschatological are unconvincing" (*The Gospel of Matthew*, 286, n. 315).

[316] For a similar line of reasoning, see Luz, *Matthew 1–7*, 317–18. Betz noted, "If one regards the aorist as an instance of the Greek aorist of prayer, the subject would not be God but human worshippers. God would then be asked to see that humanity sanctify his name, so that one should understand the petition to read as: 'cause us humans to sanctify your name'" (*The Sermon on the Mount*, 389; cp. BDF §337 [4]). Byargeon defended the moral interpretation based on parallels with the prayer of Agur in Proverbs 30 ("Echoes of Wisdom," 362–64).

Although the petition implies that Jesus' disciples have a personal responsibility to glorify the name of God through their good works, the fact that the disciple prays that God's name may be glorified in his life demonstrates that godly living is possible only through dependence on God. The good deeds of the disciple are not seen as acts of righteousness that he personally manufactures but as righteous works that God produces in and through him. The disciple cannot honor God's name in his own power. He can do so only as God graciously enables him. Once again the SM is seen to be grounded in a theology of grace rather than human ability.

"Your kingdom come." Throughout Christian history three major interpretations of this petition have arisen. The ethical interpretation sees the petition as a prayer that Jesus' disciples will live in submission to the kingly rule of God and thus obey His commands. The evangelistic interpretation views the petition as a plea for the extension of the kingdom of God throughout the world as the gospel is propagated to the ends of the earth and new believers submit to God's authority. The eschatological interpretation regards the petition as a prayer for the consummation of God's kingly rule through the second coming of Messiah Jesus.

Many interpreters conflate two or more of these interpretations. Since the time of the Reformation, many evangelical interpreters have merged all three of these views. In this eclectic interpretation, the coming kingdom is a reference to the voluntary submission of repentant sinners to God's rule, the expansion of the kingdom through mission and evangelism, and the glorious return of Jesus when all that is broken in this world is made right. Consequently, Calvin interpreted the petition as an expression of the believer's

> daily desire that God gather churches unto himself from all parts of the earth; that he spread and increase them in number; that he adorn them with gifts; that he establish a lawful order among them; on the other hand, that he cast down all enemies of pure teaching and religion; that he scatter their counsels and crush their efforts.

Calvin acknowledged that the kingdom would not come in its fullness until the final coming of Christ when "God may be all in all" (1 Cor 15:28).[317]

---

[317] Calvin, *Institutes of the Christian Religion*, 2:905–6.

In a similar approach Martin Lloyd-Jones argued that the petition had three facets. The prayer expressed the "great longing that the
kingdom of God in Christ may come in the hearts of men," in both
"our own hearts" as well as "the hearts of other men and women."
Thus when believers pray the petition, they pray "for the success of
the gospel," an "all-inclusive missionary prayer." In addition to the
ethical and evangelistic interpretations of the petition, Jones added
the eschatological interpretation:

> It is a prayer which indicates that we are "Looking for and hasting unto the
> coming of the day of God" (2 Pet 3:12). It means that disciples should antici-
> pate the day when all sin and evil and wrong and everything that is opposed
> to God shall finally have been routed. It means that we should have longings
> in our hearts for the time when the Lord will come back again, when all that
> is opposed to Him shall be cast into the lake of burning, and the kingdoms of
> this world shall have become the kingdoms of our God and of His Christ.[318]

The prayer for the coming of the kingdom resonates with one of
the most prominent themes in Jesus' teaching.[319] The various temporal aspects of the kingdom result in at least three different possible
interpretations of the petition "Your kingdom come." First, the petition could focus on the present aspect of the kingdom. The petition
could be a request to embrace fully the demands and responsibilities
of Jesus' rule here and now. This interpretation is normally associated
with the view that the kingdom consists of God's internal rule of the
believer. Luke 17:20–21 says, "The kingdom of God is not coming
with something observable; no one will say, 'Look here!' or 'There!'
For you see, the kingdom of God is among you." The latter part of the
verse may legitimately be translated "the kingdom of God is within
you."[320] However, most scholars are convinced that Jesus was referring to the presence of the kingdom in His own ministry rather than
to the internal rule of God in His disciples.[321] Thus the petition does
not seem to be a request for God's rule in the heart of believers.

The petition has sometimes been interpreted as a prayer for the
extension of God's kingdom throughout the world as the gospel is
proclaimed and new disciples are made. Bonhoeffer adopted this

---

[318] Lloyd-Jones, *Studies in the Sermon on the Mount*, 338.

[319] See the discussion on the nature of the kingdom of God in the comments on Matt 5:3.

[320] See C. Caragounis, "The Kingdom of God/Heaven," in *DJG*, 423–24.

[321] I. H. Marshall, *Luke*, NIGTC (Grand Rapids: Eerdmans, 1978), 655; and J. Green, *The Gospel of Luke*, NICNT (Grand Rapids: Eerdmans, 1997), 628–30, esp. n. 54.

missional interpretation in his paraphrase, "God grant that the kingdom of Christ may grow in his church on earth."[322] John Stott wrote, "To pray that the kingdom may 'come' is to pray both that it may grow, as through the church's witness people submit to Jesus, and that soon it will be consummated when Jesus returns in glory to take his power and reign." Interestingly both Bonhoeffer and Stott suggest that the verb "come" means "grow." One suspects, however, that if Jesus wanted to refer to the expansion of the kingdom, He would have used the verb "grow" (*auxanō*) rather than the verb "come" (*erchomai*). When Jesus spoke of the growth of the kingdom in the parables of the Mustard Seed and the Yeast, He used the verbs "grow" (*auxanō*) and "spread" (lit., "leaven;" *zumoō*). Other references to the "coming" of the kingdom in the Gospels do not appear to speak of kingdom growth through the fulfillment of the church's mission. Instead, references to the coming kingdom in Jesus' teaching are consistently eschatological or refer to events such as Jesus' transfiguration that foreshadow eschatological events (Matt 16:28; Mark 9:1; 11:10; Luke 17:20; 22:18).

The petition is thus most likely a plea for the consummation of God's kingdom through the second coming of Jesus. The suspicion that the petition is eschatological is supported by the presence of a similar petition in the *Kaddish*: "May he let his kingdom rule in your lifetime and in your days and in the lifetime of the whole house of Israel, speedily and soon. And to this, say: amen."[323]

The *Kaddish* expresses the hope that the kingdom is imminent but denies that the kingdom is present. The one who prayed the *Kaddish* hoped that he would live to see the day in which God's rule would be established, that is, might come "speedily and soon." The kingdom of God in the *Kaddish* is more than God's rule over the individual Israelite. Those who prayed the *Kaddish* likely saw themselves as already living under God's royal and divine authority as they submitted to His commandments. Rather the kingdom of God in the *Kaddish* was the full and final establishment of the rule of God that would be accompanied by the fierce punishment of the wicked, the rich reward of God's

---

[322] D. Bonhoeffer, *The Cost of Discipleship* (New York: Simon and Schuster, 1995), 166.

[323] Jeremias, *The Prayers of Jesus*, 98. The eschatological nature of the kingdom in the *Kaddish* is underscored by alternative versions. Before the phrase "in your lifetime" one version inserts "make His redemption spring forth, cause His Messiah to approach and redeem His people." Another version adds to the previous insertion "and build up His temple." See Betz, *The Sermon on the Mount*, 391.

people, and the glorious reign of the Messiah over all the earth. Jesus'
disciples would probably have heard this petition of the model prayer
as an echo of the *Kaddish* and would have automatically interpreted
the petition against that background. Jesus would probably have clarified the petition if He meant something other than what the disciples
would expect in light of their supposed familiarity with the *Kaddish*.[324]
Betz rightly concluded, "The eschatology of the Lord's Prayer expects
the kingdom of God to conquer and annex the territory at present
inhabited by the rebellious human race."[325]

Paul's letters also lend support to the eschatological interpretation.
As noted earlier, when Paul referred to inheriting the kingdom, he generally used the future tense (1 Cor 6:9–10; 15:50; Gal 5:21; cp. Eph
5:5). Paul also associated the kingdom with "the end" (*to telos*) when
Christ will conquer every ruler, power, and authority. He mentioned
the kingdom in connection with God's glory (1 Thess 2:12), eschatological judgment (2 Tim 4:1), the Second Coming (2 Tim 4:1), and
final salvation (2 Tim 4:18). He referred to the kingdom in the context
of extensive eschatological discussions (2 Thess 1:5). Although Paul
could speak of the kingdom as a present reality (Col 1:13), he much
more frequently referred to it as a future expectation. Strong evidence
supports the conclusion that Paul had extensive knowledge of Jesus'
teachings and that he was an accurate interpreter of them.[326] Paul's
testimony is thus compelling evidence in favor of the eschatological
interpretation of Matt 6:10.

Allison has pointed out that "kingdom of God" never appears as
the subject of the verb "come" in the OT, ancient Jewish literature, or
the NT outside of the Gospels. He suggested that the words of the second petition were influenced by ancient references to the "coming" of
God (Isa 35:4; 40:9–10; Zech 14:5; *1 Enoch* 1:3–9; 25:3; *Jub.* 1:22–28;

---

[324] Luz noted, "With the second petition of the Lord's Prayer, 'Let your kingdom come,' the eschatological interpretation of the prayer has its strongest pillar." He later added, "There can be no doubt about the eschatological character of this petition, even though the church's traditional interpretation has usually gone in the other direction" (*Matthew 1–7*, 1:318). See also Betz, *The Sermon on the Mount*, 390–92; France, *The Gospel of Matthew*, 246 (who described this petition as "perhaps the most clearly futuristic reference to God's kingdom in Matthew").

[325] Betz, *The Sermon on the Mount*, 391. The tensions that Betz saw between the eschatology of the Lord's Prayer and the rest of the SM are more imagined than real.

[326] See the author's discussion of this issue in A. J. Kostenberger, C. L. Quarles, and L. S. Kellum, *The Cradle, the Cross, and the Crown* (Nashville: B&H Academic, 2009), 368–77.

T. Levi 5:2; *As. Mos.* 10:1–2; *Tg. Zech.* 2:14–15).[327] Allison concluded, "It was natural for Jesus, for whom kingdom=God (as ruler) (cf. Tg. on Isa 24.23; 31.4; 52.7; and see Jeremias, *Theology*, p. 102), to speak of the 'coming' of the kingdom because, in essence, he was speaking about the 'coming' of God."[328]

This petition may be the impetus behind one of the earliest prayers of the church preserved in the NT.[329] In 1 Cor 16:22 Paul breathed the prayer, "Maranatha!" This Aramaic phrase means "Come, Lord!" This was evidently a well-known petition in the early church. Paul transliterated the Aramaic expression but did not translate it for his Greek-speaking audience. This implies that the expression was already a familiar one even among Corinthians who had no extensive knowledge of Aramaic. The same expression appears in the earliest extant collection of Christian worship material, the *Didache*, as part of a prayer to be offered at the end of the Lord's Supper. The Greek translation of the Aramaic phrase appears in Rev 22:20, "Come, Lord Jesus!"

This expression can be traced to the earliest Aramaic-speaking congregations in Palestine and probably to the church in Jerusalem.[330] The "Lord" whose coming is sought through the petition is clearly Jesus as Rev 22:20 demonstrates. The petition may be interpreted either as an appeal for Jesus' presence in corporate worship or as a prayer for His glorious return.[331] The evidence for the eschatological interpretation is most compelling.

In Revelation 22, the petition follows three promises of Jesus' eschatological coming. Verse 7 says, "Look, I am coming quickly!" Blessed is the one who keeps the prophetic words of this book." This is followed by verse 10, "Don't seal the prophetic words of this

---

[327] Davies and Allison, *A Critical and Exegetical Commentary on the Gospel According to Saint Matthew*, 1:604–5. Allison was depending on the earlier research of J. Schlosser in *Le Règne de Dieu dans les dits de Jésus* (Paris: Gabalda, 1980), 1:268–83.

[328] Davies and Allison, *A Critical and Exegetical Commentary on the Gospel According to Saint Matthew*, 1:604–5. See also Nolland, *The Gospel of Matthew*, 287.

[329] This was also suggested by Lloyd-Jones (*Studies in the Sermon on the Mount*, 338). Cp. Hill, *The Gospel of Matthew*, 137; and Wilkins, *Matthew*, 277.

[330] Larry Hurtado, *Lord Jesus Christ: Devotion to Jesus in Earliest Christianity* (Grand Rapids: Eerdmans, 2003), 173–75.

[331] See C. Blomberg, *1 Corinthians*, NIVAC (Grand Rapids: Zondervan, 1994), 342; G. Fee, *The First Epistle to the Corinthians*, NICNT (Grand Rapids: Eerdmans, 1987), 838–39; D. Garland, *1 Corinthians*, BECNT (Grand Rapids: Baker Academic, 2003), 773–74; and A. Thiselton, *The First Epistle to the Corinthians*, NIGTC (Grand Rapids: Eerdmans, 2000), 1350–52.

book, because the time is near." Verse 12 repeats, "Look! I am coming quickly, and My reward is with Me to repay each person according to what he has done." This demonstrates that the coming is eschatological and is connected to final judgment. Then immediately before the expression "Amen! Come, Lord Jesus!" Jesus testified again, "Yes, I am coming quickly!" (v. 20).

The eschatological sense of the expression is also confirmed by the usage in *Did.* 10:5–6:

> Remember your church, Lord, to deliver it from all evil and to make it perfect in your love; and gather it, the one that has been sanctified, from the four winds into your kingdom, which you have prepared for it; for yours is the power and the glory forever.
>
> May grace come, and may this world pass away. Hosanna to the God of David. If anyone is holy, let him come; if anyone is not, let him repent. Maranatha! Amen.[332]

The references in the prayer to the deliverance of the church from all evil, the perfection of the church, the gathering of the church from the four winds into the kingdom, and the passing away of the world indicate that the concluding petition, "Maranatha," is an appeal for Christ to come in all His glory to establish His kingdom on earth.

In 1 Cor 16:22 the petition "Maranatha" is likely related to Paul's teaching about inheriting the eschatological kingdom of God in 15:50–58. Thus the petition pled for Jesus to return to raise the dead, change the corruptible into the incorruptible, to finalize His victory over death, and to grant His kingdom to His transformed and resurrected people. The petition, "Maranatha," thus expresses the essence of the plea, "Your kingdom come!"[333]

---

[332] M. W. Holmes, *The Apostolic Fathers: Greek Texts and English Translations*, 3rd ed. (Grand Rapids: Baker Academic, 2007), 263.

[333] Scholars sometimes argue that Paul terribly neglected the concept of the kingdom of God that was at the center of Jesus' own teaching. However, although Paul did not discuss the kingdom as extensively as Jesus did, the paucity of references to the kingdom may have resulted from extensive oral teaching about the kingdom that made discussion in his letters unnecessary. Furthermore, Paul mentioned the kingdom more frequently than some scholars have acknowledged. The word "kingdom" (*basileia*) appears in reference to the kingdom of God/Christ 14 times in Paul's letters. These references reflect the same inaugurated eschatology as the teaching of Jesus. Paul sometimes refers to the kingdom as a present reality (Rom 14:17; 1 Cor 4:20; Col 1:13; 4:11). However, the majority of Paul's references treat the eschatological kingdom (1 Cor 6:9–10; 15:24–24; 15:50; Gal 5:21; Eph 5:5; 1 Thess 2:12; 2 Thess 1:5; and 2 Tim 4:1,18). Paul's emphasis on the eschatological kingdom was probably influenced by his knowledge of Jesus' teachings on the subject.

Jesus' followers pray fervently and frequently for the coming of
Christ's kingdom for good reason. The consummation of the kingdom
will bring about the complete fulfillment of the great blessings promised in the Beatitudes. Although Jesus' disciples now enjoy a partial
fulfillment of each of these promises, they will experience the complete and final fulfillment of these promises only after Jesus' return.
That will be the moment when His disciples will experience the full
extent of God's comfort (Matt 5:4) as He wipes every tear from their
eyes (Rev 21:4). That will be the moment when His followers "inherit
the earth" (Matt 5:5) and inhabit the new Jerusalem (21:9–22:5). That
will be the moment when believers are fully transformed into the image of the Creator and are completely filled with the righteousness for
which they so long hungered and thirsted (Matt 5:6). At the eschatological judgment they will at last experience the depths of the Father's
mercy (v. 7) when guilty sinners who are declared righteous will have
that declaration confirmed in the final judgment by God's unfathom-
able grace. At Jesus' return they will see God face-to-face (Matt 5:8).
Those who were first estranged from Him by their sin and corruption
will at last know the full joy of being His sons and daughters (Matt
5:9) and will receive from Him their heavenly inheritance (1 Pet 1:4).
At last the insulted, persecuted, and slandered disciples will receive
the great heavenly reward (Matt 5:12) that inspired their joy even in
the midst of their sufferings.

Some interpreters may be compelled to read the present aspect of
the kingdom into Jesus' petition because they fear that affirming the
eschatological interpretation may make the petition irrelevant for today. This fear is unfounded. The "blessed hope" (Titus 2:13) of Jesus'
appearing is a crucial motivation for godly living today (v. 12). Contrary to a well-worn cliché, God's people must be heavenly minded if
they are to be of any earthly good. The servant who does not eagerly
await the Master's return will probably be unprepared when He arrives to inspect the servant's work (Matt 24:45–51). Those who are
not expectantly awaiting His coming may find themselves pounding
on a locked door and be rejected by the words, "I do not know you!"
(25:1–13). Those who are not longing for Jesus' return may not expend their lives in His service and may suffer in "outer darkness"
where there will be "weeping and gnashing of teeth" (vv. 14–30).

The eschatological interpretation of the second petition has clear ethical implications. Praying for the coming kingdom prevents the disciple from being so focused on this present life that he neglects to prepare for the next. Praying for the coming kingdom empowers him to live selflessly now with the awareness that enormous reward awaits Him in the future. Praying for the coming kingdom reminds the believer that God's work is not finished and that the best is yet to come.

"Your will be done on earth as it is in heaven."   This third petition has been regarded as a clarification of the second petition. If one grants this assumption, his interpretation of the second petition will largely determine his interpretation of the third. Those who see the second petition as primarily ethical tend to interpret the third petition as a prayer of personal submission to the will of God. Those who see the second petition as eschatological tend to interpret the third petition as another plea for the consummation of God's kingdom by conquering all evil and restoring righteousness on earth.

Again many commentators conflate these interpretations. Bonhoeffer clearly affirmed the ethical view when he wrote, "The evil will is still alive even in the followers of Christ, it still seeks to cut them off from fellowship with him; and that is why they must also pray that the will of God may prevail more and more in their hearts every day and break down all defiance." However, Bonhoeffer also seems to affirm the eschatological view when he writes, "In the end the whole world must bow before that will, worshipping and giving thanks in joy and tribulation."[334] Calvin also blended the ethical and eschatological interpretations of the third petition. He argued that the petition referred to that time when "God will be King in the world when all submit to his will" and that the petition anticipated when "the earth be in like manner [as heaven] subject to such a rule, with all arrogance and wickedness brought to an end." He also saw the petition as involving personal renunciation of the desires of the flesh and a spirit of self-denial that seeks to conform one's own will to God's will.[335] The conflation of the two interpretations may well be a tacit surrender to the difficulty of choosing between the two. More

---

[334] Bonhoeffer, *The Cost of Discipleship*, 166.
[335] Calvin, *Institutes of the Christian Religion*, 3.20.42.

than one prominent scholar has argued that it is simply impossible to determine which of the two is correct.[336]

The parallel to this petition in Matt 26:39 initially seems to confirm the ethical interpretation. In Gethsemane, Jesus' first petition seems to echo the model prayer, "My Father! If it is possible, let this cup pass from Me. Yet not as I will, but as You will." This is a prayer of complete surrender to the Father's will. The second petition of Gethsemane contains a verbatim parallel to the main clause of the third petition of the model prayer. Jesus prayed, "My Father, if this cannot pass unless I drink it, Your will be done."[337] The parallel may imply that the third petition of the model prayer is a prayer of submission which embraces God's plan for the life of the disciple even if that plan entails sacrifice, suffering, and death.

In Jesus' Gethsemane prayer the word "will" (*thelēma*) seems to refer to the desire or predetermined plan of God. This is also the apparent sense of the term in 18:14: "In the same way, it is not the will of your Father in heaven that one of these little ones perish." On the other hand, three of the six uses of the term in Matthew have moral connotations (7:21; 12:50; 21:31). In these contexts God's will is the moral will that He expresses through His commandments. All three of these instances refer to "doing" (*poieō*) God's "will."

By translating Matt 6:10 as "Your will be done" most modern English translations imply that God's will in the third petition is God's moral will which the one who prays commits to obey. However, the Greek text may be better translated, "May Your will happen (*genēthētō*)." This verb choice more closely links the petition with the use of the noun "will" in 18:14 and 26:42 in which God's will is a reference to His desire or predetermined plan.[338]

Thus Jesus taught His disciples to pray that God's plan will be enacted "on earth as it is in heaven."[339] Some interpreters entertain the

---

[336] Luz, *Matthew 1–7*, 319. See also Davies and Allison, *A Critical and Exegetical Commentary on the Gospel According to Saint Matthew*, 1:605–6.

[337] Matt 6:10: *genēthētō to thelēma sou* // Matt 26:42: *genēthētō to thelēma sou*.

[338] Against Wilkins, *Matthew*, 277. Betz noted, "As parallels from the Jewish prayers show, reference is made to God's plan and intention in his governance of the universe" (*The Sermon on the Mount*, 393).

[339] Most recent commentators argue that this clause modifies all three of the first petitions. This would give all three petitions a distinct eschatological character. Despite the popularity of this view, Broadus seems to be correct in rejecting it as improbable (*The Gospel According to Matthew*, 135). The clause would be most awkward when modifying the second petition. Furthermore, no conjunctions link the three petitions as one would expect if the last clause

possibility that the phrase should be translated "both in heaven and on earth." However, the traditional translation better expresses the reading of the oldest manuscripts of the Greek text.[340] It also assumes that God already exercises complete sovereignty over heaven but that many on earth presently reject God's authority and seek to thwart His plans. Earlier in the SM Jesus urged His disciples to refrain from taking an oath by heaven since "it is God's throne" (5:34).[341] Heaven is the seat from which God exercises His rule. Since the expulsion of Satan and his demons from heaven, no rebellion against God's authority has existed there. The angels of heaven stand poised to reply immediately to God's orders and fulfill His desires. The disciples of Jesus pray that God's desires will be fulfilled on earth with the same immediacy and completeness as they are now fulfilled in heaven.

Matthew 5:35 might seem to preclude this interpretation since it describes earth as God's footstool, and this makes clear that God rules over the earth and is fulfilling His sovereign plan in the events of history even now (cp. 11:25). However, Jesus clearly recognized that life on earth was not all that God ultimately intends it to be. The problem was not that God's plan is being thwarted but simply that the implementation of this plan is incomplete. God's will on earth will not be fully and finally accomplished until all human rebellion is crushed, sinners are punished, and God's people enjoy an existence like that

modified all three petitions. Thus this, like the one in v. 12, appears to modify the petition that immediately precedes it.

[340] "Both in heaven and on earth" would lack the ὡς resulting in the construction ἐν οὐρανῷ καὶ ἐπὶ [τῆς] γῆς that appears in Matt 28:18. This reading appears in one Gk. uncial: D (5th cent.); several Old Latin manuscripts: a (4th cent.), b (5th cent.), c (12th cent.), k (4th–5th cent.); several Bohairic Coptic manuscripts (3rd cent.); and in the writings of Tertullian (after AD 220) and Cyprian (AD 258). However, the earlier uncials ℵ (AD 350), B (AD 325) as well as W (5th cent.), Z (6th cent.), Δ (9th cent.), the family 1 minuscles, and a few other manuscripts support the inclusion of the ὡς. The absence of the ὡς in some later manuscripts may have resulted from accidental error or from a scribe conforming the phrase in the model prayer to 28:18.

[341] Betz sees a distinction between Matthew's use of the plural "heavens" and the singular "heaven." He takes the plural as a reference to the transcendent abode of God and the singular as a reference to the sky. He concludes from this that the third petition sees the sun, moon, stars, and birds as already in compliance with God's will. Although the distinction between the plural and singular of οὐρανός may hold true in other NT writings, it seems to break down in Matthew. Although the singular "heaven" often has the meaning "sky" in Matthew, on numerous occasions the singular seems to refer to the abode of God (5:34; 6:20; 11:25?; 18:18; 21:25; 22:30; 23:22). See also 24:29 in which the singular and plural are used interchangeably in the Greek text (the HCSB has "sky" [sing. for "heaven"] and "celestial powers" [pl. for "heavens"]). Pennington has demonstrated that in heaven and earth pairs, "heaven" is singular in Matthew whether it refers to the sky or the abode of God (*Heaven and Earth in the Gospel of Matthew*, 125–61).

of humanity in original creation before the fall. Matthew 19:28–29 describes this era of restoration:

> "I assure you: In the Messianic age, when the Son of Man sits on His glorious throne, you who have followed Me will also sit on 12 thrones, judging the 12 tribes of Israel. And everyone who has left houses, brothers or sisters, father or mother, children, or fields because of My name will receive 100 times more and will inherit eternal life."

The Greek noun translated "Messianic Age" in the HCSB is *palingenesia*, the "remaking" or "renewal" of the cosmos.[342] This renewal had been promised in Isa 65:17–25 and is described in NT texts like Acts 1:6–7; 3:19–21,25; and 2 Pet 3:10–13. Peter concluded his discussion of the Day of the Lord with these words, "But based on His promise, we wait for new heavens and a new earth, where righteousness dwells" (2 Pet 3:13). Only after the renewal of the cosmos will righteousness conquer all evil. This is the fulfillment of the divine plan that Jesus' disciples seek through the third petition.

Jesus promised that His meek followers will "inherit the earth." Yet few would want to inherit the earth in its present condition— under the curse of sin, groaning in its corruption, and subjected to futility (Rom 8:19–25). The earth itself joins all creatures that inhabit it in "eagerly awaiting" (v. 19) the moment when "creation itself will also be set free from the bondage of corruption into the glorious freedom of God's children" (v. 21).

Although this petition is eschatological, it has clear ethical implications. Those who genuinely seek the fulfillment of God's plan for the ages will certainly desire to live in submission to His will today. Every person's moral choices are associated with one of two biblical gardens. Many exhibit the spirit of Eden where the first man and woman insisted, "Not as You will, but as I will." The true Christian disciple exhibits the spirit of Gethsemane in which the Savior agonized, "Not My will but Yours be done." The believer wants God to fulfill His plan for the cosmos by reversing the effects of sin on the world and restoring righteousness, and that same longing prompts him to strive to live righteously here and now.

The grammar of the model prayer divides the prayer into two major sections. The first three petitions are expressed in the form of third-person imperatives and are closely linked by an identical word

---

[342] See "παλιγγενεσία," BDAG, 752.

order.[343] The last three petitions are expressed in the form of second-person imperatives. Furthermore, the first three petitions each contain the second-person singular pronoun. The last three petitions all contain at least one occurrence of the first-person plural pronoun. The shift in grammar and word order signals a shift in focus for the final three petitions. The shift in person suggests that although the first three petitions focus on God, the last three focus on the personal needs of the disciple.

"Give us today our daily bread."   In many English translations the meaning of the fourth petition appears to be rather simple. The petition is a plea for God to supply the physical and material necessities for the day. However, the Greek text of the petition is more ambiguous and may allow other interpretations. The difficulties in interpretation are related to the adjective *epiousios* that is translated "daily" in the HCSB. This adjective is difficult to define precisely.[344] In the NT the adjective appears only here and in Luke's parallel to the model prayer (Matt 6:11; Luke 11:3). The adjective does not appear at all in the LXX. In fact the adjective does not appear elsewhere in any extant Greek literature that was not dependent on the usage in the model prayer.[345]

Scholars have suggested several different derivations of the adjective. First, some argue that the adjective derives from a combination of the preposition *epi* ("for") and the noun *ousia* ("existence") and thus means "necessary for existence."[346] Others suggest that the adjective developed from a shortening of the phrase "for the day which is (now)" and means "for the present day."[347] Others argue that the adjective derived from the phrase "the coming day."[348]

[343] The word order in the three petitions in the Greek text is (a) third-person singular aorist imperative, (b) definite article, (c) nominative noun, and (d) genitive singular form of the second-person pronoun.

[344] Betz commented, "A true *crux interpretum* has been and still is the apposite adjective ἐπιούσιος, for which a fully convincing explanation and translation cannot be given even today" (*The Sermon on the Mount*, 397).

[345] A. H. Sayce claimed that the adjective appeared in a Greek documentary papyrus from Egypt. Sayce's claim was first questioned by B. M. Metzger, "How Many Times Does *Epiousios* Appear Outside of the Lord's Prayer?" *ExpTim* 69 (1957): 52–54. More recently two scholars examined the papyrus known as Sb 5224.20 and demonstrated conclusively that Sayce's claim was false. See M. Nijman and K. A. Worp, "'Epiousios' in a Documentary Papyrus?" *NovT* 41 (1999):231–34.

[346] ἐπὶ οὐσία. According to BDAG this was the view of Origen, Chrysostom, and Jerome.

[347] ἐπὶ τὴν οὖσαν ἡμέραν.

[348] ἡ ἐπιοῦσα ἡμέρα was shortened to the substantive ἡ ἐπιοῦσα (Acts 7:26; 16:11; 20:15; 21:18) from which the adjective ἐπιούσιος arose. See "ἔπειμι," in BDAG, 361.

J. B. Lightfoot and Colin Hemer have argued persuasively that the last of these suggested etymologies is correct.[349] However, even when one accepts this etymology, questions of interpretation may remain. Many scholars have argued that the third petition refers to the "bread for the coming day" and interpret this as a reference to the bread that will be enjoyed in the messianic feast that accompanies the ushering in of the kingdom.[350] Scholars who affirm this view typically regard all the petitions of the model prayer as eschatological. Betz is correct in dismissing this view as "highly speculative."[351] Jesus referred to the messianic feast elsewhere in Matthew (8:11; 22:2; 26:29). The first text refers simply to reclining at the table with Abraham, Isaac, and Jacob in the kingdom. The second text refers to the slaughtering of oxen and fattened cattle in preparation for the feast. The third text refers to drinking wine in the kingdom. Strikingly absent is any mention of the consumption of bread in the kingdom in a manner that might suggest that the fourth petition of the prayer should be interpreted eschatologically.[352] Most importantly, the fourth petition is qualified by the adverb "today." Although the eschatological petitions of the prayer do ask God to hasten the arrival of the kingdom, none of them insist that the kingdom arrive now. The adverb "today" implies that the petition is focused on the needs of the present life.[353]

The bread for the coming day is the daily ration of food needed by the disciple. The "coming day" is not necessarily a reference to the following day. In Greek idiom the meaning of the phrase depended largely on the time at which it was used. When used in the morning, "the coming day" meant "today." When used at night, the phrase

---

[349] C. Hemer, "ἐπιούσιος," *JSNT* 22 (1984):81–94. Allison noted that this view is affirmed by the majority of modern scholars (Davies and Allison, *A Critical and Exegetical Commentary on the Gospel According to Saint Matthew*, 1:608).

[350] This view was affirmed by church fathers such as Athanasius and was especially popular in the early twentieth century. The eschatological view is affirmed by contemporary scholars such as Hagner, *Matthew 1–13*, 149–50.

[351] Betz, *The Sermon on the Mount*, 398.

[352] The Gospel of Luke does contain a reference to eschatological bread: "The one who will eat bread in the kingdom of God is blessed" (14:15). However, these words were spoken by one who shared a meal with Jesus and not by Jesus Himself.

[353] France, *The Gospel of Matthew*, 249. Some scholars evade this problem by suggesting that Jesus saw the bread presently consumed as an anticipation of the bread that would be enjoyed at the final feast. See Jeremias, *New Testament Theology*, 200; Davies and Allison, *A Critical and Exegetical Commentary on the Gospel According to Saint Matthew*, 1:608–10; and Hagner, *Matthew 1–13*, 149–50. For a more extensive challenge to the eschatological view, see B. Young, *Jesus and His Jewish Parables: Rediscovering the Roots of Jesus' Teaching* (New York: Paulist, 1989), 31–33.

meant "tomorrow." The best translation that incorporates both possibilities is the traditional rendering "daily." Numerous ancient texts from various Mediterranean cultures discuss the need for daily bread.[354]

Some scholars claim that interpreting the petition as an appeal for daily bread creates a conflict with Jesus' teaching in Matt 6:34: "Therefore don't worry about tomorrow, because tomorrow will worry about itself. Each day has enough trouble of its own."[355] That scholars find any tension here is puzzling. Praying for daily bread is not an expression of anxiety about tomorrow or undue concern about "what you will eat" (6:25). Proper prayer is the antithesis and corrective to the anxiety discussed later in Matthew 6. Anxiety wrings its hands; faith folds its hands. Anxiety paces the floor; faith kneels on the floor. Prayer is an exercise of faith, not a display of anxiety.

The Eighteen Benedictions, also known as the *Shemoneh Esreh* or the *Amidah*, included a prayer for food. In sharp contrast with the model prayer, the Jewish prayer asked for the year's produce. Jesus may have known of this prayer. If so, the petition for daily food is a clear corrective to the standard Jewish prayer.[356] The prayer Jesus modeled would guide the disciple to live life one day at a time in the manner Jesus taught later in the SM.

This modest petition modeled by Jesus was not only an expression of faith; also it seems designed to build and strengthen one's faith. The prayer that God will supply one's needs one day at a time is reminiscent of a couple of OT passages. In Exodus 16 God provided the manna in order to ensure the survival of His famished people in the wilderness. He ordered each family to gather only the amount of manna that was needed for that particular day (except for the day before the Sabbath when they gathered two days' supply). Maggots infested and devoured the manna of those who gathered more than they needed and dashed their hopes of storing up extra manna for the next day. God supplied the needs of each day alone and refused to give His people a surplus of food. God later explained the purpose for this constant daily provision: "So that you might know that I am the Lord your God" (Deut 29:6).

[354] E. Yamauchi, "The 'Daily Bread' Motif in Antiquity," *WTJ* 28 (1966): 145–56.

[355] Betz, *The Sermon on the Mount*, 398; Hagner, *Matthew 1–13*, 149–50.

[356] For a brief discussion of the origin of the *Shemoneh Esreh*, see D. Hare, "Liturgy: Rabbinic," in *Dictionary of New Testament Background*, 650. For a brief introduction to the current debate on the origin of the *Amidah*, see E. Fleischer, "On the Origins of the *Amidah*: Response to Ruth Langer," *Prooftexts* 20 (2000): 380–87.

This method of provision was likely motivated by the concern that God expressed in Deut 31:20, "When I bring them into the land I swore to give their fathers, a land flowing with milk and honey, they will eat their fill and prosper. They will turn to other gods and worship them, despising Me and breaking My covenant." The prosperity of God's people was also mentioned as a factor in their spiritual decline in the Song of Moses: "Then Jeshurun became fat and rebelled—you became fat, bloated, and gorged. He abandoned the God who made him and scorned the Rock of his salvation" (32:15). When God's people had an abundance of provisions, they tended to lose their sense of dependence on Him and to stray from Him.

This concern prompted a later OT saint to pray only for his daily bread. In Prov 30:7–9 Agur son of Jakeh prayed:

> Two things I ask of You; don't deny them to me before I die: Keep falsehood and deceitful words far from me. Give me neither poverty nor wealth; feed me with the food I need. Otherwise, I might have too much and deny You, saying, "Who is the LORD?" or I might have nothing and steal, profaning the name of my God.

Agur astutely observed that those who have more than they need generally cease to rely on God. Those whose bins are full of grain quickly forget the gracious One who sustains them.

The model prayer resonates with themes from the prayer of Agur. Both prayers are concerned with glorifying rather than profaning the name of God. Both prayers ask only that one's most basic needs will be met so as to avoid losing one's sense of dependence on God.

Jesus taught His disciples to seek only the needs of the day so that they could daily experience God's provision and constantly acknowledge total dependency on Him. The petition also insists that Jesus' disciples learn to be content with little. As God meets the most basic necessities of life, they should be satisfied and give Him praise. As Paul later wrote, "But godliness with contentment is a great gain. For we brought nothing into the world, and we can take nothing out. But if we have food and clothing, we will be content with these" (1 Tim 6:6–8).

"And forgive us our debts, as we also have forgiven our debtors." The word "debts" (*opheilēma*) speaks of a literal debt in the LXX and the NT except for this single occurrence. However, the Aramaic equivalent

was used in the Targums and rabbinic literature to speak of sins and transgressions of the law. Luke's parallel (11:4) says, "And forgive us our sins, for we ourselves also forgive everyone in debt to us." The original prayer likely used the word "debt," and this is implied by the fact that a reference to debt is retained in the last clause of the verse. However, Luke (or his source) correctly interpreted the "debt" as a "sin" and replaced the former word with the latter to prevent the reader from assuming the debts were financial.[357] Matthew retained the word "debts" but clearly identified these debts as "transgressions" in the commentary in verses 14–15.

The rabbinic use of the concept of "debt" to depict sins is illustrated by *m. 'Abot* 3:16. Rabbi Akiba was fond of describing God as a great shopkeeper who kept an enormous ledger in which He carefully recorded a person's debits (their sinful deeds) and their credits (their righteous deeds). Akiba warned that God would send out His collectors to collect payment for the debts at the appropriate time whether or not the debtors were prepared to pay. Akiba warned that God's people needed to make sure they performed more good deeds than bad deeds. These good deeds would add sufficient credits to their account and help ensure that the account was "in the black" rather than "in the red" on judgment day.[358]

When the verb "forgive" is used in financial contexts, the verb means to release the debtor from the legal obligation to repay the debt. However, when the "debt" is a moral one, "forgive" means to "pardon" or to "release the sinner from the consequences deserved by his actions." This petition in the model prayer is thus a plea for God to erase the sins from the disciple's moral account in the ledger that will be the basis for final judgment. Paul recognized this and later wrote that God "forgave us all our trespasses. He erased the certificate of debt, with its obligations, that was against us and opposed to us, and has taken it out of the way by nailing it to the cross" (Col 2:13–14).

The clause "as we also have forgiven our debtors" (Matt 6:12) somewhat complicates an otherwise clear petition. The word

---

[357] *Did.* 8:2 follows Matthew in using the word "debt" in the first clause of the petition. The petition in the *Didache* is identical to Matthew except that the *Didache* uses the singular form of the word "debt" (Matthew used the plural) and the *Didache*, like Luke, used a present tense form of "forgive" in the last clause.

[358] For a thorough discussion of this text and Akiba's view of salvation, see C. L. Quarles, "The Soteriology of Rabbi Akiba and E. P. Sanders's *Paul and Palestinian Judaism*," NTS 42 (1996): 185–95.

translated "as" (hōs) is a comparative particle that marks the manner
in which something is done.[359] Although in some contexts the particle can be used to identify a cause, the usage in Matt 6:12 does not
fit that pattern.[360] The "as . . . also" (hōs . . . kai) construction appears
two other times in Matthew. In Matt 18:33 the construction could be
interpreted as comparative or as causal. If the construction there is
causal, that text would teach that sinners should forgive because God
has forgiven them. Matthew 18:33 and 6:12 would then be in apparent contradiction. Matthew would likely have recognized the problems entailed in presenting divine forgiveness as a cause and result of
human forgiveness at the same time. In Matt 20:14, the construction
is clearly comparative. This analysis suggests that the construction is
consistently comparative in Matthew.

The petition thus asks that God will forgive one's sins "like we
also forgave" the sins of others. The disciple prays that the mercy with
which God forgives him will correspond to the mercy with which he
forgives others. However, the grammar implies the hope that God will
display greater mercy than the disciple displays. Matthew could have
easily translated Jesus' Aramaic prayer by using the intensive comparative article kathōs which means "just like" or "exactly as" (21:6;
26:24; 28:6). This would serve to limit the petition to asking for no
more mercy than the disciple displays himself. Matthew wisely chose
the weaker comparative particle to demonstrate that God's mercy to
the disciple corresponds to the mercy he expresses to others yet always exceeds it.

The notion that human forgiveness is a cause for divine forgiveness is prompted in part by translating the verb in the last clause of
Matt 6:12 as an English perfect "have forgiven." However, the Greek
text used the aorist tense rather than the perfect.[361] This may translate

---

[359] Of the 40 uses of ὡς in Matthew, all are comparative except 14:5 and 21:26, where it is a
marker of perspective corresponding to usage 3 described in BDAG.

[360] BDAG notes that the causal function is fairly common with participles and adds, "Only
in isolated instances does ὡς show causal force when used w. a finite verb" (1103–6). Unfortunately the only NT example of the causal force with the finite verb given in BDAG is Matt 6:12.
This is assumed completely on the grounds that the parallel in Luke 11:4 uses γάρ. However,
Green has rightly noted that "the 'for' [γάρ] of v 4b does not introduce a relationship of quid
pro quo between divine and human forgiveness, as though God's forgiveness were dependent on
human activity (cf. 6:35; 23:34!)." See Green, Luke, 443–44, including n. 27.

[361] Betz mistakenly parses the verb as a perfect form, probably because of the κα morpheme
(The Sermon on the Mount, 404). However, the verb is clearly an aorist, which often uses the κα
morpheme in the athematic conjugation.

an Aramaic *perfectum praesens*, which could be translated with a present verb "as we are also forgiving."[362] If so, God's provision of forgiveness may inspire the disciple to forgive others habitually. The believer then points to his own forgiveness of others as he appeals to God to grant more forgiveness.

The issue of forgiving others and receiving forgiveness is clearly important to Jesus and to Matthew. Although other sections of the SM and the Gospel of Matthew relate to and shed light on the petitions of the model prayer, this petition was the only one of the six to be explained in the immediate context. After completing the prayer, Jesus explained: "For if you forgive people their wrongdoing, your heavenly Father will forgive you as well. But if you don't forgive people, your Father will not forgive your wrongdoing" (vv. 14–15).

The use of the future tense to describe divine forgiveness could be gnomic, setting forth a general abiding principle about divine activity. However, the future tense is more likely eschatological and refers to the forgiveness granted in final judgment.[363] Jesus was thus teaching that if one is so hypocritical as to seek forgiveness from God and to refuse to express that same forgiveness to others, God will refuse to forgive him in the final judgment.

Jesus elaborated on this principle in the powerful parable of the Unforgiving Slave in 18:23–35. In the parable a slave (who represents the sinner) owed his king (who represents God) an enormous debt that he could not possibly repay. The enormity of the debt corresponds to the heinousness of sinners' wicked acts and the great wrath of God they deserve. Faced with the prospect of losing everything he owned and knowing the king planned to sell him, his wife, and children, the slave begged for more time to repay the debt. The request was ridiculous because the debt was clearly too great for the slave ever to repay it. However, the kind king did far more than the slave requested and graciously forgave his debt in full.

Later the forgiven slave found another slave who owed him a relatively small amount of money and demanded immediate repayment. This second slave pleaded for mercy, using words similar to his lender's own earlier plea. Although these words should have stirred the lender's memory of his king's gracious forgiveness, he refused to show

[362] See Jeremias, *New Testament Theology*, 201; Hagner, *Matthew 1–13*, 150; and Hill, *The Gospel of Matthew*, 138.
[363] Cp. Hagner, *Matthew 1–13*, 150.

the slave compassion and threw the slave into prison. Other slaves were disturbed by the forgiven slave's hypocrisy and reported his actions to the king. The king was understandably enraged. He summoned him and said, "You wicked slave! I forgave you all that debt because you begged me. Shouldn't you also have had mercy on your fellow slave, as I had mercy on you?" (vv. 32–33). The king sentenced the slave to be tortured in prison until his debts were fully repaid. Since the debt was clearly too great to be repaid, the sentence by the king appears to depict eternal punishment. Jesus concluded, "So My heavenly Father will also do to you if each of you does not forgive his brother from his heart" (v. 35).

Both the conclusion to the model prayer and the parable of the Unforgiving Slave clearly teach that gracious forgiveness of others is a condition for receiving forgiveness from God in final judgment. Personal forgiveness is not a meritorious work that somehow earns divine forgiveness. However, the willingness to forgive others graciously is a hallmark of the true disciple of Jesus. Jesus' disciples are "sons of God" (5:9). The sons of God manifest the character of their heavenly Father much as sons resemble their earthly fathers. Because God is characterized by mercy (Exod 34:6) that compels Him to forgive sinners, His children will also show mercy to others and graciously forgive those who sin against them (Matt 5:7,43–48). Furthermore, as discussed in the section on 5:7, repentance is a requirement for divine forgiveness. Those who are truly repentant will express to others the same mercy they hope God will lavish on them.

"And do not bring us into temptation, but deliver us from the evil one." Not surprisingly, a number of interpreters who see the model prayer as consistently eschatological view this petition as related to the end times as well.[364] They suggest that the "temptation" (*peirasmos*) mentioned here is the period of great trial and testing known as the Great Tribulation and discussed later in Matt 24:15–22. Perhaps the strongest evidence for the eschatological view is the use of the term *peirasmos* to describe this period of tribulation in Rev 3:10: "Because you have kept My command to endure, I will also keep you from the hour of testing (*peirasmou*) that is going to come over the whole world to test (*peirasai*) those who live on the earth."

---

[364] Jeremias, *The Prayers of Jesus*, 105–6; and Brown, "The Pater Noster as an Eschatological Prayer," 204–8.

Although the eschatological view is initially compelling, closer examination raises several problems. First, if Jesus were speaking of the great trial that will accompany the end times, one would expect Matthew to have expressed this by use of the definite article par excellence.[365] However, this argument is not decisive since in Hellenistic Greek definite objects of prepositions frequently lack the definite article.[366]

More problematic for the eschatological view is the vocabulary of the petition. When Jesus spoke of the great tribulation in Matt 24:21 and 29, Matthew translated the reference using the noun *thlipsis* that means "tribulation," "distress," "trouble," or "affliction" rather than the noun *peirasmos* ("test" or "temptation"). Other than in 6:13, the noun *peirasmos* appears only once in Matthew and appears to refer to temptation in general. One NT writer did use *peirasmos* to speak of the great trial of the end times (Rev 3:10). However, he sensed that the noun alone was inadequate to designate clearly the tribulation and used other features like the definite article, the verb *mellō* (which clearly points to the future), and descriptive clauses to clarify the expression ("the hour of testing that is going to come over the whole world to test those who live on the earth"). Luz is apparently correct in his assertion that "neither in Jewish apocalypticism nor in the NT is πειρασμός an apocalyptic technical term."[367] Matthew's own vocabulary usage gives no hint that the noun *peirasmos* is eschatological.

Furthermore requests for protection from temptation were standard fare in ancient Jewish prayers. In these prayers "temptation" normally referred to testing in the present time. An example of this appears in *b. Ber.* 60b:

> Lead my foot not into the power of sin,
> And bring me not into the power of iniquity,
> And not into the power of temptation,
> And not into the power of anything shameful.[368]

---

[365] Wallace, *Greek Grammar Beyond the Basics*, 222–23.

[366] See BDF, 133; Robertson, *A Grammar of the Greek New Testament in the Light of Historical Research*, 791; Wallace, *Greek Grammar Beyond the Basics*, 247.

[367] Luz, *Matthew: A Commentary*, 322. In note 123, Luz added, "The only exception is Rev. 3:10." However, the need for extensive clarification in Rev 3:10 suggests that even there the noun does not serve as "an apocalyptic technical term."

[368] Quoted in Jeremias, *The Prayers of Jesus*, 105. See also *b. Sanh.* 64a.

The Dead Sea Scrolls contain a similar petition: "Bring me not into situations that are too hard for me; remove from me the sins of my youth and let not my transgressions be remembered against me."[369]

The closest parallel in Matthew also suggests that the petition refers to temptation in general rather than the great tribulation. Jesus said, "Stay awake and pray, so that you won't enter into temptation" (26:41). This is remarkably similar to 6:13 since both texts relate to prayer and both have the phrase "into temptation" (*eis peirasmon*). Furthermore Matthew prefixed the preposition *eis* to the verb *elthēte* from his source (Mark 14:38). Several scholars have suggested that he edited his source in this fashion to conform the discussion in Gethsemane to the model prayer since the verb *eisenegkēs* in 6:13 has the same prefixed preposition.[370] In 26:41 *peirasmos* apparently refers to the disciples' temptation to deny Jesus during His arrest, trial, and crucifixion (26:31–35).[371]

Some scholars argue that this temptation in Matt 26:41 is eschatological.[372] This requires the great eschatological trial to begin with Jesus' arrest and extend to the glorious coming of the Son of Man. This is a difficult position to sustain. Matthew 24 shows that the period of great suffering begins with international turmoil, famines, and earthquakes. Jesus added, "These events are the beginning of birth pains" (Matt 24:8). Although one might argue that the earthquake described in Matt 27:51 signals that the "birth pains" foretold by Jesus had begun, Matthew gives no indication that nations and kingdoms were rising up against one another. On the contrary, Romans and Jews cooperated, however regrettably, in the proceedings against Jesus and in the crucifixion. This, combined with the absence of any reference to famine occurring in the last days of Jesus, makes it doubtful that Matthew intended to portray the eschatological trial as beginning with Jesus' arrest.

[369] 11QPs 24:11–12, quoted in Luz, *Matthew: A Commentary*, 1:322.

[370] Gundry, *Matthew*, 534; Nolland, *The Gospel of Matthew*, 1101. D. Senior noted, "This is the only example in the gospel where Matthew introduces the reiterated preposition in a Markan parallel" (*The Passion of Jesus in Matthew* [Wilmington, DE: Michael Glazier,1985], 110).

[371] Blomberg, *Matthew*, 397; France, *Matthew*, 373; Wilkins, *Matthew*, 842. Some who interpret the trial in Matt 6:13 as eschatological also argue for an eschatological sense in Matt 26:41. See Davies and Allison, *A Critical and Exegetical Commentary on the Gospel According to Saint Matthew*, 3:499, and Keener, *The Gospel of Matthew*, 636–37.

[372] Davies and Allison, *A Critical and Exegetical Commentary on the Gospel According to Saint Matthew*, 3:499; Hagner, *Matthew 14–28*, 783–84; Keener, *The Gospel of Matthew*, 636; and D. P. Senior, *The Passion of Jesus in the Gospel of Matthew* (Wilmington, DE: Glazier, 1985), 82.

An increasing number of scholars view Matt 24:15–20 as linking the beginning of woes to the events surrounding the fall of Jerusalem in AD 70.[373] In this view, the period of great suffering for God's people extends from the catastrophic events surrounding the Roman devastation of Jerusalem until the glorious appearance of the Son of Man at the time of the second coming (Matt 24:29–31). Blomberg observed, "It is probably best, therefore, to understand this period of great distress, or 'the great tribulation,' as it is more commonly known, as the entire period beginning with the devastation of A.D. 70 and continuing on until Christ's return."[374] If this interpretation of Jesus' eschatological discourse is correct, Matt 26:41 is not likely a prayer for protection from the great tribulation that would not begin for another generation. The view that Jesus' arrest marks the beginning of the great eschatological trial is obviously inconsistent with the popular view that the period of unmatchable suffering in Matthew 24 refers to the 42-month period that immediately precedes the second coming (Rev. 11:2–3; 13:5).[375]

Those who affirm the eschatological interpretation of 26:41 normally reach this conclusion by adopting the eschatological interpretation of 6:13 and then recognizing that 26:41 must be interpreted similarly. This procedure for determining the meaning of the texts is faulty. A wise exegete interprets obscure texts in light of clear texts rather than clear texts in light of obscure texts. Matthew 26:41 seems to be the clearer of the two texts. The immediate context strongly suggests that "temptation" is a reference to general temptation rather than to the tribulation that will afflict God's people soon before the coming of the Son of Man. Matthew 6:13 is more ambiguous since the preceding context relates both to the *eschaton* and to the present life. When one interprets 26:41 in light of its immediate context and then uses that text as a guide for understanding 6:13, the eschatological interpretation is doubtful.

---

[373] For an excellent discussion of this view, see Blomberg, *Matthew*, 352–63.

[374] Ibid., 359. See also Carson, "Matthew," 507; Keener, *Matthew*, 577. Chrysostom (*Hom. Matt.* 76) and Calvin (*Matthew, Mark, and Luke*, 3:78) saw the birth pains as events surrounding the Jewish War recorded by Josephus.

[375] See e.g., Wilkins, who commented, "The vision Jesus paints must yet be ahead. The apostle John's vision reveals such a future time of incredible horror (Rev 7–19)" (*Matthew*, 780). See also Barbieri, "Matthew," 76–77; and Stanley D. Toussaint, *Matthew: Thy Kingdom Come* (Portland, OR: Multnomah, 1980), 271–75.

The problems associated with the eschatological view are cumulatively sufficient to preclude the view. Luz did not exaggerate when he quipped, "Almost everything speaks against this view."[376] The evidence best supports the traditional view that the petition seeks protection from present temptation or trials.

The early church struggled to understand the petition since it could be taken to imply that God sometimes tempts His people. However, Jas 1:13 clearly says, "No one undergoing a trial should say, 'I am being tempted by God.' For God is not tempted by evil, and He himself doesn't tempt anyone." Two solutions have been proposed to this apparent contradiction. First, in Jesus' original Aramaic prayer, He may have used an Aramaic causative which sometimes has a permissive nuance. Thus the original petition may have been, "Do not allow us to enter into temptation."[377] The petition would then be a prayer for protection from the disciple's own sinful tendencies and the devil's allurements without any hint that God Himself is responsible for temptation. However, Matthew's Greek does not at all hint that the prohibition should be interpreted permissively. Although the imperative in Greek sometimes has a permissive nuance, this is rare,[378] and the NT contains no examples in which a prohibition using the aorist subjunctive (the construction used by Matthew in the petition) has a permissive sense.

Second, many commentators have pointed out that the Greek noun *peirasmos* may mean "temptation" (in the sense of enticement to do evil) or "testing" (in the sense of a trial which ultimately proves one's good character).[379] The use of the noun to speak of a test or trial has parallels in the LXX (Sir 6:7; 27:5,7), the NT (1 Pet 4:12), and early Christian literature (Hermas, *Mandate* 9:7).[380] However, *peirasmos* and the related verb *peirazō* are consistently used in a negative sense in Matthew (4:1,3; 16:1; 19:3; 22:18,35; 26:41). The negative sense is the most natural reading in a context that refers to the need

---

[376] Luz, *Matthew: A Commentary*, 1:322.

[377] Jeremias, *New Testament Theology*, 202; Schnackenburg, *The Gospel of Matthew*, 68; Witherington, *Matthew*, 147. The early church fathers Tertullian and Cyprian also interpreted the petition permissively. See Broadus, *The Gospel According to Matthew*, 138.

[378] Wallace, *Greek Grammar Beyond the Basics*, 288–89.

[379] France, *The Gospel of Matthew*, 136; Wilkins, *Matthew*, 279; Witherington, *Matthew*, 147.

[380] This understanding of the term was recently argued to be Matthew's intention in M. Knowles, "Once More, 'Lead Us Not Eis Peirasmon,'" *ExpTim* 115 (2004): 191–94.

for rescue from evil or the evil one (6:13b). Thus *peirasmos* in 6:13 probably refers not to testing but to actual temptation.

This does not mean that the petition portrays God as tempter in contradiction to Jas 1:13. The petition is not, "Do not tempt us." If Matthew had wished to portray God as tempter, he could have done so clearly and unambiguously. The petition, "Do not lead us into temptation" simply asks God not to lead Jesus' disciples into situations which the evil one would seize as an opportunity for temptation.[381]

Matthew likely intended for his readers to understand the petition against the background of Jesus' temptation in Matt 4:1: "Then Jesus was led up by the Spirit into the wilderness to be tempted by the Devil."[382] Several parallels between 4:1 and 6:13 suggest a connection between the two texts. First, both texts speak of God's "leading" someone into situations in which he will be tempted. Matthew 4:1 uses the verb *anagō*. Matthew 6:13 uses the verb *eispherō*. However, the two verbs have similar meanings in these two contexts. Second, both texts refer to acts of temptation. Matthew 4:1 uses the verb "tempt" (*peirazō*) while 6:13 uses the related noun (*peirasmos*). Third, both texts identify Satan as the personal agent responsible for the temptation. Matthew 4:1 identifies the tempter as "the Devil" (*ho diabolos*). Matthew 6:13 implies that the tempter is "the evil one" (*ho ponēros*).

So, when readers already familiar with Jesus' temptation experience encountered the petition in Matt 6:13, they would naturally interpret it as a request for God not to lead Jesus' disciples into a situation in which they were exposed to Satan's tempting work. Jesus' lengthy temptation in the wilderness had ended well. However, Jesus' disciples needed to recognize that they do not possess the strength that Christ exhibited in His temptation. They could not assume that they would respond to temptation with the same resolve as their Master. The allurements of a loaf of bread after a 40-day fast were more than enough to compel most to disobey. The tendency to test God and to trust Him only when He miraculously intervened to rescue His people from danger was an enduring symptom of the disciple's weak faith. The enticements of worldly wealth and power would be more than enough to dazzle Jesus' most committed disciples and prompt

---

[381] Thus the statement, "It is noteworthy that a flat contradiction to what the Lord's Prayer says is found in the Epistle of James" (Betz, *The Sermon on the Mount*, 407) is unwarranted.

[382] Luz, *Matthew: A Commentary*, 1:323.

them to direct their allegiance and worship even to the Devil himself. Jesus' disciples needed to admit humbly and honestly that, despite the amazing change they had experienced since following Jesus, they still could not withstand prolonged periods of grueling warfare with the tempter. Many might even fall on the first day of the conflict.

Much as the fourth petition encouraged Jesus' disciples to rely on God constantly for their physical survival, the sixth petition encouraged the disciples to rely on Him constantly for their spiritual survival. Jesus had promised that those who hunger and thirst for righteousness will be filled (5:6), but they would not be completely filled with righteousness until the Son of Man returns in glory. Until then, the disciples would continue to wrestle with sinful longings, be vulnerable to temptation, and be prone to moral and spiritual failure without the Father's gracious protection. Broadus aptly summarized the spirit of the petition: "The humble believer, self-distrustful because conscious of remaining tendencies to sin, and weakness in restraining them, prays that God will not bring him into temptation."[383]

The Twelve failed to see how vulnerable they truly were. The bold promises that appear in Matt 26:33 and 35 show that they thought that they were invincible and would courageously follow Jesus to their deaths. Despite Jesus' frequent warnings, they failed to acknowledge the weakness of their own flesh and to "stay awake and pray" so that they would not "enter into temptation" (v. 41). Confidence in self crowded out dependence on God. This overconfidence led to their shameful downfall when they abandoned and denied their Savior and Lord (vv. 56,69–72).

Perhaps influenced by this petition, Paul urged believers to take steps to avoid temptation. He taught that believers should enjoy sexual fulfillment in marriage "otherwise, Satan may tempt you because of your lack of self-control" (1 Cor 7:5). He taught that mature believers who lovingly correct brothers or sisters living in sin should be alert and introspective, "watching out for yourselves so you also won't be tempted" (Gal 6:1). The old adage "Pride goes before a fall" is good biblical wisdom (Prov 16:18). Jesus taught His disciples to acknowledge their weaknesses with humility and to ask for God's protection from the temptations that might overwhelm them. Bonhoeffer expressed this well: "The disciple is conscious of his weakness, and

---

[383] Broadus, *The Gospel According to Matthew*, 138.

does not expose himself unnecessarily to temptation in order to test the strength of his faith. Christians ask God not to put their puny faith to the test, but to preserve them in the hour of temptation."[384]

Since Jesus' disciples cannot completely escape temptation in this life, Jesus taught them to pray not only for protection *from* temptation but also for protection *in* temptation: "But deliver us from the evil one." The conjunction "but" (*alla*) closely connects this clause with the preceding one and suggests that 6:13 is one petition with two elements. Each clause helps in interpreting the other.

The major interpretive question is whether the petition requests deliverance from "evil" or from "the evil one." The genitive singular forms of the neuter definite article and neuter second declension adjective are identical to the masculine forms. Thus one cannot determine from the form whether Jesus was speaking of an evil act or an evil person.[385]

Several lines of evidence have been suggested to support interpreting the petition as a reference to evil acts. Some scholars see 2 Tim 4:18 as the oldest interpretation of this petition: "The Lord will rescue me from every evil work." Nevertheless the similarities between the two texts are not great. Although the verb "rescue" and the adjective "evil" are shared with the final petition of the model prayer, Paul's words are an affirmation rather than a petition. Furthermore the model prayer is addressed to the "Father," but the deliverer in Paul's text is the "Lord," which is likely a reference to Jesus (2 Tim 1:2; 4:8). An earlier text in 2 Timothy (3:11) speaks in a similar way of divine rescue from many difficulties but with no hint of an allusion to the model prayer.[386]

Scholars often appeal to *Did.* 10:5 as an example of early interpretation of the petition: "Remember your church, Lord, to deliver it from all evil." However, the eucharistic prayer of *Did.* 10:1–6 has only loose connections to the model prayer. The petition in *Did.* 10:5 is more likely an adaptation of 2 Tim 4:18 than Matt 6:13. Both texts

---

[384] Bonhoeffer, *The Cost of Discipleship*, 167.

[385] The Latin fathers tended to follow Augustine in viewing the adjective as neuter. Catholic scholars also generally adopt this interpretation. The Greek fathers and the Protestant Reformers typically interpreted the adjective as masculine. See Luz, *Matthew: A Commentary*, 1:323.

[386] Second Thessalonians 3:2 is actually a closer parallel since in this text Paul *prayed* for *rescue* from *evil* people. However, scholars do not suggest that this text is dependent on the model prayer.

describe the "Lord" as the deliverer, use the adjective "all" (*pantos*) to portray evil, and are followed by similar doxologies.[387]

Scholars also point out that there is presently no evidence that Hebrew or Aramaic literature used the title "the evil one" as a designation for Satan.[388] On the other hand several other texts in Matthew show that the title did serve this function in early Christian literature. Most scholars acknowledge that, at a minimum, "the evil [one]" is a reference to Satan in Matt 13:19,38. Matthew 5:37 probably refers to Satan as well. In Matt 5:39 the phrase refers in general to an evildoer. Similarly, the plural form of the adjective is used in Matt 13:49 to speak of evil people. One should note that even in these two examples the phrase is personal and thus masculine. Thus the independent use of the adjective *ponēros* in Matthew is always personal and thus consistently masculine. Other New Testament documents use the phrase to speak of Satan as well (John 17:15; Eph 6:16; 2 Thess 3:3; 1 John 2:13–14; 3:12; 5:18–19).[389]

· The linguistic evidence thus supports interpreting Matt 6:13 as a reference to "the evil one," that is, Satan. This interpretation establishes a close parallel between the model prayer and Jesus' prayer in John 17:15: "I am not praying that You take them out of the world but that You protect them from the evil one." The multiple references to the "evil one" in Johannine literature demonstrate that John 17:15 is a reference to Satan. As discussed earlier, this interpretation identifies Satan as the one responsible for temptation. This precludes interpretations of the first half of the petition that contradict Jas 1:13.

The use of the verb "deliver" (*hruomai*) is significant. The verb means to rescue someone from a fate from which he cannot escape on his own. The only other time the verb appears in Matthew is in the taunts of those who stood at the foot of the cross: "He has put His trust in God; let God rescue Him now—if He wants Him!" (Matt 27:43). The verb "rescue" was appropriate since Jesus' death was inevitable apart from divine intervention. To have pulled the nails that bound the Savior to the cross, to have scattered the soldiers that supervised the crucifixion, to have whisked Jesus through the angry Jewish mob,

[387] Luz, *Matthew: A Commentary*, 1:323 describes 2 Tim 4:18 and *Did.* 10:5 as "the presumably oldest interpretations of the petition." The word "presumably" offers an important qualification of the assertion.

[388] Davies and Allison, *A Critical and Exegetical Commentary on the Gospel According to Saint Matthew*, 1:615; Luz, *Matthew: A Commentary*, 323.

[389] See also *Barn.* 2:10 and *Mart. Pol.* 17:1.

and to have healed His many mortal wounds would have been rescue indeed, a task fit for legions of angels at the very least (26:53).

The use of the verb "deliver" in 6:13 implies the helplessness of the disciple apart from God's intervention. The disciple does not pray that God will assist him in battling the evil one. The disciple is so weak that he is little match for the Devil. He needs a Savior, not an assistant; a Hero, not a helper. He needs a Champion who will fight the evil one for him and who will snatch him from the clutches of the enemy who seeks to steal, kill, and destroy. Not surprisingly, Paul used the same verb to describe how God "has rescued us from the domain of darkness and transferred us into the kingdom of the Son He loves" (Col 1:13).

Calvin's comments best capture the implications of the petition:

> Here we must carefully note that it is not in our power to engage that great warrior the devil in combat, or to bear his force and onslaught. Otherwise it would be pointless or a mockery to ask of God what we already have in ourselves. Obviously those who prepare for such a combat with self-assurance do not sufficiently understand with what a ferocious and well-equipped enemy they have to deal. Now we seek to be freed from his power, as from the jaws of a mad and raging lion [1 Peter 5:8]; if the Lord did not snatch us from the midst of death, we could not help being immediately torn to pieces by his fangs and claws, and swallowed down his throat. Yet we know that if the Lord be with us, and fight for us while we keep still, "in his might we shall do mightily" [Ps. 60:12; cf. 107:14 and Comm.]. Let others trust as they will in their own capacities and powers of free choice, which they seem to themselves to possess. For us let it be enough that we stand and are strong in God's power alone.[390]

The final three petitions of the model prayer are closely linked to each other. Unlike the first three petitions that stand as independent clauses, the final three are bound together by the use of the coordinating conjunction "and" (*kai*) that appears at the beginning of verses 12–13. The petitions are closely related thematically as expressions of dependence on God. As Stott noted:

> Thus the three petitions which Jesus puts upon our lips are beautifully comprehensive. They cover, in principle, all our human need—material (daily bread), spiritual (forgiveness of sin) and moral (deliverance from evil). What we are doing whenever we pray this prayer is to express our dependence upon God in every area of our human life.[391]

---

[390] Calvin, *Institutes of the Christian Religion*, 2:914.
[391] Stott, *The Sermon on the Mount*, 150–51.

Jesus later taught that the kingdom of heaven is made up of people who are like children (Matt 19:13–15). He did not mean by this that His disciples should be characterized by a naïve faith. He meant that His disciples should depend completely on God much as children live in complete dependence on their parents. This is the reason Jesus later commented, "It will be hard for a rich person to enter the kingdom of heaven!" (v. 23). Although a child is a picture of complete dependence, a rich person is a model of independence. Jesus urged the rich young ruler to sell all that he had and follow Him so the man would learn to depend completely on God (v. 21). Sadly he was unwilling to abandon his independent lifestyle and truly depend on the Lord.

When Jesus' disciples pray, He wants them to reflect constantly on their dependence on God for everything—their survival, their salvation, and their sanctification. When God provides their daily bread, gracious forgiveness, and rescue from the temptations to which they would have otherwise succumbed, they will be reminded that all good things come from Him and grant Him the praise He is due.

The doxology that concludes the model prayer in some translations is almost certainly a later addition and not part of Jesus' original prayer as recorded by Matthew. The doxology is absent from the earliest Greek manuscripts of Matthew and early Latin, Coptic, and Syriac translations.[392] Furthermore the earliest commentaries on the Lord's Prayer show no knowledge of the doxology.[393] The parallel to the model prayer in Luke 11:4 also lacks a doxology. Manuscripts that insert a doxology in Matt 6:13 have no standard form for it. The most common form was "because yours is the kingdom and the power and the glory forever. Amen." However, some manuscripts omit reference to "the kingdom," others to "the glory," and still others to "the power." Others place a Trinitarian formula ("of the Father and of the Son and of the Holy Spirit"), which was evidently taken from Matt 28:19, after the word "glory."[394]

---

[392] ℵ (AD 350), B (AD 325), D (5th cent.), Old Latin texts (4th, 5th, 7th, 8th, 12th cent.), the Vulgate (4th and 5th cent.), Coptic texts (beginning in the 3rd cent.), and the Diatesseron (2nd cent.).

[393] These include the Greek fathers Origen (c. AD 253), Gregory of Nyssa (AD 394), Cyril of Alexandria (AD 444), and the Latin fathers Tertullian (after AD 220), Cyprian (AD 258), Ambrosiaster (after AD 384), Ambrose (AD 397), Chromatius (AD 407), Jerome (AD 419/20), and Augustine (AD 430).

[394] For an argument that the doxology did belong in the original edition of Matthew and was later deleted, see Jakob van Bruggen, "The Lord's Prayer and Textual Criticism," *CTJ* 17 (1982): 78–87.

The earliest form of the doxology was probably "because yours is the power and the glory forever. Amen." This form of the doxology appears in the *Didache* (8:2), a manual of church practice probably composed toward the end of the first century. A similar doxology also appears in the "Prayer of Paul the Apostle" from the Nag Hammadi Library. These early doxologies may have been adapted from the doxology of 1 Chr 29:11–13.[395]

The only term in the doxology that appears in the prayer itself is the term "kingdom." The nouns "glory" and "power" appear nowhere else in the entire Sermon on the Mount in reference to God. When the noun "glory" appears in Matt 6:29, it is a reference to Solomon's royal splendor.[396] When the word "power" appears in 7:22, it is in the plural and a reference to the "miracles" of false disciples.[397]

Thus, both internal evidence and external evidence suggest that the doxology was neither an original conclusion to the model prayer as spoken by Jesus nor an original part of the Gospel of Matthew. Despite this, the early Christians who developed it rightly understood that the Father to whom believers offer their petitions is more than worthy of their praise.[398] The addition of the doxology to the model prayer as the prayer was used in the corporate worship of the early church shows that God is answering the first petition of prayer, for these praises honor God's holy name.

Fasting (Matt 6:16–18)

After addressing almsgiving and prayer, Christ turned His attention to the third pillar of Judaism, fasting. He knew that His original audience understood the purpose and importance of fasting. Fasting was so characteristic of the practice of faithful Jews that Augustus bragged that he fasted even more than a Jew.[399] Thus Jesus focused His

[395] See also the doxology that followed the pronunciation of the divine name during the Day of Atonement rituals: "Blessed be the name of the glory of his kingdom for ever and ever!" (*m. Yoma* 2.8).

[396] None of the seven uses of the word "glory" in Matt refer to the glory of the Father. However, five of these refer to the glory of the Son of Man.

[397] Matt 22:29 mentions the "power" of God, and 26:64 uses the word "power" as a substitute for the divine name.

[398] Blomberg's counsel is wise: "[The doxology] nevertheless affords a very appropriate conclusion, and no one need campaign to do away with its use in churches today. Christians regularly and rightly utter many things in prayer that do not directly quote the autographs of Scripture" (*Matthew*, 121).

[399] Tacitus, *Ann.* 5.4.

instruction on the manner in which fasting was practiced. Unfortunately fasting is a foreign concept to most modern students of the SM. Thus a general introduction to fasting may be helpful.

Jewish fasting consisted of both corporate public fasts and individual fasts. The OT law required "self-denial" of all Israelites on the Day of Atonement (Lev 23:27,29,32). Traditionally this self-denial included abstaining from eating, drinking, sexual activity, washing, anointing, or putting on sandals.[400]

Corporate fasts were later required for three additional occasions. A fast was mandated for the Jewish New Year.[401] Fasting was also required on the anniversary of long-remembered tragedies from Jewish history. Two such anniversaries were the seventeenth day of the month of Tammuz and the ninth day of the month of Ab. On these two dates such calamities as the shattering of the stone tablets of the Ten Commandments, the cessation of daily whole-offerings, the divine refusal to allow Israel to enter the promised land, and the destruction of the temple had occurred.[402] Finally, fasts could be mandated during times of national crisis such as drought, famine, destructive earthquakes, crop disease, insect hoards that were destructive to crops, military attack, or attacks from wild predators.[403] All corporate fasts expressed grief and mourning and were demonstrations of repentance.[404] During times of crisis, the Israelites hoped that God would respond to the repentance expressed through the fast by granting relief or protection. As shown by Isa 58:4, through fasting the Israelites hoped to make their voices heard on high.

Fasts during national crises would intensify until God brought relief. In the initial stages those who fasted were allowed to eat and drink after nightfall. They were also permitted to work, bathe, anoint themselves, put on sandals, and have sexual relationships with their spouses. In the final stages all these activities ceased. The rabbis concluded, "If these days passed by and their prayers were not answered, they must give themselves but little to business, building or planting,

---

[400] m. Yoma 8.1.

[401] m. Roš Haš. 3.4.

[402] m. Taʿan. 4.6.

[403] m. Taʿan. 1.1–7; 3:1–8.

[404] For fasting in the OT as an expression of mourning see Judg 20:26; 2 Sam 3:35; Esth 4:3; 9:31; Ps 35:13–14. For fasting in the OT as an expression of repentance see Neh 1:4–7; 9:1–2; Zech 7:5. See also Sir 31:26; Jdt 4:9–13; and Did. 7.4.

betrothals or marriages, or greetings to one another, as becomes men that suffer God's displeasure."[405]

Private individual fasts seem to have been relatively rare. Although many commentaries insist that faithful Pharisees fasted twice each week,[406] each Monday and Thursday, this was probably uncommon. *Didache* 8:1 says, "But do not let your fasts coincide with those of the hypocrites. They fast on Monday and Thursday, so you must fast on Wednesday and Friday."[407]

However, the text does not explicitly claim that the hypocrites, a reference to non-Christian Jews, fasted every single Monday and Thursday. Most scholars interpret Luke 18:12 as proof that Pharisees fasted twice a week on a consistent basis. However, this interpretation is probably mistaken.[408] The early rabbinic evidence suggests that the allusion to fasts on Monday and Thursday in the *Didache* and the allusion to fasting twice a week in Luke refer to special fasts associated with prayer for rain.[409] These fasts normally lasted three days, a Monday, Thursday, and the following Monday. This system was developed in order to prevent upsetting local economies during the period of the fast.[410] These fasts began with the fasting of individuals. The individual fasts could begin as early as the Feast of Tabernacles and last until the Feast of Passover. Law mandated that if rain had not fallen by the seventeenth day of Marheshwan, individuals should observe a three-day fast. If rain had not fallen by the first of Chislev, the entire nation observed a three-day fast.

The individuals who began the fast for rain were Israel's first line of defense against drought, the dry periods that spelled disaster for people in an agrarian society. Only if their prayers were ineffective would the entire nation be called up to fast. These individuals were deeply respected for their piety and for the sacrifice they made for the nation. Unfortunately this deep respect by others often bred hypocrisy, the kind of hypocrisy Jesus challenged in Matthew 6.

---

[405] *m. Ta'an.* 1.7.

[406] E.g., Marshall, *The Gospel of Luke*, 221.

[407] Holmes, *The Apostolic Fathers*, 259.

[408] A. Büchler is probably correct that the Pharisee was claiming only to fast twice a week during October and November when needed rains did not come ("St Matthew VI 1–6 and Other Allied Passages," *JTS* 10 [1909]: 266–70). See also Davies and Allison, *A Critical and Exegetical Commentary on the Gospel According to Saint Matthew*, 1:618, n. 60.

[409] *m. Ta'an.* 1.1–7.

[410] *m. Ta'an.* 2.9.

The OT prophets had also challenged hypocrisy during fasts. Isaiah sternly rebuked the Israelites for transforming fasting into an empty ritual that sought to make God respond to prayers by depriving the body, bowing the head, and wearing sackcloth and ashes. The fast that God desired required freeing the oppressed, caring for the needy, relating to others peaceably, and living righteously (Isa 58:1–12).

Jeremiah 36:9 offers another example of a hypocritical fast. Although all the citizens of Jerusalem and the visitors to the city "proclaimed a fast before the Lord," they all ignored the prophecies of Jeremiah that Baruch read in the temple (vv. 9,24). Jehoiakim, king of Judah, even went so far as to cut the scroll of Jeremiah's prophecy into pieces, several columns at a time, and throw them into the fire (vv. 23,25).

When God spoke through Joel (2:12–17) urging the people to "turn to Me with all your heart, with fasting, weeping, and mourning" (v. 12), He too warned against hypocritical fasting. He insisted that the sacred fast was to be an expression of true inner repentance and not just an empty ritual. During times of national crisis, those who fasted often tore their garments in a display of mourning. Joel declared that broken hearts meant more to God than torn garments: "Tear your hearts, not just your clothes, and return to the LORD your God" (v. 13). Jesus' teaching regarding fasting is thus in the spirit of the OT prophets.

Jesus began His teaching with a construction that parallels His introduction to the discussions of almsgiving and prayer (6:2,5): "whenever you fast" (v. 15). Again Matthew's use of *hotan* rather than *ean* is significant.[411] The grammar implies that Jesus assumed His disciples would fast. This is somewhat surprising since other statements in the NT make clear that Jesus did not emphasize fasting during His ministry.

The only reference to Jesus' personal fasting in the NT is related to His 40-day wilderness temptation (Matt 4:2; Luke 4:2). Other than in the SM, Jesus mentioned fasting on only two other occasions. In Luke 18:12, the reference to fasting has negative connotations. It appears in the parable of the Pharisee and the Publican in which the Pharisee brags that he fasts twice a week. His fasting is an expression of

---

[411] BDAG claims that ὅταν often approaches the meaning of ἐάν in Hellenistic Greek (730). However, Matthew used ἐάν 64 times in his Gospel and often with a meaning distinct from ὅταν.

the spiritual arrogance and hypocrisy that Jesus condemned in Matt 6:16–18.

In Matt 9:14–17 (cf. Mark 2:18–22; Luke 5:33–39), Jesus discussed fasting in response to a challenge from the disciples of John the Baptist. They asked, "Why do we and the Pharisees fast often, but Your disciples do not fast?" (9:14).[412] Jesus replied, "Can the wedding guests be sad while the groom is with them? The days will come when the groom will be taken away from them, and then they will fast" (v. 15).

Jesus was reminding His interrogators that fasting was an expression of mourning. However, during wedding celebrations, which typically lasted seven days, participants were expected to celebrate. Jewish law even exempted brides from some of the requirements of the important fast associated with the Day of Atonement.[413] It exempted grooms from the obligation to recite the *Shemà* on the wedding night.[414] The joys of marriage overrode some of Judaism's most important ritual responsibilities.

Similarly fasting and mourning were inappropriate during this season in which the disciples enjoyed the presence of the groom, the Messiah.[415] Fasting would be proper only when the Messiah was "taken away from" the disciples, a reference to Jesus' death. Matthew recognized that fasting was appropriate during the brief period between Jesus' crucifixion and resurrection. He adapted Mark in a manner that indicates that he saw fasting as appropriate after the ascension also as believers wait for Christ's return. Mark 2:20 says, "But the time will

---

[412] The word "often" (πολλά) is probably a later scribal addition. The word is absent in the earliest Gk. manuscripts of Matthew and is uncharacteristic of Matthew's style and grammar. He does not elsewhere use the anarthrous neuter plural adjective as a temporal adverb (see Matt 9:14; 13:3; 14:24; 16:21; 19:22; 27:19). If fact, when the adjective was used temporally in Hellenistic Greek, it normally modified a noun designating a period of time such as χρόνος (Matt 25:19) or ἡμέρα. Davies and Allison noted that the adjective is used adverbially three times in Matthew (*A Critical and Exegetical Commentary on the Gospel According to Saint Matthew*, 2:108, n. 115). The present author examined all 60 occurrences of πολύς in Matthew and did not find a single clear example of an adverbial use. Gundry also noted that although Matthew frequently used the adjective, "elsewhere Matthew never uses it in the adverbial accusative" (*Matthew*, 169). However, Gundry's own word statistics appear to be mistaken. By his count the adjective appears in Matthew only 49 times (*Matthew*, 680). The use of the English adverb "often" may still be appropriate if the present tense is a customary or iterative present. This appears to be the case in light of the use of the adverb πυκνά in the Lukan parallel (5:33).

[413] *m. Yoma* 8.1.

[414] *m. Ber.* 2:5, 8.

[415] Since the OT used the image of the groom to refer to God, Jesus' words may constitute an implicit claim to deity. See Isa 54:5–6; 62:4–5; Hos 2:16–20; 2 Cor 11:2; Eph 5:22–27; Rev 19:7. Jesus' identification as the "groom" has independent attestation in John 3:29.

come when the groom is taken away from them, and then they will
fast *in that day*" (italics added). Matthew deleted the final preposition
phrase (Matt 9:15). Luke revised the phrase and made it plural "in
those days" (Luke 5:35). The revisions in Matthew and Luke seem
motivated by a similar concern—to avoid giving the impression that
fasting was proper for Christians only immediately after the crucifixion and to demonstrate that it was an approved church practice.[416]

Matthew 9:14–17 does not suggest that Jesus' disciples never fasted during Jesus' ministry among them. Jesus and His disciples likely
participated in the fast prescribed in the OT in association with the
Day of Atonement.[417] This fast was required of all Jews except children under the age of 11 (if male) or 10 (if female), pregnant wom-
en, the sick, or persons on the brink of starvation.[418] The fasts from
which Jesus' disciples refrained were likely voluntary fasts in which
one representatively expressed repentance for the nation and sought
God's blessing on Israel. Participation in these fasts would have been
problematic for more than one reason. They expressed mourning that
was inconsistent with the Messiah's advent. Furthermore those who
fasted were expected to pray standardized prayers. These prayers included the Eighteen Benedictions, which may have contained pleas
for the coming of the Messiah in this period.[419] Jesus' disciples obviously could not pray for the coming of the Messiah since this would
have amounted to a tacit denial of Jesus' identity as the Messiah.[420]

Therefore the words "whenever you fast" assume that Jesus' disciples would fast on the Day of Atonement (at least until the time Jesus
provided atonement through His death) during Jesus' earthly ministry
and that they will fast to express their longing for His return after His
ascension. Acts 13:2–3 shows that the early church also fasted and
prayed when faced with important decisions.[421]

When Jesus' disciples fasted, He insisted, "Don't be sad-faced like
the hypocrites" (Matt 6:16). "Sad-faced" (*skuthrōpos*) refers to a sullen

---

[416] See Hagner, *Matthew 1–13*, 243; Davies and Allison, *A Critical and Exegetical Commentary on the Gospel According to Saint Matthew*, 2:111.

[417] Matthew 5:23 demonstrates that Jesus' disciples participated in the temple rituals of the Day of Atonement.

[418] *m. Yoma* 8.4–6.

[419] See *m. Taʿan.* 1.6–7; 2.2–5; *Ber.* 4.1–5.5.

[420] For a similar view, see W. Lane, *The Gospel According to Mark*, NICNT (Grand Rapids: Eerdmans, 1974), 109.

[421] Acts 9:9 seems to be an example of a spontaneous fast. The experience of Saul of Tarsus on the Damascus Road was so traumatic that he had no appetite for three days.

facial expression that portrays gloom and suffering.[422] "Hypocrites" were actors putting on a show.[423] They knew well that facial expressions were essential to a convincing performance. The qualification "like the hypocrites" is important. Jesus was not condemning all sad expressions for those who fasted. If one fasted with a broken heart, putting on a happy face could be as hypocritical as the pretension Jesus condemned here. Rather, Jesus was prohibiting putting on a sad face while inwardly delighting in the attention received for one's suffering for the nation. The adjective *skuthrōpos* is associated with darkness and may have referred not only to facial expressions but also to "darkening" the face with ashes. Ancient peoples of many different cultures expressed mourning and repentance by wearing sackcloth, a dark, rough fabric made of goat or camel hair, and by rubbing ashes on their faces and bodies. Jesus referred to this practice later in Matt 11:21: "Woe to you, Chorazin! Woe to you, Bethsaida! For if the miracles that were done in you had been done in Tyre and Sidon, they would have repented in sackcloth and ashes long ago!"

Jesus added that the hypocrites made "their faces unattractive" (6:16). The verb translated "make their faces unattractive" (*aphanizō*) means "to make something disappear" either by destroying it or by covering it.[424] This is likely a reference to the practice of covering one's face with ashes as an expression of mourning or repentance.[425] Actors on a stage typically covered their faces with a wooden mask that depicted the character whose role the actor was playing. Perhaps these hypocrites knew that they needed more than good acting to win the attention of their audience. Sackcloth became their costume and ashes their mask as they sought to make their drama more convincing.

Jesus said that the hypocrites wear a sad face and cover their faces "so their fasting is obvious to people." The Greek text contains a word-play that is obscured in English translation. Verse 16 has two verbal forms that share the same root and mean "to disappear" (*aphanizō*) and "to appear" (*phainō*).[426] Ironically the hypocrites "make their faces

---

[422] See "σκυθρωπός," BDAG, 933.

[423] See comments on Matt 6:2,5.

[424] See "ἀφανίζω," BDAG, 154.

[425] E. Levine, "The Theology of Fast Day Cosmetics (Matt 6:16–18)," *JRitSt* 13 (1999): 1–6, esp. 2. Levine poses the interesting theory that Jesus prohibited the use of ashes during Christian fasting because of its association with the view that the binding of Isaac atoned for sin.

[426] Although this is not completely clear from the lexical forms, both ἀφανίζω and φαίνω share the root φαν.

disappear" so they "may appear" to men. The Greek construction clearly expresses purpose and highlights the deceptive nature of the hypocrite's self-humiliation. The hypocrites hide their faces with ash only so they may be seen. Their apparent self-abasement is merely a ploy to capture the attention and stir the admiration of others.

One can readily see why the Jewish practice of fasting sometimes bred this hypocrisy. During times of crisis individuals began to fast as a first step toward seeking God's intervention.[427] These individuals were probably highly regarded for their piety and for the effectiveness of their prayers. One rabbinic text describes the man called on to pray in time of drought as "well-versed [in prayer]" whose children were hungry and whose cupboard was bare "so that he might be whole-hearted in the prayer."[428] When one fasted and prayed and God intervened, he could attain immediate celebrity status. The Mishnah describes a man named Onias whose prayer during a national fast brought abundant rain. He was so respected that a rabbi who wished to pronounce a ban against him was forced to say: "But what shall I do to thee?—thou importunest God and he performeth thy will, like a son that importuneth his father and he performeth his will; and of thee Scripture saith, 'Let thy father and thy mother be glad, and let her that bare thee rejoice.'"[429]

Representing the nation individually in fasting and prayer probably required more than the mere willingness to go without food and drink. The rabbis discussed qualifications for an individual to represent Israel in a private fast. R. Simeon ben Eleazar argued that an individual must first be appointed by the court "as an authority for the public."[430] Other rabbis concurred, but with the qualification that anyone could fast and pray during a time of personal emotional distress. In this context fasting for the nation was a real badge of honor. Those who fasted were tempted to flaunt their fasting in order to identify themselves as spiritual heroes who suffered on behalf of the nation.

Other ancient texts show that the temptation to flaunt one's fasting was very real in the ancient world. A later rabbi warned that a Jewish woman was sentenced to hang by her breasts in hell because

---

[427] m. Ta'an. 1.4.
[428] m. Ta'an. 2.2.
[429] m. Ta'an. 3.8.
[430] t. Ta'an. 1.7.

she bragged to others about her fast.[431] Greek philosophers were also known to warn people about trying to impress others by their fasting.[432] Thus it is not surprising that Jesus found it necessary to challenge hypocritical fasting.

Jesus warned that when people fast to call attention to themselves and to impress others, "I assure you: They've got their reward" (6:16). As in Matt 6:2,5, Jesus used the verb *apechō*, which means "to receive in full what is due." The verb was originally a technical term for providing a receipt marked "paid in full."[433] The hypocrites who fast to impress others will probably achieve their goal. However, this temporary admiration is the full extent of their reward. The one who seeks temporary earthly rewards for acts of righteousness forfeits heavenly rewards for these good deeds.

Disciples could avoid fasting out of impure motives by concealing the fact that they were fasting. Jesus commanded His disciples to put oil on their heads and to wash their faces when they fasted. Although they were clearly not victims of the modern obsession with personal appearance, most Jews put on clean clothes and washed themselves before appearing in public. If they had been weeping, Jews washed their faces before appearing in public (Gen 43:30–31). Furthermore Jews often washed their feet and faces before a meal (Gen 43:24,31).

During Jewish fasts that accompanied the Day of Atonement, refraining from washing was viewed by the rabbis as a necessary expression of self-denial. The law allowed only two categories of persons, kings and brides, to wash their faces during this important fast.[434] Jewish law allowed individuals to wash their faces during the voluntary fasts that accompanied prayer for rain and even for the first three days of national fasting. However, if rain still did not come, the fast was intensified. The law specifically forbade certain activities during the later more severe national fasts, and these included eating, drinking, washing, anointing, putting on sandals, and sexual intercourse.[435]

Thus washing one's face helped conceal that one was privately mourning and abstaining from food. Perhaps most importantly, if the

---

[431] p. Hag. 2.2. Other Jewish texts emphasized the importance of fasting in secret or emphasized the importance of sincerity in fasting (Sir 34.26; T. Ash. 2.8; T. Jos. 3:4–5; Apoc. El. 1.18–19; m. Ta'an. 2:1; t. Ta'an 1.8; b. Ta'an. 16a).

[432] Epictetus, Diatr. 3.14.4–6.

[433] "ἀπέχω," BDAG, 102.

[434] m. Yoma 8.1.

[435] m. Ta'an. 1.4–6.

disciples who fasted had rubbed ashes on their faces during the private fast, these were to be washed from the face before going into the
public in order to prevent flaunting the fast before others.

Anointing, putting oil on the head or body, was also prohibited
during strict fasts or the fast accompanying the Day of Atonement.
Because they lived in a dry and sometimes hot climate and spent long
hours in the sun, Palestinian Jews often applied oil to themselves to
lubricate and sooth dry scalps and skin (Ruth 3:3; 2 Sam 12:20; Pss
23:5; 141:5; Eccl 9:8; Ezek 16:9; Luke 7:46).[436]

Washing and anointing normally marked the end of a fast (2 Sam
12:20). Thus washing and anointing the head gave no impression
that one was fasting and ensured that "you don't show your fasting
to people but to your Father who is in secret" (Matt 6:18). Following
Jesus' instructions kept the fast a matter between only the disciple and
God. Although this prevented the disciple from enjoying the temporary reward of having his ego stroked by those who were impressed
by his outward expression of piety, it assured the disciple that "your
Father who sees in secret will reward you" (v. 18). Just as the Father
saw the quiet gift and heard the prayer in the closet, He also observed
the private fast and would bless the disciple for it. The future tense of
the verb "will reward" is primarily a promise of eschatological reward.
Jesus clarified that the promised reward was heavenly and eschatological in the next section of the SM in which He urged disciples to
seek heavenly and eternal rather than earthly and temporal treasures
(vv. 19–21).

D. The Disciple's Priorities (Matt 6:19–34)

Two Kinds of Treasure (Matt 6:19–21)

Matthew 6:19–24 is related to the preceding context of the SM in
several ways. First, in verses 1–18 Jesus encouraged disciples to perform their righteous deeds driven only by the desire to please God.
This proper motivation ensured that the disciple would enjoy God's
reward. In verses 19–24 Jesus exhorted disciples to value that heavenly reward above any temporary earthly treasure. Second, in verse 11
Jesus urged disciples to be content when their basic needs were met.

---

[436] See also *t. Šeb.* 6:9; *b. Sanh.* 101a; *b. Yoma* 35b.

However, one will not be satisfied with a day's supply of bread when his real agenda is to accumulate earthly treasures. Thus verses 19–24 explicitly state the priorities that the model prayer assumes.

Jesus commanded, "Don't collect for yourselves treasure on earth." The grammatical construction that Christ used (*mē* with the present imperative) either expresses a command to stop an action already in progress or establishes a general precept.[437] Only the context can determine which of the two nuances the author or speaker intended.

A survey of Matthew's Gospel suggests that Jesus intended the former nuance. Several features in Matthew suggest that Jesus observed that His disciples were too focused on earthly treasures and that His prohibition called them to change their priorities. First, Jesus' instructions to His disciples concerning their missionary work (10:8–10) must insist that the disciples refrain from charging individuals for ministry: "You have received free of charge; give free of charge." The command, "Don't take along gold, silver, or copper for your money-belts" (10:9) suggests that although Peter claimed, "We have left everything and followed You" (19:27), the disciples still had access to wealth.

Matthew 15:19 indicates that theft, and with it the covetousness that inspires theft, is latent within the heart of corrupt humanity. This thievery accompanies several other behaviors that Jesus specifically condemns in Matthew 5–7 including sexual immorality and false testimony. This seems to imply that the tendency to accumulate earthly treasures is endemic to fallen humanity and one with which His own disciples would struggle.

The utter astonishment of the disciples in response to Jesus' teaching concerning the difficulty of the rich entering the kingdom (19:23–26) implies that the disciples had embraced a popular theology that claimed wealth was an indication of the favor one had with God. The question of Simon Peter, "What will there be for us?" (v. 27)

---

[437] Wallace, *Greek Grammar Beyond the Basics*, 724; BDF, 172 §336. The study of the syntax of prohibitions in the SM is both interesting and informative and tends to confirm what traditional grammarians have suggested about the nuance of various forms. Matthew 5–7 uses μή (a) with the aorist subjunctive in 5:2,42; 6:8,13,31,34; 7:6; (b) with the aorist infinitive in 5:34,39; and (c) with the aorist imperative in 6:3. Prohibitions with the aorist in the SM seem to prohibit the action as a whole. This is especially clear in 5:34 in which the adverb ὅλως is used. Wallace's observation that the constative use of the aorist sometimes has inceptive overtones (ibid., 723) seems accurate. Prohibitions with the present infinitive (6:1) and present imperative (6:16,19,25; 7:1) either call for the cessation of an action already in progress or establish a general precept.

seems to express the expectation that God should somehow compensate the disciples for the enormous sacrifices they had made. Jesus' promise of 100 times more houses and fields in the messianic age than those the disciples had abandoned seems to respond directly to this expectation. His teaching concerning divine reversal ("Many who are first will be last, and the last first," v. 30) clarifies that present status is not a reliable indicator of eschatological status. Many who are presently wealthy will be impoverished in the messianic age, and many who are presently poor will then become wealthy. Furthermore the request of the mother of James and John probably expresses the desire of these two disciples for material wealth as well as political authority (20:20–28).

The events recorded in 26:14–16 most clearly demonstrate that at least one disciple was characterized by obsession with earthly treasure. Although many scholars have speculated about Judas's motivation for betraying Jesus, Matthew demonstrates that Judas's greed was a significant factor. Judas approached the chief priests with the question, "What are you willing to give me if I hand Him over to you?" (v. 15). Only after an offer of 30 pieces of silver did Judas begin to look for an opportunity to betray Jesus. Judas would regret too late that infatuation with earthly treasure had prompted him to betray innocent blood (27:3–10). In light of this evidence, Jesus' prohibition in 6:19 probably means "stop collecting for yourselves treasures on earth."

The phrase "treasures on earth" is broad enough to encompass anything from the worldly applause and recognition such as the hypocrites seek to material wealth. However, the next verse makes clear that Jesus had material wealth primarily in view.

Jesus warned that earthly treasures do not last long. They are transient and temporary, here one moment and gone the next. Jesus taught that the location of one's treasure determines its long-term value. Treasures in heaven are eternal. All earthly treasures, however, are subject to decay. Treasures cannot be permanently preserved on earth where moth and rust destroy.

Rare imported fabrics were expensive in the ancient world. A beautiful Babylonian cloak was one of the tempting treasures hoarded by Achan that prompted him to defy God's command (Josh 7:21). Other texts confirm that garments were one of the more alluring spoils of war (2 Kgs 7:8). The scene in which Roman soldiers gamble for Jesus' garments at the foot of the cross shows that some callous sinners valued clothing far more than the lives of the innocent.

Among the more expensive fabrics were wool that had been specially processed to make the cloth brilliantly white and fabrics that had been dyed a deep purple (Judg 8:26; Esth 8:15; Prov 31:22; Luke 7:25; 16:19; Rev 18:16).[438] Such clothing was worn only by royalty or those who were extravagantly wealthy. Silk was worth its weight in gold in the Roman Empire.[439] But these materials of such exorbitant price could be destroyed overnight by the larvae of the moth. The OT, NT, and nonbiblical writers spoke of the ability of the moth to ruin expensive fabrics.[440]

Moths could also attack other treasures that seemed more durable than fabrics. Luke 12:33 says, "Make money-bags for yourselves that won't grow old, an inexhaustible treasure in heaven, where no thief comes near and no moth destroys." Although the destructive power of the moth could be a reference here to ruining treasures like fabrics or books, the association with "money-bags that won't grow old" has led many scholars to suggest that in this text the moth eats away at the bottom of an old moneybag made of wool and the precious coins that it contains drop out and are lost one by one.[441] When gold, silver, or copper coins dropped here and there from the moneybag, the principle "finders keepers, losers weepers" generally applied.

Books and scrolls were also treasures in the ancient world. Since writing materials were expensive and since books were copied by hand by scribes rather than produced by printing presses, a single book might cost more than the average Palestinian Jew could afford.[442] The word translated "moth" (*sēs*) was also used to describe the ancient bookworms that destroyed these precious treasures.[443]

Ancient peoples likely saw property as the most enduring earthly treasure. But the same worms that destroyed books could ruin and

---

[438] See Green, *The Gospel of Luke*, 605.

[439] Vopiscus, *Aurel.* 45.

[440] Prov 14:30 (LXX); 25:30 (LXX); Job 32:22 (LXX); Ps 39:11; Mic 7:4 (LXX); Isa 33:1 (LXX); 50:9; 51:8; Jas 5:2; Sir 43:13; Lucian, *Sat.* 1.21.

[441] See Gundry, *Matthew*, 112; Marshall, *The Gospel of Luke*, 532.

[442] On the expense of making books in the ancient world, see B. Metzger, *Manuscripts of the Greek Bible: An Introduction to Paleography* (New York: Oxford University Press, 1981), 14–19.

[443] Philo, *Abr.* 2 §11.

render illegible the title deeds to property and bring a person's ownership into question.[444]

When the Jews of Jesus' day thought about threats to one's wealth,
they probably first considered large sources of destruction like fire,
storm, and robbers. However, Jesus emphasized the transience of
earthly riches by naming as the first threat to earthly treasures a tiny
creature that any little child could crush even with her smallest finger.
In Job 4:18–19, the moth serves as a metaphor for that which is fragile
and weak:

> If God puts no trust in His servants and He charges His angels with foolish-
> ness, how much more those who dwell in clay houses, whose foundation is
> in the dust, who are crushed like a moth! They are smashed to pieces from
> dawn to dusk; they perish forever while no one notices.[445]

If treasures were vulnerable to such small and weak creatures, surely
one was unwise to depend on treasures or to spend one's life accumulating them.

Most translations also discuss the destructive powers of rust,
which could attack, tarnish, and corrode the valuable jewelry or coins
that people of the first century treasured.[446] James 5:3 warned of the
danger of corrosion: "Your silver and gold are corroded, and their corrosion will be a witness against you and will eat your flesh like fire."
However, the word translated "rust" in Matt 6:19–20 actually means
"eating" (brōsis) and never clearly refers to corrosion or tarnishing
elsewhere in the OT or NT. In the LXX the term referred to plagues of
insects or birds that destroyed crops and pastures (Deut 32:24;[447] Mal
3:11) or birds of prey and wild animals that devoured farmers' flocks
and herds (Jer 15:3; 19:7; 34:20).[448]

---

[444] m. Ketub. 2.2–4 mentions disputes over property ownership that resulted from lack of
proper documentation.

[445] Interestingly Job 27:18 used the image of a moth's cocoon to portray the fragile nature of
men's houses: "The house he built is like a moth's cocoon or a booth set up by a watchman. He
lies down wealthy, but will do so no more; when he opens his eyes, it is gone."

[446] Jerome translated βρῶσις with the Latin word erugo which means "rust." John Wycliffe
translated the NT from the Vulgate. Tyndale, the first to translate the NT from Greek, evidently
followed Wycliffe here.

[447] Although the MT refers to plagues, the LXX refers to "eating of unclean birds" (βρώσει
ὀρνέων). The genitive should probably be taken as subjective, that is, the birds eat the crops.
However, the LXX could treat the phrase as an example of the severity of famine and mean that
the starving people eat unclean birds in order to survive (objective genitive).

[448] The association of βρῶσις with locusts may have resulted from mistranslation in the LXX
because of the overlap between the Hebrew words for "food" and "eater" in an unpointed text.
Consequently some commentators have suggested that the Greek of Matt 6:19 is also an instance

The "eaters" could also be vermin who ate the foods stored in bins and barns. Exodus 10:14–15 describes the devastation that hoards of "eaters" could bring:

> The locusts went up over the entire land of Egypt and settled on the whole territory of Egypt. Never before had there been such a large number of locusts, and there will never be again. They covered the surface of the whole land so that the land was black, and they consumed all the plants on the ground and all the fruit on the trees that the hail had left. Nothing green was left on the trees or the plants in the field throughout the land of Egypt.

Exodus 10:6 says that the locusts even filled all the houses of the Egyptians, likely devouring any foods present in the homes.

Joel 1:4,10–12 expresses the horrors of such plagues:

> What the devouring locust has left, the swarming locust has eaten; what the swarming locust has left, the young locust has eaten; and what the young locust has left, the destroying locust has eaten. . . . The fields are destroyed; the land grieves; indeed, the grain is destroyed; the new wine is dried up; and the olive oil fails. Be ashamed, you farmers, wail, you vinedressers, over the wheat and the barley, because the harvest of the field has perished. The grapevine is dried up, and the fig tree is withered; the pomegranate, the date palm, and the apple—all the trees of the orchard—have withered. Indeed, human joy has dried up.

The reference to the destructive force of the eaters warned shepherds that they could not count on the wealth represented by the number of sheep in their flocks. It warned farmers that they could not depend on the wealth represented by the tons of grain in their barns and fields. These riches were just as transient as the soft and colorful fabrics worn by the wealthy in the cities.

The treasures that moths and vermin cannot destroy, thieves can easily steal away. The verb translated "break in" (diorussō) literally means "dig through." It describes a thief digging through the walls made of sun-dried brick in a first-century Palestinian home in order to retrieve its treasures that were supposedly hidden safely away.[449]

---

of mistranslation of Jesus' original Semitic saying (Luz, *Matthew: A Commentary*, 1:332). However, it is just as likely that under the influence of the LXX, the noun βρῶσις came to be used by Greek-speaking Jews and Christians to refer to a "devourer."

[449] See "διορύσσω," BDAG, 251. See also "ὀρύσσω," 725. For uses of the verb similar to that here, see Aristophanes, *Plut.* 565 (κλέπτειν καὶ τοὺς τοίχους διορύττειν); and Job 24:16. Josephus did not use the verb, but he did use a related noun, τοιχωρύχος, to refer to one who breaks into homes or invades houses (*Ant.* 16.1). Ezekiel 12:5,7,12 uses the verb to describe digging through a city wall.

Jesus made clear that no earthly treasure is secure. Larvae devour expensive clothes. Vermin devour crops, pastures, food stores, flocks, and herds. Thieves grab jewels and gold and silver coins.

Elsewhere Jesus reminded His followers that even the treasures that escape moths, vermin, and thieves will ultimately be stripped from one's hands by death. In the parable of the Rich Fool (Luke 12:13–21), Jesus told of a wealthy man who thought his future was secure because of his enormous wealth. But God said to him, "You fool! This very night your life is demanded of you. And the things you have prepared—whose will they be?" (v. 20). Jesus explained, "That's how it is with the one who stores up treasure for himself and is not rich toward God" (v. 21). Perhaps alluding to Jesus' teaching, Paul later warned the wealthy: "We brought nothing into the world, and we can take nothing out" (1 Tim 6:7). He urged those who are "rich in the present age" not to "set their hope on the uncertainty of wealth" (v. 17).

Jesus' teaching regarding the fleeting nature of riches is grounded in themes from the OT. Proverbs 23:4–5 warned, "Don't wear yourself out to get rich; stop giving attention to it. As soon as your eyes fly to it, it disappears, for it makes wings for itself and flies like an eagle to the sky."

Ecclesiastes also has much to say about the futility of investing one's life in the accumulation of possessions only so they can be enjoyed by a stranger (5:8–6:7).

Rather than accumulating earthly treasures, Jesus commanded His disciples: "Collect for yourselves treasures in heaven" (Matt 6:20). Collecting treasures in heaven refers to acquiring heavenly reward through righteous deeds. These treasures refer to the rewards Jesus promised in Matt 6:4,6,18: "Your Father who sees in secret will reward you." As previously discussed, the future tense of the verb "will reward" is likely eschatological and refers to heavenly rewards. Although Jesus' teaching about rewards in heaven may sound shocking to many modern Protestants, such teaching was completely at home in first-century Judaism. The Mishnah taught: "These are the things whose fruits a man enjoys in this world while the capital is laid up for him in the world to come: honouring father and mother, deeds of loving-kindness, making peace between a man and his fellow; and the study of the law is equal to them all."[450]

---

[450] m. Pe'ah 1.1.

In this text the "capital laid up for him in the world to come" is heavenly treasure accumulated through righteous deeds. Several commentators suggest that Jesus' focus is on using worldly wealth for the benefit of others so as to accumulate heavenly wealth.[451] This interpretation conforms Jesus' teaching to the precedent in Tobit 4:8–9: "If you have many possessions, make your gift from them in proportion; if few, do not be afraid to give according to the little you have. So you will be laying up a good treasure for yourself against the day of necessity." This interpretation is correct, so far as it goes, but it is unduly restrictive. Interpreters certainly should not ignore the implications of this text for one's responsibilities to the needy as modern Christians sometimes tend to do. However, one should also avoid interpreting the text so narrowly that charitable gifts are seen as the exclusive or primary means of accumulating heavenly treasure.[452] This interpretation shows proper sensitivity to the following context in which Jesus emphasized a proper perspective on possessions. However, the instruction about heavenly treasures also has a clear connection to the preceding context. In the SM the actions that are specifically described as accumulating reward include suffering persecution for Jesus' sake (Matt 5:12), loving one's enemies (5:46), generous gifts to the poor (6:2–4), fervent and sincere prayer (6:5–6), and humble fasting (6:16–18). No doubt this list is representative rather than exhaustive. Clearly almsgiving, prayer, and fasting are examples of important acts of righteousness mentioned in 6:1. Matthew 10:41–42 adds that those who show hospitality to prophets, righteous people, and followers of Jesus will receive a reward as well. Disciples accumulate heavenly treasures through all these means and still others. Thus Jesus' teaching more closely parallels *Pss. Sol.* 9:5: "He that does righteousness layeth up for himself life with the Lord," and 2 *Bar.* 24:1: "For behold! The days come and the books shall be opened in which are written the sins of all those who have sinned, and again also

---

[451] Betz, *The Sermon on the Mount*, 434; Keener, *The Gospel of Matthew*, 230–32; Bruner, *The Churchbook: Matthew 1–12*, 321–32; Lloyd-Jones, *Studies on the Sermon on the Mount*, 355. Lloyd-Jones was concerned to avoid any tension between the accumulation of heavenly treasures and justification by faith alone. Thus he interpreted: "If you have money, so use it while you are here in this world that, when you arrive in glory, the people who benefited by it will be there to receive you." In his interpretation the heavenly treasures are the souls won through the believer's acts of love.

[452] Davies and Allison also affirm broader means of accumulating heavenly treasure (*A Critical and Exegetical Commentary on the Gospel According to Saint Matthew*, 1:632).

the treasures in which the righteousness of all those who have been righteous in creation is stored."[453]

Although Paul clearly taught that eternal life is a free gift rather than a wage earned, he too used the imagery of storing up treasure to speak of the accumulation of heavenly reward through good works. In 1 Tim 6:18–19 he commanded Timothy to instruct the rich "to do what is good, to be rich in good works, to be generous, willing to share, storing up for themselves a good reserve for the age to come, so that they may take hold of life that is real." The verb translated "storing up" in the HCSB is *apothēsaurizō*, an intensification of the verb *thēsaurizō* used in Matt 6:19–20.

Jesus did not define the nature of these heavenly treasures. They probably consist of the special blessings and privileges mentioned in texts like Matt 19:29 and 25:14–30: family, houses, lands, and increased authority in the eschatological kingdom. In fact 19:29 seems to have revised Mark 10:29–30 (=Luke 18:29–30) in order to clarify that houses and lands will be enjoyed by Jesus' disciples.

The individual rewards that constitute one's treasures in heaven are expressions of God's grace. Jesus taught in the Beatitudes that God fills those who hunger and thirst for righteousness with righteousness. Amazingly God imparts righteousness to His disciples and then rewards them for it.

Jesus contrasted the transience of earthly treasures with the permanence of heavenly treasures. Jesus taught that heavenly riches are superior to earthly ones because they are incorruptible. Moths cannot devour the disciple's heavenly robes and worms cannot destroy the title to his heavenly inheritance. Rust cannot corrode his heavenly crown. Vermin cannot destroy the fertility of the new earth or prevent the abundance of wine, fruit, and grain promised for the new era.

Heavenly treasures are also invulnerable to theft. No one can seize them from Jesus' followers. Jesus' statement implies the doctrine of the preservation of the saints. Peter may have been reflecting on the significance of these words when he described the believer's heavenly inheritance as "imperishable, uncorrupted, and unfading, kept in heaven for you" (1 Pet 1:4).

In summary, Jesus commanded His disciples to devote their lives to deeds of righteousness through which they would accumulate

[453] See also *4 Ezra* 7:97; *2 Enoch* 50:5.

heavenly treasures rather than striving to amass worldly wealth. Worldly wealth was transient; only heavenly treasures would endure. Jesus concluded His teaching about heavenly versus earthly treasures with the warning: "For where your treasure is, there your heart will be also" (Matt 6:21). Here one's "treasure" refers to what one values most and in which he has chosen to invest his life. A person's treasure shows where his heart truly is. In Judaism the "heart" did not merely refer to an organ in the chest responsible for the circulation of blood through the body. Instead it referred to the center of a person's existence, the seat of spiritual, moral, and emotional life. The heart was the source of a person's thoughts, desires, decisions, and actions. Jesus taught that the heart is ultimately what determines a person's behavior (Matt 5:28; 15:18–19). Most importantly, both the OT and NT show that the heart is the organ with which a person loves (Deut 6:4–5; 1 Pet 1:22).

One of the fundamental teachings of Judaism was that the heart should belong to God. At least three times a day, faithful Jews were expected to recite the *Shemà*, which reminded them of the obligation to "love the LORD your God with all your heart" (Deut 6:5). Jesus taught that this was the greatest of all the commandments (Matt 22:37). However, when a person chooses to devote his life to the accumulation of earthly possessions, his heart truly belongs to those earthly treasures rather than to God.

Materialism, which treasures earthly things more than God Himself, is thus a subtle but certain form of idolatry. Paul calls it such in Eph 5:5 and Col 3:5. Jesus had already taught that when a man looks on another woman and longs for her as he should long for his wife alone, he has committed adultery of the heart. Now He taught that when a person loves material possessions as he should love heavenly treasures alone, he has committed idolatry of the heart. In Matt 13:44–45 Jesus taught that the kingdom of heaven is the greatest of treasures, like a pearl of great price for which a merchant gladly sacrifices all he has. However, the materialist values the kingdoms of the world (4:8) more than the kingdom of heaven and cherishes the creation more than the Creator.

Matthew 6:24 confirms that a man loves and is devoted to the master whom he serves. If a person's life is devoted to the acquisition of possessions, those possessions are the object of his love and devotion. His heart belongs to them.

Matthew 6:21 begins with the conjunction *gar* which means "since" or "because." Thus this verse provides the rationale for accumulating heavenly and enduring treasures. The tight grammatical connection between verses 20 and 21 could imply that what a person treasures not only expresses his deepest affections but also determines his destiny. Doriani seems to support this view: "If we place our treasure in heaven, our heart will follow and be as safe as the treasure."[454] Since the heart is with one's treasures, if the treasures are in a place where they are exposed to corruption and destruction, then the heart is subject to destruction with them. If the treasures are in a place where they are vulnerable to thieves, then one's heart can be stolen away with them.[455] This view, however, is doubtful since the illustrations that follow in 6:22–24 focus on a person's internal spiritual condition rather than his final destiny.

The implication of Jesus' teaching is that materialism is such a serious form of idolatry that it is absolutely incompatible with genuine Christian discipleship. Jesus made this even clearer in verse 24. This seems severe, but Paul confirmed this principle. In Eph 5:5 he counted covetousness or greed along with sexual immorality as among sins so heinous that those who are doing such things will not inherit the kingdom of God.

Two Conditions of the Eye (Matt 6:22–23)

Jesus viewed materialism with seriousness because one's perspective on earthly possessions determines how he views the whole of life. Matthew 6:22–23 presents serious challenges to the interpreter. Betz, who has written extensively on this text both in his commentary and in a more detailed essay, commented, "The saying 'On Vision' (6:22–23) is one of the most difficult and yet most interesting passages of the

[454] Doriani, *The Sermon on the Mount*, 158.

[455] Filson seems to accept this view since he commented, "To make possessions one's consuming concern is eternally ruinous" (*A Commentary on the Gospel According to St. Matthew*, 100). Similarly Stott (*The Sermon on the Mount*, 155) noted, "Here Jesus declares that our heart always follows our treasure, whether down to earth or up to heaven." Nolland seems to entertain this view as a possibility when he mentions that the verse could mean "the heart will follow the stockpiled treasure" (*The Gospel of Matthew*, 299). Nolland rejected this view in favor of the consensus view.

SM."[456] Scholars debate what Jesus meant when He stated, "The eye is the lamp of the body." They also disagree on the meaning of the "good eye" and the "bad eye."

Before examining each phrase of this text, a few observations about the context of the passage are appropriate. Jesus' parable of the eye and the body is immediately preceded by a text that urged disciples not to collect earthly treasures. The parable is immediately followed by a discussion of God and money. Furthermore the connection between verses 22–23 and verse 24 is especially strong. The adjective "good" (*haplous*; lit., "single") in verse 22 sharply contrasts with the references to duality in verse 24. Other displays of Matthew's literary artistry suggest that this contrast was intentional rather than accidental. These contextual features provide important clues to guide the interpreter in understanding an otherwise difficult text. Unless the specifics of verses 22–23 show otherwise, the interpreter may assume that these verses deal with the issue of the disciple's relationship to money and/or possessions.

Jesus stated the essential principle of His parable: "The eye is the lamp of the body." Betz outlined two different understandings of the nature of the SM that lead to a great divide in specific interpretations of this verse. If the SM is classed as Jewish wisdom literature that is prephilosophical in nature, parallels in biblical and Jewish literature will be sufficient to guide the interpreter in discovering the meaning of the text. However, if the SM is an assembly of theological arguments of a more developed and sophisticated philosophical nature, the interpreter must appeal to the extensive discussions of various theories of "sense perception, cognition, ophthalmology, light and darkness, and colors" by the Greek philosophers. Betz adopts the latter approach. This commentary chooses the former.

Betz's approach to the interpretation of this passage seems to be at odds with some of his own conclusions about the nature of the SM. In the introduction to his commentary, he wrote:

> In terms of religion, the Sermon on the Mount and the Sermon on the Plain have their origins in Judaism, a Judaism, however, that has been disturbed or inspired (depending on one's point of view) by Jesus of Nazareth, who is assumed by the Sermons as their author and speaker. The particular brand

---

[456] Betz, *The Sermon on the Mount*, 438.

of Judaism that produced the Sermon on the Mount may be called "the Jesus movement," or, perhaps at a later stage, "Jewish Christianity."[457]

He later added, "As Jesus was a Jew, all the teachings of the Sermon on the Mount are Jewish in theology and cultural outlook."[458] He contrasted Matthew's SM with Luke's SP, explaining that the former addressed disciples from a Jewish milieu while the latter addresses disciples from a Greek milieu, although these different emphases were not mutually exclusive.

Given the Jewish background of both Jesus and Matthew, one should not expect the intricate discussions of sense perception among the Greek philosophers to be crucial to understanding Matt 6:22–23. The various theories of the Greek philosophers may be deemed a necessary guide for interpretation only if evidence suggests that such discussions were widely known in Palestinian Judaism of the Second-Temple period or in early Jewish Christianity. At present such evidence is lacking.[459] Thus Betz's theory that 6:22–23 is a deliberate polemic against the Platonic-Stoic concept of an internal light is unlikely.

The majority of commentators understand verse 22 to mean that the eye is the instrument by which external light passes into the body.[460] Allison has challenged this view at length.[461] He has attempted to prove that the majority position is anachronistic since early Jewish texts that compare the eye to a lamp consistently affirm the extramission theory of vision rather than the intromission theory of vision. Although Westerners since around AD 1500 universally have adopted the view that external light passes through the eye, ancient Jewish texts consistently expressed the view that the eye is itself a source of

[457] Ibid., 1.

[458] Ibid., 2.

[459] Betz does show that Philo (*Abr.* 150–66) adopts the theory of vision set forth in Plato's *Timaeus* Philo, in Betz's own words, "explicitly takes up the whole of Platonic tradition" (Betz, *The Sermon on the Mount*, 448). However, the views of an Alexandrian Jew so deeply influenced by Greek philosophy are not likely to be representative of the views of a Palestinian Jewish rabbi or the Jewish Christian who preserved His teachings in written form. The other allusions to Greek philosophical ideas regarding vision in Jewish literature, which Betz mentioned earlier, are too general to confirm a connection between Jewish views and the Greek philosophical writers (ibid., 442).

[460] France compares the eye to a window (*The Gospel of Matthew*, 138). Davies and Allison admit that this is the view of "the vast majority of commentators" (*A Critical and Exegetical Commentary on the Gospel According to Saint Matthew*, 1:635).

[461] D. C. Allison Jr., "The Eye Is the Lamp of the Body (Matt. 6:22–23=Luke 11.34–36)," *NTS* 33 (1987): 61–83. See the helpful summary of his view in *A Critical and Exegetical Commentary on the Gospel According to Saint Matthew*, 1:635–36.

light which it casts on surrounding objects. Consequently, the primary lesson taught in verses 22–23 is "Just as the healthy, good eye sends light into the world, so too do the righteous, filled with the light of God, dispel the shades around them."[462]

Although a few scholars have found Allison's view convincing, his arguments suffer from several serious flaws.[463] First, although the intromission theory was not universally held until the Middle Ages, the theory was not unknown. Democritus, Epicurus, Plato (at the writing of his *Republic*), and possibly Pythagoras affirmed that images, appearances, or air-imprints emanated from objects and were cast into the eye.[464]

Second, many of the Jewish texts that Allison claims support the extramission theory are purely figurative and cannot bear the weight imposed on them. For example Dan 10:6 describes a heavenly figure as having "eyes like flaming torches." However the figure's face is described as "like the brilliance of lightning" and his arms and feet "like the gleam of polished bronze." These are mere descriptions of the glorious radiance of this figure and do not imply any theory of sight. Similar objections may be made about Allison's appeal to the epiphanies in Zech 4 (describing the eyes of God) and 2 *Enoch* 42:1 (here describing guardians of the keys to hell). Literary descriptions of divine and demonic persons do not likely serve as helpful explanations of the human eye.[465]

Allison's appeal to *b. Šabb.* 151b is also problematic. The reference to a lamp appears in the *gemara* commenting on the mishnaic

---

[462] Ibid., 1:636.

[463] Several scholars show awareness of Allison's theory but reject it. These include Betz, *The Sermon on the Mount*, 449–53; Hagner, *Matthew 1–13*, 158–59; Luz, *Matthew: A Commentary*, 1:333; Morris, *Matthew*, 154; Charles Talbert, *Reading the Sermon on the Mount: Character Formation and Decision Making in Matthew 5–7* (Grand Rapids: Baker, 2004), 123; and Wilkins, *Matthew*, 294. Nolland stated that "the thought in vv. 22–23 is clarified and unified by assuming that the metaphorical construction involved appeal to imagery based on this ancient view [extramission theory]" (*The Gospel of Matthew*, 300). Yet he later claimed, "The imagery is of light coming into the body through the eyes and illuminating the whole interior of the person" (ibid., 301).

[464] See Betz, *The Sermon on the Mount*, 442–48. Plato seems to have affirmed what might be labeled an intromission theory in *Resp.* 6, 508b when he claimed that the eye receives "the power which it possesses as an influx, as it were, dispensed from the sun." In *Tim.* 45c-d, Plato seems to have affirmed the extramission theory.

[465] Furthermore, the most reliable text of 2 *Enoch* 42:1 says that the demonic eyes are like "extinguished lamps," which would not support the extramission theory anyway; and 3 *Enoch* 35:2 says that the eyes of angels are like torches of fire, but this description is intended to contrast the angels with humanity much like the description of their amazing height ("as the Great Sea in height").

statement that "he who closes the eyes [of a dying person] at the point of death is a murderer." The rabbis explained, "This may be compared to a lamp that is going out: If a man places his finger upon it, it is immediately extinguished." The *gemara* does not intend to compare the eyes to a lamp. Rather it compares the fragile flicker of a dying flame to the fragility of life at the brink of death. No theory of sight seems to be implied.

Third, Allison's appeal to *Testament of Job* 18:3 is most crucial since this text is his single example of the eye/lamp simile in ancient Jewish literature. However, Allison depends on a questionable emendation proposed by R. A. Kraft (which Kraft appears to mistranslate) to support his view.[466] Fourth, Allison's theory depends on imperfect parallels. Although he lists six Jewish texts that "liken the eye to a lamp," several actually compare the eye to a torch instead.[467] Fifth, Allison argues that Luke 11:36 shows that the earliest interpreter of Jesus' saying understood Jesus' words in light of the extramission theory. However, this required Allison to adopt C. C. Torrey's view that the Greek text of Luke 11:36 mistranslates an Aramaic original. Although any student of the SM in particular and Matthew in general must be grateful to Allison for his many keen insights, in this case his view is unconvincing.

Most commentators recognize that Matt 6:22 simply portrays the eye as the source of light for the body. Ultimately, whether Jesus affirmed the intromission or extramission theory of sight probably matters little for understanding this analogy. Even philosophers who affirmed the extramission theory imagined that light beamed from the eye merged with light from the sun and from the object in focus, then entered the body through the eye.[468] Jesus was referring to the universally recognized truth that the eye is the organ that makes sight possible.

[466] The reference to lamps appears only in manuscript S (AD 1307/1308) of *T. Job* but is absent from P (generally recognized as the most reliable text) and V (see R. P. Spittler, *OTP* 1:830). The Gk. text of P should read οἱ ἐμοὶ ὀφθαλμοὶ τοὺς λύχνους ποιοῦντας ἔβλεπον, not, as Kraft emended, οἱ ἐμοὶ ὀφθαλμοὶ τοὺς λύχνους ποιοῦντες ἔβλεπον. Spittler properly translated the Gk. text: "My eyes saw those who make lamps" (*OTP* 1:846, n. 18.b). Kraft translated his emended text: "My eyes, acting as lamps, searched out" (*The Testament of Job* [Missoula, MT: Scholars, 1974], 40. Kraft's translation would require the addition of ὡς before τοὺς λύχνους and does not seem to comport with the use of the definite article before λύχνος.

[467] Daniel 10:6 (LXX) and *3 En.* 35.2 both use the term λαμπάδες rather than λύχνους. See Betz, *The Sermon on the Mount*, 449, n. 214.

[468] See Nolland, *The Gospel of Matthew*, 301.

Jesus drew an important inference from this general principle. The Greek text introduces the second sentence of verse 22 with the inferential particle *oun*, which shows that He was stating a conclusion based on the preceding premise. The conclusion is that since the eye is the source of light for the body, the condition of the eye is important and determines the degree of light that enters the body. "If your eye is good, your whole body will be full of light. But if your eye is bad, your whole body will be full of darkness."

The adjective translated "good" in verse 22 is *haplous*, which literally means "single."[469] The meaning of the phrase "single eye," however, is not immediately obvious. The best procedure is to seek to understand the clearer reference to the "bad eye" that immediately follows, and then recognize that the "good eye" is the opposite of the bad eye. The adjective *haplous* likely functions as the opposite of the adjective *ponēros* since (a) the conjunction *de* that begins verse 23 bears an adversative sense ("but") in this context and establishes a clear contrast between verses 22b and 23a; and (b) the adjectives "full of light" (*phōteinon*) and "full of darkness" (*skoteinon*) are clearly opposite.

Given the focus on wealth and possessions in the surrounding context, one immediately suspects that the eye portrays an outlook or perspective on money or material objects. This suspicion is confirmed by numerous associations of the "eye" and riches in Jewish literature. The OT describes the eye as the organ susceptible to temptation by materialism. In Eccl 2:10, after the Teacher described how he amassed houses, vineyards, gardens, parks, servants, herds, flocks, silver, gold, treasures, and concubines in his pursuit of enjoyment, he adds, "All that my eyes desired, I did not deny them." Ecclesiastes 5:10–11 says, "The one who loves money is never satisfied with money, and whoever loves wealth is never satisfied with income. This too is futile. When good things increase, the ones who consume them multiply; what, then, is the profit to the owner, except to gaze at them with his eyes?" The eye serves a similar function in intertestamental literature. Tobit 4:7 says, "Give alms from your possessions, and do not let your eye begrudge the gift when you make it." Sirach 14:8–10 says, "The miser

---

[469] The translators of the HCSB recognize that the condition of the eye is a referent for a person's moral condition. They sought to express this in their translation by describing the eye as "good" or "bad" rather than merely "healthy" or "sick." Such a translation provides the English reader with helpful clues for understanding the correct interpretation of the passage.

is an evil person; he turns away and disregards people. The eye of the greedy person is not satisfied with his share; greedy injustice withers the soul." Sirach 31:13–14 says, "Remember that a greedy eye is a bad thing. What has been created more greedy than the eye? Therefore it sheds tears for any reason. Do not reach out your hand for everything that you see, and do not crowd your neighbor at the dish."

Thus Jewish literature associates the "bad eye" with greed and stinginess. For example, Deut 15:7–10 urges Israelites to lend money generously to the poor even when the year for canceling debts was near. Verse 9 warns Israelites not to be "stingy toward your poor brother and give him nothing." In the MT, the expression for stinginess is "the evil eye." The LXX translated the expression literally, "Do not let your eye be evil toward your brother." The verb translated "be evil" is *ponēreuō*, the verb form related to the adjective *ponēros* ("bad") in Matt 6:23.

Proverbs 23:6, "Don't eat a stingy person's bread," translates the Hebrew expression, "Don't eat the bread of the evil eye." The phrase translated "a greedy man" in Prov 28:22 is literally "a man with an evil eye." Especially relevant to the discussion here, Matt 20:15 appears to use the "evil eye" in reference to selfishness. In this text a worker who labored all day was upset because the master paid another worker who labored only a short time the same amount that he received. The master asked the resentful servant, "Is your eye evil (*ponēros*) because I am good?"[470] In context, this appears to mean, "Are you stingy (or resentful of what others have) because I am generous?" In light of this evidence the "bad eye" in 6:23 represents greed, stinginess, covetousness, and miserliness.[471]

Due to the sharp contrast between the "good" or "single" eye and the bad eye in verse 23, one would expect the "good eye" to represent generosity. Several parallels in Jewish texts confirm this usage. In Prov 22:9, the Hebrew text translated "a generous person" is literally "he who has a good eye." The fact that Matthew spoke of a single (*haplous*) eye rather than a good (*agathos* or *kalos*) eye is easily explainable. The adjective "single" can mean "generous" since the related adverb *haplōs* sometimes means "generously" (Jas 1:5), and the related noun

---

[470] Present author's translation. See the marginal reading in the HCSB.
[471] See Hagner, *Matthew 1–13*, 158; G. Harder, "πονηρός," *TDNT*, 6 (1968):555–56; and Luz, *Matthew: A Commentary*, 1:333.

haplotēs may, in some contexts, mean "generosity" (Rom 12:8; 2 Cor 8:2; 9:11,13). This meaning also finds support in extrabiblical texts.[472]

The use of the adjective "single" implies more than mere generosity. In its most basic sense the adjective means "consisting of one" as opposed to double (*diplous*), which meant "consisting of two." The next section of the SM warns about seeking to maintain a double allegiance to both God and money by warning, "No one can be a slave to two masters" (Matt 6:24). This suggests that the "single eye" is one that does not allow the allurement of wealth and possessions to distract him from God. Those who seek to divide their loyalties between God and financial success are victims of a blinding form of double vision. This double vision is as dangerous as the "double mind" or the "double heart."[473] Thus the good eye is one whose focus is fixed on God and whose vision is not blurred by focusing on two objects at the same time, God and possessions. Thus the adjective "single" is a double entendre.[474] In this adjective the themes of generosity toward others and singlehearted devotion to God coalesce to define the disciple's proper view of possessions and riches.

The contrast between "full of light" and "full of darkness" (vv. 22–23) demonstrates the great impact that one's view of material possessions and health ultimately has on his life. The contrast between "light" and "darkness" is common in Jewish literature. When used metaphorically, "light" may symbolize knowledge or revelation and "darkness" symbolizes ignorance or failure to see and understand the truth. Many commentators take the usage of the metaphors in verse 23 in this sense. Keener, for example, wrote, "Those who justify their pursuit of material possessions by comparing themselves with others will blind themselves (cf. 7:3–5) to the truth of their disobedience and affect their whole relationship with God."[475] Similarly, France suggested: "If the idea of the lamp was of that which enables the body to find its way, the thought is of a purposeful life, directed toward its true goal. The alternative is a life in the dark, like a blind man, because the 'evil eye' of selfish materialism gives no light to show the

---

[472] See *T. Iss.* 3:8.

[473] The adjective δίψυχος ("double-minded") is used in Jas 4:8 (see also Ps 119:113). The noun διπλοκαρδία ("double-heartedness") is used in *Did.* 5:1 and *Barn.* 20:1.

[474] See also Broadus, *The Gospel According to Matthew*, 146; France, *The Gospel of Matthew*, 262; and Keener, *The Gospel of Matthew*, 232–33.

[475] Keener, *The Gospel According to Matthew*, 232.

way."[476] In this view a person's greed is said to sentence him to live in darkness, unable to see and understand the truth, and vainly groping to find his way.

Several features of the passage suggest that Jesus intended to communicate more than this. The adjectives used to describe the eye, "single" and "evil," refer not to knowledge and ignorance but to moral categories. This is clearly true of the adjective "evil" (*ponēros*).[477] This is also true of the adjective "single" (*haplous*).[478] Aquila's Greek translation of Job 1:1 used the adjective to describe Job's righteous character.[479] The LXX used the related noun (*haplotēs*) to translate the Hebrew terms for "integrity" (2 Sam 15:11; HCSB: "innocently") and "uprightness" (1 Chr 29:17).[480] Intertestamental Jewish literature used the adjective to describe personal integrity.[481] The NT also uses the noun in a positive moral sense to speak of sincerity, integrity, and righteousness (2 Cor 1:12; 11:3; Eph 6:5; Col 3:22). Other early Christian literature used the adjective to describe those who love God with all their hearts and detest all that displeased Him.[482]

Given the prominence of moral terms in Matt 6:22–23, the images of light and darkness probably refer not merely to knowledge and ignorance, sight and blindness, but to good and evil. Jesus' contemporaries often used the imagery of light and darkness in this moral sense. For example in 2 Cor 6:14–15, Paul asked, "What partnership is there between righteousness and lawlessness? Or what fellowship does light have with darkness? What agreement does Christ have with Belial?" In this series of parallel questions, light is associated with righteousness and with Christ, and darkness is associated with lawlessness and Belial.[483] Use of "light" and "darkness" to portray

---

[476] France, *The Gospel of Matthew*, 139.

[477] The adjective is used 26 times in Matthew (5:11,37,39,45; 6:13,23; 7:11,17,18; 9:4; 12:34,35 [three times], 39,45 [twice]; 13:19,38,49; 15:19; 16:4; 18:32; 20:15; 22:10; 25:26). In every instance its moral connotations are clear.

[478] See "ἁπλοῦς," BDAG, 104.

[479] Davies and Allison, *A Critical and Exegetical Commentary on the Gospel According to Saint Matthew*, 1:638.

[480] Keener claimed that LXX translators used the adjective to translate the Hebrew word for "perfect." This appears to be mistaken. The adjective appears in the LXX only in Prov 11:25 where it appears to refer to one who generously blessed others by sharing possessions with the needy. The noun form appears with greater frequency in the apocryphal section of the LXX (1 Macc 2:37,60; 3 Macc 3:21; Wis 1:1; Dan 13:63).

[481] *T. Reu.* 4:1; *T. Sim.* 4:5; *T. Levi* 14:1; *T. Job* 26:6; *T. Iss.* 4:2.

[482] *Barn.* 19:2.

[483] See also Rom 13:12; Col 1:12–13; 1 Thess 5:5.

good and evil is a prominent feature of literature from the Qumran community. 1QS 3.19–24 says:

> Upright character and fate originate with the Habitation of Light; perverse, with the Fountain of Darkness. The authority of the Prince of Light extends to the governance of all righteous people; therefore, they walk in the paths of light. Correspondingly, the authority of the Angel of Darkness embraces the governance of all wicked people, so they walk in the paths of darkness.
>
> The authority of the Angel of Darkness further extends to the corruption of all the righteous. All their sins, iniquities, shameful and rebellious deeds are at his prompting, a situation God in His mysteries allows to continue until His era dawns. . . . All the spirits allied with him share but a single resolve: to cause the Sons of Light to stumble.[484]

Matthew himself earlier made two references to light in which light is associated with righteousness or goodness. In Matt 5:16 Jesus' disciples let their light shine by doing good works to the glory of God. In 5:14, "light" seems to have some association with righteous living as well. This evidence suggests that "full of light" means "full of righteousness" and "full of darkness" means "full of evil."[485] Similar considerations led Zöckler to conclude:

> The two alternatives with which the listener is confronted allude to different moral conditions. The single eye gives light to the whole body, which is another metaphor for a person's wholeness—it denotes the morally intact person. A bad eye has the opposite result; it causes the person's darkness, that is, a corrupt ethical condition.[486]

Greediness corrupts the entirety of a person's life with evil. Generosity, on the other hand, is essential to being truly and thoroughly righteous.

Allison has argued that Jesus' point was not that greediness corrupts a person's life but instead that greediness is a symptom of a pre-existing inner corruption. In his view a person is generous because of

---

[484] M. O. Wise, M. G. Abegg Jr., and E. M. Cook, *The Dead Sea Scrolls: A New Translation* (San Francisco: Harper San Francisco, 1996), 120.

[485] For a similar view, see Blomberg, *Matthew*, 123–24. He concluded, "The way that people handle their finances affects every other part of their lives, either for good or for bad." See also E. Sjöberg, "Das Licht in dr. Zur Deutung von Matth. 6,22ff. Par," *ST* 5 (1951): 89–105, esp. 103–4; Guelich, *The Sermon on the Mount*, 332. Schnackenburg described the light as "fellowship with God and to the God-given inclination to good." Darkness, he described, as "separation from God" and, apparently from the God-given inclination to good as well (*The Gospel of Matthew*, 71).

[486] T. Zöckler, "Light within the Human Person: A Comparison of Matthew 6:22–23 and Gospel of Thomas 24," *JBL* 120 (2001): 487–99, esp. 490.

the light with which he is filled, and a person is greedy and selfish because of the darkness that inhabits him. Thus the thought of 6:22–23
would parallel Matt 12:34–35; 23:27–28; and Mark 7:20–23.[487]

Some scholars contest Allison's view on the ground that he has
turned the grammar of Jesus' statement upside down by making the
condition into the consequence and the result into the cause.[488] However, Allison's view is grammatically possible.[489] Wallace discusses a
category of conditional sentences which he called "evidence-inference"
in which the "if clause" (protasis) states evidence demonstrating
the validity of the "then clause" (apodosis). Wallace correctly notes
that in such constructions "often, though not always, the ground-
inference condition will semantically be the *converse* of the cause-
effect condition."[490]

The problem for Allison's view is the temporal relationship between the "if" and "then" clauses in Matt 6:22–23. In every other example of the evidence-inference use of conditional sentences given by
Allison and Wallace, the tense of the verb in the apodosis is either past
(perfect, aorist, imperfect) or present. Neither lists any examples in
which an apodosis using a future tense verb fits this category.[491] Furthermore in these examples the tense of the verb in the apodosis is
consistently either antecedent in time to the tense of the protasis or
contemporaneous with the tense of the protasis.[492] However, in Matt
6:22–23, the first two conditional statements use the present tense in
the protasis and the future tense in the apodosis. This seems to imply
that the state described in the apodosis follows and is a consequence
of the condition expressed in the protasis.[493] More simply put, the self-

---

[487] More recently S. Turan has come to the conclusion that the condition of the eye displays
the condition of the soul based on an old rabbinic principle of matchmaking ("A Neglected
Rabbinic Parallel to the Sermon on the Mount (Matthew 6:22–23; Luke 11:34–36)," *JBL* 127
[2008]: 81–93).

[488] Luz, *Matthew: A Commentary*, 1:333, n. 26.

[489] See his own defense of his handling of the grammar in Davies and Allison, *A Critical and
Exegetical Commentary on the Gospel According to Saint Matthew*, 1:637–38. Examples include
Matt 12:28; John 9:41; Rom 7:20; 8:9; 14:15.

[490] Wallace, *Greek Grammar Beyond the Basics*, 683.

[491] This seems significant since 8 of the 10 examples are first-class conditional sentences in
which any tense might have been used in the apodosis.

[492] The tenses of the protasis and apodosis are as follows: Num 16:29 (future/perfect); 1 Kgs
22:28 (aorist/aorist); Matt 12:26 (present/aorist); 12:28 (present/aorist); John 9:41 (imperfect/
imperfect [2nd class]); Rom 7:20 (present/present); 8:9 (present/present); 14:15 (present/pres-
ent); Rom 8:17 (no stated verbs); 1 Cor 15:44 (present/present).

[493] This last argument assumes that the future tense in Matt 6:22–23 is predictive. If the
future were gnomic, the tense could describe a state that is concurrent with the condition. The

ish greed mentioned in the "if clause" leads to the horrible internal darkness described in the "then clause."

Other Jewish texts from this era alert readers to the spiritual dangers of wealth.[494] They also warn of the potentially disastrous effects of the love for financial success. One text warns of a great affliction that will "fill everything with evils with disgraceful love of gain, ill-gotten wealth."[495] It speaks of "love of money, which begets innumerable evils for mortal men."[496] The source warns of the ravaging of Greece because "men will come face to face in strife among themselves because of gold and silver. Love of gain will be shepherd of evils for cities."[497] Sirach 31:5–8 warned:

> One who loves gold will not be justified; one who pursues money will be led astray by it. Many have come to ruin because of gold, and their destruction has met them face to face. It is a stumbling block to those who are avid for it, and every fool will be taken captive by it. Blessed is the rich person who is found blameless, and who does not go after gold.

Perhaps the most jolting warning appears in the NT:

> But those who want to be rich fall into temptation, a trap, and many foolish and harmful desires, which plunge people into ruin and destruction. For the love of money is a root of all kinds of evil, and by craving it, some have wandered away from the faith and pierced themselves with many pains. (1 Tim 6:9)

Jesus concluded, "So if the light within you is darkness—how deep is that darkness!" (Matt 6:23). When greed forces out any trace of inner good and only evil remains, the inner person is indescribably evil. The greedy person's corruption is complete. No room remains for love for God or pursuit of the kingdom and its righteousness (vv. 24,33).

Modern readers may be shocked by Jesus' teaching about the corrupting influence of greed. However, other ancient Jewish writers recognized that greed could be categorized among the worst of evils. The disdain of some Jews for greed is expressed in *T. Levi* 17:11–12 in

---

gnomic future is rare in the NT according to Wallace (*Greek Grammar Beyond the Basics*, 571). However, the verbs in verse 24 appear to be rare examples of this category.

[494] *1 Enoch* 63:10; 94:8; 96:4; 97:8; 1QS 10:18–19; 11.2; CD 4.17; 8.7; Sir 31:8–11; *Let. Aris.* 211; Josephus, *J. W.* 2.250; id., *Ant.* 4.190; and *m. Abot* 2:7.

[495] *Sib. Or.* 3.189.

[496] Ibid., 3.235–36.

[497] *Sib. Or.* 3.640–42.

which the writer lists "money lovers" among such sinners as "idolators," "adulterers," "pederasts," and "those who practice bestiality."

Two Masters (Matt 6:24)

"No one can be a slave of two masters, since either he will hate one and love the other, or be devoted to one and despise the other. You cannot be slaves of God and of money." Jesus continued His instruction on the theme of money and possessions by insisting that devotion to God and obsession with money and possessions are mutually exclusive. The "single eye" must have a single focus, and the single heart must have a single devotion.

Jesus' statement was absolute and seems to allow for no exceptions. "No one" (*oudeis*) demonstrates that not even one individual is capable of equally divided loyalties between God and riches. When this negative pronoun is combined with the verb "can" (*dunamai*), the construction excludes the possibility of submitting one's life to both service to God and fulfillment through financial gain.

The Mishnah ruled that a man could not be half slave and half free. Originally the school of Hillel taught that a half-slave should work for his master one day and for himself the following day. The school of Shammai argued that this was impossible. The slave had to be released by the master, and the slave had to write a certificate of debt to the master for half of the value of a slave. Ultimately the school of Hillel also adopted the position of the school of Shammai.[498]

Although a Jew could not be half slave and half free, the law did make provisions for slaves who were jointly owned by two different masters. Thus Jesus was not claiming that joint ownership of a slave by two masters was legally prohibited, as some commentators have suggested.[499] Both the NT (Acts 16:16) and the Mishnah mention slaves who belonged to joint owners. Joint ownership might result from the sale of a slave to a new master with the proviso that the slave remain under the old master's authority for a specific amount of time or perhaps because the slave was part of an estate divided between two heirs.[500] However, the rulings of the Mishnah indicate that jointly owned slaves could not eat the Passover offering from the

---

[498] *m. ʿEd.* 1.13; *Giṭ.* 4:5.

[499] Hill, *The Gospel of Matthew*, 143; A. H. McNeile, *The Gospel According to Matthew: The Greek Text with Introduction and Notes* (London: Macmillan, 1915), 85.

[500] *b. B. Qam.* 90a.

table of both masters (*m. Pesaḥ.* 8.1). The Mishnah does not indicate who decided which master would provide the Passover meal to the slave or what factors influenced this decision. The decision was probably made based on who had the greater authority and responsibility for the slave or which master the slave preferred. In any event the Mishnah makes clear that two masters cannot have completely equal authority and responsibility for a slave and a slave cannot equally divide his loyalties between two masters. Thus the legal complications related to joint ownership of slaves confirm the principle that Jesus taught. The people in Jesus' audience may have been familiar with slaves who rushed through tasks assigned by one master so they could devote their service to their favorite master.

Readers of Matthew's Gospel who were familiar with the LXX would likely have read the command to choose one Master as an echo of several familiar OT texts. Three times a day faithful Jews recited the *Shemà*, which insisted that "the Lord our God is one Lord." The word "Lord" (*kurios*) is the same word used in Matt 6:24 for the master of a slave. Every faithful Jew recognized that there could be no lord beside Yahweh. He alone deserved to be Lord and Master, and His people were to love Him with all their heart, soul, and strength (Deut 6:4–5).

Jesus insisted that when a person attempts to divide his loyalty between two masters, he will inevitably "hate one and love the other, or be devoted to one and despise the other." The verb "hate" (*miseō*) in contrast to "love" (*agapaō*) may reflect a Semitic idiom and mean to "love less" (Matt 10:37; Gen 29:30,33).[501] The addition of the parallel clause "be devoted to one and despise the other" does not preclude this interpretation. Jesus recognized that each person has a limited amount of love, devotion, and service to offer. The greater one's love for money grows, the more one's love for God is diminished. The more one's obsession for money increases, the more one's passion for God decreases.

Jesus drew an application from His illustration: "You cannot be slaves of God and of money." The Greek word translated "money" (*mamōnas*, "mammon") appears only here (and in the Lukan parallel; 16:9,11,13) in the NT. It is actually a transliteration of an Aramaic term that referred to property, possessions, or money and appears in

---

[501] See the discussion in Gundry, *The Gospel of Matthew*, 115.

other Jewish texts of the era.[502] Jesus' use of the term is a personification. He portrayed mammon as a master seeking to enslave and to rule
over a person's life in competition with God, the one true and rightful
Master.

Although scholars of an earlier generation claimed that mammon was the name of a Syrian deity, no evidence supports this view.
Others portray mammon as a demon, a view popularized by Milton's
Paradise Lost (1.679–80). This view has some merits. The Gospels of
Matthew and Luke appear to be the first surviving Greek texts to use
the Aramaic term.[503] Betz has suggested that for readers unfamiliar
with the Semitic background, "naming this pseudo-deity by a foreign
name indicates its demonic and even magical character."[504] Similarly
Hengel observed, "Perhaps the early church left this Semitic loan-
word untranslated because they regarded it almost as the name of
an idol: the service of mammon is idolatry."[505] These observations
are probably correct since the Evangelists could easily have translated the term for their Greek audience. The mysterious term would
function like a personal name for a Greek audience and warn that
money and possessions are essentially deified by those who serve
them above God.

Other Jewish teachers of this era saw love for God and love for
wealth and possessions as mutually exclusive. One source insists,
"Those who love God have loved neither gold nor silver, nor all the
good things that are in the world."[506] In the *T. Jud.*, love for money
and sexual lust led to Judah's downfall and doomed his tribe to wickedness. Judah warned his people, "Guard yourselves therefore, my
children, against sexual promiscuity and love of money; listen to Judah, your father, for these things distance you from the Law of God,
blind the direction of the soul, and teach arrogance." In words reminiscent of Jesus' warning in Matt 6:23 about the potential of greed to
darken and corrupt a person inside, Judah warned that sexual passion

[502] A translation expresses the meaning of a foreign term in a different language. Transliteration merely expresses the pronunciation of the foreign term in the alphabet of the second
language. For other usages of the term in Jewish texts of this era, see Sir 31:8; 1QS 6.2; 1Q 27.1,
2, 5; CD 14.20; *m. Abot* 2.7 [BDAG incorrectly cites 2.17]; *m. Sanh.* 1.1; *j. Pe'ah* 1.1; *b. Ber.* 61b.

[503] See Nolland, *The Gospel of Matthew*, 304, n. 387.

[504] Betz, *The Sermon on the Mount*, 458.

[505] M. Hengel, *Property and Riches in the Ancient Church: Aspects of a Social History of Early
Christianity* (Philadelphia: Fortress, 1974), 24, cited in Davies and Allison, *A Critical and Exegetical Commentary on the Gospel According to Saint Matthew*, 1:643.

[506] 1 Enoch 108.8.

and greed "deprive [a person's] soul of all goodness." These passions "enslave him, so that he is unable to obey God: They blind his soul, and he goes about in the day as though it were night." Judah also associated greed with idolatry: "My children, love of money leads to idolatry, because once they are led astray by money, they designate as gods those who are not gods. It makes anyone who has it go out of his mind." Judah also claimed that his greed had been stirred by Satan himself: "The prince of error blinded me."[507]

Jesus' teaching and the ancient Jewish parallels clearly portray materialism as more than a mere cultural phenomenon. On the contrary, it is false religion at its worst. It honors created things more than the Creator and makes idols of the blessings of God that should have prompted thanks to Him. Jesus described materialism even more explicitly as idolatry in verse 32. Its subtle allurements are the whispers of Satan and his demons. Just as Satan attempted to lure Jesus to false religion of the worst sort, the worship of the Devil himself, by the offer of the kingdoms of the earth, so now Satan uses the offer of worldly treasures to draw people away from God to worship property, possessions, and money. People still speak of those who "sell their souls for the sake of the almighty dollar." By describing the dollar as "almighty," an adjective properly used only in description of God, they subtly acknowledge that materialism is in essence idolatry.

Furthermore materialism enslaves those who should serve God as their Master. The slavery imagery of this passage reminds readers how quickly they may be possessed by the things they possess. Materialism turns the owner into chattel and possessions into masters. It blinds, shackles, and imprisons the greedy much like the Philistines blinded, shackled, and imprisoned the mighty Samson. The blinded slave cannot easily find a way of escape from his cruel master so that he can flee to the arms of the gracious Master who loves him and desires the best for him. Allison warned, "Mammon, once it has its hooks in human flesh, will drag it where it wills, all the time whispering into the ear dreams of self-aggrandizement."[508]

---

[507] T. Jud. 17–18. H. C. Kee, "Testaments of the Twelve Patriarchs," OTP 1:777–828. These testaments probably date to the second century BC.

[508] Davies and Allison, A Critical and Exegetical Commentary on the Gospel According to Saint Matthew, 1:642.

E. The Result of Proper Priorities (Matt 6:25–34)

Matthew 6:25–34 is closely connected to the preceding section (vv. 19–24). The phrase "This is why I tell you" indicates that verses 25–34 draw an application from the preceding verses. The antecedent of the pronoun "this" (*touto*) clearly points to at least verse 24 and probably beyond it to the entire discussion of riches and possessions. Focusing on heavenly treasures (vv. 19–21), being characterized by generosity (vv. 22–23), and refusing to allow materialism to compete with one's devotion to God (v. 24) should free disciples from many of their anxieties. Failure to view riches and possessions from a proper perspective only promotes anxiety.[509]

One of Jesus' contemporaries, the rabbi Hillel, was reported to have said, "The more flesh the more worms; the more possessions the more care."[510] Hillel's words focused on the transience of the present life. The more one feeds the body, the more worms will have to devour in the grave. This body is temporary and will die. Possessions inspire "care" or anxiety because they are even more transient than the body. These possessions will be abandoned at death, but even more significant is the fact that they can easily be lost because of the moths, vermin, and thieves that Jesus discussed earlier. Earthly possessions are in a continual state of risk. Ironically, when a person seeks happiness through riches and possessions, he only guarantees that anxiety will chase away any prospect of happiness. Even the most foolish should recognize that they cannot hold on to these treasures forever.

Anxiety is one of the sad symptoms of slavery to mammon. Just as the shackles of the bondslave prevent him from escaping from his master, worry over riches and possessions shackles the materialist to the master mammon and prevents him from enjoying real freedom.

Jesus exhorted His disciples, "Don't worry about your life, what you will eat or what you will drink" (v. 25). The KJV reads, "Take no thought for your life." This translation may give modern readers the false impression that Jesus prohibited even thinking about and

---

[509] Allison sees a connection of a different sort. He proposed that Matthew foresaw a possible objection to the claims of the preceding material on the part of the reader: "How can I eat and clothe myself if I whole-heartedly serve God and am relatively indifferent to mammon?" Matthew 6:25–34 provides Matthew's response. See Davies and Allison, *A Critical and Exegetical Commentary on the Gospel According to Saint Matthew*, 1:646.

[510] *m. ʾAbot* 2.7.

planning for the future.[511] However, as the HCSB shows, the Greek verb *merimnaō* refers to apprehension, anxiety, or worry rather than wise planning.[512]

Hagner has pointed out that the cognate noun *merimna* occurs twice in the Apocrypha in contexts where it is associated with insomnia.[513] This implies that the word group describes an anxiety so severe that it robs its victims of their sleep. Another text warns that anxiety "brings on old age too soon."[514] Hagner aptly described this form of worry as a "paralyzing anxiety," worry that cripples its victims with dread.[515]

The grammatical form of the prohibition, *mē* with the present imperative, may urge the audience to cease an action already in progress ("Stop worrying!"), or it may express a general prohibition.[516] Matthew used the negative with the aorist subjunctive in verses 31 and 34 to express a general prohibition. Thus the use of the present tense here probably suggests that the grammatical form in verse 25 calls the disciples to stop worrying. Furthermore the portrayal of the disciples as men of "little faith" (v. 30) implies that they struggled with worry and were being corrected by Jesus. Finally, the question in verse 28, "Why do you worry?" clearly implies that Jesus' disciples did worry at least periodically. Jesus knew that anxiety was endemic to the human race and that all people who have the confused priorities He challenged in verses 19–24 will be plagued with worry.

Although the word translated "life" (*psuchē*) may mean "soul" as the "seat and center of inner human life," the connection of the term to food and drink shows that it here refers simply to physical life. Jesus thus urged His disciples to avoid worrying about their survival. Worry about "what you will eat or what you will drink" (v. 25) did not reflect concern about the variety or quality of one's menu. The concern was whether one would have anything to eat or drink at all. Jesus was speaking largely to poor members of an agrarian society in which

---

[511] The translation was a good rendering in the early 1600s when the KJV was produced. Broadus noted that contemporary writers like Francis Bacon and Shakespeare used the word "thought" to express the idea of worry, e.g., "he died of thought" (Broadus, *The Gospel According to St. Matthew*, 148).

[512] See "μεριμνάω," BDAG, 632.

[513] See 1 Macc 6:10 and Sir 42:9.

[514] Sir 30:24.

[515] Hagner, *Matthew 1–13*, 163.

[516] Wallace, *Greek Grammar Beyond the Basics*, 724–25.

food resources depended on adequate rainfall and crops could be easily destroyed by hoards of insects, disease, wild fires, or high winds. The disciples' ancestors had faced periods of such fierce hunger that parents cannibalized their own children (Deut 28:53–57; 2 Kgs 6:25–29; Jer 19:9; Lam 2:20; 4:10). Memories of these dire circumstances stirred fears among Jesus' contemporaries that they too might go hungry and resort to drastic measures.

Although the phrase "or what you will drink" is probably original, it is absent from some early manuscripts and ancient translations of Matthew.[517] However, even if the phrase did not appear here, it definitely appears in verse 31. Thus Jesus also discouraged His followers from being anxious about what they would drink. Most of the wells in ancient Palestine were hand-dug shallow wells that quickly dried up during periods of drought. Few rivers in ancient Israel were perennial sources of water. Most were wadis that raged during the rainy season but turned to mud and dust soon thereafter. Many first-century Jews from the region were acquainted firsthand with the pain and weakness that accompanied dehydration. They knew what it was like for a parched tongue to cleave to the roof of their mouths and for their voices to grow hoarse from intense thirst.

Famine and drought were not the only threats to the survival of the poor. Sickness, injury, or old age could also rob a man of his ability to work. Rabbi Nahorai once argued that a father should teach his son the law rather than a craft or trade since knowledge of the law promised reward in this life and the life to come, "but with all other crafts it is not so; for when a man falls into sickness or old age or troubles and cannot engage in his work, lo, he dies of hunger."[518] In this setting worry about whether a person would have enough to eat and drink was understandable.

Jesus also prohibited His disciples from worrying about the clothes they would wear on their bodies. The poor of Palestine typically wore a different wardrobe from wealthier members of society. The wealthy

---

[517] The phrase is present in B but does not appear in ℵ. The UBS⁴ apparatus includes the phrase with a "C" rating. The phrase may have been omitted by scribes who were more familiar with the Lucan version of this pericope, since it also lacks the phrase. On the other hand, scribes tended to conform Luke to Matthew rather than vice versa. Furthermore variations in the phrase among ancient manuscripts, particularly the appearance of καὶ in the place of the ἤ, may imply that the phrase was a later addition. See Metzger, *A Textual Commentary on the Greek New Testament*, 17.

[518] *m. Qidd.* 4:14.

might wear imported silk dyed a rich purple. The poor generally wore wool, which was relatively inexpensive. Sheep were the most common grazing animals in Palestine, and wool was readily available. The poor normally wore either undyed wool, or they stained their garments with a cheap dye that made their clothing gray or brown. Even this inexpensive clothing might be unaffordable for the most extremely impoverished. Matthew 25:36,43–44 mentions those who had no clothing and needed assistance from Jesus' followers. Although the Greek text described these needy persons as "naked" (*gumnos*), this adjective does not necessarily imply that they lacked any clothing. In most NT contexts it refers to lacking adequate clothing. A person who lacked a warm outer cloak to protect himself from the rain, wind, and chill was normally described by this adjective. As seen earlier, the outer cloak was a necessary item of clothing that often served as one's blanket on cold, crisp nights and functioned as a jacket on blustery days. This cloak was so important for survival that OT law forbade a lender to hold it as collateral overnight (Exod 22:26). Paul listed among the hardships of his apostolic ministry that he was "often without food, cold, and lacking clothing" (2 Cor 11:27). During both Jewish and Roman beatings, outer garments could be removed and not returned, and inner garments were often torn and destroyed. Paul would have needed to replace these garments after severe beatings and often could not afford to do so immediately. One recalls Paul's request that Timothy bring his cloak to Rome before the arrival of winter (2 Tim 4:12,21). James 2:15 also describes poor believers who were "without clothes" and lacked food.

When garments were seized by unscrupulous lenders, or were aged and dry-rotted, became moth eaten, were torn, or simply wore out, the poor might wring their hands and wonder how they could possibly obtain replacements. Their concern was not high fashion or even mere modesty. Since these garments protected their bodies from the sun and the cold, they were necessary to their survival.

Jesus asked a rhetorical question to demonstrate that worry over food, drink, and clothing was unnecessary: "Isn't life more than food and the body more than clothing?" (Matt 6:25). The grammatical form of the question in the Greek text implies an affirmative response: Yes! Life is more important than food. The question used a common style of rabbinic argumentation called the argument "from the greater to the lesser" (*qal waḥomer*). Some interpreters read the question as an attempt to redefine the priorities of the disciples. Worry about food, drink, and clothing does not enhance life but only spoils it. Since life is more important than these things, disciples should avoid worry.[519] Morris commented:

> Put this way, even the poorest must agree that, important as are food and clothing, they are not the most important things of all. There is more to life than food; there is more to the body than its clothing. This attitude removes people from preoccupation with their own worldly success; it discourages the wealthy and the comfortable from concentrating on their own success and the poor and uncomfortable from concentrating on their own misery. We belong together, whatever our worldly goods, and this encourages the idea of sharing.[520]

This interpretation takes the comparative adjective "more" in a quantitative sense, that is, life involves more things than just food. However, when this adjective is followed by a genitive of comparison, it more likely has a qualitative sense, that is, life is greater or more important than food.[521] The statement anticipates the argument in verses 26–30, which insists that God will graciously provide for His people, so worry is unnecessary. The statement emphasizes God's power by arguing that if God is capable of granting life to humans (an act requiring greater power), surely He can sustain their lives by providing food for them (an act requiring less power). If God created the human body (an act requiring greater power), surely He can clothe the body (an act requiring less power).[522]

Scholars who reject this interpretation appeal to two arguments. First, some point out that the text does not explicitly refer to God's creative power and activity. Thus this meaning would be unclear to the original audience and Matthew's readers.[523] However, the two

---

[519] See Luz, *Matthew: A Commentary*, 1:342. He wrote under the influence of Luther's view. Luther reduced the statement to a formula: "Food is supposed to serve the body, but among you the body serves the food." Talbert seems to adopt this view as well (*The Sermon on the Mount*, 127).

[520] Morris, *The Gospel of Matthew*, 157.

[521] See "πολύς," BDAG, 849 2.B.b. See Matt 12:41–42 where the same construction describes something as "greater than" Jonah and Solomon.

[522] This interpretation was affirmed by Broadus, *The Gospel According to Matthew*, 148; Davies and Allison, *A Critical and Exegetical Commentary on the Gospel According to Saint Matthew*, 1:648; France, *The Gospel of Matthew*, 140; Hagner, *Matthew 1–30*, 163; and Wilkins, *Matthew*, 297.

[523] See Luz, *Matthew: A Commentary*, 1:342.

illustrations that dominate the immediately following verses do, in fact, emphasize God's power and gracious providence. Verse 26 introduces these illustrations in a manner that suggests that they depict the truths of verse 25 and perhaps specifically 25b.

Some commentators also object that this interpretation is so similar to the illustrations in verses 26–30 as to make the passage cumbersomely redundant. On the other hand the similarity between the illustrations regarding the birds and the wildflowers shows that Jesus did not shy away from redundancy. Anxiety dies hard, and Jesus likely intended for His repetition to chip away at His disciples' worries one blow at a time. Furthermore the point of the rhetorical question is not the same as the point of the two illustrations. The illustrations argue from the superiority of humans to birds and wildflowers. The rhetorical question argues from the superiority of the activity of creation to the activity of provision.

Jesus' point then is that the God who formed Adam's body and gave it life is more than capable of providing for human needs in order to sustain life. The recognition that the Provider is none other than the Creator should alleviate all concern over whether He is capable of granting the food, water, and clothing necessary for survival. He is certainly able to supply all the needs of Jesus' disciples.

Jesus appealed to the "birds of the sky" as His first illustration of God's gracious providence (v. 26). Although the birds did not plant crops, harvest them, or store up the harvest in barns in order to provide for their future needs, they did not go hungry.[524] The reason was simple: "Your heavenly Father feeds them." The OT insisted that animals survived through God's gracious providence: "All of them [the creatures that fill the earth and seas] wait for You to give them their food at the right time. When you give it to them, they gather it; when You open your hand, they are satisfied with good things" (Ps 104:27–28).[525]

---

[524] Although some scholars have alleged that the claim that animals do not harvest contradicts Prov 6:6–11, the form of Prov 6:6–11 preserved in the LXX, Targum, and Peshitta differs from the MT by reading "without having any harvest" rather than "without having any chief." J. Healy argued that the originator of Matt 6:26 was dependent on this alternative reading. See his "Models of Behavior: Matt 6:26 (//Luke 12:24) and Prov 6:6–8," *JBL* 108 (1989): 797–98.

[525] This text also indicated that God could choose to withhold His provision: "When You hide Your face, they are terrified; when You take away their breath, they die and return to the dust."

Luke's parallel (12:22–32) speaks of God's provision for "the ravens" specifically, rather than the birds of the air in general. Luke
probably best preserves Jesus' precise language. The OT associated
God's providence with the feeding of the ravens several times. In Job
38:41, the Lord asked Job, "Who provides the raven's food when its
young cry out to God and wander about for lack of food?" Similarly
Ps 147:7–9 says, "Sing to the LORD with thanksgiving; play the lyre to
our God, who covers the sky with clouds, prepares rain for the earth,
and causes grass to grown on the hills. He provides the animals with
their food, and the young ravens, what they cry for." These OT texts
and Jesus emphasized God's care for ravens in particular because they
were unclean animals (Lev 11:15; Deut 14:14) that most Jews would
consider least worthy of God's attention and provision. In His argument from lesser to greater, Jesus pointed out that if God made sure
an unclean creature like a raven had adequate food, He would surely
provide for His own children whom He regarded as the pinnacle of
His creation.

The description of God as "your heavenly Father" indicates that
Jesus' followers have a claim on God's provision that other creatures
do not. Although the description of God as Father serves merely as a
reference to His identity as Creator in some contexts (Isa 64:8; Acts
17:28; Jas 1:17), here the title clearly implies more. Jesus did not describe God as "their [the birds'] heavenly Father." Jesus' followers
have a relationship with God that is unique. If God met the needs
even of an unclean bird, surely He will meet the needs of His own
children. The description of God as "your heavenly Father" anticipates Matt 7:9–11:

> "What man among you, if his son asks him for bread, will give him a stone?
> Or if he asks for a fish, will give him a snake? If you then, who are evil, know
> how to give good gifts to your children, how much more will your Father in
> heaven give good things to those who ask Him!"

The description of God as "your heavenly Father" also indicates
that the promises of the Beatitudes have been and are being fulfilled
in the lives of Jesus' disciples. Jesus promised that the peacemakers
"will be called sons of God." The description of God as "your heavenly Father" confirms that Jesus' followers are already His sons who
have been brought into a special relationship with Him and manifest
the Father's character.

Jesus contrasted His followers with the birds that enjoyed God's faithful and gracious care with the question: "Aren't you worth more than they?" (Matt 6:26). Again the question is posed in a grammatical form that implies an affirmative answer: "Of course, God's people are worth more than birds!" If God cherishes Jesus' followers far more than He cares for the birds, He will surely meet the needs of Jesus' disciples as faithfully and consistently as He meets the needs of the birds.

Jesus' teaching seems to have contradicted the teaching of the rabbis. Simeon ben Eleazar taught that it was necessary to teach one's son a craft since every person forfeited his right to God's provision because of his evil deeds:

> Hast thou ever seen a wild animal or a bird practicing a craft?—yet they have their sustenance without care and were they not created for naught else but to serve me? But I was created to serve my Maker. How much more then ought not I to have my sustenance without care? But I have wrought evil, and [so] forfeited my [right to] sustenance [without care].[526]

Like Jesus, Simeon taught that God graciously provided for the birds and other animals. Like Jesus, Simeon taught that humans are superior to animals and thus are more fit to be beneficiaries of His providence. In contrast to Jesus, Simeon argued that sin had robbed God's people of the assurance of His gracious provision so that each person had to provide for his own needs.

If Simeon's view was widely held by Jews in the time of Jesus, Jesus' teaching would have been revolutionary. Jesus' teaching would have implied that God's people were now enjoying a new eschatological era in which the consequences of sin were being reversed and removed. Although humankind lost the assurance of God's gracious provision because of the fall (Gen 3:17–19), and although the Jews forfeited these blessings by forsaking the Mosaic covenant (Deut 28:15–24,38–40), God was now promising to provide for the needs of His people. This promise likely signals that God was initiating the promised new covenant through the ministry of Jesus.[527]

The new covenant promised that God would grant His Spirit to His people: "I will place My Spirit within you and cause you to follow My statutes and carefully observe My ordinances" (Ezek 36:27). The

---

[526] *m. Qidd.* 4.14. Simeon ben Eleazar belonged to the fifth generation of the *tannaim* (AD 165–200).

[527] Keener saw Jesus' teaching as an indication that He "regards God's original purpose at creation as still valid." He cited in support Matt 19:4–6 (*The Gospel of Matthew*, 235).

new covenant also promised that God's people would return to their land and that God will make the land amazingly fruitful:

> I will summon the grain and make it plentiful, and will not bring famine on you. I will also make the fruit of the trees and the produce of the field plentiful, so that you will no longer experience reproach among the nations on account of famine. . . . The desolate land will be cultivated instead of lying desolate in the sight of everyone who passes by. Then they will say: "This land that was desolate has become like the garden of Eden." (Ezek 36:29–30,34–35)

Similarly the new covenant promise in Deut 30:1–10 climaxed in verse 9 with the assurance of God's gracious provision: "The LORD your God will make you prosper abundantly in all the work of your hands with children, the offspring of your livestock, and your land produce. Indeed, the LORD will again delight in your prosperity, as He delighted in that of your fathers."

Thus the assurance of God's generous provision for Jesus' followers is likely confirmation that the new covenant was being initiated through Jesus. Jesus' death was the sacrifice that initiated the new covenant (Matt 26:28). He baptized His followers with the Spirit (Ezek 36:27; Matt 3:11) and gave His followers the assurance of God's gracious provision in fulfillment of the new covenant.

It is important to note that the new covenant did not promise that work would become unnecessary. Deuteronomy 30:9 says, "The LORD your God will make you prosper abundantly *in all the work of your hands.*"[528] Jesus' teaching should not be taken as implying that work is unnecessary in the new covenant era. France wisely commented,

> If this light-hearted illustration were pressed too literally, it might suggest that the disciple has no need to grow and harvest food. But the point is that God sees that even the birds are fed, and a disciple is more valuable to him than a bird. What is prohibited is worry, not work. Even the birds have to spend a lot of energy in hunting or searching for their food, but the point is that it is there to be found.[529]

Even in the NT era some members of the Christian church concluded that work was unnecessary. Paul had to insist repeatedly that believers should work diligently to provide for their needs (1 Thess 5:14;

---

[528] Italics mine.
[529] France, *The Gospel of Matthew,* 140.

2 Thess 3:6–12). Jesus' teaching is fully consistent with Paul's since the birds are not examples of laziness or idleness. Instead they are pictures of freedom from worry through dependence on a gracious Provider. Ancients recognized that even wild animals labored for their food (Prov 6:6,8; 30:25; Deut 25:4; Sir 11:3) and were not likely to have heard Jesus' words as a denial of this obvious fact.

Jesus immediately turned to an illustration of the futility of worry: "Can any of you add a single cubit to his height by worrying?" (Matt 6:27). The general point of Jesus' illustration is clear: worry accomplishes nothing. However, the specific meaning of His statement has long been a topic of debate, and no consensus on this text has emerged. The ambiguity of the statement is due to the fact that the key terms in the sentence can be interpreted temporally or spatially. The Greek word *hēlikia* may refer to a person's physical stature (thus the translation "height" in the HCSB) or a person's age or life span. The interpreter must infer which meaning is intended based on contextual factors. For example, the noun clearly refers to physical stature in the description of Zacchaeus in Luke 19:3 since Luke's reference to the man's *hēlikia* serves as an explanation of his inability to see over the heads of the crowds that blocked his view of Jesus. Both meanings are attested in the only two occurrences of the noun in the LXX. The noun clearly serves as a reference to a person's age in Job 29:18 (LXX), "My age will grow old, like the stump of a palm tree I will live a long time."[530] On the other hand Ezek 13:18 uses the noun to refer to a person's height: "Woe to the women who . . . make veils for the heads of people of every height." In the Apocrypha, the noun normally refers to a person's age.[531]

The early versions of the New Testament and most of the early church fathers view Matt 6:27 as a reference to increasing one's stature.[532] Recent commentators who see the noun as a reference to one's

---

[530] Author's translation.

[531] Twenty-one of the 22 occurrences seem to refer to age (2 Mac 4:40; 5:24; 6:18,23–24; 7:27; 15:30; 3 Mac 4:8; 4 Mac 5:4 [twice], 7,11,36; 8:10,20; 9:26; 11:14; Wis 4:9). Only Sir 26:17 uses the term in reference to physical stature.

[532] See Broadus, *The Gospel According to Matthew*, 149. Broadus stated that the "Latin, Peshito, Memphitic, Gothic" versions all translate the term with words referring to physical stature. Luz noted that the Old Latin, Vulgate, and Peshitta translate the term as a reference to height. The African version (k) and Erasmus's *Annotationes* affirmed the temporal translation. See Luz, *Matthew: A Commentary*, 1:344, n.51.

height include Garland, Luz, and Morris.[533] Those who hold this view argue that the term "cubit" (*pēchus*) requires viewing *hēlikia* as a spatial category and thus a reference to height. "Cubit" normally referred to a measurement of distance equal to about 18 inches, roughly the distance from a man's elbow to the tip of his middle finger.[534] However, this argument is not conclusive since the term "cubit" could be used in a figurative sense to speak of measurements of time. Mimnermus (2.3), a sixth-century BC writer, used the term in this sense in his expression "for only a cubit of time." The OT also used measurements of length as figurative measurements of time: "You, indeed, have made my days short in length [lit., 'a few handbreadths'] and my life span as nothing in Your sight" (Ps 39:5). Thus, although the normal meaning of "cubit" makes reading *hēlikia* as a reference to height the most natural reading, the temporal interpretation is possible and should be adopted if the context with the SM best supports it.[535]

Commentators who see *hēlikia* as a reference to one's life span include Betz, Blomberg, Broadus, Davies and Allison, Filson, France,

[533] Garland, *Reading Matthew*, 83; Luz, *Matthew: A Commentary*, 1:344; Morris, *The Gospel of Matthew*, 159. This is also the interpretation affirmed by BDAG, 812.

[534] See "πῆχυς," BDAG, 812.

[535] Although those who adopt the spatial interpretation fail to mention this, perhaps the strongest evidence in support of the view is the usage of the verb αὐξάνω ("to cause to grow in size, extent, or quality") in 6:28. The illustration of the wildflowers might teach two points: God causes the flowers to grow and He clothes them. Thus the illustration could serve the dual purpose of confirming that God is responsible for the physical growth of humans (v. 27) and that He clothes them as well (vv. 29–30).

The presence of the verb "grow" in 6:28 has been questioned since one of the earliest extant texts of Matthew, ℵ (AD 350), uses the verb ξαίνω ("comb wool in preparation for making thread"). This reading had been erased from the codex by a later corrector but was discovered by T. C. Skeat with the aid of ultraviolet light in 1938. See Skeat, "The Lilies of the Field," *ZNW* 37 (1938): 211–14. Skeat's photograph of this text from Sinaiticus appears in the end papers of Robinson, Hoffman, and Kloppenborg, *The Critical Edition of Q*. See also their Excursus on the Scribal Error in Q 12:27 on xcix–ci. After the discovery of the reading, many scholars concluded that this was the original reading of Matthew. This reading may also find support in P. Oxy. 655, an early Greek manuscript of the *Gospel of Thomas*. See D. Jongkind, "'The Lilies of the Field' Reconsidered: Codex Sinaiticus and the Gospel of Thomas," *NovT* 48 (2006): 209–16. Some scholars such as K. Brunner ("Textkritisches zu Mt 6,28," *ZKT* 100 [1978]: 251–56) still view the original reading of ℵ as the original reading of Matthew and/or of Q. This verb seems to fit the context better than "grow" since it is the preliminary step to spinning thread. However, the manuscript evidence for the reading "grow" is strong. The editors of the UBS4 assigned the reading a "B" rating and Metzger argued that the reading of Sinaiticus "arose as a scribal idiosyncrasy that was almost immediately corrected" (*Textual Commentary on the Greek New Testament*, 18). Furthermore, the reading "grow" is uncontested in the extant manuscripts of the parallel in Luke 12:27. Even ℵ uses the verb "grow" there. Thus the large majority of recent scholars accept the reading "grow."

Gibbs, Gundry, Hagner, Hill, Keener, Schnackenburg, Wilkins, and Witherington.[536] Most point out that Luke's explanation in 12:26 describes the addition of the cubit as a "little thing." Certainly, adding an entire 18 inches to one's height would be a drastic increase in stature that would unlikely be described as a "small thing." Luz argued that the "cubit" was the normal unit for measuring the body in the ancient world and that ancient people generally regarded the cubit as something small rather than large. His argument in support of this latter point is rather weak. He points out that a derivative of the word "cubit" was used to describe small children. However, although a cubit seems small when it is the measure of a person's entire height, it remains a relatively large measure when one speaks of increasing height by that amount. Alcaeus, a lyric poet from the sixth century BC, described an enormous giant as less than five cubits tall.[537] Description of an increase of a foot and a half in height as a "small thing" would only make sense as some kind of humorous understatement. Stott points out that growth by a cubit could be considered a "small thing" from God's vantage point since "God does it to all of us between our childhood and youth."[538] On the other hand Jesus was not speaking about what God does. He was speaking about human ability or inability. Nor was He speaking to children for whom growth by a cubit might seem to be natural or normal. He was speaking to adults for whom growth by a cubit would seem truly spectacular. Furthermore the concern of the context is not the growth of the body but personal survival. Thus the context best supports the temporal interpretation.[539]

[536] Betz, *The Sermon on the Mount*, 475–76; Blomberg, *Matthew*, 125; Broadus, *The Gospel According to St. Matthew*, 149; Davies and Allison, *A Critical and Exegetical Commentary on the Gospel According to Saint Matthew*, 1:652–53; Filson, *A Commentary on the Gospel According to St. Matthew*, 101; France, *The Gospel of Matthew*, 140; Hagner, *Matthew 1–13*, 164; Gibbs, *Matthew 1:1–11:1*, 360–61, 364–65; Gundry, *The Gospel of Matthew*, 117; Hill, *The Gospel of Matthew*, 144; Keener, *The Gospel of Matthew*, 237; Schnackenburg, *The Gospel of Matthew*, 73; Wilkins, *Matthew*, 297–98; and Witherington, *Matthew*, 152.

[537] See "πῆχυς," BDAG, 812.

[538] Stott, *The Sermon on the Mount*, 163.

[539] Some commentators, like Stott, think that the evidence is inadequate to guide interpreters in choosing between these two options (*The Sermon on the Mount*, 163). Nolland blazes a somewhat different trail. He affirms a temporal meaning for *pēchus* and *hēlikia*, but he suggests that Jesus was referring to adding a period to one's age in order to qualify for a position like that of priest or community leader that required maturity and seniority (*The Gospel of Matthew*, 311). Nolland's interpretation is more sensitive to the temporal use of the noun *hēlikia* in Hellenistic Gk. texts but less suited to the context in Matthew 6 where the concern is not rapid advancement in age or maturity but physical survival.

Jesus' point is that worry is futile and pointless. It serves no positive purpose. If a person cannot add months, weeks, days, or minutes to his life by worrying, he should not assume that worrying about the things necessary to his survival will benefit him either. Jesus' question may have been especially ironic to His original audience since they were probably aware that worry was unproductive and actually counterproductive. Sirach 30:24 says, "Jealousy and anger shorten life, and anxiety brings on premature old age." Even before the advances of modern medicine, wise people recognized that anxiety negatively impacted its victims' health. Many people in Jesus' audience would likely have recognized that rather than adding time to a person's life, anxiety actually subtracted from it. All knew that worry affects the quality of a person's life even if it does not affect its length.

More importantly Jesus' question is based on the conviction that God is Lord over human life. In His great sovereignty, He has determined the length of life for each individual. God has determined both the moment of one's birth and the moment of one's death.[340] Deuteronomy 32:39 says, "See now that I am He; there is no God but Me. I bring death and I give life; I wound and I heal. No one can rescue anyone from My hand." First Samuel 2:6 says, "The Lord brings death and gives life; He sends some to Sheol, and He raises others up." Similarly, Eccl 3:1–2,11 indicate that God has appointed a time for every event: "There is an occasion for everything, and a time for every activity under heaven: a time to give birth and a time to die. . . . He has made everything appropriate in its time." Psalm 139:16 says, "All my days were written in Your book and planned before a single one of them began." Job 14:5 says, "Since man's days are determined and the number of his months depends on You, and since You have set limits he cannot pass." Psalm 104:29–30 insists that all creatures are dependent on Him for life: "When You take away their breath, they die and return to the dust. When You send Your breath, they are created, and You renew the face of the earth." Psalm 39:4 also implies that God has fixed the length of a person's life: "Lord, reveal to me the end of my life and the number of my days." Since life and death are completely in God's hands, no one can prolong his life by wringing his hands.

---

[340] Hagner noted, "Behind this view [Matt 6:27] lies the Hebraic concept of the sovereignty of God in life and death, including the predetermined hour of one's death" (*Matthew 1–13*, 164).

Since God has determined the duration of each person's life, lack of food will not result in premature death and abundance of food will not prolong life. A person's survival depends on divine sovereignty, not human anxiety. By reminding His audience of the limitations of their power ("Who among you is able"), Jesus reminded them of God's unlimited power in which they are to place their trust.

Jesus then turned to another illustration of God's providence over nature to calm the anxieties of His followers. Although Jesus had directly prohibited anxiety earlier (6:25), He now questioned the reasons for worry: "And why do you worry about clothes?" The question assumes that Jesus' followers were plagued by anxiety. Jesus wanted them to probe the underlying cause of their anxiety. Ultimately the cause for their worry was not the circumstances of their lives but a warped view of God.

Jesus pointed to the wildflowers of the Palestinian countryside as examples of God's ability to clothe His people.[541] These flowers are beautifully clothed even though "they don't labor or spin thread." Matthew 6:26 seems to have been primarily addressed to men since planting and harvesting belonged to the tasks assigned to men in first-century Jewish culture. Verse 28 seems to have been primarily addressed to women since working with wool and spinning thread were deemed women's work.[542] Among the tasks a wife was expected to perform every day was "working in wool."[543]

The need to clothe a family could stir anxiety for several reasons. First, working with wool was time-consuming. Once the wool had been sheared from the sheep, it had to be combed to remove the tangles. The individual strands were then spun into thread. The thread was then woven into fabric on a loom. The fabric was softened and made watertight by pounding it with a fuller's mallet. Sometimes the fabric was dyed. Only after these time-consuming processes was the wool ready to be made into garments. When a wife was already expected to grind flour, bake bread daily from scratch, prepare meals, clean the home, wash clothes, tend to children, and meet her husband's needs, concern for finding the time to keep her family clothed could become a source of anxiety. Many of the wife's other duties had to be performed on a daily basis. If any duty was put off for another

---

[541] On the text critical issues related to 6:28, see n. 536.

[542] Hagner, *Matthew 1–13*, 165; Luz, *Matthew: A Commentary*, 1:343.

[543] *m. Ketub.* 5.5.

day because she simply could not complete all her tasks, she would likely choose to put off her wool work. However, if she did not stay on schedule with each step of the long process of preparing clothing, it would eventually catch up with her. As winter approached or clothes wore out, the stresses of work could easily overwhelm her. Buying clothes premade from a tailor or seamstress was rarely an option.

Clothing a family not only required a huge amount of time. It also required one either to have enough sheep in his flocks to provide an adequate amount of wool or enough money to purchase the wool from others. When a family barely had enough money to purchase food, saving for occasional expenses like the purchase of wool presented a real challenge. Thus clothing a family could be difficult for the poor, and it added to the many other stresses of life.

Jesus reminded His disciples that although wildflowers did not frantically work to card, spin, weave, and sew, "not even Solomon in all his splendor was adorned like one of these!" The OT describes Solomon's great wealth (1 Kgs 4:20–28), which implies that he dressed in the finest garments of his day but does not specifically describe his clothing. However, by the first century Solomon's opulence had become proverbial.[544] People of Jesus' day would have imagined Solomon dressed in royal purple and decked out in gold and jewels. Although rulers of the day were known to dress lavishly, in the Jews' minds no imperial garb could begin to compare with the royal robes of the great Solomon.[545]

As grand and glorious as Solomon's wardrobe was, Jesus insisted that the splendor of the wildflowers was far greater. The wildflowers Jesus had in mind may have been the anemones that were a rich purple, the color one expected royal robes to bear.[546] Isaiah 28:1,4

---

[544] Josephus, *Ant.* 8.4; *m. b. Meṣiʿa* 7.1.

[545] Josephus said that the royal apparel of Herod Agrippa I (briefly mentioned in Acts 12:21) consisted of a garment woven entirely of silver thread that reflected the sunlight with such brilliance that some observers assumed that he was divine (*Ant.* 19.8.2 §§340–47). Warren Carter has argued that the textual and intertextual clues show Jesus' intention to use the reference to Solomon negatively. Solomon served as an example of one who failed to trust God and thus sought wealth through the oppression of others ("'Solomon in All His Glory': Intertextuality and Matthew 6.29," *JSNT* 65 [1997]: 3–25). John Jones has argued that the appeal to Solomon is intended to remind readers of the reliance on human industry which Solomon taught in Prov 6:6–11. In his view Jesus' teaching was designed to correct this faulty perspective ("'Think of the Lilies' and Prov 6:6–11," *HTR* 88 [1995]: 175–77.

[546] For Jewish texts describing royal robes as purple, see 1 Macc 10:20, 62, 64. In 1 Macc 14:43–44, King Demetrius ruled that Simon, the high priest and ethnarch of the Jews, should be clothed in purple and prohibited all other Palestinian Jews from wearing that royal color. For

describes the "beautiful splendor" of the gorgeous flowers that grew at the summits of the Palestinian mountains. The Creator had painted these flowers with such beautiful hues that no robe stained with man-made dyes could possibly compare to their splendor.

Although the OT described the glorious beauty of the flowers that God made, these flowers were even more notorious for their fragile and transient nature. The beauty of the flower was fleeting because it was prone to fade and wither (Job 14:2; Ps 103:15; Isa 28:1,4; 40:6; Nah 1:4; Jas 1:10–11; 1 Pet 1:24). Jesus alluded to this prominent OT theme by emphasizing not only the beauty but also the transience of the wildflowers. They are "here today and thrown into the furnace to-morrow" (Matt 6:30). In a single day the wildflowers that adorned the grassy hillside could dry up so completely that their withered, crisp petals and stems became highly flammable and could serve as tinder in the earthen ovens where the Palestinians cooked their food. Coals nearly dead would suddenly burst into flame when fed the brittle rem-nants of the flowers that had stunned beholders with their beauty only hours before.

Jesus stressed the transience of the wildflowers in order to stress the greater worth of humanity. Rather than asking, "Aren't you worth more than they?" (v. 26) a second time, Jesus implied the supremacy of humanity to flora by describing the fate of the flowers. Jesus clearly assumed that humans have far greater longevity than wildflowers. His illustration and its application could imply that human existence is eternal. Jesus might also have been implying that His disciples would enjoy a much better destiny than the wicked. Matthew had already quoted John the Baptist's comparison of the wicked to trees that do not produce good fruit and that "will be cut down and thrown into the fire" (3:10). John had warned that those who do not receive the bap-tism of the Spirit will be baptized with fire (3:11). He had compared the wicked to chaff that "He will burn up with fire that never goes out" (3:12). Jesus would use similar imagery to describe the destiny of those who refused to follow Him (7:19; 13:40; 18:8; 25:41). If Jesus had merely wished to emphasize the transience of the flower, then like the OT writers He could have described it withering or fading. Instead

information regarding the identity of the "wildflowers" of Matt 6:28, see Davies and Allison, *A Critical and Exegetical Commentary on the Gospel According to Saint Matthew*, 1.654. They men-tion the purple anemone, gladiolus, crocus, poppy, the white Madonna lily, or flowers in general as possibilities. See also "κρίνον," BDAG, 567.

He may have chosen to describe the flowers being thrown into the furnace in order to remind the disciples that God loved them so much, He had rescued them from this frightening fate.[547]

Jesus' disciples, who were created to live eternally and who would be rescued from the inextinguishable fire, were far more precious to God than grass and could thus be certain that God would "do much more" for them than He did for the grass. God will faithfully clothe His people. He will ensure that they have what they need to wear. God could make sure that they were clothed by causing their garments to last far longer than they otherwise would. The OT emphasized God's gracious provision for the Israelites by testifying that God caused their garments and sandals to last the entire 40 years of their wilderness wanderings (Deut 8:4; 29:5), a miracle still well remembered in Nehemiah's day (Neh 9:21). When clothing became worn or torn, He was more than able to provide new garments. Jesus did not promise that this clothing would have a designer label, but He would make sure His people were protected from the elements.

Jesus had earlier asked, "Why do you worry?" (Matt 6:28). He now answered His own question by describing His disciples as "you of little faith" (v. 30). The adjective "of little faith" (*oligopistos*) appears only five times in the NT. All five occurrences are descriptions of the disciples spoken by Jesus in the Synoptic Gospels. Four of the five NT occurrences appear in Matthew.[548] In 8:26 the small faith of the disciples made them terrified in the face of a violent storm. Their fear turned into amazement when Jesus stilled the storm. In 14:31 the small faith of Peter distracted his attention from the one who walked on the water and made him frightened by the strength of the wind. Jesus challenged Peter's doubt and demonstrated again His power over wind and waves. In 16:8, the small faith of the disciples led them to believe that Jesus told them to beware of leaven because they had no bread to eat. Jesus reminded them of how He fed the five thousand and the four thousand and explained that His instruction forbidding leaven related to the teaching of the Pharisees and Sadducees, not to bread, which He was more than able to supply.

The same small faith that led the disciples to doubt Jesus' ability to control the weather, walk on water, or miraculously supply food

---

[547] The word "fire" (πῦρ) occurs 12 times in Matthew (3:10–12; 5:22; 7:19; 13:40,42,50; 17:15; 18:8–9; 25:41). Every instance except 17:15 involves an allusion to eternal punishment.

[548] Outside of Matthew the adjective appears only in Luke 12:28.

to His disciples was the underlying cause of the disciples' anxiety. If they truly believed in God's power, their fears and worries would vanish. Worry is ultimately prompted by faith that is too small. Other Jewish teachers recognized this. Rabbi Eleazar once said, "Whoever has a mouthful yet remaining in his basket, and says, 'What shall I eat tomorrow,' belongs to the number of those who have little faith."[549] Worry assumes that God is ignorant of His peoples' needs, lacks the power to meet their needs, or does not care enough about them to meet their needs. Worry is an expression of doubt in God's knowledge, strength, or compassion. The two illustrations of God's providence show that He has the power to meet needs. Jesus' question, "Aren't you worth more than they?" (v. 26) shows that He cares enough to meet our needs. His assurance, "Your heavenly Father knows that you need them [all these things]" (v. 32), shows that He is perfectly aware of our needs.

Jesus again urged His disciples not to worry about food, drink, or clothing. This prohibition in verse 31 assumes a different grammatical form from the one in verse 25. The earlier prohibition urged the disciples to stop their constant worrying. This prohibition offers an urgent appeal never to worry at all.[550] The blanket prohibition shows that worry is never justified or excusable.

Jesus equated worry with pagan notions of deity. Disciples should not worry about food, drink, or clothing because "the idolaters eagerly seek all these things" (v. 32). Although the HCSB uses the translation "idolaters" here, Matthew did not use the normal term for an idolater (*eidōlolatrēs*). Instead he used the term *ethnos*, which is normally translated "Gentile." However, the translation is legitimate since the term often refers to "those who do not belong to groups professing faith in the God of Israel, *the nations, gentiles, unbelievers* (in effect='polytheists')."[551] Such a translation is especially appropriate in Matthew in contexts in which the term has negative connotations since one of Matthew's major themes is Jesus' acceptance of non-Jews. Jesus clearly did not view Gentiles negatively because of

---

[549] *b. Soṭah* 48b.

[550] The form is μή with the aorist subjunctive. See Wallace, *Greek Grammar Beyond the Basics*, 723. This is a "summary" use that prohibits "the action as a whole."

[551] "ἔθνος," BDAG, 276. Hagner also noted that "'the Gentiles,' here is a negative word, referring to those outside the family of faith, i.e., the pagans (cf. v. 7 for the same use of the word)" (*Matthew 1–13*, 165).

their ethnicity. Thus negative references to "Gentiles" in Matthew must relate to their practice of false religion.

Jesus' statement clearly indicates that the Gentiles typically had warped priorities. The verb "eagerly seek" (*epizēteō*) has a prefixed preposition that gives the verb new intensity and speaks of an unusually strong desire to obtain something. Gentiles were notorious for being obsessed with the necessities of life. The Letter of Aristeas, a document probably dating to the second century BC, contrasts Gentiles and Jews in this manner:

> [Gentiles] are those who are concerned with meat and drink and clothes, their whole attitude (to life) being concentrated on these concerns. Such concerns are of no account among the people of our race, but throughout the whole of their lives their main objective is concerned with the sovereignty of God. (140–41)[552]

This Gentile obsession with the necessities for survival was prompted by their pagan notions of deity. Since their idol gods were deaf, dumb, blind, and impotent, most felt that they needed to rely entirely on themselves to meet their own needs.[553] Even those who actually believed that the idol could provide for them felt that they had to manipulate, placate, or bribe their god if he was to act. Jewish legend says that Abraham turned from idolatry because he recognized that an idol cannot "save a man, or hear a man's prayer, or give him any gift."[554] Rather than supplying food to their worshippers, most idol gods instead demanded food from the worshipper. The food was believed to have been consumed by the god himself when it really filled the bellies of the pagan priests and their families.[555]

The God of Israel is no impotent idol. He is more than capable of supplying the food, drink, and clothing His people need. God is also completely aware of the needs of His people: "Your heavenly Father knows that you need them" (v. 32). The verb "need" (*chrēzō*) shows that the necessities of life rather than mere wants or desires are in view. One of the reasons the petition in the model prayer for God to supply the necessities for life is so brief is that God already knows the needs of His people. So His people do not need to be consumed with

---

[552] R. J. H. Shutt, "Letter of Aristeas," *OTP*, 2:22.

[553] See the critiques of idolatry in Hab 2:18–19 and Isa 44:9–20.

[554] *Apoc. Ab.* 3:8. See R. Rubinkiewicz, "Apocalypse of Abraham," *OTP*, 1:690.

[555] See the account of Daniel's expose of this scam in "Bel and the Dragon," Dan (LXX) 14:1–22.

worry over these needs and can focus on matters of greater importance—the kingdom of God and His righteousness.

Rather than worrying about the necessities of physical survival,
Jesus' disciples should "seek first the kingdom of God and His righteousness" (v. 33). Betz emphasizes the great importance of this verse
and urges interpreters to examine it carefully and thoughtfully: "Since
v. 33 encapsulates the theology of the SM, one must carefully examine the terms. Indeed, no word is superfluous or ambiguous in this
statement, and each word is reflected through the SM in one form or
another."[556] The verb "seek" (*zēteō*) in this context means "to devote
serious effort to realize one's desire or objective, *strive for, aim (at), try
to obtain, desire, wish (for)*."[557] The verb shares the same root as the
verb "eagerly seek" in verse 32. However, in verse 32 the preposition
epi is prefixed to the verb. Matthew now dropped the prefix in order to
distinguish the striving of the disciple for the kingdom from the vain
and anxious striving of the idolater.[558]

Nevertheless, the adverb "first" (*prōton*) greatly intensifies the
verb. This adverb can mean "first in time" or "first in priority, importance, rank." Thus Jesus' command could mean first give attention to
these spiritual matters, then afterwards attend to physical matters or
seek the kingdom and righteousness above all else. Both uses occur
elsewhere in the Gospel of Matthew. However, Jesus seems to use the
word here in the same sense as Matt 20:16,27 to indicate that spiritual
and heavenly things must be the believer's highest priorities.[559] Thus
Jesus commanded His disciples to strive for the kingdom of God and
His righteousness above all else. These were to be their highest priorities. These were to be their sacred obsessions. The ancients recognized that physical concerns could override and distract someone
from greater spiritual concerns. Rabbi Simeon b. Yohai once asked,
"How can a man be sitting and studying [the Scriptures] when he
does not know where his food and drink will come from nor where he
can get his clothes and coverings?"[560]

---

[556] Betz, *The Sermon on the Mount*, 482.

[557] "ζητέω," BDAG, 428.

[558] Betz, *The Sermon on the Mount*, 482.

[559] Thomas Schmidt, "Burden, Barrier, Blasphemy: Wealth in Matt 6:33; Luke 14:33; and
Luke 16:15," *TJ* 9 (1988): 171–89, esp. 177–78.

[560] *Mek.* on Exod 16:6, cited in Talbert, *The Sermon on the Mount*, 127.

Seeking the kingdom involves endeavoring "to become admitted into it, and share the privileges and duties of its subjects."[561] The present tense of the imperative verb implies that the disciple is to seek the kingdom constantly and continually. France notes that "the primary emphasis is on submission to God's sovereignty here and now, i.e., obedience to his will, though the idea of looking forward to, and working for, the ultimate establishment of his kingdom cannot be ruled out."[562] Seeking the kingdom is similar to the rabbinic notion of assuming the "yoke of the kingdom of heaven."[563] Accepting the yoke of the kingdom of heaven involves submitting to God's authority out of reverence and love as a precursor for obeying His commands. The rabbis discussed why the Decalogue began with the commandment, "Do not have other gods besides Me." They explained:

> The matter may be compared to a human king who entered a province. Said his servants to him: "Impose decrees upon the people." He answered them: "No; when they accept my sovereignty, I shall impose decrees upon them; for if they do not accept my sovereignty, they will not accept my decrees either."[564]

Twice each day faithful Jews were expected to recite in order three passages of Scripture: Deut 6:4–9; 11:13–21; and Num 15:37–41. The Mishnah taught that the *Shemà* (Deut 6:4–9) preceded the next major section of the recitation which dealt with obedience to God's commands to show "that a man may first take upon him the yoke of the kingdom of heaven and afterward take upon him the yoke of the commandments."[565] Urbach cited numerous rabbinic texts to demonstrate that assuming the yoke of the kingdom of heaven involved submission to God's rule with reverent fear and devotion. When Jesus referred to the kingdom of heaven as a present phenomenon, as He did here, the kingdom refers to God's rule over His people.[566]

---

[561] Broadus, *The Gospel According to Matthew*, 151.

[562] France, *Matthew*, 141. See also Davies and Allison, *A Critical and Exegetical Commentary on the Gospel According to Saint Matthew*, 1:660–61 and Wilkins, *Matthew*, 299. Against Betz (*The Sermon on the Mount*, 483) and Luz (*Matthew: A Commentary*, 1:344–45) who see the kingdom here as eschatological. Present righteousness leads to entrance into the eschatological kingdom.

[563] See E. Urbach, *The Sages: Their Concepts and Beliefs*, trans. Israel Abrahams (Jerusalem: Magnes, 1987), 1:400–419.

[564] Mekhilta de R. Ishmael, quoted in ibid., 1:400.

[565] *m. Ber.* 2.2.

[566] Urbach, *The Sages*, 1:400–419.

The addition of "and His righteousness" confirms that the focus is submission to God's rule here and now. Interestingly the order of the two nouns, "kingdom" and "righteousness," matches the order of taking the yoke of the kingdom of heaven and taking the yoke of the commandments in rabbinic teaching.[567] By this order Jesus taught that a disciple first submits to God's rule in the person of His Messiah and then pursues righteousness by obeying the Messiah's teachings. The righteousness the disciple seeks is not the imputed righteousness described by Paul in his letters to the Romans and the Galatians. Instead this righteousness is the righteousness actually imparted by God to the disciple and expressed in his daily living. Jesus' disciples desperately hunger and thirst for righteousness. God graciously satisfies this hunger and quenches this thirst by filling them with this righteousness (Matt 5:6).[568] Since this righteousness is imparted by God, others who witness the disciples' good works give glory to the Father in heaven (v. 16). This righteousness is extraordinary, exceeding even the impressive righteousness of the scribes and Pharisees (v. 20). This righteousness consists not only of outward acts that comply with God's law but also of internal character that comports with God's own character (v. 48). Jesus described this righteousness at length earlier in the SM. This is the righteousness of those who control their anger and are quick to resolve disagreements with others. This righteousness involves sexual purity, fidelity to one's word, an eagerness to forgive others, and love for one's enemies. Disciples seek this righteousness not to impress other people but for the glory of God and pursuit of heavenly reward. Since seeking the kingdom involves eager submission to God's reign over the disciple, the demand to seek the kingdom and the command to seek God's righteousness are inseparable.

The pronoun "His" (*autou*) could be a possessive genitive, in which case it would describe the righteousness that disciples seek as the

[567] In Codex B, the order of the two nouns is reversed: "His righteousness and kingdom." However, other manuscripts do not support this order. The reading in B seems to be completely idiosyncratic. The Textual Commentary is probably correct in the suggestion that the scribe responsible for B transposed the two nouns "to suggest that righteousness is prerequisite to participation in the kingdom" (18).

[568] Against Davies and Allison, who argue that "the notion of gift can only be read into the text" (*A Critical and Exegetical Commentary on the Gospel According to Saint Matthew*, 1:661). In favor of the position affirmed here see Guelich, *The Sermon on the Mount*, 347.

righteousness that characterizes God Himself.[569] However, since 5:6 insists that God fills the disciples with the righteousness for which they hunger and thirst, the pronoun is more likely a genitive of source indicating that God supplies the righteousness that the disciples seek.[570] Again, properly understood, the SM never degenerates into some taxing legalism that imposes demands on Jesus' followers without empowering them to satisfy those demands. Instead God imparts the righteousness He demands in keeping with the promise of the new covenant.

When disciples seek to submit to God's reign in Christ and live righteously by obeying Jesus' teachings, they are assured that God will meet their needs for food, drink, and clothing: "All these things will be provided for you" (6:33). The translation "will be provided" may fail to capture an important nuance of the Greek verb *prostithēmi.* The verb commonly means "to add to something that is already present or exists."[571] Although the verb may be translated "give" or "provide" in some situations, it often bears the nuance of "giving again,"

---

[569] Nolland explored three possible interpretations of the genitive pronoun: (a) possessive or "exemplary" genitive, (b) genitive of source, and (c) genitive of reference that describes the righteousness that God requires (*The Gospel of Matthew*, 314–15). Nolland opted for the third interpretation. He dismissed the second interpretation on the grounds that it would "introduce a new thought not encouraged either by the main drift of the Sermon or by earlier uses of 'righteousness.'" Nevertheless in note 425 Nolland acknowledged that since the initiative of God stands behind Jesus' ministry, righteousness that results from Jesus' ministry can be described as "from God." He admitted that 3:15 and 5:6 "come closest to reflecting this," but he saw no clear connection between those texts and 6:33. However, the connections between 5:6 and 6:33 are more extensive that Nolland sees. "Seek" is roughly synonymous with "hunger and thirst for." The divine passive "will be filled" parallels the genitive expression "of (from) God."

[570] Complex, text-critical questions surround the genitive modifier that follows the noun "kingdom." Some manuscripts have the modifier "of God," others "of the heavens," and others lack the modifier entirely. The committee responsible for the UBS4 was torn between the first and last of these readings. The original reading was likely "the kingdom and his righteousness." This reading is supported by the earliest uncials ℵ and B. Furthermore, it seems to be the reading that best accounts for the other readings. Originally "kingdom" was unqualified as in Matt 8:12; 13:38; and 24:7,14. Scribes recognized that this was unusual for Matthew and felt that the pronoun "His" (αὐτοῦ) required an antecedent closer than "your heavenly Father" in the preceding verse. Thus they supplied "of God" (τοῦ θεοῦ). Others sought to improve the style by deleting "His" and replacing it with "of God" with the intent that this phrase modify both "kingdom" and "righteousness." Other scribes recognized that Matthew preferred to refer to the kingdom as the kingdom of heaven and introduced yet another change, although, in some cases, this made the "His" (the original ground for revision) awkward and led scribes to drop the phrase "His righteousness" entirely. This reconstruction is similar to the one proposed by W. Hatch ("A Note on Matthew 6:33," *HTR* 38 [1945]: 270–72). However, the pronoun "His" (αὐτοῦ) appears in the early uncials ℵ and B and is widely attested.

[571] "προστίθημι ," BDAG, 885. The verb is a divine passive that reverently expresses the conviction that God Himself will supply the needs of Jesus' followers.

"providing more," or "increasing."[572] The word choice seems to indicate that those who seek the kingdom and righteousness will find
them and that God will provide for the disciple's physical needs in
addition to these greater spiritual blessings.

This has two important implications. First, the kingdom and righteousness are present and not just eschatological realities for Jesus'
disciples. If the kingdom and righteousness were not experienced until the eschaton, as many commentators claim, God's provision for
daily needs would not be "added" to the kingdom and righteousness.
Instead the kingdom and righteousness would be added to the blessings disciples presently enjoy. Jesus' language strongly implies that
the kingdom and righteousness are present realities for His disciples.

Second, the kingdom, righteousness, and material provisions are
all gracious gifts from God's hands.[573] God grants the kingdom and
righteousness to the disciples, but He does not stop there. He satisfies
their hunger, quenches their thirst, and clothes their bodies as well.

These provisions should probably be seen as the firstfruits of the
material blessings of the kingdom.[574] Jesus alluded to these material
blessings when He promised that the sacrifices His disciples make will
be more than compensated for in the future: "Everyone who has left
houses, brothers or sisters, father or mother, children, or fields because of My name will receive 100 times more and will inherit eternal
life" (19:29). The text does not specify how God will meet the needs
of His people. He undoubtedly uses a variety of means. However, God
will often meet the needs of the disciples by blessing other disciples
and urging them to share generously with those in need. The righteousness that should be the top priority of the disciple's life includes
generosity (5:42) and gifts for the poor (6:2–4).[575]

Jesus urged His disciples, "Don't worry about tomorrow" (v. 34).
"Tomorrow" (aurion) clearly refers to a greater stretch of time than
the next 24-hour period. "Tomorrow" is an example of synecdoche, a
figure of speech in which a part of something represents the whole. In

---

[572] Contrary to BDAG, Luke 17:5 seems to mean "increase our faith" rather than merely
"grant us faith."

[573] This does not imply that kingdom and righteousness are antecedents of the pronoun
ταῦτα. The kingdom and righteousness are first enjoyed and then food, drink, and clothing are
granted as added blessings.

[574] Blomberg, Matthew, 126.

[575] See ibid.; Keener, The Gospel of Matthew, 237; and Green, The Gospel of Luke, 659.

this context "tomorrow" represents all future life in this present age.[576] The word served this function so frequently in proverbs about worry that the term had practically become an idiom. For example, the Talmud said, "Care not for tomorrow's cares; for you do not know what a day brings forth. Perhaps tomorrow you will not exist; and then you will have cared for a world no longer yours."[577] The broad phrase "about tomorrow" shows that food, drink, and clothing represent many other concerns about the future that stir anxiety in the hearts of Jesus' disciples. Focusing on the present will alleviate many of the disciples' worries since God has already shown His faithfulness in meeting their present needs. The focus on the present was already encouraged in the model prayer: "Give us today our daily bread" (v. 11).

Jesus offered two reasons for relinquishing worries about the future. First, "tomorrow will worry about itself." Jesus personified the future and imposed on this humorous imaginary character all of the emotions typically associated with the future. He imagined the future as a fretting, floor-pacing, hand-wringing, hyperventilating fellow on the brink of an anxiety attack who does more than enough worrying for everyone.[578] Jesus did not say, as some modern Christians do, "God worries about the future, so you don't have to." If worry was inconsistent with the faith of the Christian disciples, how much more was it inconsistent with God's nature and power. "Father Time" may be a nervous wreck, but the heavenly Father never is.

Second, Jesus warned that "each day has enough trouble of its own." This is a candid reminder that God does not promise a trouble-free life. Even the life of a faithful disciple who stubbornly trusts in God may be fraught with problems. However, guessing about what problems one may encounter in the future is seldom a helpful exercise.

---

[576] Davies and Allison, *A Critical and Exegetical Commentary on the Gospel According to Saint Matthew*, 1:662; Luz describes this usage as *pars pro toto* and lists Gen 30:33; Exod 13:14; and Josh 4:6 as examples (*Matthew: A Commentary*, 1:346). One might add Prov 27:1.

[577] *b. Sanh.* 100b. For other parallels see C. Carlston, "Matthew 6:24–34," *Int* 41 (1987): 179–83.

[578] Nolland adopted a slightly different view. He wrote, "The goal here is to take from us our sense of worrisome responsibility for tomorrow. The rhetorical strategy used to achieve this is to relocate to a credible somewhere else the worry about tomorrow which comes so naturally to us. . . . [I]t is tomorrow and only tomorrow which is located in the appropriate time for paying attention to the needs of tomorrow" (*The Gospel of Matthew*, 316). However, if Jesus were speaking seriously about the one whom disciples should trust with tomorrow's worries, surely God, rather than a personification of tomorrow, would have been mentioned since this is the primary point of the entire section on worry. Far more likely, Jesus' statement was intended to be humorous, and the original audience recognized it as such.

Focusing on potential difficulties that a person may (or may not) face in the future often distracts him from attending to matters at hand. A person has to get through today to even experience a tomorrow. Thus focusing on the present rather than the future is wise.

F. The Disciple's Relationships (Matt 7:1–12)

Relating to Brothers (Matt 7:1–5)

At first glance chap. 7 seems to have little connection to the preceding context.[579] The focus on judging appears to introduce a completely new topic. Further reflection, however, suggests that chap. 7 returns to the topic of hypocrisy that Jesus began to address in 6:1. The word "hypocrite" appeared in 6:2,5, and 16 and now reappears in 7:5. This suggests that Jesus' teaching beginning in 6:1 through much of chap. 7 is directed against hypocrisy. Matthew 6:19–34 contained developments of truths introduced in Jesus' earlier attack on hypocrisy. The hypocrite's focus on present reward rather than future reward betrayed a perverted set of priorities that promoted materialism and anxiety. Thus Jesus addressed these two ills associated with hypocrisy and now treats another symptom of it: hypocritical judgment.

"Do not judge, so that you won't be judged." These are probably the most frequently quoted verses from the NT in twenty-first-century America. They are also among the most misunderstood. The verses are typically used to argue that no one is qualified to comment on whether another person's actions are right or wrong, even if that person's behavior is clearly condemned in the Scriptures. This interpretation of the verses is clearly mistaken.[580] It ignores the grammar of Jesus' command, Jesus' illustration of the command (vv. 3–5), Jesus'

---

[579] Hagner commented, "We encounter a relatively abrupt break with the preceding material as this new subject is addressed." However, he later acknowledged a general relationship of the passage to preceding material (*Matthew 1–13*, 168).

[580] See Betz, *The Sermon on the Mount*, 488; Gundry, *Matthew*, 120–22; Hagner, *Matthew 1–13*, 169. Some commentators see the text as prohibiting all acts of judging. These include Hill (*Matthew*, 146–47) and Guelich (*The Sermon on the Mount*, 349–53). Davies and Allison suggested that Jesus intended to prohibit all acts of judging but that the evangelist only regarded the saying as prohibiting hypocritical judgment (*A Critical and Exegetical Commentary on the Gospel According to Saint Matthew*, 1:673–74). The notion that 7:1 prohibits all judging dates to at least as early as the end of the second century. Irenaus had to defend a bishop's right and responsibility to reprove those who err. His defense was largely a response to the misinterpretation of this passage (*Haer.* 4.30.3).

teaching about discerning false prophets and false disciples by their behavior (vv. 15–23), Jesus' own stern warning about failing to obey His teachings (vv. 24–27), as well as later teachings of Jesus such as His instructions about relating to a sinning brother (18:15–20).

The prohibition "Do not judge" uses the negative *mē* with the present imperative. This could call the hearers and readers to stop an action already in progress or express a general precept.[581] The context suggests that Jesus intended the former. The query in verse 3 does not question whether the disciples judged others hypocritically. Instead, it assumed that they did so and urged the disciples to explore the motivations for their hypocritical judgment. Thus Jesus had observed a judgmental attitude among His disciples, and He now urged His disciples to abandon that outlook: "Stop your [hypocritical] judging."

Disciples should avoid harsh and hypocritical judgment "so that you won't be judged." Although it is possible that Jesus was referring to judgment by other people,[582] Matthew often used passive verbs without a stated agent to describe reverently the activity of God. Grammarians refer to this usage as the "divine passive."[583] This usage is especially probable in this context in light of the parallel between this statement and Jesus' teaching in 6:12,14–15. Jesus taught that a person should expect to be treated by God in a manner similar to the one in which he has treated others. If a person forgives others, he can expect to be forgiven by God. If he refuses to forgive others, he can expect God to withhold His forgiveness. Similarly in the Beatitudes Jesus taught, "Blessed are the merciful, because they will be shown mercy" (by God—divine passive). Matthew 7:1 repeats and rephrases the principle expressed in these earlier statements. If a person judges others harshly, he can expect harsh judgment from God. However, if he judges others mercifully, he can expect merciful judgment from God.

---

[581] Wallace, *Greek Grammar Beyond the Basics*, 724; BDF 172 §336.

[582] Betz suggested that 7:1 teaches the simple principle of reciprocity, that is, those who judge others will be judged by others. Betz argued, however, that in 7:2, divine eschatological judgment was in view (*The Sermon on the Mount*, 490–92).

[583] Wallace, *Greek Grammar Beyond the Basics*, 437–38. The divine passive is most common in the sayings of Jesus. Jeremias saw the usage of the divine passive as a hallmark of the *ipsissima verba* (the actual words) of Jesus (*New Testament Theology*, 9–14). Most commentators recognize the passives in 7:1–2 as divine passives (e.g., Hagner, *Matthew 1–13*, 169; and Gundry, *Matthew*, 120).

Jesus elaborated in verse 2: "For with the judgment you use, you will be judged, and with the measure you use, it will be measured to you." The second half of the verse is identical to an expression that appears in another context in Mark 4:25. In Mark the expression referred to listening to and obeying Jesus' teaching.[584] An almost identical expression in Luke 6:38 urged disciples to share generously with others. If they were stingy, God would be stingy with them. If they were generous, God would be generous with them.[585] In Matthew the application of the expression is different from these parallels. However, Jesus likely used similar expressions in various ways in different contexts. The usage in Matthew is most similar to the way in which the rabbis used the expression.[586] For example in the Mishnah the expression referred to God's poetic justice in which His sentence was especially appropriate for the sinner's offense.[587] According to the rabbis examples of this abound in the OT. Because Samson's lustful eyes led him to sin, the Philistines put out his eyes. Since Absalom gloried in his hair, he was hanged by his hair. Similarly if a person lacks mercy in his judgment of others, he can expect God to judge him mercilessly.

Verse 3 clarifies that the topic under discussion is the judgment of one's "brother." Throughout Matthew's Gospel, the term "brother" frequently refers to a fellow disciple of Jesus.[588] This suggests that Jesus was treating a Christian's judgment and correction of others within the Christian community. This observation necessarily restricts application of Jesus' words. Tolstoy thought that Jesus' teaching required the abolishment of the entire system of public justice and prohibited any human from ever donning a black robe, taking gavel in hand, and sitting at the judicial bench.[589] However, Jesus' words were not political statements about the illegitimacy of court systems. His words

---

[584] J. A. Brooks, *Mark*, NAC (Nashville: Broadman, 1991), 84; Lane, *The Gospel According to Mark* (Grand Rapids: Eerdmans, 1974), 167.

[585] D. L. Bock, *Luke* (Downers Grove, IL: InterVarsity 1994), 607–8; Green, *The Gospel of Luke*, 275; Marshall, *The Gospel of Luke*, 266–67.

[586] See *m. Soṭa* 1:7; *Mek.* on Exod 13:19a; *b. Roš Haš.* 16b; *Gen. Rab.* 9:11; Tg. on Isa 27:8; and Palestinian Tg. on Gen 38:26.

[587] *m. Soṭa* 1.7–8.

[588] H. F. von Soden, "ἀδελφός," *TDNT*, 1 (1964): 144–46; Davies and Allison, *A Critical and Exegetical Commentary on the Gospel According to Saint Matthew*, 1:512–13; Hagner, *Matthew 1–13*, 169–70; Luz, *Matthew: A Commentary*, 1:352. Against Betz, *The Sermon on the Mount*, 492.

[589] L. Tolstoy, *My Religion*, trans. H. Smith (London: Walter Scott, 1889), 39–54. The contrast between the views of Tolstoy and Wellhausen is presented in Betz, *The Sermon on the Mount*, 487. H. Thielicke argued that Matt 7:1–2 showed that "the human being transcends the legal order" (*Theologische Ethik* [Tübingen: Mohr/Siebeck, 1964], 3:337–38).

related to members of the family of God who must lovingly correct
one another without haughty or hypocritical condemnation of others.

Jesus challenged hypocritical judgment by asking "Why do you
look at the speck in your brother's eye but don't notice the log in
your own eye?" (v. 3). The question is not merely a rebuke but a sincere call to probe the motive and rationale (the "why") for this judgment. The present tense of the verb "look" (blepeis) not only implies
that members of Jesus' audience were judging others inappropriately
but also insinuates that this biased and harsh judgment was habitual.
The hearers were not just judging; they were judgmental. Their judgmental attitudes were expressed by a tendency to scrutinize the minor faults of others while overlooking their own much more serious
faults. Significantly Jesus did not see this tendency as characteristic
of only the scribes and Pharisees. Jesus' followers would also struggle
with an inclination toward hypocritical judgment.

A "speck" (karphos) was a tiny piece of straw, chaff, or wood.[590]
The word was often used to denote that something was small and
insignificant. In a context dealing with the judgment of others the
"speck" is a relatively small and insignificant sin.[591] No sin is small
and insignificant, but a sin may be relatively small in comparison with
much more heinous offenses. Jesus portrayed these far greater sins as
"the log in your own eye." The word "log" (dokos) refers to "a piece
of heavy timber such as a beam used in roof construction or to bar a
door."[592] Josephus used the term to describe a huge beam of wood as
long and thick as the mast of a ship that was used by Vespasian for
a battering ram. The massive beam was armed with a huge piece of
iron on the front that had been cast in the shape of a ram's head. The
battering ram was so heavy and powerful that even one blow from it
caused the mighty walls of Jerusalem to shake.[593] The huge and heavy
beam signified the grievous offences of the hypocrite.

---

[590] "κάρφος," BDAG, 511.

[591] Turner, Matthew, 206.

[592] "δοκός," BDAG, 256. Hagner pointed out that although the contrast between a piece of
sawdust and a beam appeared in the Talmud (b. ʿArak. 16b; b. B. Bat. 15b), the illustration was
especially appropriate for a teacher who spent most of his life working in a carpenter's shop
(Matthew 1–13, 169). Based on the evidence of the carpentry illustration, Davies and Allison
infer that 7:3–5 is likely authentic material from Jesus (A Critical and Exegetical Commentary on
the Gospel According to Saint Matthew, 1:671).

[593] Josephus, J.W. 3.19 §§213–21.

Some interpreters will likely object to the notion that some sins are more grievous than others. Popular theology teaches that all sins are equal in the eyes of God. However, this popular theology is not biblical theology. The NT teaches that all sins are serious and that any sin is deserving of God's fierce wrath. Yet this does not mean that all sins are equal. In John 19:11 Jesus told Pilate, "You would have no authority over Me at all . . . if it had not been give to you from above. This is why the one who handed Me over to you has the greater sin." The sin of Annas or Caiaphas in handing Jesus over for execution by Pilate was a greater sin than Pilate's sentencing Jesus to death.[594] Jesus clearly taught that some sins may be greater or less than others. The contrast between the speck and the beam confirms this with graphic imagery.

Jesus then used the humorous illustration to demonstrate that disciples cannot aid their brothers in addressing their smaller sins until they first deal with their own more grievous ones. The question "how can you say?" (Matt 7:4) expresses shock at the audacity of a person attempting to attend to the spiritual needs of others when he is in far worse spiritual condition. The illustration shows that the sinning brother will fail to do his patient any good when he attempts to remove his speck, and he will likely do him great harm. Removal of a speck from the fragile and sensitive eye is a delicate procedure. The man with a huge beam protruding from his own eye is poorly equipped to perform this procedure. The beam can only hinder him from seeing clearly. Verse 5 shows that only after the beam is removed can he see well enough to perform his surgery. Until then, his hindered vision ensures that he will make a mess of the procedure, permanently damaging the delicate eye of his patient and robbing him of his precious sight. Even worse, every movement of his own head will only whack his poor patient's skull with the mighty beam. Such a physician is destined to be like the ones described in Mark 5:26—his treatments will only make his patient worse.

The rebuke "hypocrite" repeats the challenge from Matt 6:2,5, and 16. The harsh judge is a play actor who assumes the role of a spiritual physician when in reality he himself is a patient sicker than the

---

[594] G. Borchert, *John 12–21*, NAC (Nashville: Broadman & Holman, 2002), 254; R. Brown, *The Gospel According to John XIII-XXI*, AB (New York: Doubleday, 1970), 878–79; D. A. Carson, *The Gospel According to John*, PNTC (Grand Rapids: Eerdmans, 1991), 601; and A. Kostenberger, *John*, BECNT (Grand Rapids: Baker, 204), 535.

one he attends. The rebuke in 7:5 answers Jesus' question in verse 3. Why does someone lock his eyes on someone's smaller sins while ignoring his own more heinous ones? He does so because of his hypocrisy. With this use of the term, Jesus expanded the meaning of the term "hypocrite." The "hypocrite" is not only someone who performs deeds of righteousness out of a desire for self-aggrandizement. He is also consumed with pride and self-deception.[595] He is blind to his own sin but keenly aware of the faults of others. He is devoted to inspection without introspection, careful examination of others without any sincere evaluation of himself.

Paul may have had this saying of Jesus in mind when he challenged the hypocrisy of some of his fellow Jews in Rom 2:1. He wrote, "Therefore, anyone of you who judges is without excuse. For when you judge another, you condemn yourself, since you, the judge, do the same things." In Paul's context the hypocrite seemed to think that he could distract attention from his own guilt by pointing to the guilt of others. Paul insisted that this evasive tactic was ineffective. In fact it only heightened the sinner's guilt.

If Jesus had ended His teaching on the issue here, it would confirm the popular impression that Jesus wanted His disciples to mind their own business and refrain from ever commenting on the sins of others. Yet Jesus did not wish to leave that false impression. He added, "First take the log out of your eye, and then you will see clearly to take the speck out of your brother's eye" (Matt 7:5). Jesus clearly taught that abandoning one's own more heinous sins was a prerequisite for addressing the more minor sins of others.[596] Nevertheless Jesus affirmed that His disciples should humbly and compassionately aid others in abandoning their own sins.[597] A person who has removed a beam from an eye successfully (and his own eye at that!) is well qualified to assist in removing a speck from another's eye. A person who has renounced

---

[595] See D. Via, "The Gospel of Matthew: Hypocrisy as Self-deception," SBLSP 27 (1988): 508–16.

[596] Broadus, The Gospel According to Matthew, 157.

[597] Several scholars recognize that this statement stands in contradiction with the view that Jesus prohibited all acts of judgment. They seek to reconcile this statement with their interpretation of 7:1 by viewing 7:5 as ironic. See Hill, The Gospel of Matthew, 147; Guelich, The Sermon on the Mount, 352–53; Schweizer, The Good News According to Matthew, 169. Luz has pointed out that both the adverb "first" (πρῶτον) and the future indicative form of διαβλέπω argue against interpreting the statement ironically. The ironic interpretation requires that one understand the future indicative as a "kind of sarcastic possibility." However, the future indicative does not elsewhere serve this function (Matthew: A Commentary, 1:353, esp. n. 43).

and abandoned particularly heinous sins is likewise well equipped to assure others that they can conquer their relatively smaller sins. One cannot aid his brother in addressing his sins in the manner that Jesus desires unless he recognizes sin as sin and lovingly confronts the brother with his sin. Thus Jesus' teaching requires the evaluation and confrontation that many readers wrongly assume Jesus forbade in 7:1. Although 7:1–5 has sometimes been used to argue against the practice of church discipline, the text actually commands loving church discipline.[598]

Relating to Dogs and Pigs (Matt 7:6)

Verse 6 appears to be loosely connected to verses 1–5. The preceding verses address how one should correct a brother and assist him in overcoming his sin. Verse 6 relates to those who desire no assistance in overcoming their sin but intend to persist in their wicked behavior. No matter how humbly or lovingly the disciple approaches such a person, the efforts to assist will only prove disastrous.

Verse 6 has long puzzled interpreters. Many scholars have concluded that the text makes no sense in its present form. Several suggest that the confusing reading is a result of either mistranslation from the Aramaic or a textual corruption. In 1792 Johann Adrian Bolten pointed out that the consonants for the words "holy" and "ring" were identical in Aramaic. He suggested that the word meaning "ring" was mistranslated "holy" in the Greek Gospel.[599] Bolten's suggestion has been accepted and improved by modern scholars such as Perles, Jeremias, and Schwarz.[600] These scholars speculated that the saying in Matt 7:6 is an allusion to Prov 11:22 which says, "A beautiful woman who rejects good sense is like a gold ring in a pig's snout."

Several problems make this ingenuous interpretation doubtful. First, if one substitutes the translation "ring" for "what is holy," the word "ring" is associated with "dogs" and not with "pigs." This makes

---

[598] See R. E. Olson, "To Judge or Not to Judge," *Christianity Today* (July 2005): 52. See also Matt 18:15–20; 1 Cor 5:1–13; 2 Cor 2:5–11; Gal 6:1–5; 1 Thess 4:14; 2 Thess 3:6–15.

[599] Luz, *Matthew: A Commentary*, 1:354.

[600] F. Perles, "Zur Erklärung von Mt 7:6," *ZNW* 25 (1926): 163–64; J. Jeremias, "Matthäus 7,6a," *Abba* (Götlingen: Vandenhoeck to Ruprecht, 1966), 83–87; G. Schwarz, "Matthäus vii 6a: Emendation und Rückübersetzung," *NovT* 14 (1972): 18–25. S. Llewelyn has suggested that although the original Aramaic saying referred to a ring, the change to "what is holy" was a product of intentional interpretation that applied the reference to the Eucharist, rather than accidental mistranslation ("Mt 7:6a: Mistranslation or Interpretation," *NovT* 31 [1989]: 97–103).

an allusion to Prov 11:22 unlikely. In order for the theory of this allusion to remain viable, one would have to argue not only for the mistranslation of a single word but also for the insertion of the references to both dogs and pearls in order to smooth out and clarify the mistranslated statement. Second, the text in its present form makes better sense if we retain the word *hagion* ("what is holy"). This reading is also better suited to discussions within first-century Judaism. Third, as Betz has insisted, "The Greek text must be the basis of the interpretation, and not a hypothetical Aramaic source, which, if it ever existed, has disappeared without a trace."[601]

The statement "Don't give what is holy to dogs" likely refers to the Jewish concern for protecting sacrificial meat from misuse.[602] Portions of sacrificial meat that were not burned on the altar were reserved for the priests and their families (Lev 8:31; 10:14). Meat from an animal that had been killed by wild predators was to be thrown to the dogs (Exod 22:31). Thus to feed sacrificial meat to dogs was to treat what was holy as if it were profane.

The Sectarian Manifesto of the Qumran community, now known as 4QMMT, is greatly concerned with guarding the separation of the profane from the holy. 4QMMT 51–54 says,

> (Concerning dogs,) one may not bring dogs into the holy camp because they may eat some of the [b]ones from the sanc[tuary and] the meat which is still on them. For Jerusalem is the holy camp. It is the place that He chose from all the tribes of Israel, for Jerusalem is the foremost of the camps of Israel.[603]

The author of the scroll believed that dogs should be banned from the holy city in order to prevent them from having access to sacred meat.

The dogs (*kuōn*) spoken of in Matt 7:6 and 4QMMT were not domesticated pets. In 15:26, the evangelist used a different word, the diminutive form *kunarion*, to speak of house dogs that eat scraps from their master's table. The dogs mentioned in 7:6 are wild street dogs that were known for both their viciousness and their ravenous appetite for disgusting foods. Such dogs licked leper's sores (Luke 16:21). They ate decaying foods that their stomachs rejected and then turned

---

[601] Betz, *The Sermon on the Mount*, 494–95.

[602] The LXX frequently used the plural form τὰ ἅγια to refer to sacrificial meat. However, Hb. and Aram. texts normally used the sing. form and the LXX sometimes retains the sing. (Lev 2:3; 22:14; Ezra 2:63; Neh 7:65). See Llewelyn, "Mt 7:6a: Mistranslation or Interpretation," 100.

[603] Wise, Abegg, and Cook, *The Dead Sea Scrolls*, 459. See also *m. Ṭehar.* 4:3, which deals with dogs conveying uncleanness by carrying carrion in their mouths.

and lapped up their own vomit (Prov 26:11; 2 Pet 2:22). Not only
were dogs considered unclean (Exod 22:31); also they lacked the sen-
sibility to distinguish sacrificial meat from the rotting meat they scav-
enged from the garbage heaps in the valley of Hinnom. They would
treat as profane what was most holy. To feed them holy meat would
thus be an act of horrible sacrilege.

Although the words of 4QMMT are reminiscent of the words of
Jesus, they address a slightly different scenario. The author of 4QMMT
was concerned about dogs accidentally being allowed to scavenge the
leftovers from holy sacrifice. Jesus, on the other hand, prohibited His
disciples from intentionally giving holy meat to dogs. Since such an
act would be unthinkable for a reverent Jew, the interpreter immediately suspects that Jesus' words were allegorical.

Although the majority of commentators recognize the allegorical
nature of Jesus' statement, identifying "what is holy" and the "dogs"
is no easy task.[604] The earliest known interpretation appears in *Did.*
9:5. The *Didache* interpreted "what is holy" as a reference to the Lord's
Supper and the "dogs" as unbaptized persons.[605] This interpretation
may have been prompted by the assumption that the Lord's Supper
was a sacrificial act that replaced temple sacrifices. Gregory of Nazianzus interpreted "what is holy" as Christian doctrines and "dogs"
as those with unholy ears and hearts.[606]

Jesus added that His disciples should not "toss your pearls before
pigs" (Matt 7:6). Since this statement appears in parallel with the following statement about pigs and pearls and seems to teach the same
truth, the two statements are best examined and interpreted together.
The verb "toss" is equivalent to the verb "give." Pearls, like sacred
meat, are valuable and worthy of careful treatment. Like dogs, "pigs"
were described in the OT as unclean (Lev 11:7; Deut 14:8). Both species of animal were often lumped together as unclean or despised animals.[607] Neither animal would appreciate the value of what was set

[604] Luz wrote, "I am going to permit myself not to interpret the logion." He argued that the
multitude of interpretations in the early church reflected "the erratic character of this logion, a
logion that is not understandable in the Matthean context" (*Matthew: A Commentary*, 1:356).

[605] "Do not let anyone eat or drink from your Eucharist, except those who were baptized in
the name of the Lord, because the Lord also has spoken about this matter: 'Do not give what is
holy to the dogs'" (author's translation).

[606] For a good survey of the history of interpretation of Matt 7:6, see T. J. Bennett, "Matthew
7:6: A New Interpretation," *WTJ* 49 (1987): 371–86.

[607] *1 Enoch* 89:42; 2 Pet 2:22; Oxy. Prap. V 840.33; *b. Šabb.* 155b; Horace, *Ep.* 1.2.26; 2.2.75.

before them. Thus the two halves of the compound sentence in Matt
7:6 seem completely synonymous.

"Pearls" clearly refer to something that is precious, but what does
it refer to? In Job 28:18 pearls represent the enormous value of wisdom. In Matt 13:45 a priceless pearl represents the enormous value
of the kingdom of God that, like a great treasure, is worthy of any
sacrifice necessary to obtain it. In light of that verse, one suspects
that the pearls represent the message about the kingdom that was first
preached by John (3:2) and Jesus (4:17) and would soon be preached
by Jesus' disciples (10:7) Ancient Jewish literature used pearls as a
symbol for excellent teaching.[608] Thus it appears that the common
Jewish usage (pearls as teaching) and the meaning in Matthew (pearls
as kingdom) have coalesced and refer here to teaching about the
kingdom.

Matthew 7:6 describes those from whom the message about the
kingdom should be withheld as "pigs." Jews sometimes referred to
Gentiles as "pigs" or "dogs."[609] Thus some interpreters regard verse
6 as a prohibition against ministry to Gentiles that reinforces the instruction in 10:5–6 and 15:24.[610] The response of Luz to this interpretation is fully justified: "Theologically it is not at all in keeping with
Matthew."[611] Although Jesus had prioritized the spiritual needs of the
Israelites during His ministry, the inclusion of four Gentile women in
Jesus' genealogy (1:3,5–6), the fact that Jesus was first worshipped by
Gentiles (2:11), Jesus' selection of Capernaum in "Galilee of the Gentiles" as the headquarters for His ministry, and many other features of
this Gospel all anticipate the climactic command to "make disciples
of all nations" (28:19). Matthew clearly did not regard the statement
as a prohibition of Gentile mission.

Much more likely, "dogs" and "pigs" refer to wicked people who
will despise and mock the Christian message. Both terms could serve
as general terms of contempt. "Dog" was a word of reproach in numerous OT texts (1 Sam 17:43; 24:14; 2 Sam 9:8; 16:9; Ps 22:20; Prov
26:11; Isa 56:10–11). It also serves this function frequently in the NT.
In Phil 3:2 the term "dogs" was used by Paul to identify the Judaizers.
Revelation 22:15 associates dogs with sorcerers, the sexually immoral,

---

[608] *Mek.* on Exod 13:2; *'Abot R. Nat.* 18; *b. Ḥag.* 3a; *b. Ber.* 33b; *b. Yebam.* 94a; *b. Qidd.* 39b.
[609] Matt 15:26; *'Abot R. Nat.* 34.
[610] T. W. Manson, *The Sayings of Jesus*, 2d ed. (London: SCM, 1949), 174.
[611] Luz, *Matthew: A Commentary*, 1:355.

the murderers, the idolaters, and everyone who loves and practices lying, all of whom are excluded from the holy city and barred from access to the tree of life. Jewish texts that combine metaphorical references to "dogs" and "pigs" typically emphasize their uncleanness and use the terms to symbolize the wicked. In *1 Enoch* 89:42, "dogs, foxes, and wild boars" represent the pagan enemies of Israel who were destroyed in the conquest. In 2 Pet 2:22 a "dog" and a "sow" portray false teachers who are "slaves of corruption" entangled in the world's impurity and who have turned back from the holy commandment delivered to them.

Just as dogs will fail to show proper reverence for sacrificial meat and pigs will fail to value precious pearls, the wicked will fail to value and show reverence for the message about the kingdom. On the contrary, they will only spurn, mock, and ridicule it. Pigs often ate white peas or acorns that were similar to pearls in appearance.[612] A pig would be angered when he saw pearls in his trough, mistook them for some part of his normal diet, and then felt a sharp pain when the hard inedible pearls crunched between his teeth. The furious pig would trample the pearls until they were buried beneath the muck of his wallow. The verb translated "trample" (*katapateō*) not only describes the pigs as walking on the pearls with their hard hooves, but it also refers primarily to treating them with disdain.[613] This scene pictured the utter contempt the wicked would show for the gospel. They would not politely reject it; they would trample it underfoot with complete scorn. The gospel of the kingdom is too glorious to be dragged through the mud. Reverence for the Christian message demands that it be protected from those who will not merely reject it but also repudiate it.

Similarly dogs who do not appreciate sacrificial meat may turn and attack the one who fed them. Common Jewish wisdom warned against feeding wild street dogs because they might stalk the one who showed them compassion. Rabbis advised their disciples to feed hungry dogs in the open field but to drive them away immediately afterwards with a stick in order to avoid an attack.[614] The danger of a dog

---

[612] A. B. Bruce, "The Gospel According to Matthew," in *The Expositor's Greek Testament*, ed. W. Robertson Nicoll (Grand Rapids: Eerdmans, 1979), 1:129–30; and Keener, *The Gospel of Matthew*, 243.

[613] "καταπατέω," BDAG, 523. See Matt 5:13; Heb 10:29; Isa 28:3. The verb is quite common in the LXX, appearing 51 times.

[614] See *b. Šabb.* 155b.

biting the hand that feeds him is proverbial to this very day.[615] Jesus warned His disciples that if they attempted to force their message on the wicked who showed no appreciation for it, they were only inviting persecution. The wicked would soon begin to snarl, bare their fangs, and tear the flesh of those who showed compassion to them by sharing the good news.[616]

The pigs and dog thus represent the wicked who persecute the disciples because of their allegiance to Jesus (Matt 5:11). They are those who are hardened in their rejection of the good news, spiritually deaf, and spiritually blind (13:10–15; 15:14; 21:34–39; 24:9; 27:27–31,38–44). Consequently Matt 7:6 urges disciples to withhold the message about the kingdom, the Christian gospel, from those who treat it with contempt. The two prohibitions in verse 6 are expressed in a grammatical form (*mē* with the aorist subjunctive) that prohibits an action as a whole. The form often forbids one to begin an action.[617] Thus the form typically commands, "Do not ever . . ." or "Do not . . . at all." Jesus thus forbade efforts to impose the gospel on wicked people who showed only contempt for it at all times and under all circumstances.

Jesus' instruction here raises many practical questions. Should believers implement these instructions by attempting to read the minds and hearts of others to determine whether they should share the gospel with them? Does any rejection of the gospel so dishonor it that one's witness should be silenced or only harsh and adamant rejection? Difficult questions such as these have prompted some commentators to suggest that the instructions in verse 6 should not be followed by the modern church at all. When Luz's treatment of this verse climaxed in a discussion of the "meaning for today," he asked,

> What is one to do with this biblical word in the church today? My advice is
> radical: one should not use it as a biblical word. The history of interpretation

[615] T. Bennett overlooked this consideration when he claimed that one cannot explain a dog attacking someone who fed it sacrificial meat. Bennett argued that Matt 7:6 was simply an illustration of how those who judge others (giving their holy opinion of their conduct) will be judged (turned on and attacked) ("Matthew 7:6—A New Interpretation," *WTJ* 49 [1987]: 371–86).

[616] The majority of commentators see a chiastic arrangement in Matt 7:6. See T. F. Glasson, "Chiasmus in St Matthew 7:6," *ExpTim* 68 (1957): 302; Davies and Allison, *A Critical and Exegetical Commentary on the Gospel According to Saint Matthew*, 1:677. The reference to "trampling" best suits the behavior of a pig. "Tear you to pieces" could describe the behavior of a wild boar, but the illustration apparently refers to domesticated pigs that were fed. Thus this element of the illustration best describes the behavior of a wild street dog.

[617] Wallace, *Greek Grammar Beyond the Basics*, 723–24; BDF, 173, sec. 337.

shows that such a saying whose context has become totally unrecognizable
was able to be used only as a secondary biblical legitimation for ecclesiastical
or theological divisions that for other reasons already existed.[618]

Nevertheless one cannot dismiss the teachings of Jesus as a "biblical word" simply because the church may have abused or misapplied
His instruction in the past. Furthermore, the claim that this text was
"used only as a secondary biblical legitimation for ecclesiastical or
theological divisions" is untrue.

Later texts in Matthew's Gospel demonstrate how Jesus intended
for His instructions to be applied. When Jesus sent out the Twelve for
ministry in Matt 10:11–15, He commanded:

> When you enter any town or village, find out who is worthy, and stay there
> until you leave. Greet a household when you enter it, and if the household is
> worthy, let your peace be on it. But if it is unworthy, let your peace return to
> you. If anyone will not welcome you or listen to your words, shake the dust
> off your feet when you leave that house or town. I assure you: It will be more
> tolerable on the day of judgment for the land of Sodom and Gomorrah than
> for that town.

Jesus' teaching demonstrates that the disciples were not to presume
that any person would reject the gospel. They were to offer it to anyone. However, when the gospel was rejected, the disciples were to
refocus their evangelistic efforts on others. Allison seems to capture
the spirit of the command: "The saying is an admonition about the
necessity to limit the time and energy directed towards the hard-
hearted. . . . They were not to throw away wittingly the words of the
gospel. . . . There has to be an economy of truth."[619]

The apostle Paul provided an excellent model of obedience to
this principle in his missionary work. He patiently explained the gospel to a group over periods of weeks, even if they did not accept the
message, so long as they remained open to it. However, when the
audience adamantly rejected the gospel, he turned his attention to
others (Acts 13:42–14:20; 17:1–15,32–34; 19:23–20:1). Believers in
the modern church would do well to follow Paul's example and Jesus'
instructions.

---

[618] Luz, *Matthew: A Commentary*, 1:356.
[619] Davies and Allison, *A Critical and Exegetical Commentary on the Gospel According to Saint
Matthew*, 1:676.

Relating to the Father (Matt 7:7–12)

The verb "ask" suggests that Jesus' instruction addresses, at least partially, the issue of prayer. The Lucan context of this saying confirms
this view since the saying follows soon after the model prayer, sepa-
rated from it only by a parable that emphasizes persistence in asking (Luke 11:2–13). Matthew 7:11 repeats the verb "ask" and thereby
forms an inclusio that suggests the primary focus of the text is prayer.
"Seek" and "knock" do not introduce distinct ideas. Instead, these
verbs serve as metaphors for asking in prayer. "Knocking" in particular served as a metaphor for prayer in rabbinic sayings.[620] Furthermore, the verbs translated "will be given" and "will be opened" are
passive verbs that are almost certainly to be taken as examples of the
divine passive that is so common in the SM.[621] "Asking," "seeking,"
and "knocking" are thus pleas for God to act, different metaphors for
prayer.

The verb "ask" (*aiteō*) appeared earlier in the SM in 5:42 and 6:8.
In the former occurrence the verb referred to one person asking another to supply a need. More importantly the latter occurrence referred
to a person asking God to supply one's needs. Matthew 6:25–34 (esp.
v. 32) implies that these needs are primarily food, drink, and clothing. The illustration that Jesus used to confirm his teaching speaks of
a child asking his father for bread and fish (7:9–10). These foods are
examples of the "good gifts" evil fathers give their children. Consequently one expects the "good things" the heavenly Father grants His
children to include food as well.[622] This initially seems to suggest that
Jesus' teaching here returns to the themes of 6:11,25–34 by focusing
on the disciple's dependence on God for the resources necessary to
life.

Unfortunately readers naturally interpret 7:7–11 as a blanket
promise that God will positively answer the sincere prayers of His
people. Hill represents this view: "The imperatives ask . . . seek . . .
knock . . . are emphatic, and express a confident attitude towards the
Father in heaven. No limitations or conditions are attached to the

---

[620] France, *The Gospel of Matthew*, 144.

[621] Against Betz who remarked, "The one to be asked is another person, not necessarily only
God" (*The Sermon on the Mount*, 504). Support for the divine (or theological) passive appears in
Davies and Allison, *A Critical and Exegetical Commentary on the Gospel According to Saint Mat-
thew*, 1:679; and Hagner, *Matthew 1–13*, 174.

[622] France, *The Gospel of Matthew*, 145.

statement, though presumably sincerity is required."[623] Similarly Morris noted, "The general expression (ask) shows that no particular kind of prayer is in mind; Jesus is concerned with praying as such and telling his hearers that prayer is efficacious."[624] Most commentators have noticed the dangers latent within this view and quickly clarify that Jesus elsewhere imposed limitations on what seems to be an unlimited promise. Morris added, "This is not Jesus' complete teaching on prayer; for that we must remember the importance of forgiving as we pray for forgiveness, of asking in faith, asking in accordance with the will of God (cf. 6:12; 21:21–22; 26:39), and more."

Stott keenly sensed the problem when he wrote:

> The best way to approach this problem is to remember that the promises of Jesus in the Sermon on the Mount are not unconditional. A moment's thought will convince us of this. It is absurd to suppose that the promise "Ask, and it shall be given you" is an absolute pledge with no strings attached; that "Knock, and it will be opened to you" is an "Open, Sesame" to every closed door without exception; and that by the waving of a prayer wand any wish will be granted and every dream will come true. The idea is ridiculous. It would turn prayer into magic, the person who prays into a magician like Aladdin, and God into our servant who appears instantly to do our bidding like Aladdin's genie every time we rub our little prayer lamp.[625]

Stott also noted that if Jesus promised to grant every single request expressed in prayer, the wise person would never pray again because he recognizes that he lacks the insight to know what is truly best in all circumstances.

Several commentators note that the grammar of the passage itself imposes certain limitations on Jesus' promise. The three imperatives of verse 7 are present imperatives. Present imperatives normally command a person to begin and continue an action (ingressive-progressive), perform an action continually (customary), or perform an action repeatedly (iterative present).[626] All three varieties of usage

---

[623] Hill, *The Gospel of Matthew*, 148.

[624] Morris, *The Gospel According to Matthew*, 169.

[625] Stott, *The Sermon on the Mount*, 188.

[626] Wallace, *Greek Grammar Beyond the Basics*, 721–22. Wallace suggests this rule of thumb for distinguishing between these three usages: "Normally, a good rule of thumb is that when an *attitude* is commanded, the force of the present imperative will either be *ingressive-progressive* or *customary*; when an *action* is commanded, the force of the present imperative will usually be *iterative*." Although the categories suggested by Wallace are helpful, the suggested rule of thumb for distinguishing between the varieties of the present imperative is less so. Several of the examples of the various categories do not fit this rule of thumb.

for the present imperative stress the importance of continuing to perform an action. For this reason the Holman Christian Standard Bible
adopts the translation, "keep asking," "keep searching," and "keep
knocking." These grammatical forms suggest to some commentators
that the primary purpose of Jesus' instruction was to stress the importance of persistence in prayer.

This hypothesis finds support in the Lukan parallel (Luke 11:9–
13). The Lukan version is immediately preceded by the parable of
the man who knocks on the door of a friend at midnight to request
several loaves of bread (Luke 11:5–8). Although the friendship between the two men was not sufficient to ensure that the man's request
would be granted, the friend would get out of bed and give the visitor
what he needed "because of his persistence." Luke 11:9 introduces
the commands "keep asking . . . keep searching . . . keep knocking"
with the words, "So I say to you."[627] The word *kagō* closely connects
verse 9 to the preceding parable and suggests that verses 9–13 state
the moral of the preceding parable.[628] Allusions to Jesus' saying in the
Gospel to the Hebrews, the Oxyrhynchus Papyrii, and the Gospel of
Thomas show that early interpreters also regarded it as stressing the
importance of persistence in prayer.[629] The nuance of the present imperatives and the context of the saying in Luke prompted Jeremias to
view that saying as an expression of what he called "beggar's wisdom."
He explained, "If the beggar, although harshly repulsed at first, knows
that persistent appeals will open the hands of his hard-hearted fellow
men, how much more certain should you be that your persistence in
prayer will open the hands of your heavenly Father."[630]

Nevertheless God does not always choose to grant even that for
which one persistently prays. Although the interpreter should recognize an emphasis on persistence in prayer as central to this text, one
still doubts that Jesus intended to teach that one will receive whatever
he persistently prays for.[631] Such an interpretation would make Jesus'

[627] Literally, "and I say to you."
[628] See "κἀγώ," BDAG, 487.
[629] Clement of Alexandria, *Strom.* 2.9.45.5; 5.14.96.3; Oxy. Pap. 654.1; *Gos. Thom.* 2 (see also 92 and 94). By contrast, the allusion to this text in the Shepherd of Hermas seems to emphasize the importance of avoiding doubtfulness in prayer (Herm. *Sim.* 9.4).
[630] J. Jeremias, *The Parables of Jesus*, 2nd rev. ed. (New York: Charles Scribner's Sons, 1972), 159–60.
[631] Morris recognized that the emphasis on human persistence could make the text danger-ously anthropocentric. Thus he warned, "The point is not that human persistence wins out in

teaching patently false.[632] Furthermore Matthew's usage of this saying in the SM lacks the features which in Luke's Gospel place emphasis on persistence. This makes it unlikely that Matthew saw persistence in prayer as the primary point of the saying.

A closer examination of Jesus' teaching in Matt 7:7–12 suggests that Jesus' primary purpose in these statements was not to teach about prayer or to call His disciples to persistence in prayer. Rather this text focuses on appeal to a gracious God for entrance into the kingdom. Jesus' intention was to stress that eschatological salvation is a gift granted to His disciples who approach God as spiritual beggars (5:3) and humbly plead for God to give them the undeserved privilege of entering His kingdom.

The key to the correct interpretation of this text requires the student of the SM to look beyond the mere grammatical form of the imperatives to the specific vocabulary Jesus chose for His imperatives. The word choices immediately suggest that these imperatives are closely connected to the surrounding context in the SM, a context that serves to clarify Jesus' promise.[633]

Despite the connection between "ask" and physical needs in 5:42 and 6:8, other considerations raise doubts that 7:7–8 focuses primarily on petition for physical needs. First, the Lukan parallel (which is otherwise almost identical to Matthew's version) supplies an important key to interpretation of the passage by replacing the words "good things" from Matt 7:11 with the words "Holy Spirit" (Luke 11:13). This suggests that the "good things" for which the disciple pleads in prayer refer to the Holy Spirit, whose baptism (Matt 3:11; Luke 3:16) transforms Jesus' disciples in fulfillment of the promise of the new covenant (Ezek 36:26–27).

Second, several features of the SM suggest that Luke did not spiritualize Jesus' teaching but was faithfully interpreting the original intent of Jesus' words in a manner with which Matthew would himself

the end but that the heavenly Father who loves his children will certainly answer their prayer" (*The Gospel According to Matthew*, 169).

[632] Luz commented, "Once again we see Jesus' unconditional trust in the Father. Such faith evokes admiration but also criticism. In 'the full magnificence and simplicity of his faith' is Jesus not also naïve and blind to reality? Does he really think that every request will be answered?" (*Matthew: A Commentary*, 1:359).

[633] Many commentators see 7:11–11 as a floating saying of Jesus that has little relationship to its context in the SM. Hill claimed that although the saying was closely linked to its context in Luke, "here the verses seem to have no connection in thought with the passages which precede and follow" (*The Gospel of Matthew*, 148).

agree. Although idolaters are obsessed with their need for food, drink, and clothing (6:31–32), Jesus' disciples have a different set of priorities. They hunger for righteousness more than they crave their next bite of bread, and they thirst for holiness more than they long for their next sip of water (5:6). Jesus' disciples prioritize the kingdom of God and the righteousness that pertains to it far above food, drink, and clothing (6:31–33). After these statements Jesus' audience would recognize that the requests for kingdom entrance and righteous living were the most urgent and important requests.

Third, with the exception of 7:11a in which "good gifts" refers to food, all other occurrences of the adjective *agathos* in Matthew have connotations of moral goodness.[634] The adjective describes righteous people, righteous deeds, and righteous words. In 5:45 the adjective appears in parallel with the adjective *dikaios* (righteous) and is contrasted with the adjective *ponēros* ("evil"). In 7:17–18 the adjective was used twice to describe a healthy tree that produces good fruit, allegorical references to a righteous man who produces righteous words and deeds. In 12:34 the adjective describes the good words that evil men are incapable of speaking because of their corrupt hearts, the good words and deeds that issue from the pure hearts of good people. In 19:16 it refers to the good deeds the rich young ruler assumed necessary to inherit eternal life. In 19:17 it described the holy character of God Himself. In 20:15 it describes a landowner's generosity that symbolically portrayed the mercy of God. In 22:10 the adjective described good people in contrast with evil people. In 25:21 and 23 the adjective described a "good and faithful servant" who served his Lord well. This consistent use of the adjective "good" in Matthew would prompt sensitive readers to view the "good things" of 7:11 as righteous character, deeds, and words produced by the Holy Spirit.

The next imperative, "seek" (*zēteō*), supports this conclusion.[635] This verb appears only one other time in the SM. In 6:33 an identical form of the verb (present active imperative second-person plural) was used in the command, "But seek first the kingdom of God and His righteousness." This implies that the command "seek" in 7:7 means

[634] Even in 7:11a, moral connotations are present. The "good gifts" are contrasted with the evil character of earthly fathers. Gifts of stone and serpents to hungry children would be evil because they would leave a child hungry, possibly break a trusting child's teeth, and put the child at risk of injury, pain, and death. Bread and fish are "good gifts" because they express a desire to sustain life and meet the needs of others.

[635] The HCSB translates the verb "keep searching."

"Keep seeking the kingdom of God and the righteousness that God grants." The related promise "and you will find" is also closely connected to teaching about the kingdom in the SM. The verb "find" (*heuriskō*) appears only one other time in the SM (v. 14), in which the verb speaks of true disciples who "find" the difficult road that leads to life. This further confirms that Jesus commanded His hearers to seek the kingdom and promised that those who seek it will find it.[636]

Although the case for interpreting "good things" as a reference to kingdom entrance and kingdom righteousness is already strong, the final imperative "knock" makes the interpretation almost certain. The verb "knock" does not appear elsewhere in the SM or the Gospel of Matthew. However, just as the verbs "ask" and "seek" closely connect to other passages in the SM, this verb seems to relate closely to a passage in the SM too. Although the other imperatives allude to the preceding context, the imperative "knock" appears to relate to the paragraph that immediately follows 7:7–12.

Matthew 7:13–14 refers to a narrow gate. Although in modern times most readers assume that one would pass without permission through a gate and then knock on a door to request permission to gain entrance, ancient readers would have approached the text with a different set of assumptions. In the NT era one not only knocked on doors (*thura*) but also on gates (*pulōn, pulē*). Acts 12:13 says that Simon Peter "knocked at the door in the gateway." The next verse describes this door as a "gate." Consequently "knock" may mean "knock at the narrow gate through which one enters the kingdom."[637]

This implies that "ask . . . seek . . . knock . . ." constitute something along the lines of an evangelistic invitation. Jesus' urged His hearers to ask for kingdom entrance, to seek the kingdom and the righteousness of God above all else, to seek the difficult path to life that so few find, to knock on the narrow gate that is the only means of access to salvation. The nature of these commands suggests that they were not directed to those who were already disciples but to those who were contemplating a life of discipleship. Perhaps at this point in His sermon, Jesus shifted His attention from His disciples to people

---

[636] In Matt 13:44 the kingdom is compared to a treasure that a man "found" in a field. See Jer 29:13 for a classic OT promise to those who seek the Lord.

[637] Keener likewise asserted: "The door to be opened is the gate of salvation (7:13; contrast Luke 11:5–13). Thus it is possible that Matthew's emphasis in this section is prayer for God's rule (cf. 6:9–10)" (*The Gospel of Matthew*, 245).

in the crowds (7:28–8:1). Matthew 7:13–14 seems to require this shift in primary audience, but the transition more likely began here at 7:7. This view is supported not only by the meaning of the imperatives in this section but also by the description of those to whom Jesus spoke in verse 11, "You . . . who are evil." This suggests that the imperatives in verse 7 are likely inceptive progressive. They command the hearers to begin asking, seeking, and knocking and to continue to ask, seek, and knock until they enjoy all the benefits of the kingdom of God.

Several other commentators arrive at positions similar to this one. Hagner stated: "These 'good things' can be thought of as the eschatological blessings that accompany the presence of the kingdom (cf. Luke's 'Holy Spirit'), so that the work of the disciples in proclaiming the kingdom is primarily in view."[638] Closer is the view of D. A. Carson Jr., who suggests that the "good things" are the character qualities demanded by the SM such as love, righteousness, humility, and purity.[639] Closer still is the view of Keener:

> Contextually, the supreme object of "seeking" is the kingdom (6:33; for the food he mentions, cf. also 8:11; on "finding" cf. 10:39; 11:29; 13:44; 16:25); though disciples ask God to supply their material needs (6:11), they do not "seek" them zealously (6:32–33; cf. 1 Tim 6:5–11). The door to be opened is the gate of salvation (7:13; contrast Lk 11:5–13). Thus it is possible that Matthew's emphasis in this section is prayer for God's rule (cf. 6:9–10).[640]

If the interpretation above is correct, the popular interpretation of 7:8 must also be slightly revised. The verse is often interpreted as if it said, "One who asks *always* receives" when in fact it reads, "*Everyone* who asks receives." Betz, for example, commented:

> That this experience happens to everyone may be an exaggeration, but we count on it as being generally true; otherwise we would not continue to do these things. Thus, the suggestion is, one has not reason to be overly skeptical or pessimistic. Under normal circumstances, and maybe even under extraordinary circumstances, people will help when asked. People can expect to find when they seek. Doors will open when one knocks. The message is that

[638] Hagner, *Matthew 1–13*, 174.

[639] Carson, "Matthew," 186–87. Similarly Blomberg suggests, "The 'good gifts' God gives include everything that pertains to seeking first his kingdom and its righteousness" (*Matthew*, 130).

[640] Keener, *The Gospel of Matthew*, 244. A similar view is supported by Nolland (*The Epistle of Matthew*, 325). Although Davies and Allison offer no real support for the view, they also conclude that "the 'good things' are precisely all that is required to live the life of faithful discipleship as this is set forth in the great sermon" (*A Critical and Exegetical Commentary on the Gospel According to Saint Matthew*, 1:685).

we do this all the time, and we are right in doing it. It may not always happen, but surprisingly these things do happen most of the time.[641]

However, if 7:7 is an invitation to seek the kingdom, 7:8 need have
no exceptions. The point of the statement is that no one who seeks
the kingdom will be denied entrance. The "all" (*pas*) may fit with
the prominent theme of inclusion of the Gentiles in God's redemptive plan (28:19–20). It may also imply that even though people are
evil, those who seek to enter the kingdom by the narrow gate will be
granted access. Thus "all" includes not only Gentiles but also notorious sinners that most would expect to be excluded from the kingdom.
Even these would be invited into the kingdom when they repented
and followed Jesus (Matt 21:31–32).

Jesus illustrated the Father's eagerness to meet the spiritual needs
of His children by pointing to an earthly father's eagerness to meet the
physical needs of his children. Both the grammar and the context of
7:9–10 show that Jesus assumed a negative response to His questions.
In the Greek language, one may phrase a question in a manner that
implies an affirmative response, a negative response, or implies no
response at all. Here Jesus phrased His question using the negative *mē*
which anticipates a negative response: "of course not."[642]

Interestingly Jesus saw the need to limit the pool of fathers under
consideration to those in His immediate audience. Rather than simply asking "What man," He qualified, "What man among you." Some
fathers are so wicked as to offer stones to starving sons or snakes to
hungry daughters, and Jesus knew it. By limiting the example to His
current audience, Jesus prevented these unusual cases from spoiling
His illustration.

The small loaves of bread that constituted the normal daily diet
of Palestinians Jews in the first century resembled both in shape and
color the small round and flat stones that littered the countryside.
In Matt 4:3, the tempter had appealed to the similar appearance of
stones and bread in his command, "If You are the Son of God, tell
these stones to become bread." Earthly fathers cannot turn stones into
bread, but through a wicked bait and switch, they could substitute
stones for bread. The stones were not only inedible but could easily

---

[641] Betz, *The Sermon on the Mount*, 505.
[642] See "μή," BDAG, 646. Usage 3 is "marker of expectation of a negative answer to a question." See also BDF §427.

break the teeth of a trusting child who attempted to bite and chew them or choke a child who attempted to swallow them. Similarly, serpents bear some resemblance to fish. Like fish they have scales and propel themselves with a winding movement. Yet, rather than serving as a healthy and acceptable diet, serpents were declared unfit for human consumption in OT dietary laws. Because snakes belong to the category of anything that moves on its "belly" (Gen 3:14), they were "detestable" and were not to be eaten under any circumstances. Furthermore, if the snake were alive or improperly prepared and cooked, its venom could kill the one to whom it was given.

Jesus acknowledged that none among His hearers would give a hungry child a stone or snake even though "you are evil." The choice of the pronoun "you" (*humeis*) rather than "we" (*hēmeis*) implies that Jesus has a different moral nature than those in His audience. The specificity of the pronoun recalls 3:15 in which Jesus claimed that by the act of baptism He fulfilled "all righteousness." The pronoun suits well the doctrine of Jesus' sinless perfection affirmed elsewhere in the NT (2 Cor 5:21; Heb 4:15; 7:26–28; 1 Pet 1:19; 1 John 3:3).[643] The statement may also imply that Jesus has shifted attention from His disciples to others in His audience. In light of the use of the adjective "evil" in Matthew, it is difficult to imagine that Jesus intended to describe His disciples in this manner. Earlier He described His disciples as "pure in heart" (5:8), those "who are persecuted for righteousness" (v. 10), those whose good works "give glory to your Father in heaven" (v. 16), and those whose righteousness "surpasses that of the scribes and Pharisees" (v. 20). The new Moses has led His people on a new exodus that liberates them from slavery to sin (1:21). In Him the new covenant has been sealed and enacted (26:28; Jer 31:31–33) so that God's law is written on their hearts and they have become like good trees bearing good fruit (Matt 7:17–19), good men who produce good things from their storeroom filled with good things (12:35).[644]

Verse 11 does not necessarily imply that those in Jesus' audience were already children of God. It does imply that the blessings of the

[643] See also Davies and Allison, *A Critical and Exegetical Commentary on the Gospel According to Saint Matthew*, 1:683–84.

[644] Alternatively the description of Jesus' audience as "evil" may include even the disciples and simply be part of the argument from the lesser to the greater. Although Jesus' disciples have experienced a radical transformation and are characterized by a righteousness that vastly exceeds that of others, in comparison to God's holiness the good of the disciple ranks as evil. See Luz, *Matthew: A Commentary*, 1:359.

kingdom are reserved only for those who are children of God. The entire argument from lesser to greater depends on the hearers' identity as children of the heavenly Father, for it is His fatherly love that compels Him to grant entrance into the kingdom and to bestow kingdom blessings.

It is difficult to determine when the promises in 7:7–8 and 11 will be fulfilled. Verses 7 and 11 use the future tense, and it is possible, perhaps likely, that these tenses are eschatological futures.[645] The future tense was used in 6:33 to speak of a promise fulfilled in the immediate future. Matthew 7:5–6 also uses the future to speak of events that will soon occur. The gnomic future, the use of the future tense to state a general timeless principle, was used in 6:24 and 7:16,20. Still, the context of the SM strongly suggests that these promises will be finally and completely fulfilled only at Jesus' return. As shown above, these promises relate to kingdom entrance. Matthew 7:21–24 shows that kingdom entrance occurs "on that day." This great day is the day of reckoning and judgment that will occur at the time of Jesus' return. The eschatological reference must be understood, however, in light of the inaugurated eschatology that was apparent in the Beatitudes. Jesus' disciples experience many of the blessings of the kingdom here and now although these blessings will only be fully experienced in the eschaton. The commands to begin and keep on asking, seeking, and knocking show that those who are contemplating a life of discipleship should not delay. They should regard entrance into the kingdom as an urgent priority now. Nevertheless they will enjoy the full benefits of the kingdom only when Jesus returns.

The "therefore" (oun) that begins verse 12 clearly demonstrates that the verse draws an inference or makes an application of principles stated in the preceding context. At the very least, the "therefore" points to the immediately preceding verses (7–11) that focused on the generous nature of the heavenly Father.[646] Repeatedly in the SM, Jesus had applied the principle of the "imitation of the Father" in His instructions for His disciples. The disciples are children of the heavenly Father who have partaken of His holy character and are to imitate His example (5:44–45,48). Since the Father selflessly gives to meet the

---

[645] See Matt. 6:4,6.
[646] Adolph von Schlatter, *Der Evangelist Matthäus: seine Sprache, sein Ziel, seine Selbständigkeit* (Stuttgart: Calwer, 1959), 246; Gundry, *Matthew*, 125.

needs of His children, disciples should also seek to treat others the way they want to be treated.[647]

Strong evidence suggests, however, that the "therefore" looks both to and beyond the immediately preceding verses. The mention of "the Law and the Prophets" in both 7:11 and 5:17 intentionally form an *inclusio* that brackets this major section of the Sermon.[648] Consequently 7:12 summarizes and concludes Jesus' interpretation and application of the Law (5:17–48), His instruction related to deeds of righteousness (6:1–18), and His instruction for life in this world including both one's relationship to possessions (6:19–34) and to people (7:1–6), as well as 7:7–11. This structural clue led Allison to conclude that 7:12 is "in true rabbinic fashion—a general rule which is not only the quintessence of the law and the prophets but also the quintessence of the sermon on the mount and thus the quintessence of Jesus' teaching in general."[649] Matthew 7:12, like 5:48, stands as the highest expression of the extraordinary righteousness that should characterize Jesus' disciples (5:20).

This principle is known to many as the "Golden Rule," a name for the principle that dates to at least as early as the end of the Middle Ages.[650] Contrary to popular opinion, this name was not inspired by the preciousness of this important moral principle. This name relates to accounts claiming that the Emperor Alexander Severus had Matt 7:12 inscribed in gold on the wall of his throne room.[651]

Jesus described this principle as "the Law and the Prophets." The point is that verse 12 is the summation of the essence of the character God required of His people in the OT. This statement is similar to 22:34–40 in which Jesus answered the question, "Which

[647] Chrysostom suggested another kind of connection with 7:7–11 (*Hom. Matt.*). He saw 7:12 as a statement of the requirement for God hearing and answering one's prayers as promised in the preceding verses. However, the use of the οὖν elsewhere in the sermon (5:19,23,48; 6:2,8–9,22–23,31,34; 7:11–12,24), better supports the view above.

[648] Davies and Allison, *A Critical and Exegetical Commentary on the Gospel According to Saint Matthew*, 1:685–86; France, *The Gospel of Matthew*, 145; Guelich, *The Sermon on the Mount*, 361–62; McNeile, *The Gospel According to St. Matthew*, 93. Guelich affirmed this not on structural grounds but because the conjunction "does not follow logically from what precedes." Broadus (*The Gospel According to Matthew*, 160) appears to have noticed the *inclusio* and agreed with Luther that 7:12 is a "recapitulary inference, from all that he has been teaching concerning the righteousness required of his people."

[649] Davies and Allison, *A Critical and Exegetical Commentary on the Gospel According to Saint Matthew*, 1:686.

[650] Betz, *The Sermon on the Mount*, 509. Compare Keener, *The Gospel of Matthew*, 248.

[651] France, *The Gospel of Matthew*, 145.

commandment in the law is the greatest?" Jesus pointed to Deut 6:5 and Lev 19:18, which called for love for God and love for others respectively. Jesus then concluded, "All the Law and the Prophets depend on these two commands" (Matt 22:40). Matthew 5:43–48 also demonstrates that expressing the Father's love to others including one's enemies is the most crucial factor in being holy as He is holy (Lev 11:44–45; 19:2; 20:7).

Several parallels to Jesus' teaching are known to have existed in Jewish literature from the Second Temple period. Tobit 4:15 said, "And what you hate, do not do to anyone."[652] Similarly *b. Šabb.* 31a said,

> A certain heathen came before Shammai and said to him, "Make me a proselyte, on condition that you teach me the whole Torah while I stand on one foot." Thereupon he repulsed him with the builder's cubit which was in his hand. When he went before Hillel, he said to him, "What is hateful to you, do not do to your neighbour: that is the whole Torah, while the rest is commentary thereon; go and learn it."

Other Jewish texts from the period show that the principle of not treating others in a manner in which one did not want to be treated was prevalent and popular. Jesus' teaching is more powerful and demanding than the more commonly affirmed principle. It calls for disciples to do more than merely refrain from undesirable treatment of others; it urges them to act positively for the benefit of others.

Although earlier generations of Christian scholars have insisted that the positive form of Jesus' teaching was completely novel, at least one Jewish text comes close to the principle that Jesus taught. Sirach 31:15 said, "Judge your neighbor's feelings by your own, and in every matter be thoughtful."[653] The command to be considerate of others' feelings and to recognize that their feelings are probably similar to those one would have in an identical situation resonates with the underlying principle of Jesus' command. Positive expressions of the principle also appear in the writings of ancient figures such as Homer, Herodotus, Isocrates, and Seneca.[654] However, the force of Jesus' command does not depend on its innovation. Much of the material in the sermon is an insightful application of principles of righteousness

---

[652] Cp. NRSV.
[653] Cp. NRSV.
[654] J. P. Meier, *Matthew*, New Testament Message (Wilmington, DE: Glazier, 1980), 70.

revealed in the OT. It is not surprising that others observed these principles as well.[655]

Despite some commonality between the Golden Rule and Jewish moral principles, Jesus developed and modeled the principle in ways that were truly unique. This uniqueness made His teaching astonishing and led the crowds to recognize His superiority to the scribes (Matt 7:28). Broadus recognized the similarity between Jesus' teaching and that of His predecessors. However, he noted, "The real novelty of Christian ethics lies in the fact that Christianity offers not only instruction in moral duty, but spiritual help in acting accordingly."[656] Jesus not only commanded His disciples to live in accord with the Golden Rule; He also empowered them to do so through the new exodus, the new creation, and the new covenant.[657]

---

[655] Some commentators have heavily criticized the negative expression of the principle in order to demonstrate the superiority of the form in the SM. However, negative critiques of the standard form of the principle are unwise since both a variant reading of the NT (Acts 15:20,29) and another early Christian text (*Did.* 1:2) quote the principle favorably.

[656] Broadus, *The Gospel According to Matthew*, 161.

[657] See the section "Theological Framework for the Interpretation of the Sermon on the Mount" in the introduction.

Chapter 7

THE CONCLUSION TO THE SERMON (7:13–8:1)

A. *Two Roads and Gates (7:13–14)*

Jesus commanded His disciples to "enter" (from *eiserchomai*) through the narrow gate. He typically used this same verb to describe entering the kingdom of heaven (Matt 5:20; 7:21; 18:3; 19:23–24; 23:13) or entering into life (18:8–9; 19:17). The two expressions mean roughly the same thing as a comparison of 19:17 with 19:23 shows.[1] Thus the narrow gate probably marks the entrance into the kingdom and into life. The use of the aorist imperative *eiselthate* ("enter") stresses both the huge importance and great urgency of entering the kingdom.[2]

Matthew 7:7–11 stressed the ease with which one enters the kingdom. Kingdom entrance is a divine gift prompted by the grace of a good and thoughtful Father. One gains entrance into the kingdom through simply asking, searching, and knocking. God grants entrance into the kingdom in response to the disciple's request. He reveals the kingdom for which the hopeful disciple searches. He opens the door which no man has the ability to open on his own.[3] Verses 13–14 now balance that earlier teaching by candidly warning the disciples that kingdom entrance and kingdom living will be accompanied by difficulty.

Jesus first warned that the entrance into the kingdom is restrictive: "Enter through the narrow gate." The gate is metaphorical. Jesus did not intend to suggest that an actual gate grants entry through a literal wall that surrounds His domain. Instead the gate is a metaphor for the entrance of the disciple into the kingdom. Depending on the view that one adopts regarding the relationship of the gate to the road in verses 13–14, the gate may represent either repentance of sin and confession of Jesus as Lord here and now (3:2; 4:17; 7:7–11,21)[4]

---

[1] Broadus, *The Gospel According to Matthew*, 163–64.

[2] Wallace, *Greek Grammar Beyond the Basics*, 720.

[3] See Rev 3:7.

[4] This is apparently the interpretation adopted by the author of Hermas *Sim.* 9.12.5 §89: "For if you want to enter some city, and that city is walled all around and has only one gate, can you enter that city except by the gate it has?" "How, sir," I said, "could it be otherwise?"

or passing the scrutiny of eschatological judgment on the last day (7:21–23). As discussed earlier, people in the first century knocked on gates seeking entrance into the outer courtyard of an estate (Acts 12:13). Thus the reference to knocking in Matt 7:7 likely anticipates this reference to the gate of the kingdom.

The adjective "narrow" (*stenos*) in Matt 7:13 demonstrates that entrance into the kingdom is restrictive and highlights the exclusive nature of the kingdom. Because the gate is narrow, few people enter through it at a time. The definite article that modifies the noun "gate" is probably monadic and indicates that this gate is the only one of its kind, the only gate that leads to life.[5] One cannot enter the kingdom except by this single means. The mention of the narrow gate would probably have prompted the ancient reader to envision a small door-like passage in a city wall whose location was known only to the citizens of the city. This small gate would be the only means of entrance into the city at night or during times of danger when the large gates were closed and barred.[6]

This narrow gate that leads to life stands in stark contrast to the wide gate that leads to destruction (v. 13). A wide gate permitted people to enter *en masse* and thus portrays the popularity of the route to destruction. Those who choose the kingdom may find that they do so alone. Those who reject the strict demands of the kingdom will have plenty of company. The word order initially suggests that the clause "there are many who go through it" refers to the broad road that leads to destruction. However, the Greek verb *eiserchomai* refers to the act of entering and the phrase "through it" probably identifies the point of entrance.[7] Thus the clause is most likely a brief commentary explaining the significance of the wide gate specifically.

"If, therefore, you cannot enter the city except through its gate," he said, "so too a man cannot enter the kingdom of God except by the name of his Son, who was loved by him." Parable 9 may have been part of a later interpolation from the first half of the second century. See Holmes, *The Apostolic Fathers*, 331.

[5] Wallace, *Greek Grammar Beyond the Basics*, 223–24. See Hermas *Sim.* 9.12.5 ("That city is walled and has only one gate."); and 4 *Ezra* 7:6–10.

[6] See J. Jeremias, "πύλη," *TDNT*, 6 (1968):923 for the use of "gate" in eschatological passages.

[7] This view takes the διά as spatial. For parallels see 2 Chr 23:20; Jer 17:25; Lam 4:12; Ezek 44:2; John 10:1–2. Broadus argued that the antecedent of the αὐτῆς could be "road" since Matt 8:28 used a compound of ἔρχομαι and the prepositional phrase διὰ τῆς ὁδοῦ to speak of passing through by means of a road. Nevertheless the distinct meanings of εἰσέρχομαι and παρέρχομαι create a difficulty for reading 7:13 in light of 8:28. See "εἰσέρχομαι," BDAG, 293, esp. 1.a.g.

The road that leads to destruction is broad, and the road that leads to life is tight or constrictive. The adjectival participle *tethlimmenē* is translated "difficult" in the HCSB because the verb often refers to experiencing difficulty or persecution (2 Cor 1:6; 4:8; 7:5; 1 Thess 3:4; 2 Thess 1:6–7; 1 Tim 5:10; Heb 11:37). However, when the verb is used to describe places, cities, or living quarters, it typically means "tight," "cramped," "congested," or "narrow." Furthermore, since the word is clearly contrasted with an adjective meaning "broad," "spacious," or "roomy" (*euruchōros*) in this context, it likely means "narrow."

This does not mean that the narrow gate and the narrow road both depict the restrictiveness and exclusivity of the kingdom. Although many leading commentators argue that the two metaphors have the same referent (i.e., the rigors of discipleship), the two images are probably not entirely redundant.[8] The gate is an entry point into the kingdom. One passes through it in a moment. A road or path, however, is something on which one travels for a more prolonged period of time. Indeed, the Greek term "road" (*hodos*) frequently referred metaphorically to the course of one's behavior or a way of life.[9] The gate thus seems to symbolize some critical moment of decision while the road symbolizes a lifestyle.

Scholars debate whether the long narrow path leads up to the gate or the path commences at the gate. Those who see the path leading up to the gate view the path as a metaphor for one's way of life and the gate as a metaphor for the critical moment at which one is assigned his eternal destiny in eschatological judgment.[10] Thus the

---

The verb παρέρχομαι would normally require the accusative of direct object to identify the area through which one passed. See "παρέρχομαι," BDAG, 776, esp. 6.

[8] Hagner (*Matthew 1–13*, 179) states, "The two metaphors refer together to the same thing." A similar position was taken by Guelich, *The Sermon on the Mount*, 388; Gundry, *Matthew*, 127; Davies and Allison, *A Critical and Exegetical Commentary on the Gospel According to Saint Matthew*, 1:698. France also coalesces the two metaphors but does so based on the doubtful conclusion that the words ἡ πύλη ("the gate") were originally absent from 7:14 (*The Gospel of Matthew*, 146). However, the manuscript evidence supporting the inclusion of the words is, in the words of the editorial committee, "overwhelming." For a defense of the inclusion of these words see Metzger, *Textual Commentary on the Greek New Testament*, 19.

[9] "ὁδός," BDAG, 692.

[10] Gibbs, *Matthew 1:1–11:1*, 383–84; Nolland, *The Gospel of Matthew*, 332–33; Luz, *Matthew: A Commentary*, 1:372; Schnackenburg, *The Gospel of Matthew*, 77. Betz affirmed this order but argues that the "rough road" is not a result of the difficult teachings of the SM or anti-Christian persecution but is instead a reference to the ordinary struggles of life (*The Sermon on the Mount*, 521–23).

narrow road represents a life guided by the precepts of the SM and the gate represents the entrance into the eschatological kingdom that will be granted by God to the faithful disciple. Those who see the gate as marking the beginning of the path view the gate as a metaphor for the disciples' initial commitment to follow Jesus and the path as a metaphor for the life of discipleship.[11] Morris summarized this latter view well: "Matthew's Jesus is appealing *both* for an evangelical decision (the gate) *and* for an ethical endurance (the way)."[12]

A decision between these two options is difficult. Several considerations favor viewing the gate as the beginning point of a road that leads to another destination. First, the word order lends support to this interpretation. In both verses 13 and 14, the gate is consistently mentioned before the road. Second, the similarities between Matt 7:13–14 and Luke 13:24 favor this view. Some commentators argue that since Luke 13:24 is clearly eschatological, the parallel supports an identification of the gate with eschatological judgment.[13] However, Luke's "door" represents a decision that must be made in this life before one faces eschatological judgment, before the door to the kingdom is closed and locked by the Master.[14] Thus if Luke's narrow door and Matthew's narrow gate share the same referent (and this is uncertain given the significant differences between the two texts), the gate must represent the decision to repent and follow Jesus that marks the beginning of the Christian life. Also if the narrow road led to the narrow gate, the reference to "finding" the narrow gate would be odd.[15]

On the other hand, several weighty considerations favor the view that the road leads up to and ends at the gate. First, the vocabulary

---

[11] Carson, "Matthew," 189 (citing Groschiede and Hendrickson in support); Keener, *The Gospel of Matthew*, 250–51; Morris, *The Gospel of Matthew*, 175; and Wilkins, *Matthew*, 322. Wilkins described this view as the majority position. However, this is doubtful. Most of the commentators that Wilkins listed as affirming this position (Betz, France, and Davies-Allison) actually seem to hold other views. Betz argues that the gate lies at the end of the road. He entertained the possibility that the narrow gate refers to the Beatitudes and the road referred to the lifelong struggle to implement the teachings of the SM, but he viewed this interpretation as "less probable." France and Davies-Allison suggest that the gate and the road are two different metaphors for the same referent.

[12] Morris, *The Gospel of Matthew*, 175 (italics his).

[13] See Allen, *A Critical and Exegetical Commentary on the Gospel According to Saint Matthew*, 68.

[14] See Green, *The Gospel of Luke*, 528–29; Marshall, *The Gospel of Luke*, 564–65; Plummer, *A Critical and Exegetical Commentary on the Gospel According to Saint Luke*, 346.

[15] This point is acknowledged even by scholars who adopt the former view. See Nolland, *The Gospel of Matthew*, 334.

of the text supports this view. In Matthew, the word "road" (*hodos*) seems to refer exclusively to the roads outside the city.[16] When Matthew spoke of wide roads inside the city, he used the term *plateia* (Matt 12:19); and when he spoke of narrow lanes inside the city, he used the term *hrumē* (6:2). Furthermore when Matthew referred to the exit from a city at which a highway to another city begins, he used the term *diexodos* (Matt 22:9). One would expect to find this term here as well if Matthew intended to portray the gate as opening up to the road. Instead, Matthew used the term *pulē*, thus prompting his readers to imagine a gate to which the road leads. This vocabulary would likely prompt readers to envision a road leading to a city gate.

Second, the term "gate" was frequently associated with eschatological images in ancient literature. The expression "gates of Hades" appears in the OT, later Jewish literature, and even in the works of pagan writers.[17] Matthew used the expression in 16:18[18] and the metaphor also appears in Rev 1:18. The ancients also spoke of the "gates of the blessed" or "the gates of heaven."[19] Third, Matt 7:21 uses the future tense of the verb *eiserchomai*, the verb translated "enter" in 7:13, to describe entrance into the kingdom at eschatological judgment.[20] This suggests that the use of the verb in 7:13 points to an eschatological event as well.

Fourth, the command "enter" probably has an implied object "kingdom" or "life," as discussed earlier. Nearly all other references to entering the kingdom in Matthew are clearly eschatological (5:20; 18:3; 19:23–24; 25:10).[21] References to entering life are exclusively eschatological (18:8–9; 19:17). Although "life" and the "kingdom"

[16] Besides his quotations of the LXX and his metaphorical uses, Matthew used the word ὁδός 13 times. These occurrences are 2:12; 5:25; 8:28; 10:10; 13:4,19; 15:32; 20:17,30; 21:8,19; and 22:9–10.

[17] OT occurrences include Pss 9:13; 107:18; Job 38:17; Is 38:10. See also Wis 16:13; 3 Macc 5:51; *Pss. Sol.* 16:2; 1QH 6:24; *Sib. Or.* 2.228. For occurrences in pagan literature, see Keener, *The Gospel of Matthew*, 428–29.

[18] For a good overview of the history of interpretation, see J. P. Lewis, "The Gates of Hell Shall Not Prevail Against It (Matt 16:18): A Study of the History of Interpretation," *JETS* 38 (1995): 349–67.

[19] For the former expression, see *Sib. Or.* 3.770. For the latter, see *1 Enoch* 9.10; *3 Enoch* 10.102; *3 Bar.* 6.13. For the phrase "gates of heaven" in secular Greek, see Homer, *Il.* 5.749.

[20] See comments on Matt 7:21–23.

[21] A possible exception is Matt 23:13. Davies and Allison seem correct when they note: "The present tenses (contrast Luke) probably imply the presence of the kingdom" (*A Critical and Exegetical Commentary on the Gospel According to Saint Matthew*, 3:287).

are virtually synonymous, as argued earlier, "life" is explicitly mentioned in 7:14 and the kingdom is not. "Life" (*zōē*) forms a more natural contrast with "destruction" (*apōleia*) than does "kingdom." This serves to enrich the eschatological flavor of the parable.

The closest parallel to Jesus' teaching in Second-Temple Jewish literature also supports this understanding. *Fourth Ezra* 7:6–10 said:

> There is a city built and set on a plain, and it is full of all good things; but the entrance to it is narrow and set in a precipitous place, so that there is fire on the right hand and deep water on the left; and there is only one path lying between them, this is, between the fire and the water, so that only one man can walk upon that path. If now that city is given to a man for an inheritance, how will the heir receive his inheritance unless he passes through the danger set before him?

Metzger correctly identified this passage as among several close parallels between *4 Ezra* and the NT, but he qualified this observation by noting that "none of them suggests direct dependence." However, the document dates to AD 100–120 and was written by a Jewish author. Thus it illustrates how members of Jesus' audience might have envisioned the scene described in His illustration.[22]

Finally, the evidence in favor of the gate-to-road view is not compelling. The word order does not require that the gate precede the road. The gate is mentioned first because of the great importance of the eschatological judgment that is the focus of 7:15–27, a topic introduced in verses 13–14. The parallel with Luke 13:24 is a loose one. Most commentators admit that they are unsure whether Matt 7:13–14 and Luke 13:24 belong to the same traditions.[23] Although it is difficult to imagine how some might fail to "find" the gate if the narrow road leads directly to it, the antecedent of the pronoun *autēn* in Matt 7:14 could be "road" or "life" rather than "gate." Difficulty in locating a small path leading to a narrow gate would be fully comprehensible.

Although the choice between these two interpretations cannot be easily made, the balance of evidence favors the view that Matthew describes a road leading to a gate. Thus the road refers to a person's

---

[22] See Metzger, "The Fourth Book of Ezra," *OTP*, 1:517–59.

[23] Hagner concluded, "It may well be that here we see two independent, though similar, logia passed down by oral tradition" (*Matthew 1–13*, 178). See the sane judgment regarding the issue in Davies and Allison (*A Critical and Exegetical Commentary on the Gospel According to Saint Matthew*, 1:695). Luz, on the other hand, argued that the two parallels both derive from Q (*Matthew: A Commentary*, 1:370).

life, and the gate refers to the eschatological judgment that will result from his life choices.

The description of the path as narrow could constitute a warning that the disciple's life will be plagued with hardship and will entail persecution. Since the verb *thlibō* can mean "narrow" or refer to an act of persecution, the Greek text may entail a double entendre in which a narrow path portrays a persecuted life. On the other hand this is the only occurrence of this verb in Matthew. Matthew does not elsewhere use this verb to describe the persecution of believers.[24] Instead he preferred the verb *diōkō* to refer to persecution.[25] Furthermore the perfect tense of the participle is rather odd if Matthew wished to use the narrow path to portray the persecution of believers. The perfect tense normally describes an action that was completed in the past but has present, ongoing results. One would have expected Matthew to have used a present participle if he wished to describe the continuing experience of persecution by the disciples. Finally this interpretation ignores the rich OT background which likely informed Jesus' usage of the imagery of the narrow and wide paths.

Several evidences suggest that the narrow road depicts the restrictive nature of the life chosen by Jesus' disciples. First, later in Matthew's Gospel, the word "road" (*hodos*) was used in an ethical sense. In 21:32 the word refers to the "way of righteousness." In 22:16 the word is used in the phrase "the way of God," which is apparently a lifestyle of obedience to God. This suggests that the metaphorical use of the word "road" in 7:13–14 may have ethical connotations as well.

Second, both the OT and the NT use the metaphor "walk" to describe one's ethical or moral lifestyle. This same usage was prevalent in rabbinic literature. Literature addressing the way one should live was described as Halakah, a Hebrew word meaning "the walk." The "path" or "road" on which one walks typically portrayed ethical or moral guidelines that direct behavior (Judg 2:22; Isa 30:21; Jer 6:16; 2 John 6).

The OT does not specifically mention a wide road or narrow road. However, it offers several descriptions of the road that leads to destruction and the road that leads to life. These descriptions confirm

---

[24] Matthew did use the related noun θλῖψις four times in his Gospel to refer to persecution or tribulation. See Matt 13:21; 24:9,21,29.

[25] Matthew used διώκω six times (5:10–12,44; 10:23; 23:34). See also the related term διωγμός in 13:21.

the hypothesis that the metaphor of the "road" in Matthew refers to one's ethical or moral lifestyle.

First, the OT portrays the road that leads to destruction as a path traveled by the wicked who urge all others to join them in their sins. Proverbs 1:10–16 says,

> My son, if sinners entice you, don't be persuaded. If they say—"Come with us! Let's set an ambush and kill someone. Let's attack some innocent person just for fun! Let's swallow them alive, like Sheol, still healthy as they go down to the Pit. We'll find all kinds of valuable property and fill our houses with plunder. Throw in your lot with us, and we'll all share our money"—my son, don't travel that road with them or set foot on their path, because their feet run toward trouble, and they hurry to commit murder.

Sinners entice others to join them as they engage in their wicked acts. "Come with us," they shout. "Throw in your lot with us," they cheer. But God urges His people, "Don't travel that road with them or set foot on their path." Like the wide road of the SM, this road leads inevitably to destruction. Proverbs 1:17–19 concludes, "It is foolish to spread a net where any bird can see it, but they set an ambush to kill themselves; they attack their own lives. Such are the paths of all who make profit dishonestly; it takes the lives of those who receive it."

Proverbs 4 calls this road "the path of the wicked," and "the way of evil ones" (v. 14), and "the way of the wicked" (v. 19). Proverbs 5 confirms that the path of the wicked leads to destruction. Though the forbidden woman's lips "drip honey and her words are smoother than oil," (v. 3), "her feet go down to death; her steps head straight for Sheol. She doesn't consider the path of life: she doesn't know that her ways are unstable" (vv. 5–6).

Jesus described this path that leads to destruction as a wide road, in part, because it is traveled by the majority of people. The number of the sinners who travel on it seems to grow continually as they prod others to join with them. Jesus may also have described the road as wide because a wide road allows plenty of room for weaving back and forth and provides a vivid picture of a lifestyle with few moral constraints. The wide road offers enough moral latitude that each person can do what is right in his own eyes.[26]

---

[26] Broadus came close to this view when he contrasted the wide road with the narrow road thusly: "In the one, men can wander heedlessly, and roam about at pleasure in the broad spaces; the other requires to be pursued with great care and exactness" (*The Gospel According to Matthew*, 164). He later added, "The way to life is fenced in on either side by God's requirements

The OT also described the path of righteousness that leads to life. The OT portrayed the law as a narrow path from which the godly should not deviate "to the right or the left." After the Ten Commandments were given, Moses commanded, "Be careful to do as the LORD your God has commanded you; you are not to turn aside to the right or the left" (Deut 5:32). Similarly the Law commanded Israel's king to write a copy of the instructions for the king on a scroll in the presence of the priests and to read it every day for as long as he lived "so that he may learn to fear the LORD his God, to observe all the words of this instruction, and to do these statutes . . . he will not turn from this command to the right or the left" (Deut 17:19–20). After God announced the blessings that His people would enjoy if they fulfilled their covenant with Him, God urged, "Do not turn aside to the right or the left from all the things I am commanding you today" (28:14). God instructed Joshua, "Above all, be strong and very courageous to carefully observe the whole instruction My servant Moses commanded you. Do not turn from it to the right or the left, so that you will have success wherever you go" (Josh 1:7).

Second Kings 22:2 portrayed Josiah as one who fulfilled the instructions for the king in Deuteronomy 17: "He [Josiah] did what was right in the LORD's sight and walked in all the ways of his ancestor David; he did not turn to the right or the left."

God's commands were "narrow" in the sense that they left no room for deviation. They required a straight walk from which one could not turn either to the right or to the left. In contrast to a wide road that leaves plenty of moral latitude, the narrow road is restrictive and morally and ethically confining. It establishes clear boundaries for one's behavior that are not to be crossed. Jesus taught His disciples

(Deut 5:32; Prov 4:27; Isa 30:21)" (ibid., 165). Although Calvin's commentary leaps immediately to application of the passage, his application hints that he too saw the broad road as a metaphor for complete moral freedom and the narrow road as a life with tight moral restrictions: "Men are so permissive towards themselves, so uncontrolled, and lax, that Christ here tells His disciples to get themselves onto the narrow and thorny road. As it is unpleasant to force our desires away from their free and unrestricted career, He relieves the pain, by the glad compensation of telling us, that by this narrow gate and path, we enter life" (A Harmony of the Gospels, 232). Hagner also approaches this view when he writes, "There are no significant demands to be met, no discipline to acquire, in order to go through this gate and down this path" (Matthew 1–13, 179). Filson likewise stated, "Those who take the broad, spacious way resent the limiting demands of loyalty and discipline; their way seems comfortable and sensible, but it leads to full and final spiritual disaster" (A Commentary on the Gospel According to St. Matthew, 106). Similarly, Gundry remarked: "The broad way represents the antinomian course of least resistance" (Matthew, 127).

that the parameters for their walk were clearly defined by the moral teachings of the OT (Matt 5:19) and His own teachings about kingdom living in the SM (5:1–7:27). Thus the narrow road is probably to be understood as a lifestyle that respects the ethical parameters for life that God has established; it is the path of obedience.

The book of Proverbs offers several descriptions of this path of righteousness. Proverbs 4:18 says, "The path of the righteous is like the light of dawn, shining brighter and brighter until midday." Proverbs 4:25–27 adds, "Let your eyes look forward; fix your gaze straight ahead. Carefully consider the path for your feet, and all your ways will be established. Don't turn to the right or to the left; keep your feet away from evil."

Significantly Prov 5:6 and 15:24 call the path of righteousness "the path of life" and contrast it with the path that leads to Sheol. Jesus' reference to the narrow road that leads to life and the path that leads to destruction would be reminiscent of these OT references to His original first-century Jewish audience.[27] Luz is thus correct when he concludes, "The difficult way, which under afflictions leads the few to the narrow gate, is the way of righteousness described in the Sermon on the Mount."[28] Likewise Betz suggested, "The motif of the Two Ways also operates as a literary device in the sense that the teachings of the SM describe 'the way of life' to be lived by the faithful disciples."[29]

This interpretation is an ancient one. The *Didache* begins by announcing, "There are two ways, one of life and one of death, and there is a great difference between these ways." The *Didache* defines the way of life by quoting Deut 6:5; Lev 19:18, a paraphrase of the Golden Rule, and with numerous other references to the SM.[30] The way of death is a lifestyle opposite that demanded by the SM.[31]

The restrictive nature of the gate and the road are emphasized by the exclamation "how" (*ti*), which expresses shock or amazement at extent or degree.[32] The gate is exclusive, and the path is restrictive.

---

[27] See also Isa 35:1–10, esp. 8–10; and Jer 21:8.

[28] Luz, *Matthew: A Commentary*, 1:372. Gundry noted, "By setting the two roadways alongside the two gates, Matthew shows that entrance into life at the last day requires traveling the narrow way—living the life of surpassing righteousness—in the present time" (*Matthew*, 127).

[29] Betz, *The Sermon on the Mount*, 523.

[30] See *Did.* 1:1–4:12.

[31] Ibid., 5:1–6:2.

[32] Some manuscripts have the causal conjunction ὅτι ("because") instead of τί. These include both ℵ and B. The use of τί as an exclamatory expression was distinctively Semitic. The LXX frequently used τί to translate the Hebrew מָה (Pss 3:2; 139:17; Song 1:10; 7:7). The omicron

The narrowness of the gate and the path make them easy to overlook. Thus few people "find" it (Matt 7:14). As discussed earlier, the antecedent of "it" (*autēn*: feminine singular) could be "gate," "road," or "life." Since Matt 10:39 and 16:25 refer to a person "finding life," a strong case can be made that the antecedent is "life" herein. Admittedly, the noun often translated as "life" in those two texts is *psuchē* ("soul") rather than the noun *zōē* that Matthew used in 7:14. However, Matthew contrasted the reference to "finding life" with "losing one's life" in a manner that suggests that "finding life" (*zōē*) is roughly equivalent to "finding life" (*psuchē*). The reference in 11:29 to finding rest for one's soul in Jesus' allusion to Jer 6:16 is also similar. Nevertheless the pronoun in Matt 7:13 in the clause "there are many who go through it" likely refers either to the road or gate. The parallelism between verses 13 and 14 suggests that the pronoun in verse 14 refers to either the road or gate as well.

The verb "find" in verse 14 also recalls verse 7 and implies that the masses of humanity pass by this narrow gate or road because they do not properly seek it. Furthermore the verb "find" is used in 13:44 and 46 to describe one who finds a great treasure and a priceless pearl, both metaphors for the kingdom. Thus like the verb "enter," the verb "find" implies that both the gate and the road are associated with the kingdom. In light of its usage in these parables, the verb may hint that the kingdom is so great and precious that one should expend any effort necessary to find the way to enter it.

Because the path is restrictive, few will choose to take it. Most will choose the path that gives them the greatest moral latitude, the freedom to live as they desire whether or not God approves. Although they think they are living life to the fullest, in reality they have forfeited life and embraced a path to destruction. "Destruction" (*apōleia*) speaks of the utter ruin and eternal punishment that those who repudiate Jesus and His teaching will face after eschatological judgment. In the context of the Gospel of Matthew, the term clearly refers to eternal conscious torment and not to annihilation, the mere cessation of existence. John the Baptist described this destruction as "the coming wrath" (3:7). This evoked reminiscences of OT descriptions of God's fury against the unrepentant wicked. John also described this

---

was probably added by a scribe who was unfamiliar with this Semitic use of τί. See "τὶς," BDAG, 1007. See also Metzger, *Textual Commentary on the Greek New Testament*, 19.

destruction as a baptism of fire in which the wicked are burned "with fire that never goes out" (v. 12). Jesus used the image of fire in numerous parables to describe this destruction as well (7:19; 13:30). Jesus used the familiar term "hell" (*geenna*) to refer to this place of punishment (5:22,29–30; 10:28; 18:9; 23:15,33).[33] Jesus described gehenna as a "blazing furnace where there will be weeping and gnashing of teeth" (13:42,50). In 18:8–9 He used the phrases "eternal fire" and "hell-fire" (lit., "gehenna of fire") interchangeably. In the parable of the Unforgiving Servant Jesus portrayed this destruction as an imprisonment in which the wicked are perpetually tortured (18:34).[34] In the parable of the Wedding Banquet and that parable of the Talents Jesus described the eternal state of the wicked as "the outer darkness, where there will be weeping and gnashing of teeth" (22:13; 25:30). He described the destiny of the wicked as "the eternal fire prepared for the Devil and his angels" and "eternal punishment" (25:41,46). The path of moral laxity is thus a dead-end road in the most frightening sense. Horrifying punishment is the destination to which the world insanely rushes.

People need not stumble blindly along, uncertain of where the path they have chosen will ultimately lead. The SM is a road map that marks out the narrow path that leads to life in God's kingdom. Those who ignore the map do so to their own peril.

B. Two Trees and Fruits (Matt 7:15–20)

The relationship of this paragraph to the preceding discussion is not entirely clear. Most likely the topic shifts to false prophets because they were popular leaders who guided the masses on their path to destruction. Jesus urged His disciples to be on a constant alert for these false prophets. The present imperative form of the verb translated "beware" (*prosechō*) implies that the disciples must never let their guard down. The threat of the false prophet is continual; thus the disciples' vigilance must be tireless.

False prophets are those who claim to speak for God but actually deceive people instead. Their lies are effective, and Jesus later warned that they will "deceive many" (24:11). Their ability to deceive would

---

[33] See the discussion on Matt 5:22.

[34] The term βασανιστής (*basanistēs*) that is translated as "jailer" in the main text of the HCSB probably means "torturer" as the marginal reading shows. The term is related to βασανίζω (*basanizō*) which means "to torture." See "βασανιστής," and "βασανίζω," BDAG, 168.

sometimes be enhanced by their performance of "great signs and wonders" (v. 24). The phrase "signs and wonders" appears 19 times in the LXX almost exclusively in reference to the plagues and miracles of the exodus.[35] This implies that some false prophets would have the ability to perform feats that were truly stupendous. That such feats would almost deceive the elect, were it not impossible to do so, is not surprising. Jesus also warned that false prophets would not be a rarity for "many false prophets will rise up" (v. 11).

The threat of false prophets is repeatedly mentioned in ancient Jewish literature. Three different passages in the Mishnah are related to false prophets. The Sages argued that only the greater Sanhedrin could try a suspected false prophet (m. Sanh. 1:5), that the penalty for a convicted false prophet was death by strangulation (m. Sanh. 11:1), and that a false prophet was "one who prophesies concerning something which he has not actually heard or concerning something which was not actually said to him" (m. Sanh. 11:5).

Philo also dealt with the issue of false prophets in his exposition of the ninth commandment against bearing false witness. He described the false prophets as:

> all those persons who pursue the spurious and pretended kind of prophecy are inverting the order of truth by conjectures and guesses, perverting sincerity, and easily influencing those who are of unstable dispositions, as a violent wind, when blowing in a contrary direction, tosses about and overturns vessels without ballast, preventing them from anchoring in the safe havens of truth. For such persons think proper to say whatever they conjecture, not as if they were things which they themselves had found out, but as if they were divine oracles revealed to themselves alone, for the more complete inducement of great and numerous crowds to believe a deceit. Such persons our lawgiver very appropriately calls false prophets, who adulterate the true prophecy, and overshadow what is genuine by their spurious devices. . . . [They are] persons who deliver predictions, practising a lying art of prophecy, and disguising themselves under the specious name of prophetic inspiration, falsely taking the name of God in vain.[36]

Jesus warned that false prophets come "in sheep's clothing but inwardly are ravaging wolves" (Matt 7:15). The expression "ravaging wolves" was probably derived from the OT. Genesis 49:27 says,

---

[35] See LXX Exod 7:3,9; 11:9–10; Deut 4:34; 6:22; 7:19; 11:3; 13:2–3; 26:8; 28:46; 29:2; 34:11; Pss 77:43; 104:27; 134:9, where the plagues and miracles of the exodus are in view. Compare LXX Esth 10:9; and Wis 8:8.

[36] Philo, Spec. Leg. 4:50–52.

"Benjamin is a wolf; he tears his prey."[37] More importantly Ezek 22:27 used the simile of the roaring lion tearing its prey to depict the false prophets of Jerusalem and the image of "wolves tearing their prey, shedding blood, and destroying lives" to portray corrupt officials who use their positions of authority and influence to pursue "unjust gain."[38] Matthew 7:15 may be an intentional allusion to Ezek 22:27. If so, the allusion may hint that greed was a primary motivation of the false prophet, a prominent theme in the early commentary on Matt 7:15 in the *Didache*.

These ravenous wolves wear "sheep's clothing." Elsewhere in Matthew, the term "sheep" was used to refer to Jesus' disciples (Matt 10:16; 26:31). In Jesus' teaching on final judgment, "sheep" represented the nations that received Jesus' representatives and their message (25:32–33). Hence the false prophets disguise themselves as Jesus' disciples in order to live undetected among the sheep of the flock and thus devour the sheep with great ease.

The image of a wolf in sheep's clothing may express awareness of one of Aesop's fables. Aesop was a Greek slave who lived from the seventh to the sixth century BC. Among the hundreds of fables ascribed to him is the fable of the wolf in sheep's clothing:

> Once upon a time a wolf resolved to disguise his appearance in order to secure food more easily. Encased in the skin of a sheep, he pastured with the flock deceiving the shepherd by his costume. In the evening he was shut up by the shepherd in the fold; the gate was closed, and the entrance made thoroughly secure. But the shepherd, returning to the fold during the night to obtain meat for the next day, mistakenly caught up the wolf instead of a sheep, and killed him instantly. Harm seek; harm find.[39]

If Jesus' original hearers or Matthew's original readers were aware of this parable, this allusion might remind them not only of the deceptive nature of the false prophet but also of the coming judgment on the false prophet in which the angry and protective Shepherd would destroy the wolves that had threatened His flock.[40]

[37] LXX: λύκος ἅρπαξ which differs from the phrase in Matt 7:15 only in that it is singular while λύκοι ἅρπαγες is plural.
[38] LXX: λύκοι ἁρπάζοντες. See also Ezek 22:27–28 and Zeph 3:3–4, which mention wolves and prophets.
[39] G. F. Townsend, *Aesop's Fables* (New York: Globusz, 2004), 79.
[40] Keener (*The Gospel of Matthew*, 253) and Davies and Allison noted that Aesop's fables may have circulated during the time of Jesus in Palestine since they clearly influenced some rabbinic texts (*A Critical and Exegetical Commentary on the Gospel According to Saint Matthew*, 1:704).

According to some scholars the "sheep's clothing" worn by the false prophet was a reference to the prophet's mantle like the one described in 1 Kgs 19:13,19; 2 Kgs 2:8,13–14; and Heb 11:37.[41] *First Clement* 17:1 says, "Let us be imitators also of those who went about 'in goatskins and sheepskins,' preaching the coming of Christ. We mean Elijah and Elisha, and likewise Ezekiel, the prophets, and alongside them those ancient men of renown as well." However, most writers in the early church interpreted the sheep's clothing as merely symbolic. The symbolic interpretation is probably correct since, if Matthew had wished to refer to the prophet's distinctive garb, he would likely have used the term "mantle" (*mēlōtē*) instead of clothing (*enduma*) as the former term was used in 1 Kgs 19:13,19; 2 Kgs 2:8,13–14; Heb 11:37; and *1 Clem.* 17:1 to describe the prophet's distinctive garment.

Despite the false prophets' clever attempts to disguise themselves as Christian disciples, Jesus exclaimed, "You'll recognize them by their fruit" (Matt 7:16). The Gospel of Matthew consistently uses the term "fruit" to speak of deeds that reveal the moral character of a person. John the Baptist urged sinners to produce fruits worthy of repentance (3:8). The Gospel also frequently contrasts "good" (*kalos*) fruits with "evil" (*ponēros*) fruits (3:10; 7:17–19; 12:33). Thus the false prophet will lack the extraordinary righteousness that characterizes the genuine disciple (5:20), the righteousness described at length in the SM. This will reveal his true identity.

The prepositional phrase "by their fruit" is in an emphatic position and hints that evaluating the prophet by other means may lead to unreliable conclusions. Attempting to determine whether one was a true prophet by evaluating the accuracy of their prophecies, the effectiveness of their exorcisms, or the power displayed in their miracles might prompt the disciples to accept the false prophet as a true one (7:22–23; 24:24). The prophet's fidelity to and fulfillment of Jesus'

This influence is discussed in H. Schwarzbaum, "Talmudic-Midrashic Affinities of Some Aesopic Fables," *Laographia* 22 (1965): 466–83.

[41] See O. Böcher, "Wölfe in Schafspelzen: Zum religionsgeschichtlichen Hintergrund von Matth 7:15," *ThZ* 24 (1968): 405–26; D. Hill, "False Prophets and Charismatics: Structure and Interpretation in Mt. 7:15–23," *Bib* 57 (1976): 327–48. Luz, who rejects this view, states that it was "often advocated in the early church" (*Matthew: A Commentary*, 1:377). However, Davies and Allison demonstrate that the symbolic interpretation of the "sheep's clothing" was affirmed by most early Christian writers (*A Critical and Exegetical Commentary on the Gospel According to Saint Matthew*, 1:704).

teachings in the SM was the critical criterion for evaluating one who claimed to be a prophet.

This principle was clearly important. The statement "You will recognize them by their fruit" in 7:16 is repeated verbatim in the conclusion of the section in verse 20. Thus the statement forms an *inclusio* that brackets Jesus' teaching about recognizing false prophets.

Jesus explained and confirmed this principle with an agricultural illustration. "Are grapes gathered from thornbushes or figs from thistles?" (v. 16). The question utilizes the negative *mēti* to imply that the question should receive a negative response. The nuance of the grammar may be expressed through the translation, "Grapes are not gathered from thornbushes, are they?" The implied answer is "Of course not!"[42]

The primary point of the statement is that a plant of one species does not produce the fruit of a plant of another species. Grapes and thornbushes as well as figs and thistles are two completely different kinds of plants. In *m. Kil.* 5:8, Rabbi Eliezer argued that the "law of diverse kinds" (Lev 19:19; Deut 22:9–11) prohibited a farmer from allowing thorns to grow in his vineyard. If he allowed thorns to grow in the vineyard, he was not allowed to harvest the surrounding grapes. The analogy demonstrated that even though the false prophets disguised themselves as disciples, true disciples and false prophets were two different kinds of people who would be characterized by two different kinds of behavior.

Such statements were fairly common among ancient teachers. Seneca wrote, "Good does not spring from evil any more than figs grow from olive trees."[43] Epictetus taught, "Such a powerful and invincible thing is the nature of man. For how can a vine be moved to act, not like a vine, but like an olive, or again an olive to act, not like an olive, but like a vine? It is impossible, inconceivable!"[44] Similarly Plutarch argued, "We do not expect the vine to bear figs nor the olive grapes."[45]

Matthew's version of the statement is slightly different from Luke's parallel (Luke 6:44). The most significant difference is that

---

[42] "μήτι," BDAG, 649 describes the particle as a marker that invites a negative response to the question that it introduces and notes that it is more emphatic than the simple μή.

[43] Seneca, *Ep. Mor.* 87.25.

[44] Epictetus, *Diss.* 2.20.18.

[45] Plutarch, *Tranq. An.* 13.

Luke's version associated thorns with figs (rather than grapes as in Matthew) and thistles with grapes (rather than figs as in Matthew). Several explanations of this difference are possible. Jesus may have used this analogy in His teaching on different occasions, and Matthew and Luke may have each preserved one of two different versions of the analogy. However, given the similar literary contexts for the analogy in Matthew and Luke, the two Gospels seem to be referring to the same saying.[46] This suggests that one or both of the Gospels have slightly adapted Jesus' saying.[47] If so, Matthew's version is more likely a refinement of Luke's than vice versa. Both the form and vocabulary of the saying support this.[48] For example, the negative *mēti* that appears in Matthew's version of the saying instead of Luke's more common negative *ou* occurs four times in Matthew, but only twice in Mark and twice in Luke.[49] Thus it is likely a feature of Matthew's revision. Furthermore although Luke's Gospel mentions thorns and a "bramble bush" (*batos*), Matthew refers to thorns and thistles. One can more easily explain reasons why Matthew may have adapted the vocabulary of the saying preserved by Luke than vice versa. The "bramble bush" was the species through which Yahweh manifested His presence to Moses, and Matthew's reverence may have prompted hesitation about associating the plant with evil.[50] More importantly thorns and thistles

[46] See the discussion of the relationship of the SM to the SP in the introduction.

[47] Such adaptations cause no problem for biblical inerrancy since many of the sayings of Jesus in the Gospels are the ancient equivalent of modern indirect quotations that rephrase a statement but faithfully preserve the original intent of the statement.

[48] Matthew's version is phrased as a question while Luke's is phrased as a statement. The form may be a feature of Matthean redaction since statements in material shared with Luke are often phrased as questions in Matthew and since, if one assumes the two-source hypothesis, Matthew rephrases Markan statements as questions while Luke preserves the Markan form. For example see Matt 5:46//Luke 6:32; Matt 5:47//Luke 6:33; Matthew 6:25//Luke 12:23; Matt 6:26//Luke 12:24; Matt 6:30//Luke 12:28; Matt 6:31//Luke 12:29. Matthew 8:29 forms a question from the statement preserved in Mark 5:7//Luke 8:28. Furthermore Matt 19:4–5 forms questions from statements in Mark 10:6–8. Matthew occasionally preserves a question from Mark that Luke deleted entirely. Compare Matt 22:18//Mark 12:15//Luke 20:23; Matt 24:2//Mark 13:2//Luke 21:6; Matt 26:8//Mark 14:4//Luke 7:39. On the other hand Luke sometimes rephrases a Markan question as a statement while Matthew preserves the interrogatory form. See Matt 9:14//Mark 2:18//Luke 5:33. Thus the evidence from form is ambiguous and does not clearly demonstrate whether Matthew or Luke preserved the more original form of the saying. Nevertheless, especially when one considers that material unique to Matthew has a high concentration of questions, the scales tip slightly in favor of Matthew redacting a more original form preserved in Luke.

[49] The negative μήτι appears .18 times in Matthew, .15 times in Mark, and .09 times in Luke for every 1,000 words. Thus even when one accounts for variations in length between the Gospels, the negative is twice as frequent in Matthew as in Luke.

[50] See Exod 3:2–4; Deut 33:16; Mark 12:26; Luke 20:37; Acts 7:30,35.

are far more frequently associated with each other in the LXX and would stir memories of the fall of man (Gen 3:18), so Matthew may have thought that this pair of plants would more clearly represent wickedness to his audience.[51]

This leads the interpreter to suspect that the grouping of grapes with thorns and figs with thistles is a Matthean contribution as well. One scholar has suggested that Matthew's grouping was designed to point out the similarity in appearance shared by the paired plants. According to Carson, "From a distance the little black berries on the buckthorn could be mistaken for grapes, and the flowers on certain thistles might deceive one into thinking figs were growing."[52]

More likely, the association of grapes and thornbushes is an allusion to a familiar OT text full of theological significance. The Song of the Vineyard in Isa 5:1–7 portrayed Israel as a vineyard in which Yahweh invested much care. Although Yahweh expected the vineyard to produce good grapes, it produced only worthless grapes. The parable is important in Matthew since Jesus clearly alluded to it in His introduction to the parable of the Wicked Tenants in Matt 21:33–46. Although the MT states that the vineyard produced bad grapes, the LXX says that God "waited for it to make a bunch of grapes, but it produced *thorns*" (Isa 5:2,4, italics added). These thorns that overtook the vineyard were obviously incapable of producing the fruit God demanded. By pairing grapes and thorns, Matthew has produced an allusion to this familiar text that reminds his readers of Israel's failure to produce the good works God expected.[53] The allusion hinted at the judgment that would result from Israel's moral failure (Isa 5:3–7; Matt 21:41,43). The allusion also identifies the fruits God expects from His people: "He looked for justice, but saw injustice, for righteousness, but heard cries of wretchedness" (Isa 5:7).

---

[51] See Hos 10:8; Heb 6:8. Davies and Allison entertain the possibility that Matthew reworked the saying preserved in Luke and drawn from Q for the reasons suggested here (*A Critical and Exegetical Commentary on the Gospel According to Saint Matthew*, 1:707). Nevertheless they favored the view that Matthew and Luke utilized two different versions of Q. Hagner, on the other hand, stated, "Luke and Matthew here probably depend on Q, with Matthew making slight adjustments of the logion in its application to false prophets" (*Matthew 1–13*, 181).

[52] Carson, "Matthew," 191.

[53] Davies and Allison also posed the possibility that Matthew associated grapes and thorns under the influence of Isa 5 (*A Critical and Exegetical Commentary on the Gospel According to Saint Matthew*, 1:707). This is far more likely than Gundry's suggestion that "perhaps . . . Matthew thinks of the thornbushes as a figure for wild grapevines and of the thistles as standing for fig trees of poor quality" (*Matthew*, 129).

Just as grapes cannot be gathered from thorns, figs cannot be reaped from thistles. The mention of grapes and figs may also constitute an allusion to the OT. Both grapes and figs served as symbols of Israel. The vineyard portrayed Israel in the important parable of Isaiah 5, and grapes and figs represented Israel in Hos 9:10: "I discovered Israel like grapes in the wilderness. I saw your fathers like the first fruit of the fig tree in its first season. But they went to Baal-peor, consecrated themselves to Shame, and became detestable, like the thing they loved."

Interestingly, Jer 8:13 combines reference to grapes and figs to describe the fruitlessness of Israel under God's judgment: "I will gather them and bring them to an end. This is the Lord's declaration. There will be no grapes on the vine, no figs on the fig tree, and even the leaf will wither. Whatever I have given them will be lost to them." Allusions to false teachers and false prophets in the immediate context of the Jeremiah passage are especially intriguing. Jeremiah 8:8 asked, "How can you claim: We are wise; the law of the Lord is with us? In fact, the lying pen of scribes has produced falsehood." More importantly Jer 8:10–11 said, "From the least to the greatest, everyone is gaining profit unjustly. From prophet to priest, everyone deals falsely. They have treated superficially the brokenness of My dear people, claiming: Peace, peace, when there is no peace."

The vineyard and the fig tree also appear to represent apostate Israel in the account of the cursing of the fig tree and the parable of the Vineyard in Matt 21:18–21,33–46. Against this background, reference to the inability of thorns and thistles to produce grapes and figs warns that the false prophets do not represent the true people of God, will not produce the fruits of righteousness demanded by God, and are destined for divine judgment. These themes are clarified and reiterated in the analogy of 7:17–19.

Just as one species of plant does not produce the fruit of another, a plant of one quality cannot produce the fruit of another. Every good tree produces good fruit. Every bad tree produces bad fruit. The use of the adjective "every" (*pan*) implies that there are no exceptions to this principle. Similarly the use of the verb *dunamai* with the negative in verse 18 shows that it is absolutely impossible for a tree of one quality to bear fruit of a radically different quality. The phrase "bad tree" describes a tree that is diseased, rotten, and decaying (*sapron*).[54] Good fruit could not possibly come from such a source. The adjective *ponēros* translated "bad" in the phrase "bad fruit" normally means "evil" in the sense of a moral category in Matthew (5:11,37,39,45; 6:13,23; 7:11, etc.). The adjective makes clear that the health of the two different trees portrays the moral and spiritual condition of two different kinds of people and the condition of the fruits portrays good and evil deeds. "Fruit" is frequently a figurative reference to a person's deeds and words in Matthew (e.g., 3:8; 12:33–37).[55] Thus sheep's clothing cannot mask the inner evil of false prophets. This inner evil will express itself through evil behavior.

Matthew 7:19 reiterates a theme from the preaching of John the Baptist in 3:10: "Even now the ax is ready to strike the root of the trees! Therefore, every tree that doesn't produce good fruit will be cut down and thrown into the fire." Since "fire" is frequently used to describe eternal punishment in Matthew (3:12; 5:22; 13:40,42,50; 18:8–9; 25:41), the statements of both John and Jesus are clear warnings that false prophets will be consigned to hell. Those who embrace their teachings and are characterized by behavior like theirs will receive the same sentence.

Josephus referred to several false prophets both from OT history and from among his contemporaries as well. He demonstrated that some false prophets intentionally deceived their hearers by prophesying what they knew to be contrary to the truth.[56] He shows that Deut 18:20–22 was still seen as a guideline for distinguishing true and false prophets in the intertestamental period, that is, if a single prediction of a prophet failed to be fulfilled, he would be regarded as a false prophet.[57]

References to false prophets also appear in the *Didache*. Although the final composition of the *Didache* probably dates to the middle of the second century AD, it incorporates earlier material that seems to date to the mid and late first century.[58] The *Didache* identifies

---

[54] See "σαπρός," BDAG, 913. BDAG argues that if the normal meaning "rotten" applies here, then the statement must be a hyperbole.

[55] Early Christians recognized this. Ignatius commented on this text in Ignatius, *Eph.* 14:2, "No one professing faith sins, nor does anyone possessing love hate. 'The tree is known by its fruit'; thus those who profess to be Christ's will be recognized by their deeds" (Holmes, *The Apostolic Fathers*, 147).

[56] Josephus, *Ant.* 8.9 §§236–245; 10.7.3 §111; id., *J.W.* 2.13.5 §261; 6.5.2 §285.

[57] Josephus, *Ant.* 13.11.2 §312.

[58] See Holmes, *The Apostolic Fathers*, 247–48.

false prophets as those who seek to take advantage of the church's generosity and hospitality, who utter prophesies for their own selfish benefit (such as "Give me money!"), who fail to follow the example of Christ, or even those who teach truth yet do not practice what they teach.[59]

Scholars debate the precise identity of the false prophets discussed in Matt 7:15–20. Suggestions include Gnostics,[60] Essenes,[61] Pharisees,[62] zealots,[63] charismatic enthusiasts,[64] and Judaizers (Jewish Christians who were overly zealous for the law and opposed to Gentile mission).[65] The view held by the majority of scholars is that the false prophets were Hellenists who overly emphasized believers' freedom from the law.[66] This view suggests that the false prophets are the false disciples who will be rejected by Christ in the final judgment because of their lawlessness.

A growing number of scholars argue that the data of Matthew 7 are insufficient to develop a precise identification of the false prophets.[67] They suggest that the warning was intended to be a general one and has many different applications.

C. Two Confessions (Matt 7:21–23)

Jesus taught in 7:13–14 that the gate by which one enters the kingdom is exclusive and that this narrow gate will elude most people.

---

[59] *Did.* 11–12.

[60] Bacon, *Studies in Matthew*, 348.

[61] C. Daniel, "Faux prophètes: Surnom des Esséniens dans le sermon sur la montagne," *RevQ* 7 (1969): 45–79.

[62] D. Hill, "False Prophets and Charismatics: Structure and Interpretation in Matthew 7,15–23," *Bib* 57 (1976): 327–48. This is a reversal of his earlier view (*Matthew*, 151).

[63] Schlatter, *Der Evangelist Matthäus*, 252–54.

[64] Käsemann, *New Testament Questions*, 82–107.

[65] Guelich, *The Sermon on the Mount*, 408–9.

[66] G. Barth, "Matthew's Understanding of the Law," in *Tradition and Interpretation*, ed. G. Bornkamm, G. Barth, and H. J. Held (Philadelphia: Westminster, 1963), 89–164, esp. 159–64; Gundry, *Matthew*, 126–36. Gundry claimed that the false prophets were characterized by "antinomian teaching" and "antinomian behavior," but he argued that for Matthew the permissive interpretations of the law by Judaizers was paramount to antinomianism. One may classify Gundry as identifying the false prophets as both antinomians and as Judaizers. See also Turner, *Matthew*, 217–18.

[67] See D. Aune, *Prophecy in Early Christianity and the Ancient Mediterranean World* (Grand Rapids: Eerdmans, 1983), 222–24; Betz, *The Sermon on the Mount*, 534; Carson, *Matthew*, 190–91; Davies and Allison, *A Critical and Exegetical Commentary on the Gospel According to Saint Matthew*, 1:701–2; Hagner, *Matthew 1–13*, 182–83; Luz, *Matthew: A Commentary*, 1:376–77; Nolland, *The Gospel of Matthew*, 335–36; Schnackenburg, *The Gospel of Matthew*, 178.

Now Jesus likely shocked His hearers by exclaiming that the narrow gate that excluded all who were not Jesus' disciples would also exclude many who claimed to be His disciples. Just as false prophets were ravenous wolves who disguised themselves as sheep, some goats (25:31–46) attempted to masquerade as sheep as well.

Jesus said, "Not everyone who says to Me, 'Lord, Lord!' will enter the kingdom of heaven" (7:21). The confession of Jesus as Lord reflects a high and early Christology. The title "Lord" (*kurios*) appeared 11 times in Matthew prior to 7:21. Ten of the previous occurrences clearly refer to Yahweh. Matthew 1:20,24; 2:19 use the term in the expression "the angel of the Lord" which is a clear reference to the angel of Yahweh from numerous OT texts.[68] Twice the term "Lord" is used in Matthew's fulfillment formula to identify God as the One who inspired the Scriptures (1:22; 2:15). Three times the title "Lord" appeared in quotations of the OT in which the Hebrew Scriptures used the divine name Yahweh (3:3; 4:7,10). In 5:33 the title referred to Yahweh as the One to whom vows must be paid. The single exception (prior to 7:21) in which the title does not refer to Deity is 6:24. Nevertheless connotations of Deity are present since the term was used in the plural to refer to God and mammon as two different masters between which every person must choose (6:24). In light of the earlier usages of the title in Matthew, the natural reading of the term in 7:21 regards it as a title of Deity.

The frequency of uses of "Lord" as a title of Deity drops significantly after the SM. Eighteen of the 80 total occurrences of *kurios* clearly refer to Yahweh since the term appears in phrases like "the angel of the Lord," Matthew's fulfillment formula, or direct quotations of the OT.[69] "Lord" also often serves to identify the owner of property or the master of a slave and even functions as a polite noun of address that may in some instances be the equivalent of the modern "sir." Nevertheless a number of uses of "Lord" as a title of authority or ownership serve as allegorical references to God in the parables of Jesus.[70]

Several key texts clearly use the title to ascribe deity to Jesus. First, Matt 3:3 described John the Baptist as the fulfillment of Isa 40:3. John was a voice crying in the wilderness to prepare for the coming

---

[68] This usage occurs over 50 times in the OT (e.g., Gen 16:7,9–11).

[69] See Matt 1:20,22,24; 2:13,15,19; 3:3; 4:7,10; 5:33; 11:25; 12:8; 21:9,42; 22:37; 23:39; 27:10; and 28:2.

[70] E.g., Matt 18:25,27,31–32,34; 21:30,40.

of the Lord. The early chapters of Matthew appear to identify Jesus as the Lord for whom John prepared the way. John spoke of One who would come after him who was vastly superior to him since He would baptize people with the Holy Spirit (Matt 3:11–12). John's initial refusal to baptize Jesus and his protest, "I need to be baptized by You, and yet You come to me?" (v. 14) identify Jesus as the great One who would come after John. The Hebrew word in Isa 40:3 that is translated "LORD" is Yahweh. Thus in applying Isa 40:3 to John and to Jesus, Matthew clearly identified Jesus as the LORD ("Yahweh").[71]

Equally dramatic is Matt 12:8 in which Jesus identified Himself as "the Lord of the Sabbath." Most hearers in Jesus' audience would have recognized that Yahweh is the Lord of the Sabbath since He instituted the Sabbath by His rest at the conclusion of the creation week and by the fourth commandment of the Decalogue (Exod 20:8–11). The word "Lord" (*kurios*) appears three times in the Sabbath commandment, and all three occurrences are clear references to Yahweh. Thus it is highly likely that Jesus' original Jewish audience would have regarded this self-identification as a divine claim.[72]

Similarly Jesus argued that King David referred to the Messiah as his "Lord" and that this implied that the Messiah would be far more than merely David's son (Matt 22:41–46).[73] Interestingly the LXX used the double vocative "Lord, Lord" a total of 18 times.[74] Every occurrence is a reference to Yahweh and normally translates the combined title and name Adonai Yahweh. The original readers of Matthew would likely have recognized the double vocative here as an echo of the LXX and regarded "Lord" as having divine connotations.[75]

---

[71] "There is a remarkable Christological claim involved in applying Isaiah's depiction of God's forerunner to the man who prepared the way for the coming of Jesus" (France, *The Gospel of Matthew*, 105). See also M. Öhler, "The Expectation of Elijah and the Presence of the Kingdom of God," *JBL* 118 (1999): 461–76, esp. 468–73; Turner, *Matthew*, 108–9.

[72] France, *The Gospel of Matthew*, 462–63; A. Saldarini, *Matthew's Christian-Jewish Community*, Chicago Studies in the History of Judaism (Chicago: University of Chicago Press, 1994), 129. Keener describes this identification as speculative (*The Gospel of Matthew*, 356, n. 56).

[73] Davies and Allison, *A Critical and Exegetical Commentary on the Gospel According to Saint Matthew*, 3:254–55; France, *The Gospel of Matthew*, 849.

[74] Deuteronomy 3:24; 9:26; Judg 6:22; 16:28; 1 Kgs 8:53; 1 Chr 17:24; Esth 13:9; Pss 68:7; 108:21; 129:3; 139:8; 140:8; Jer 28:62; Ezek 21:15; Amos 7:2,5; 2 Macc 1:24; 3 Macc 2:2. See also Judg 2:1; 2 Sam 7:18–20,22,25,28–29.

[75] France did not consider this evidence when he hesitantly commented that "it would go beyond the philological evidence to claim *kyrie* as in itself an attribution of divinity." However, France recognized that the divine sense of the title fit best with the portrayal of Jesus as eschatological judge (*The Gospel of Matthew*, 293).

Hagner aptly commented on the confession of 7:21: "Matthew's community can hardly have failed to think here of the primary Christian confession, that Jesus is Lord (cf. Rom 10:9; Phil 2:11; 1 Cor. 12:3)." Similarly Davies and Allison confidently asserted, "The early Christian confession, 'Jesus is Lord' (Rom 10:9; 1 Cor 12:3; Phil 2.11), stands in the background."[76] The contexts of the Pauline texts related to this confession demonstrate that "Lord" functions as a title of Deity in the confession. Romans 10:9 is Paul's exposition and application of Joel 2:32 (Rom 10:13) in which calling on the name of the Lord refers to calling on Yahweh. Similarly the title "Lord" in the confession of Phil 2:11 is identified as the name that is above every other name, a clear substitute for the ineffable name of God, and is drawn from the description of Yahweh in Isa 45:23 that Paul quoted. The confession affirms Jesus' authority and His Deity.

Jesus warned that as significant as this confession is, not all who make it are guaranteed entrance into His kingdom. The future tense "will enter" implies that entrance into the kingdom is an eschatological event. Although the future tense could be gnomic, in which case it would depict Jesus' statement as a general timeless principle, this eschatological interpretation is confirmed in Matt 7:22, which refers to "that day," that is, the day of final judgment.[77] Other texts in Matthew associate entrance into the kingdom with final judgment. Matthew 5:20 says that only those whose righteousness exceeds that of the scribes and Pharisees will enter the kingdom. This seems to imply that entrance into the kingdom is permitted only after an evaluation of the professing disciple's behavior and character. Similarly 18:8–9 contrasts entering into life, which is associated with entering into the kingdom (v. 3), with being cast into eternal fire or the fiery Gehenna. Two of the three occurrences of the verb "enter" (*eiserchomai*) in the indicative mood with reference to the kingdom of heaven in Matthew are in the future tense (7:22; 19:23). Matthew 23:13 uses the present tense. Most scholars view the use of the present tense as implying that the kingdom is present in some sense, although at least one commentator has argued that this reference is also eschatological.[78]

---

[76] Davies and Allison, *A Critical and Exegetical Commentary on the Gospel According to Saint Matthew*, 1:713.

[77] This verse uses the remote demonstrative pronoun.

[78] Gibbs, *Matthew 1:1–11:1*, 266.

Jesus insisted that entrance into the kingdom required that one do "the will of My Father in heaven" (7:21). The grammar and context of the statement imply that those who do the will of the Father are a sub-group of those who confess that Jesus is Lord. This may be expressed in English by the insertion of the word "also": "Not everyone who says to Me, 'Lord, Lord!' will enter the kingdom of heaven, but only the one who does the will of My Father in heaven." Although confession of Jesus as Lord is not sufficient to guarantee kingdom entrance, it remains essential to kingdom entrance. Still mere verbal profession is not enough. The true disciple expresses the sincerity of his confession of Jesus' identity as the Lord through obedient living. Jesus was not pitting obedience against faith but was insisting that obedience is the necessary expression of true faith.

The "will" of the Father is God's moral will as expressed through the commandments of the OT and the teaching of Jesus, especially the teachings of the SM.[79] Modern readers tend to regard references to God's will as allusions to His secret eternal plan for individuals. Matthew used the term "will" (*thelēma*) in this sense in 6:10; 18:14, and 26:42. Yet, when he referred to "doing" the will of the Father, he clearly had in mind obedience to God's moral will as expressed in His commands.[80] The phrase "will of the Father in heaven" appears to have been a stock term in Judaism for the deeds commanded in the law. For example *m. 'Abot* 5:20 says:

> Judah b. Tema says, "Be strong as a leopard, fast as an eagle, fleet as a gazelle, and brave as a lion, to carry out the will of your Father who is in heaven." He would say, "The shameless go to Gehenna, and the diffident to the garden of Eden. May it be found pleasing before you, O Lord our God, that you rebuild your city quickly in our day and set our portion in your Torah."[81]

Matthew referred to doing the will of the Father on two other occasions. In 12:50 Jesus taught that "whoever does the will of My Father in heaven, that person is My brother and sister and mother." Obedience to the Father demonstrates a person's identity as His son or daughter. Matthew 21:31 used the phrase in the interpretation of the parable of the two sons: "Which of the two did his father's will?" The chief priests and elders correctly replied that the one who did

---

[79] Blomberg, *Matthew*, 133.
[80] Broadus, *The Gospel According to Matthew*, 167; Hill, *The Gospel of Matthew*, 152.
[81] Judah lived at the end of the second century AD.

the father's will was the one who obeyed his command to work in the vineyard despite his previous protest. When Jesus interpreted the parable, He identified the one who did the father's will as those who believed John's teaching about the "way of righteousness." The son who did the father's will represented tax collectors and prostitutes who obeyed John's commands: "Repent, because the kingdom of heaven has come near!" (3:2) and "Produce fruit consistent with repentance" (v. 8).

The closest parallel to 7:21 is Luke 6:46: "Why do you call Me 'Lord, Lord,' and don't do the things I say?" Although the only direct verbal parallel between the two sayings is the double vocative "Lord, Lord," the context suggests that the two sayings are true parallels. Luke 6:46 appears in the SP between the parallel to Matt 7:16–20 (Luke 6:43–44) and the parallel to Matt 7:24–27 (Luke 6:47–49). Thus "the will of My Father in heaven" is equivalent to "the things I [Jesus] say." Consequently Jesus' teaching, particularly the Sermon on the Mount/Plain, expresses the Father's will.

The substantival participle translated "the one who does" is in the present tense. The tense emphasizes the true disciple's commitment to continue doing the Father's will as a manner of life.[82] Thus the true disciple not only confesses Jesus as Lord; he also walks the narrow path that leads to the gates of the kingdom as described in Matt 7:13–14.

"That day" (v. 22) is the day of final judgment, the Great Assize. The use of the remote demonstrative pronoun "that" (*ekeinos*) implies that this Day of Judgment belongs to the distant future.[83] Jesus explicitly referred to the "day of judgment" in 10:15; 11:22,24; and 12:36. In 24:36, the phrase "that day" refers to the time of the Second Coming when the Son of Man comes on the clouds of heaven with power and great glory and sends His angels to gather the elect from the four winds. Jesus said, "Now concerning that day and hour no one knows—neither the angels in heaven, nor the Son—except the Father only" (24:36). This use of the phrase "that day" is similar to a common usage in the LXX in which "that day" refers to the day of Yahweh's wrath or vengeance (e.g., Jer 46:10; Zeph 1:15).

---

[82] The present tense is "customary." See Wallace, *Greek Grammar Beyond the Basics*, 521–22.

[83] BDAG ("ἐκεῖνος," 302) points out that the remote demonstrative functions with the noun "day" especially "of God's climactic judgment day Mt 7:22; Lk 6:23; 10:12; 2 Th 1:10; 2 Ti 1:12,18; cp. Rv 16:14 v.l. ὁ αἰὼν ἐ. (opp. αἰὼν οὗτος) *the age to come* Lk 20:35 (s. αἰὼν 2b)."

The high Christology of the saying is reflected not only in the confession of Jesus as Lord but also by the need to appeal to Jesus for entrance into the kingdom.[84] Matthew 7:21–23 clearly places Jesus in the role of eschatological judge. Jesus' role in eschatological judgment was already implied by John the Baptist in his reference to the Messiah's baptism of fire (3:11–12). It was later confirmed by Jesus' exercise of the divine prerogative of forgiving sins (9:1–8). The parable of the Wheat and the Weeds (13:24–30,37–43) stated that the Son of Man "will send out His angels, and they will gather from His kingdom everything that causes sin and those guilty of lawlessness. They will throw them into the blazing furnace where there will be weeping and gnashing of teeth" (13:41–42). In Matt 16:27 Jesus said, "For the Son of Man is going to come with His angels in the glory of His Father, and then He will reward each according to what he has done." Later in the parable of the Sheep and the Goats (Matt 25:31–46), also unique to Matthew, Jesus described Himself as the Son of Man who sits on the throne of His glory and judges the nations. He will say to the righteous, "Come, you who are blessed by My Father, inherit the kingdom prepared for you from the foundation of the world" (v. 34). And He will say to the wicked, "Depart from Me, you who are cursed, into the eternal fire prepared for the Devil and his angels" (v. 41).

The OT insisted that God is the ultimate judge of all human beings. The patriarch Abraham described Yahweh as "the Judge of all the earth" (Gen 18:25). The psalms likewise repeatedly affirm that Yahweh is the eschatological Judge.

> The LORD judges the peoples; . . . God is a righteous judge and a God who shows His wrath justice every day. (Ps 7:8,11)

> For You have upheld my just cause; You are seated on Your throne as a righteous judge. You have rebuked the nations: You have destroyed the wicked; You have erased their name forever and ever. The enemy has come to eternal ruin; You have uprooted the cities, and the very memory of them has perished. But the LORD sits enthroned forever; He has established His throne for judgment. He judges the world with righteousness; He executes judgment on the peoples with fairness. (Ps 9:4–8)

> Our God is coming; He will not be silent! Devouring fire precedes Him, and a storm rages around Him. On high, He summons heaven and earth in order to judge His people. . . . The heavens proclaim His righteousness, for God is the judge. (Ps 50:3–4,6)

[84] Carson, "Matthew," 193; France, *The Gospel of Matthew*, 293–94.

> Exaltation does not come from the east, the west, or the desert, for God is the
> Judge; He brings down one and exalts another. For there is a cup in the Lord's
> hand, full of wine blended with spices, and He pours from it. All the wicked
> of the earth will drink, draining it to the dregs. (Ps 75:6–8)

The visions of Daniel associated judgment with the coming of the Son of Man. The vision immediately before the Son of Man vision ends with the statement, "The court was convened, and the books were opened" (Dan 7:10). Daniel 7:22 and 26 also associate judgment with granting the kingdom to the Son of Man. Although judgment is associated with the coming of the Son of Man, the Ancient of Days rather than the Son of Man serves as judge (see esp. v. 22). Thus Jesus' claim to serve as eschatological judge strongly implies that He recognized himself as Deity.

Although the double vocative "Lord, Lord" seems to function as a confession of Jesus' Deity in Matt 7:21 and Luke 6:46, it seems to be an expression of desperation in Matt 7:22. This parallels the use of the construction in 25:11 in which the construction expresses the desperation of the foolish virgins who were shut out of the marriage celebration, a picture of sinners who are shut out from the kingdom.

The negative *ou* modifies all three of the questions in 7:22 and implies a positive response in Greek grammar. Thus the translation in the HCSB is fitting: "Didn't we prophesy in Your name, drive out demons in Your name, and do many miracles in Your name?" In this context the questions are framed to compel Jesus to nod His head in agreement and acknowledge the qualifications of the one making the appeal to enter the kingdom. Nevertheless the clever ploy fails. As Blomberg reminded readers, "Signs and wonders can come from sources other than God, including both the demonic world and human manufacture (cf. Acts 19:13–16; Rev 13:13–14)."[85]

The verb "prophesy" means "to proclaim an inspired revelation" or "to foretell something that lies in the future."[86] In Matt 11:13 and 15:7 the verb has the latter meaning, for it refers to predictions made by the Law and the Prophets and by the prophet Isaiah. In Matt 26:68 it has the former meaning since it refers to supernatural knowledge of present rather than future events.

Jesus did not dispute the claim that these individuals had uttered prophecies in His name. The ability to foretell the future or express

[85] Blomberg, *Matthew*, 133.
[86] "προφητεύω," BDAG, 890.

knowledge that was not attained by ordinary human means need not necessarily come from God. Acts 16:16–19 tells of a slave girl who was inhabited by a demon who granted her the ability to foretell the future. The term used by Luke to describe this spirit was sometimes used to refer to individuals who had the gift of ventriloquism.[87] However the account in Acts strongly implies that the slave girl was no mere ventriloquist. After Paul cast out the spirit that inhabited her, she lost her abilities and was unable to feign the gift to the satisfaction of her previous customers. Thus a prophetic gift, even an authentic prophetic gift, does not prove that the one who possesses it is a genuine disciple of Jesus or a servant of the true God.

Although Josephus wrote about several contemporaries that he regarded as false prophets who merely pretended to have a prophetic gift, he also wrote about a member of the sect of Essenes named Judas, who "never missed the truth in his predictions." Judas once wished for death when a prophecy foretelling the death of Antigonus, brother of Aristobulus, on a particular day seemed to fail, thus identifying him as a false prophet. Yet the moment Judas had lost all hope that his prophecy would be fulfilled, news arrived that Antigonus had been killed in the place and on the day the prophet had foretold.[88] Even accurate prophecies do not positively identify a person as a true follower of Jesus.

The claimants would also appeal to exorcisms that they had performed as grounds for entrance into the kingdom. As with their appeal to their prophecies, Jesus did not dispute their claim. Matthew 12:27 states that members of the sect of the Pharisees sometimes cast out demons. Acts 19:11–17 shows that some Jewish exorcists even attempted to perform exorcisms in Jesus' name:

> God was performing extraordinary miracles by Paul's hands, so that even facecloths or work aprons that had touched his skin were brought to the sick, and the diseases left them, and the evil spirits came out of them. Then some of the itinerant Jewish exorcists attempted to pronounce the name of the Lord Jesus over those who had evil spirits, saying, "I command you by the Jesus whom Paul preaches!" Seven sons of Sceva, a Jewish chief priest, were doing this. The evil spirit answered them, "Jesus I know, and Paul I recognize—but who are you?" Then the man who had the evil spirit leaped on them, overpowered them all, and prevailed against them, so that they ran out of that

[87] See, e.g., *m. Sanh.* 7:7. The text contrasts the soothsayer who speaks with his lips and the "Python which speaks from his armpits."

[88] Josephus, *Ant.* 13.11.2, §§310–13.

house naked and wounded. This became known to everyone who lived in Ephesus, both Jews and Greeks. Then fear fell on all of them, and the name of the Lord Jesus was magnified.

Josephus also mentions exorcisms that were performed by his contemporaries. He claimed to have been an eyewitness of exorcisms performed by a Jew named Eleazar in the presence of Vespasian:

> God also enabled him [Solomon] to learn that skill which expels demons, which is a science useful and sanative to men. He composed such incantations also by which distempers are alleviated. And he left behind him the manner of using exorcisms, by which they drive away demons, so that they never return, and this method of cure is of great force unto this day; for I have seen a certain man of my own country whose name was Eleazar, releasing people that were demoniacal in the presence of Vespasian, and his sons, and his captains, and the whole multitude of his soldiers. The manner of the cure was this: He put a ring that had a root of one of those sorts mentioned by Solomon to the nostrils of the demoniac, after which he drew out the demon through his nostrils; and when the man fell down immediately, he abjured him to return into him no more, making still mention of Solomon, and reciting the incantations which he composed. And when Eleazar would persuade and demonstrate to the spectators that he had such a power, he set a little way off a cup or basin full of water, and commanded the demon, as he went out of the man, to overturn it, and thereby to let the spectators know that he had left the man.[89]

Jesus also mentioned those who claimed to have performed miracles in His name, although they were not true disciples. Jesus would later warn that false prophets in the last days would "arise and perform signs and wonders to lead astray, if possible, even the elect" (Matt 24:24). As mentioned earlier, the phrase "signs and wonders" in the LXX typically refers to the plagues and miracles of the exodus and suggests that the feats of the false prophets would be truly stupendous. Josephus mentions that false prophets who were his contemporaries promised and sometimes attempted miracles including miracles that were reminiscent of the exodus and the conquest. A self-professed prophet named Theudas promised his followers that he would part the waters of the Jordan River so they could cross on dry land.[90] Theudas was captured and beheaded by the Fadus, the procurator of Judea, before he could attempt his miracle.

---

[89] Ibid., 8.2.5, §§43–48.
[90] Ibid., 20.5.1, §97.

Rabbinic literature speaks of several Jewish miracle workers. The best-known of these were Honi the Circle-drawer and Hanina ben Doza. The Mishnah states:

> C. M'SH S: They said to Honi, the circle drawer, "Pray for rain."
> D. He said to them, "Go and take in the clay ovens used for Passover, so that they not soften [in the rain which is coming]."
> E. He prayed, but it did not rain.
> F. What did he do?
> G. He drew a circle and stood in the middle of it and said before Him, "Lord of the world! Your children have turned to me, for before you I am like a member of the family. I swear by your great name—I'm simply not moving from here until you take pity on your children!"
> H. It began to rain drop by drop.
> I. He said, "This is not what I wanted, but rain for filling up cisterns, pits, and caverns."
> J. It began to rain violently.
> K. He said, "This is not what I wanted, but rain of good will, blessing, and graciousness."
> L. Now it rained the right way, until Israelites had to flee from Jerusalem up to the Temple Mount because of the rain.
> M. Now they came and said to him, "Just as you prayed for it to rain, now pray for it to go away."
> N. He said to them, "Go, see whether the stone of the strayers is disappeared."
> O. Simeon b. Shatah said to him, "If you were not Honi, I should decree a ban of excommunication against you. But what am I going to do to you? For you importune before the Omnipresent, so he does what you want, like a son who importunes his father, so he does what he wants."[91]

Josephus also offers a brief description of Honi, though he refers to him by a slightly different name, Onias the Righteous. Josephus's account dates the miracle worker to the first century BC.

> Now there was one, whose name was Onias, a righteous man he was, and beloved of God, who, in a certain drought, had prayed to God to put an end to the intense heat, and whose prayers God had heard, and had sent them rain. This man had hid himself, because he saw that this sedition would last a great while. However, they brought him to the Jewish camp, and desired, that as by his prayers he had once put an end to the drought, so he would in like manner make imprecations on Aristobulus and those of his faction.
>
> And when, upon his refusal, and the excuses that he made, he was still by the multitude compelled to speak, he stood up in the midst of them, and said,

---

[91] m. Ta'an. 3:8.

"O God, the king of the whole world! since those that stand now with me are
thy people, and those that are besieged are also thy priests, I beseech thee,
that thou wilt neither hearken to the prayers of those against these, nor bring
to effect what these pray against those." Whereupon such wicked Jews as
stood about him, as soon as he had made this prayer, stoned him to death.[92]

The references to Hanina ben Doza in the Mishnah are relatively
brief. One passage says, "When R. Hanina b. Dosa died, wonder workers came to an end."[93] Another adds:

> A. One who prays and errs—it is a bad sign for him.
> B. And if he is a communal agent [who prays on behalf of the whole con-
> gregation], it is a bad sign for them that appointed him.
> C. [This is on the principle that] a man's agent is like [the man] himself.
> D. They said concerning R. Haninah b. Dosa, "When he would pray for
> the sick he would say, 'This one shall live' or 'This one shall die.'"
> E. They said to him, "How do you know?"
> F. He said to them, "If my prayer is fluent, then I know that it is accepted
> [and the person will live]."
> G. "But if not, I know that it is rejected [and the person will die]."[94]

The Babylonian Talmud mentions two stories of Hanina's heal-
ings. The first shares the background of Hanina's teaching regarding
prayer. The second explains one of the keys to his effectiveness in
prayer.

> Our Rabbis taught: Once the son of R. Gamaliel fell ill. He sent two scholars
> to R. Hanina b. Dosa to ask him to pray for him. When he saw them he went
> up to an upper chamber and prayed for him. When he came down he said
> to them: Go, the fever has left him; They said to him: Are you a prophet?
> He replied: I am neither a prophet nor the son of a prophet, but I learnt this
> from experience. If my prayer is fluent in my mouth, I know that he is ac-
> cepted: but if not, I know that he is rejected. They sat down and made a note
> of the exact moment. When they came to R. Gamaliel, he said to them: By
> the temple service! You have not been a moment too soon or too late, but so
> it happened: at that very moment the fever left him and he asked for water to
> drink.
>   On another occasion it happened that R. Hanina b. Dosa went to study To-
> rah with R. Johanan ben Zakkai. The son of R. Johanan ben Zakkai fell ill. He
> said to him: Hanina my son, pray for him that he may live. He put his head
> between his knees and prayed for him and he lived. Said R. Johanan ben Zak-
> kai: If Ben Zakkai had stuck his head between his knees for the whole day, no
> notice would have been taken of him. Said his wife to him: Is Hanina greater

---

[92] Josephus, *Ant.* 14.2.1, §22–24.
[93] *m. Soṭah* 9:15.
[94] *m. Ber.* 5:5.

than you are? He replied to her: No; but he is like a servant before the king, and I am like a nobleman before a king.[95]

Just as Jewish exorcists sometimes performed exorcisms in Jesus' name, some sought to perform miracles in his name. The Tosefta, Palestinian Talmud, Babylonian Talmud, and other texts forbid Jews to heal or to receive healing in Jesus' name.[96]

The phrase "in your name" is in an emphatic position in each of the claimant's appeals. The phrase indicates and emphasizes that the claimants had invoked the power and authority of Jesus to perform their supernatural feats.[97]

By listing prophecy first among the supernatural activities of these claimants, a close connection is established between Matt 7:21–23 and the preceding paragraph about false prophets. On the basis of this connection, many scholars conclude that the false prophets mentioned earlier were charismatic enthusiasts who practiced prophecy, exorcism, and performed miracles.[98] This does not mean Jesus intended to denounce all charismatic activity. As Hagner noted:

> These persons are not criticized for their charismatic activities but for their dependence upon them as a substitute for the righteousness taught by Jesus. We may conclude that charismatic activities, done apart from this righteousness, have no self-contained importance and are in themselves insufficient for entry into the kingdom of heaven.[99]

Although the focus on charismatic activities in the judgment scene is pronounced, Matt 7:15–20 is broad enough to refer to any purported prophet whose life is not consistent with the teachings of the SM.

"I never knew you!" (v. 23) denies that Jesus ever had the personal relationship with the individuals that they claim. The words serve as a formula of repudiation (25:12; 26:70,72,74). Similar expressions

---

[95] *b. Ber.* 34b.

[96] *t. Ḥul.* 2:22–23; *y. Šabb.* 14:4; *y. ʿAbod Zar.* 2:2; *b. ʿAbod Zar.* 27b; *Qoh. Rab.* 10:5.

[97] H. Bietenhard, "ὄνομα," *TDNT* 5 (1967):242–83, esp. 271. See the discussion and rejection of alternative views in Davies and Allison, *A Critical and Exegetical Commentary on the Gospel According to Saint Matthew*, 1:715–16.

[98] D. Aune, *Prophecy in Early Christianity and the Ancient Mediterranean World* (Grand Rapids: Eerdmans, 1983), 223; D. Hill, "False Prophets and Charismatics: Structure and Interpretation in Matthew 7,15–23," *Bib* 57 (1976): 327–48 [7:15–20 refer to Pharisees and 7:21–23 refer to charismatic enthusiasts]; Hagner, *Matthew 1–13*, 182–83; Keener, *The Gospel of Matthew*, 252; Luz, *Matthew: A Commentary*, 1:376–77.

[99] Hagner, *Matthew 1–13*, 188.

were used by the rabbis when placing persons under the mildest category of ban.[100] The words here are clearly more serious than a mild ban and lead to a permanent exclusion from Jesus' presence and the kingdom of heaven.

"Depart from me, you lawbreakers" is an allusion to Ps 6:8 that shares six out of eight words with the LXX.[101] In its original context the command was uttered against enemies who shake with terror as they face sudden disgrace (Ps 6:10). This terror is a response to God's anger and wrath (6:1–3). The phrase "lawbreakers" (lit., "you who are working lawlessness") expresses the depths of the depravity of these defendants in final judgment. In Matt 23:28 the term described the internal corruption of the scribes and Pharisees. In 13:41 the word describes the sinfulness of those destined for fire, weeping, and gnashing of teeth after the final judgment. In 24:12 the term refers to the horrible wickedness that is rampant as God's judgment approaches. Thus the false disciples are clearly deserving of the punishment to which Jesus consigned them. They will rightly suffer God's wrath because of their rebellion against Him.

D. Two Hearers and Builders (Matt 7:24–27)

"Therefore" shows that Matt 7:24–27 draws an inference from the preceding material in the SM. Since the paragraph emphasizes the necessity of obeying Jesus' words, it is closely connected with verses 15–20, which stress the necessity of the fruits of righteousness as a hallmark of the true prophet, and verses 21–23, which stress the necessity of doing the Father's will in order to pass the scrutiny of eschatological judgment. If the narrow path that leads to the kingdom in verses 13–14 refers to obedience to Jesus' teaching, as suggested earlier, then the entire section (vv. 13–23) is tightly connected with the concluding illustration in verses 24–27.

Jesus' teaching was addressed to everyone who "hears these words of mine." This commentary argued earlier that the "will of My Father in heaven" (v. 21) referred to the moral will of God as expressed in the teachings of Jesus and particularly the SM. That is clearly the case here. If Jesus had merely spoken of "My words," He might have

---

[100] Carson, "Matthew," 193; Keener, *The Gospel of Matthew*, 254.

[101] The parallel in Luke (13:27b) replicates the portion of Ps 6:8 which Matthew rephrased, making clear that Ps 6:8 was being quoted by both evangelists.

referred to His teaching in general. By the use of the near demonstrative pronoun "these" (*toutous*), He clearly showed that He was referring to the content of the SM in particular.

In His concluding parable Jesus first offered an analogy of one who hears the teachings of the SM and "acts on them." The present tense of the verb "acts" (*poieō*) is likely a customary present that indicates that obedience to Jesus' teaching characterizes these hearers' lifestyle. Although they do not perfectly keep all of the commands of the SM all the time and hence must appeal to the Father for forgiveness on a daily basis (6:12), their overall pattern of life is marked by submission to Jesus' teachings.

The verb translated "will be like" (*homoiōthēsetai*) is in the future tense and is probably an eschatological future that offers a description of the obedient hearer of Jesus' teaching on "that day," the day of judgment, mentioned in 7:22.[102] Matthew normally used the aorist tense of the verb (13:24; 18:23; 22:2) in the introductions to his parables in the familiar phrase "the kingdom of God is like . . ." Matthew shifted to the future tense of the verb when introducing the parable of the Ten Virgins (25:1), a parable that focused on preparation for the Second Coming. He also added the temporal adverb "then" (*tote*), which clarified that the future kingdom was the topic of the parable. Thus the use of the future tense in 7:24 is significant and hints that the parable relates to the return of Christ and eschatological judgment.[103]

The obedient hearer of Jesus' sermon will be like a "sensible man." The adjective "sensible" (*phronimos*) appears a total of seven times in Matthew and most frequently describes one who wisely prepares for the coming of the Messiah through faithful service and obedient living (24:45; 25:2,4,8–9). In Matt 10:16, the adjective has a slightly different sense and describes the shrewdness of serpents that Jesus' disciples are to imitate as they seek to survive in a world committed to their extinction. The snake's shrewdness is probably related to its

---

[102] See also Nolland, *The Gospel of Matthew*, 343.

[103] Initially this suggestion for the significance of the future tense of ὁμοιόω seems to be undermined by the use of the future tense of the verb alongside the use of an equivalent phrase "is like" (ὁμοία ἐστίν) in the present tense in Matt 11:16. However, the future tense in 11:16 is deliberative, the use of the future in a rhetorical question (Wallace, *Greek Grammar Beyond the Basics*, 570). The deliberative future appears only in the first person. Since the future tense of ὁμοιόω in 7:24 and 25:1 is part of a third-person construction, the future tense cannot be deliberative.

ability to lie undetected due to its ability to blend in with its sur-
roundings.[104] In this eschatological context, the former meaning is
clearly intended. Those who are characterized by wisdom and insight
will both hear and heed the teaching of Jesus.

The obedient disciple is like a wise man "who built his house on
the rock." The rock symbolizes a place of safety and security. Psalm
27:1–6 uses the term "rock" in a similar manner:

> The LORD is my light and my salvation—whom should I fear? The LORD is the
> stronghold of my life—of whom should I be afraid? When evildoers came
> against me to devour my flesh, my foes and my enemies stumbled and fell.
> Though an army deploys against me, my heart is not afraid; though a war
> breaks out against me, still I am confident. I have asked one thing from the
> LORD; it is what I desire: to dwell in the house of the LORD all the days of my
> life, gazing on the beauty of the LORD and seeking Him in His temple. For He
> will conceal me in His shelter in the day of adversity; He will hide me under
> the cover of His tent; He will set me high on a rock. Then my head will be
> high above my enemies around me.

The introduction to the parable identifies the rock as a symbol for
"these words of mine," the teachings of the SM.[105] Only obedience to
Jesus' teaching provides security and safety in the coming storm.

The house will be assaulted by a violent storm. First, "the rain fell"
(Matt 7:25). Although the rain mentioned in 5:45 was a divine blessing,
a gentle rain that watered thirsty crops and assured an abundant harvest
in an expression of God's indiscriminate love, this rain was a torrential
downpour that caused rivers, streams, and wadis to swell and overflow.
"The rivers rose" and spilled over their banks, flooding villages, and
softening the earthen foundations and mud walls of the simple homes.
Furthermore "the winds blew and pounded that house." The verb translated "pounded" (*prospiptō*) means to "move against something with
great force."[106] Josephus used the verb to describe the actions of a group
of zealots who assaulted and killed the rich and eminent Zacharias, son
of Baruch.[107] The storm that assaulted the house was so violent that it
would surely have toppled it if it were built on any other foundation.
"Yet it didn't collapse, because its foundation was on the rock."

---

[104] Nolland, *The Epistle of Matthew*, 423.
[105] Oddly Betz has suggested that the rock imagery of Matt 7:24–25 should be interpreted
in light of the equation of Peter and the rock in 16:13–19 (*The Sermon on the Mount*, 563–65).
[106] "προσπίπτω," BDAG, 884.
[107] Josephus, *J.W.* 4.5.4, §343.

Although many in the history of interpretation have assumed that this storm represents the "storms of life," most contemporary scholars recognize the "storm" as an allusion to eschatological judgment.[108] The "therefore" that begins this section (v. 24) links it with the judgment scene in verses 22–23. Furthermore Jesus' contrast between the "wise man" and the "foolish man" appears again in Matthew only in chap. 25 in the parable about the Ten Virgins, a clear warning calling people to prepare themselves for the judgment that will occur at the time of the Second Coming. Also 24:37–39 uses the storm and flood of Noah's day to prefigure eschatological judgment.[109]

Also, the OT frequently used the metaphor of the storm to depict divine wrath.[110] This theme is especially pronounced in the Prophets. Jeremiah 23:19–20 says, "Look, a storm from the LORD! Wrath has gone forth, a whirling storm. It will whirl about the heads of the wicked. The LORD's anger will not turn back until He has completely fulfilled the purposes of His heart."

Jeremiah 30:23–24 repeats the refrain. Jeremiah 25:32 also alludes to this storm of divine wrath: "This is what the LORD of Hosts says: Pay attention! Disaster spreads from nation to nation. A great storm is stirred up from the ends of the earth."

Isaiah 28:17–22 also utilized this imagery:

"And I will make justice the measuring line and righteousness the mason's level." Hail will sweep away the false refuge, and water will flood your hiding place. Your deal with Death will be dissolved, and your agreement with Sheol will not last. When the overwhelming scourge passes through, you will be trampled. Every time it passes through, it will carry you away; it will pass through every morning—every day and every night. Only terror will cause you to understand the message. Indeed, the bed is too short to stretch out on, and its cover too small to wrap up in. For the LORD will rise up as He did at Mount Perazim. He will rise in wrath, as at the Valley of Gibeon, to do His work, His strange work, and to perform His task, His disturbing task. So now, do not mock, or your shackles will become stronger. Indeed, I have heard from the Lord GOD of Hosts a decree of destruction for the whole land.

---

[108] See Augustine, *Serm. Mont.* 2.25; and Betz, *The Sermon on the Mount*, 566, for the former view. For the latter view, see Carson, "Matthew," 194; Davies and Allison, *A Critical and Exegetical Commentary on the Gospel According to Saint Matthew*, 1:721–22; Guelich, *The Sermon on the Mount*, 412; Filson, *A Commentary on the Gospel According to St. Matthew*, 108; Luz, *Matthew: A Commentary*, 1:386–87; Nolland, *The Gospel of Matthew*, 343–44.

[109] Schnackenburg, *The Gospel of Matthew*, 79.

[110] Later Jewish literature also depicted the difficulties of the last days as a storm. See 1QH 3.14; *Sib. Or.* 3.689–92; 5.377–80; *2 Bar.* 53.7–12.

Significantly the only security available in this storm of judgment is a rock that serves as a symbol for the Messiah (Isa 28:16).[111]

Ezekiel 13:10–16 also used the imagery of a storm to depict divine wrath:

> "Since they have led My people astray saying: Peace, when there is no peace, for when someone builds a wall they plaster it with whitewash, therefore, tell those who plaster it that it will fall. Torrential rain will come, and I will send hailstones plunging down, and a windstorm will be released. Now when the wall has fallen, will you not be asked: "Where is the coat of whitewash that you put on it?"
>
> "So this is what the Lord GOD says: I will release a windstorm in My wrath. Torrential rain will come in My anger, and hailstones will fall in destructive fury. I will tear down the wall you plastered with whitewash and knock it to the ground so that its foundation is exposed. The city will fall, and you will be destroyed within it. Then you will know that I am the LORD. After I exhaust My wrath against the wall and against those who plaster it with whitewash, I will say to you: The wall is no more and neither are those who plastered it—those prophets of Israel who prophesied to Jerusalem and saw a vision of peace for her when there was no peace. This is the declaration of the Lord GOD."

Ezekiel's prophecy constitutes the closest parallel to Jesus' words.[112] Ezekiel warned of both torrential rain and wind rather than merely a flood as in Isaiah. Ezekiel also warned of the downfall of a white-washed wall that was built on a poor foundation in a symbolic representation of the downfall of Jerusalem.

The depiction of the unleashing of God's wrath as a fierce storm is a theme of several of the psalms too. Psalm 50:3–4 warns, "Our God is coming; He will not be silent! Devouring fire precedes Him, and a storm rages around Him. On high, He summons heaven and earth in order to judge His people." Psalm 83:13–17 uses similar imagery in a prayer for the judgment of God's enemies:

> "Make them like tumbleweed, my God, like straw before the wind. As fire burns a forest, as a flame blazes through mountains, so pursue them with Your tempest and terrify them with Your storm. Cover their faces with shame so that they will seek Your name, Yahweh. Let them be put to shame and terrified forever; let them perish in disgrace."

---

[111] The verse is quoted in Rom 9:33; 10:11; 1 Pet 2:6 and alluded to in 1 Cor 3:11; Eph 2:20; and 1 Pet 2:4.

[112] Nolland noted, "There is likely some influence from Ez. 13:10–16" (*The Gospel of Matthew*, 343).

The moral of the parable is clear: wise people prepare themselves to face the approaching storm of divine judgment by hearing and doing Jesus' words. Jesus' teaching merges OT depictions of eschatological judgment as a storm with the theme in wisdom literature that the righteous endure catastrophes that destroy the wicked.[113] Proverbs 10:25 says, "When the whirlwind passes, the wicked are no more, but the righteous are secure forever." Similarly Prov 12:7 says, "The wicked are overthrown and perish, but the house of the righteous will stand." Proverbs 14:11 adds, "The house of the wicked will be destroyed, but the tent of the upright will stand."

Jesus contrasted the wise person who both heard and obeyed Jesus' teaching in the SM with a "foolish man" who heard but disobeyed (Matt 7:26). The adjective "foolish" (mōros) appears six times in Matthew. Half of the occurrences are related to the contrast between the wise and foolish virgins in the parable of the Ten Virgins in 25:1–13. Since this parable clearly has an eschatological focus, the contrast between the wise and foolish builders likely has an eschatological focus as well.

The adjective was also used in 5:22 as discussed earlier. In 23:17, the adjective was used to describe the scribes and Pharisees who used perceived loopholes in the law to justify deceptive vows. The context suggests that Jesus used the term to portray someone who rebelled against divine authority. Although the adjective is generally translated "foolish" or "stupid,"[114] in some contexts it is clearly more than a criticism of someone's intellectual capacity. It was a judgment of one's spiritual and moral condition.

The foolish person who disregarded Jesus' teaching was like a builder who constructed his house on the sand. In contrast with the rock, the sand depicts something that is unstable and fragile. Although "sand" most often depicts large numbers in ancient imagery (Gen 13:16; 22:17; 28:14; 32:12), on rare occasions it depicts something that is fragile.[115] An example appears in the works of Philo, who wrote:

[113] Nolland, The Gospel of Matthew, 343–44.
[114] "μωρός," in BDAG, 663.
[115] Betz suggested that "sand" symbolizes the multitude of nations and that the parable contains a veiled polemic against Paul's mission to the Gentiles (The Sermon on the Mount, 566–67). Such an interpretation not only ignores the meaning of the parable suggested in the introduction but also introduces tension with the climax of the Gospel in 28:19–20.

> Again, if the new world is to be exactly like the old one, then the maker is
> only wasting his labour, and differs in no respect from infant children who,
> very often while playing on the sea shore raise up little mounds of sand, and
> then pull them down again with their hands and destroy them; for it would
> have been much better than making another world exactly like the former,
> neither to take anything from, nor to add anything to, nor to change either
> for the better or for the worse, what existed originally, but to let it remain just
> as it was.[116]

Sand was obviously a poor foundation for a house since it was easily swept away by wind or washed away by water. The foolishness of the builder is heightened by the fact that the house he constructed on the sand was "his" house. This home would not be inhabited by strangers or even by clients. It was intended for the builder and his own family. A builder would be expected to invest special care in the construction of his own home, but the builder carelessly constructs his home on the poorest of foundations.

The description of the storm of eschatological judgment that struck the house is almost identical to the description given in verse 25. The only difference is a change in the verbs translated "pounded" in the HCSB. The verb translated "pounded" in verse 27 means "to strike against" or "to make contact with something in a bruising or violent manner."[117] The verb was used in 4:6 in Satan's quotation of Ps 91:12 regarding painfully striking one's foot against a stone.

As any reasonable person would have expected, the house collapsed "and its collapse was great!"[118] Like the collapse of the Philistine temple in the days of Samson (Judg 16:26–30) or the collapse of the tower of Siloam (Luke 13:4) in Jesus' time, the terrible collapse not only reduced the house to rubble but claimed the lives of all those who sought refuge from the storm in the trusted walls of the home. The roof that was trusted to protect the inhabitants from the rain and the walls that were trusted to protect them from the wind would snap their bones and crush their skulls as they toppled to the ground.

The point of the parable is clear. Just as confessions of faith without expressions of obedience do not guarantee salvation (Matt 7:21–23), hearing Jesus' teaching without heeding His teaching leaves one

---

[116] Philo, Set. Mund. 42.

[117] "προσκόπτω," BDAG, 882.

[118] Davies and Allison suggest in light of parallels in Philo that "its collapse was great" was proverbial language for a complete collapse (A Critical and Exegetical Commentary on the Gospel According to Saint Matthew, 1:724). See Philo, Mut. Nom. 55; id, Migr. Abr. 80; id, Ebr. 156.

unprepared for divine judgment. Those who do not obey Jesus' teaching in the SM will be destroyed in the coming storm of eschatological judgment.

Once again Jesus' words imply a high Christology. Jewish teachers often spoke of the necessity of obeying God's law as well as hearing God's law. One second-century teacher illustrated this claim with a parable that is similar to the parable in 7:24–27. He compared one who studies the Torah and has good works to a builder who erected a foundation of stones and then built walls of bricks on the stone foundation so that floodwaters would not dissolve the bricks and cause the house to fall. One who studies the Torah but has no good works was like a man who built his home with mud bricks on the ground. Even a small amount of water dissolved the bricks and caused the walls to collapse. This parable is almost as similar to Matthew's parable as Luke's version (6:46–49).[119]

In Jesus' parable, obedience to His teaching is substituted for obedience to the Torah. As Keener noted:

> Jesus here refers to his own words as Jewish teachers generally referred to God's law. . . . The language at least implies that Jesus is God's prophetic spokesperson (Ezek 33:32–33) but is more authoritative than is typical even for prophets; in this context (7:21–23; cf. 18:20), the claim is far higher. Neither Matthew nor his tradition allows a reader to be content with calling Jesus a great teacher or prophet (16:13–16); one must either accept all his teachings, including those that demand submission to his Lordship, or reject him altogether.[120]

Furthermore this conclusion to the SM shares much in common with the covenantal blessings and curses that conclude the Torah.[121] One was blessed for keeping the Torah but cursed for disobeying it. Interestingly among the curses for disobedience were destructive rain (Deut 28:24) and building a home but being unable to occupy it (v. 30). These similarities may hint that Jesus is the new Moses, presenting a new Torah. Nevertheless the key statements of Deut 28:1–2,15 were: "If you faithfully obey the LORD your God . . . all these blessings will come" and "If you do not obey the LORD your God . . . all these curses will come." Jesus was demanding the same obedience to His teachings

---

[119] See Gundry, *Matthew*, 135; Keener, *The Gospel of Matthew*, 255.

[120] Keener, *The Gospel of Matthew*, 255.

[121] Meier, *The Gospel According to Matthew*, 75; Schweizer, *The Good News According to Matthew*, 190; Turner, *Matthew*, 221.

that Yahweh demanded to His commands. Thus the parable that concludes the SM seems to imply Jesus' deity.

E. The Response (Matt 7:28–8:1)

The conclusion to the SM in 7:28–8:1 points back to 5:1–2 by referring to the "crowds" and to Jesus' "teaching." It also contains an important word, "authority," that introduces a prominent theme in the next main section of the Gospel (8:9; 9:6,8; 10:1). Thus the conclusion serves as a suitable bridge between the sermon and the narrative that follows it. It also anticipates the conclusion of the Gospel as whole (28:16–20) in which Jesus insists, "All authority has been given to Me in heaven and on earth."

The words "when Jesus had finished this sermon" (7:28) are an important feature for understanding the structure of the Gospel of Matthew. The Greek phrase recurs in 11:1; 13:53; 19:1; and 26:1 at the conclusion of important collections of Jesus' teaching. Based on this feature, Bacon suggested that Matthew intended to divide his Gospel into five major sections plus a Prologue (chaps. 1–2) and Epilogue (26:3–28:20).[122] Each major section concluded with the statement "And when Jesus finished," followed by some reference to Jesus' sayings, instruction, or parables (7:28–29; 11:1; 13:53; 19:1; and 26:1). These major sections were similarly designed because they contained narrative segments followed by major discourses. Bacon suggested that the organization of Matthew into five major sections was a part of Matthew's attempt to present his Gospel as a new Pentateuch. The five sections mirrored the five books of Moses in the Old Testament.

The repetition of the concluding formula after segments of narrative followed by a discourse seems too consistent to be merely coincidental. Furthermore the division into five sections fits tightly with one of Matthew's major theological emphases, Jesus' identity as the new Moses. Other ancient books had a five-part arrangement that reflected the influence of the Pentateuch. Such books include the book of Psalms, the Megilloth, the history of the Maccabees by Jason of Cyrene, 1 Enoch, the original Perekim that lay behind the Pirke Aboth, and Papias's "Expositions of the Lord's Sayings."[123]

---

[122] Bacon, *Studies in Matthew*, 80–90, 145–263.
[123] Gundry, *Matthew*, 10–11.

Nevertheless certain features of Matthew strain the view of a simple five-section arrangement that reflected the Pentateuch. First, the contents of Matthew's five books do not parallel the contents of the five books of Moses. Second, Matthew had five major discourses but six major narrative sections. Gundry concluded from this that the Gospel of Matthew is "structurally mixed" and that modern scholars should avoid imposing an outline on Matthew.[124]

Gundry's caution seems wise. Detailed outlines of Matthew should be viewed as a convenient means of summarizing the contents and highlighting the progression of the Gospel. They should be recognized as constructs of modern scholars rather than as indications of an original structure intended by Matthew.

Jesus amazed the crowds with an authority in His teaching that greatly surpassed the authority of His contemporaries. First-century Jewish teachers appealed to the authority of their rabbinic predecessors in their teaching.[125] The Jerusalem Talmud notes that Rabbi Hillel lectured on a controversial topic all day but that his followers did not accept his teaching until he cited the authority of his predecessors Shemaiah and Abtalion.[126] However, Jesus introduced His teaching with the contrast, "You have heard that it was said . . . but I tell you" (5:21,27,31,33,38,43). In these words Jesus was assuming an authority for interpreting the law that was independent of Jewish oral tradition. He was claiming an authority greater than that of the most esteemed Jewish rabbis.

The amazement of the crowds was intense yet superficial. Though the crowds listened to Jesus with initial amazement (22:33), they eventually turned into a bloodthirsty mob that demanded His execution (26:55; 27:20–22). Sadly, by their response (or lack of it) to Jesus' teaching, these crowds identified themselves as the "many" who took the wide road of hearing but not heeding the road that leads to destruction (7:13).

These concluding words stand as a stark warning to all who read the SM. The study of this sermon is not a mere academic exercise that satisfies a person's curiosity about a great Teacher or stirs interest in the ethical instruction of an ancient Jewish philosopher. The SM demands that hearers and readers obey its commands. The SM calls

[124] Ibid., 11.
[125] See *m. ʾAbot* 1:1–12.
[126] *y. Pesaḥ.* 6.1.33a. See also *b. B. Meṣiʿa* 58b–59b.

every reader to begin a long and difficult journey on a narrow path, a path marked by pain and persecution, but also a path that leads to a narrow gate beyond which the weary traveler will enjoy wonders too great to describe.

NAME INDEX

Hengel, M. *256*
Heth, W. *132*
Hill, D. *44, 60, 79, 91, 175, 189, 198,*
    211, 254, 269, 283, 288, 296–97,
    299, 323, 329, 333, 341
Hoffman, P. *43, 268*
Holler, Z. N. *8*
Holmes, M. W. *199, 225, 310, 328*
Hughes, P. *167*
Hunter, A. M. *1, 48, 59*
Hurtado, L. *198*

Iko, A. *138*
Isaksson, A. *130*

Janzen, D. *131*
Jeremias, J. *96, 101, 111, 143, 167,*
    188–89, 192, 196, 198, 206,
    211–13, 216, 284, 289, 298, 310
Jerome *109, 115, 205, 222, 236*
Johnson, L. T. *1*
Jongkind, D. *268*
Jordan, C. *148, 149*
Josephus *22, 127, 142–43, 146–47,*
    155, 159, 182, 215, 237, 253,
    272, 286, 328, 337–40, 344
Justin *132*

Käsemann, E. *329*
Kee, H. C. *257*
Keener, C. *3, 32–34, 47, 59, 63, 76, 90,*
    94, 96, 98–100, 115, 124, 129,
    139, 141, 153–54, 156, 176, 185,
    189, 192, 214–15, 239, 249–50,
    265, 269, 281, 293, 301–2, 306,
    312–13, 322, 331, 341–42, 349
Keil, C. F. *127*
Kellum, L. S. *197*
Kinnaman, D. *3*
Kissinger, W. S. *2, 5–7, 9*
Klausner, J. *73*
Kloppenborg, J. S. *43, 268*
Knowles, M. *216*
Köstenberger, A. J. *197, 287*
Kraft, R. A. *246*

Lane, W. *28, 79, 228, 285*

Levine, E. *229*
Lewis, J. P. *313*
Lewis, N. *155*
Lightfoot, J. B. *140, 160, 206*
Llewelyn, S. R. *155, 289–90*
Lloyd-Jones, M. *195, 198, 239*
Lohmeyer, E. *99*
Luck, W. F. *134*
Luther, M. *7, 9, 60, 189, 262, 306*
Luz, U. *14–16, 19, 25, 42, 49, 53, 55,*
    58, 60, 67–68, 77, 81–82, 84, 87,
    90, 95–96, 100, 102, 104, 107,
    114–16, 122, 129–30, 133, 148,
    153, 161, 168, 189, 192–93, 197,
    202, 213–14, 216–17, 219–20,
    237, 245, 248, 252, 262, 267–69,
    271, 278, 282, 285, 288–89,
    291–92, 294–95, 299, 304, 311,
    314, 318, 323, 329, 341, 345
Lyons, G. *3*

Malina, B. *83*
Mann, C. S. *27, 82*
Manson, T. W. *292*
Marcion *104*
Marshall, I .H. *43, 195, 225, 235, 285,*
    312
Mavrodes, G. *148*
McEleney, N. J. *41, 175*
McNeile, A. H. *254, 306*
Meier, J. P. *43, 96, 103, 105, 133, 307,*
    349
Melanchthon *60*
Merrill, E. *67, 127–28, 131–32*
Metzger, B. *55, 79, 205, 235, 260, 268,*
    311, 314, 319
Michaelis, C. *41*
Mitchell, M. *5*
Moo, D. J. *97*
Moore, G. F. *181*
Morris, L. *80, 189, 245, 262, 268,*
    297–98, 312

Nijman, M. *205*
Nolland, J. *33–34, 48, 50, 56–57, 59,*
    64, 72, 80, 85, 91, 104, 110, 114,
    122, 151–53, 158–59, 163–64,

SUBJECT INDEX

SCRIPTURE INDEX